THREE GENRES

The Writing of Poetry, Fiction, and Drama

THIRD EDITION

STEPHEN MINOT

Trinity College
Hartford, Connecticut

PRENTICE–HALL, INC., ENGLEWOOD CLIFFS, N.J. 07632

Library of Congress Cataloging in Publication Data

MINOT, STEPHEN.
  Three genres.

  Includes index.
  1. Creative writing. I. Title.
PN145.M5 1981   808'.02   81-12002
ISBN 0-13-920397-4   AACR2

Editorial/production supervision by Daniel Mausner
Cover by Zimmerman Foyster Design
Manufacturing buyer: Harry P. Baisley

Printed in the United States of America

10 9 8 7 6 5

ISBN 0-13-920397-4

Grateful acknowledgment is made to the authors, publishers, and individuals mentioned below for permission to reprint or to quote from the following works.

  The Service for Joseph Axminster from *Oilers & Sweepers* by George Dennison. Copyright © 1963. Reprinted by permission of **Random House, Inc.**

  "Girl" by Jamaica Kincaid. Reprinted by permission; © 1978 The New Yorker Magazine, Inc.

  "The Windmill Man" by Tim McCarthy. Volume XXVI, Number 2, *Colorado Quarterly.* Copyright Registration No.
B268517. Publication date July 6, 1977.

  "Sausage and Beer" by Stephen Minot, copyright © 1962 by The Atlantic Monthly Company. Reprinted with permission of the publisher.

PRENTICE-HALL INTERNATIONAL, INC., *London*
PRENTICE-HALL OF AUSTRALIA PTY. LIMITED, *Sydney*
PRENTICE-HALL OF CANADA, LTD., *Toronto*
PRENTICE-HALL OF INDIA PRIVATE LIMITED, *New Delhi*
PRENTICE-HALL OF JAPAN, INC., *Tokyo*
PRENTICE-HALL OF SOUTHEAST ASIA PTE. LTD., *Singapore*
WHITEHALL BOOKS LIMITED, *Wellington, New Zealand*

To Ginny

Contents

Preface

Three Genres is about the *process* of literary writing. It examines the way poets, writers of fiction, and dramatists create and develop new works.

This third edition, like the first two, is not intended as a "how to" book. It does not promise commercial success. Instead, it treats each of these three genres as a genuinely sophisticated art form and describes each genre's special characteristics from a writer's point of view.

I have had three kinds of readers in mind: students taking courses in literary or creative writing, students in reading courses, and individuals not in school who are working on their own to develop their abilities as writers or readers of literature.

Courses in literary writing (also called *creative* and *imaginative* writing—the terms are interchangeable) deal with complex art forms. Can they be taught? Only those who have never taken such courses ask that question. A good writing seminar will speed development just as conservatories help musicians and art schools unfold new possibilities for painters and sculptors.

Part of this process stems from the teacher's own experience and training, but much of it comes from the interchange of ideas and reactions of those in the class. Everyone should feel free to participate regularly and informally. This is what distinguishes a seminar from a lecture course, and most teachers feel that the seminar is by far the best vehicle for writers.

There are, however, certain basic concepts that must be introduced to each new class. Without a text, an instructor may find it necessary to give occasional lectures. One of the purposes of this book is to reduce the need for these and thereby increase the time available for a relaxed and open seminar discussion.

Although *Three Genres* was originally conceived as a textbook for writers, it has been adopted increasingly as an innovative approach to introductory literature courses. While most critical texts deal with literature in its finished form, *Three Genres* is concerned with the dynamics of the creative process. How, for example, is the beat of metered verse muted so as not to be obtrusive? How do writers of free verse find alternative forms of rhythm? What happens to the means of perception when a writer converts a short story into a stage play or a television script? When a literary work is seen as the product of a long, complex chain of conscious and unconscious decisions, it takes on a living quality. Reading becomes a far richer experience.

In addition to classroom use, *Three Genres* has also served writers and active readers who are not taking a course. Writers out of college often complain that they find themselves cut off from useful criticism. Well-meaning friends are often too polite ("Well, it's different") or subjective ("That character reminds me of my landlord—yuch!") or personal ("Did that really happen to you?"). And publishers are frequently terse ("It does not meet our editorial needs"). How does one evaluate one's own work?

This text won't read manuscripts and respond, but it should help independent writers to ask the right questions about their own work and in this way develop the critical sense which is necessary for revision and artistic growth.

Three Genres first appeared in 1965 and since then has been used in over two hundred universities, colleges, and schools in forty-five states. Comments and suggestions I have received over the years have been incorporated in this third edition. I am particularly grateful to three readers who, after using the text in class for a number of years, reviewed it carefully and provided me with valuable critiques. They are Professor Enid S. Friedman, Essex County College, Newark, New Jersey; Professor Russell M. Griffin, University of Bridgeport, Connecticut; and Professor Sheila Juba, Lane Community College, Eugene, Oregon. With the help of these three from highly different sections of the United States plus many others who have offered their impressions, this third edition has come to reflect the experiences of teachers and writers across the country.

I am also indebted to Dick Tuttle for his illustrations and to William Ritman for permission to reproduce his set design of Harold Pinter's *The Collection.* My thanks to George E. Nichols III for his advice and the use of his resources.

Among the many changes, the poetry selections have been strengthened with the addition of more work by women—an infusion of vitality and conviction which has given new life to the genre as a whole. The woman's experience is also represented in two of the four stories. Both the poetry and the fiction sections have been enriched by the addition of more work by black writers. And the drama portion now contains a chapter on television writing, along with a sample script.

All three sections now have more space devoted to the complex business of getting started—how to draw on experience and how to make use of what one has read to stimulate one's own private vision. I have also added a third appendix suggesting the resources available both to those who will continue writing and to those who will be more active readers. These are substantive changes, which I hope will make the present volume even more helpful than the second edition.

The principle which has guided me from the beginning and which has remained unchanged in all three editions is that a text on literary writing has no business telling a reader *how to write;* its single task is to show writers *how to develop as writers.* There is a crucial difference. The first strives for uniformity. A "how to" book, for example, is highly proscriptive. Craft is presented as a set of rules and tricks; innovation and personal expression are discouraged. But a sophisticated writer develops the way a work of art does—individually. What one needs is more options.

A writer increases the number of options available by studying a variety of techniques and trying different approaches. A short-story writer, for example, may well choose to avoid dialogue in a particular work, but if this is done because the author is unsure about how to suggest speech on paper, no choice is involved. In the same way, poets who have not taken the time to explore meter cannot *choose* to write free verse; they are forced to. And a playwright who persists in writing highly expressionistic, dreamlike plays cannot be sure this is a genuine free choice until she or he has worked through at least one realistic script.

This principle applies even to the original choice of genre. A particular experience or a vivid ironic contrast may lend itself to a poem or a story or may even be the kernel of a dramatic work, but the writer is not able to choose freely between those alternatives without having first spent some time working with each form.

A writer, then, develops by discovering the full range of what is possible in each genre. Much of this is done by reading. An equal amount is done by practice writing. Both have to be active, conscious efforts. Later, this familiarity will be internalized in what is best described as "a feel for the medium." When that is achieved, this book will have served its purpose.

S. M.

Part 1
The Writing of Poetry

Chapter **1**

The Distinction of a Poem

The value of basic *definitions;* defining *literature; verse* distinguished from prose by its use of *the line,* the *sound* of words, the *rhythm* of phrases, and *compression* of suggestion; *sophisticated* poetry distinguished from simple verse by complexity of suggestion and the employment of poetic *conventions.*

Writers do not wrestle with definitions of literary terms as much as critics do. A writer's first obligation, after all, is to write.

But if you spend much time writing without having the vocabulary to describe your own work and that of others, you will have serious problems. You may "have a feeling" about a poem, but unless you can express it accurately in words, your ability to evaluate and revise the work is seriously limited. Those who lack practical critical ability often remain "first-draft writers." And amateurs.

In order to develop as a writer—or a reader—one should master and use whatever basic terms seem to be helpful when writers talk among themselves about their work. Subjective responses ("Why don't you write something happy?") usually tell us more about the speaker than the poem. Precise analysis ("This vehicle has the wrong overtones for its tenor") leads to understanding and usually to revision. We have to understand both the strengths and the failings of our own writing before we can develop.

WHAT IS LITERATURE?

Writers need to share a general, working definition of *literature* if they are going to understand each other. A great deal of time can be wasted if this term is used as a synonym for *good*. "I like your poem," a self-proclaimed critic says, "but is it literature?" And the next four hours are then spent trying to define the term.

For practicing writers, the most useful definition is the one proposed by Northrop Frye (see *Anatomy of Criticism*, Princeton University Press). He divides all writing into two categories, *descriptive* and *literary*.

In *descriptive writing* "the final direction of meaning" is tied to the real world about us. That is, its primary purpose is to describe or interpret some aspect of our environment. This category includes such forms as the essay, thesis, editorial, article, or a text such as this. When we evaluate such works we use terms like *valid, true,* and *helpful* (or *false* and *useless*), each of which implies that such writing should reflect accurately the world about us.

Literary writing, on the other hand, creates its own world. The poem, the story, the novel, and the play are judged largely by internal criteria: unity, consistency, complexity, and fresh use of literary conventions. Such works may also make suggestions about the "real" world, but the primary concern of the writer is not to convince or inform, it is to create. Viewed this way, the poem is closer to a sculpture than it is to utilitarian writing such as an essay. Even when literary writing becomes highly thematic—satiric poetry, for example—it tends to be not so much an argument as a human response. It is possible, of course, to thrust poetry, fiction, or drama directly into the area of argumentation in the form of advertising jingles, propagandistic fiction, and political skits. But then we judge them for their "message," treating them quite correctly as descriptive writing.

This definition of literary writing is particularly helpful for us when we write poetry. It describes how our work is related to fiction and drama. It is more precise than phrases like *creative writing*. And it avoids value judgments. There is an enormous difference, of course, between the verse of Edgar Guest and that of Ezra Pound, but it does not help us as writers to shrug off Guest's work as "nonliterary."

Most important of all, Frye's precise use of the term "literary writing" reminds us that our work as poets is not just an elaborate way to present some philosophical truth. It provides an antidote to the emphasis on "theme" and "message" which has dominated many English literature classes. After all, we can listen to a song without demanding that it give us some deep truth. And we can enjoy a painting in the same spirit. A poem exists largely for its own sake, a pleasure in itself.

THE CHARACTERISTICS
OF A POEM

All literary writing is composed either in verse or in prose. What is the difference? There is only one absolute distinction: in poems, the length of the line is a part of the art form. This is one distinguishing factor found in all poetry regardless of the period.

Prose, on the other hand, is continuous. That is, the length of a line has nothing to do with the form. It varies according to the size of the page on which it is being printed. When we write fiction we leave this up to the typist or printer because it is not an aspect of our art.

Poets do not allow their typists or printers to change the number of words in any line because in most cases they have used those lines to create rhythmical effects or sound patterns. They are a part of the art form, a valuable part that is not available for the writer of prose.

This is more than a technical distinction. Poets tend to *think* in lines, using them as a base for the construction of images, rhythms, and sound patterns. It is for this reason that many poems are begun with what eventually may become the fifth, the twelfth, or the last line. Poems often develop by association rather than by the prose writer's concern for what happens next.

By controlling the line length, poets also control the shape of their poems. Whether they are using traditional meter or free verse, they can make their poems snake down the page in brief lines or fill each page with long ones. These differences control to some degree the way the reader responds to the work. In addition, poets can make extreme use of typography so that the shape of the poem becomes a picture in itself.

When we write prose—as we all do most of the time—we have only one typographical device, the paragraph. With the exception of that, our work will fill the page in a block of print. But when we shift to poetry, we usually become far more concerned with the visual aspect of our work. Through line length we can influence the meaning, the tone, and the rhythmical patterns of our work.

There are three additional characteristics of poetry, each of which will be treated in a separate chapter. I mention them here as an overview so that each can be kept in perspective. They are *sound devices, rhythmical patterns,* and the *compression of statement.* None of these is as absolute as the use of the line—individual poems can be found which fail to use one or even two of these devices. But a great majority of poems contain all four characteristics.

The use of sound is enormously important to most poets. Generally, this is a matter of linking two or more words by matching final sounds (rhyme), initial consonants (alliteration), or sounds within words (assonance and consonance). In addition, the sound of the word itself may echo what it describes (onomatopoeia) as in "buzz," "cuckoo," and "hiss."

Analysis and examples of all these devices appear in Chapter 5, but it is worth noting here how intense the element of sound can become even when buried within words. In the first stanza of Dylan Thomas' "Fern Hill," for example, the poet describes how as a child he felt like a young prince among the trees and in the sunlit fields. These three lines ripple with assonance. I have italicized only the most obvious examples—six pairs in three lines!

> And once below a *time* I lordly had the tr*ees* and l*eaves*
> Tr*ail* with d*aisies* and barl*ey*
> Down the r*ivers* of the w*indfall* light.

It is possible, of course, to write a poem which contains no sound devices whatever. It is still a poem. But the use of sound is a significant part of most poetry regardless of period.

The third of these four characteristics of verse is the use of rhythm. In simplest terms, rhythm is a systematic variation in the flow of sound. All speech varies the flow of sound, of course; otherwise it would be a steady hum. But the key word here is "systematic." Such systems vary enormously. Traditional meter, a fairly regular repetition of stressed and unstressed syllables, is the most common form. A looser method involves counting just the stressed syllables in a line. *Beowulf* was written in this way, as is a good deal of contemporary verse. Quantitative meter, rarely used in English, depends not on stress but on the length of duration in the pronunciation of a syllable. Varied as these approaches are, they all constitute systematic variations in the flow of sound.

But there are also nonauditory rhythms. Striking effects have been achieved by patterning the number of syllables in each line regardless of stress (Marianne Moore), by balancing syntactical elements (Walt Whitman), by repeating key words and phrases (Allen Ginsberg), and by arranging the length of lines (E. E. Cummings). We respond to these signals from what we see on the page as well as through what we hear when we read the poem aloud. Rhythm in poetry is like a heartbeat, giving this genre a special kind of life.

Prose can also contain samples of rhythm, as seen in the fiction of Thomas Wolfe and Dylan Thomas. Such rhythms, however, tend to be more fragmentary and are often created from the sentence structure. They are never based on line length.

The fourth and final characteristic of poetry is compression of statement. Poems usually say a lot in a few words. That is, most poems have a range of suggestion with subtle shadings of feeling. Often they require several readings.

This does not mean, of course, that poems have to be short. But within even the most sweeping epics like the *Iliad* or *Beowulf* there are stanzas which reverberate with implications. And now that story telling is so closely identified with prose fiction and film, the tendency for poets is to concentrate on the subtleties of personal experience, packing their lines with varied implications. Even when poems make blunt social or political statements, they usually are distilled from the poet's own experience.

This compression—drawing broad implications from specific details or images—is achieved partly through similes but mostly by metaphors and symbolic suggestion. Dylan Thomas, for example, built a simple word like "green" into a symbol that would require pages of prose to explain.

Poetry, then, is distinguished from prose by its special use of the line, the sound of words, the rhythm of phrases, and the compression of suggestion. There is no law which forces us as poets to develop all four in every poem; but we cannot call ourselves poets in the full sense until we *can* use any of them when we choose.

SOPHISTICATED VS.
SIMPLE POETRY

So far, I have been describing poetry, not evaluating it. But we make value judgments all the time. Teachers of writing classes occasionally give an "F" or a "D" for what they consider inferior work, and this is only a gentle prelude to the grades which editors hand out regularly in the form of rejection slips. A poet spends a lifetime being publicly "graded" by reviewers. But just what do we mean by "good" and "bad"?

Standards obviously vary from person to person. Many people really prefer greeting-card verses about ideal mothers and dear old dads; others reject work on that level as "rubbish" but secretly believe that the last "genuine poetry" was written by Tennyson. And then there are those who with equal sincerity admire the song lyrics of Bob Dylan or the poetry of Amiri Baraka. How does one develop as a poet with so many conflicting standards?

The solution comes from two terms used in science. To a biologist, simple forms of life are *simple* and complex forms are *sophisticated*. Thus, the bird is not *better* in any objective sense than the jellyfish, but it is far more sophisticated in that the potential of living matter has been developed much further.

As an individual, the biologist may prefer a canary to a jellyfish as a pet or may feel that the jellyfish is *better* as an example of living tissue; but acting as a biologist, his or her use of the terms *simple* and *sophisticated* are objective.

Does all poetry have to be sophisticated? Of course not. Judging by the verse of greeting cards, far more people prefer their poetry simple—regular meter, conventional sentiments, and the cozy familiarity of time-tested clichés. Writing simple verse is a craft and there are books that teach it. But this is not one.

Sophisticated literature is the subject of this text. It is by definition complex, but it is not necessarily cluttered or obscure. A fly's eye, for example, is in some ways more complex in structure than a human eye, but as an instrument of sight it is far from sophisticated. It cannot see as well. In the same way, a villanelle (see p. 83) with its complex systems of rhyme and repeated lines is structurally more complicated than, say, a three-line haiku; but in some cases the haiku is more sophisticated because it *does* more—it has a wider, more subtle range of suggestion.

Varieties of *complexity* can be created in any of the four characteristics already discussed: use of the line (Herbert, Thomas, Ginsberg), sound devices (Poe), rhythmical effects (Vachel Lindsay), and compression of statement (an example by Ezra Pound appears later in this chapter). And in addition, complexity may involve refashioning an old convention, such as Coleridge's use of the ballad form in "The Rime of the Ancient Mariner," Dylan Thomas's ironic use of the elegy in "Refusal to Mourn. . .," or Ginsberg's use of syntactical rhythm, which has its roots in Biblical prose.

In some cases, complexities such as these have resulted in sophisticated verse. But in others they have become ends in themselves and the poem becomes more of a trick, a stunt—and simple.

Joyce Kilmer's "Trees" has been used many times in battles over what is and what is not "good" poetry. I cite it here not for one last hatchet job but to illustrate what makes a poem *simple*. Here are the first three of its six stanzas:

> I think that I shall never see
> A poem lovely as a tree.
>
> A tree whose hungry mouth is pressed
> Against the earth's sweet flowing breast;
>
> A tree that looks to God all day
> And lifts her leafy arms to pray; . . .

Setting aside all concern for evaluation, we can see certain specific characteristics which, first, indicate that it is indeed verse and, second, that it is simple verse. It uses lines, but the lines are arranged in rhyming couplets that soon become monotonously regular. There are three samples of sound devices, but each is an end rhyme which lands bluntly on a stressed, one-syllable word. This mathematical regularity is not softened by assonance, consonance, double rhyme, slant rhyme, or any other sound device.

The rhythm is based on a simple, unvaried use of meter. No attempt has been made to integrate rhythmical patterns with tone or statement. In this respect, it resembles the simple chants used by children ("Eeny meeny miny mo / Catch a tiger by the toe"), but there is no indication that Kilmer's work is intended to be chanted.

The degree of compression varies. The first stanza contains none. It is denotative, direct, and without any figure of speech. It is a good prose sentence. But the second and third stanzas do use metaphors: The tree's roots are likened to one suckling at a breast; and the branches, to one lifting arms upward in prayer. Since only an unweaned contortionist could manage this, we must assume that we are not dealing with an extended metaphor. The use of two separate, visually unrelated metaphors in two adjoining couplets intensifies the separation between stanzas already established by the meter and the rhyme. Further, the images themselves are essentially unchanged and undeveloped borrowings from two well-used metaphors: Mother Nature and a tree as a man reaching toward heaven.

By way of contrast, here is Ezra Pound's two-line poem, "In a Station of the Metro":

The apparition of these faces in the crowd;
Petals on a wet, black bough.

Because this is so short, many readers are tempted to make a quick judgment and pass on. But my concern here, as with Kilmer's poem, is not evaluation; the poem can be examined with the same objective sense the biologist uses when dissecting.

As with "Trees," the line is an intentional part of the form and can't be changed by the typesetter. The title sets the scene—assuming that the reader knows that "Metro" refers to the Paris subway. The first line presents a more or less literal description of the faces in the subway, and the second offers a metaphorical association—a comparison which intensifies our view of the scene.

But the first line is not entirely denotative in the sense that Kilmer's first stanza was. The word "apparition" has overtones which we do not normally associate with subway stations. First, it suggests that something has appeared suddenly or unexpectedly; further, it has the meaning of ghosts or phantoms. In some way, then, the faces of those in a crowded subway station remind the poet of apparitions.

The second line develops this in an intricate fashion. The image is one of petals presumably torn loose in a rain storm and plastered on a black bough. Each word is significant. "Petals" has a conventional association with youth (spring) and innocence; "wet" is our only clue that there has been a storm; "black bough" not only establishes a contrast with the lightness of petals but provides the picture of faces in the black subway car which rushes in with the suddenness of an apparition when viewed from the platform.

There is no moral here and not even a "message" such as some school children are taught to seek in every poem. But there is the sense of suddenness when the subway car rushes into a station, a touch of fear, and a highly original suggestion about the relationship between that solid, black metallic product of modern society and the faces one sees through the window, pale and fragile.

The first reason for calling this poem sophisticated, then, is the complex use of imagery and the subtlety of the suggestions which result. But the rhythm is also complex. The first line is iambic (ta-*tum*, ta-*tum*) throughout. The second breaks the pattern with a trochee which stresses the first syllable (*Pet*-als) and then abandons meter for the sake of those three heavy stresses which demand a pause between them: ". . .wet, black bough." Just why iambic followed by a trochaic foot moves the poem from light to heavy tone is a matter for Chapter 6, but it is enough to point out here that in this poem, rhythm, with all its variations, is bound quite consciously with meaning and tone.

There is no true rhyme in this brief poem, but there are other samples of sound devices. The final words in each line are bound with similar vowel sounds (cr*ow*d and b*ou*gh) in what is called a slant rhyme or assonance. The second line is constructed with two linked pairs: p*e*tals and w*e*t joined with assonance, and *b*lack and *b*ough with alliteration.

Beyond these technical distinctions, the poems differ in their basic intent. Kilmer makes two clear and highly conventional statements: that trees in general are "lovely" and that they are in his opinion made by God. Pound's poem, on the other hand, doesn't make any philosophical statement. Instead, it catches a vivid visual impression and presents it to the reader. Like a photographer, Pound has selected his subject with care. It is as if he seized our arm and said, "Hey, look at that!" What we see, though, comes to us through the words he selected.

Simple poetry often makes simple, conventional statements that may be soothing but are soon forgotten because they do not really touch us. We are told that love, like trees, is beautiful, Christmas is merry, and mothers are wonderful. Sophisticated poetry is more often rooted in a personal experience: faces in a subway station which look like petals plastered on a bough after a storm, a particular tree which was important to the writer years ago, a specific Christmas or mother or brother who evokes a complex and perhaps contradictory set of emotions.

Simple verse has its function. It soothes. Sophisticated poetry, the subject of this text, has more complex and intricate rewards: it gives pleasure in its form and fresh insights in its statement.

CONVENTIONS VS. INDIVIDUALITY

A poetic convention is any pattern or device which is repeated in a large number of poems. Meter is a poetic convention, and so are the varieties of typography in free verse; rhyme is a convention, and so are those more muted methods of linking words by sound—assonance, alliteration, and consonance.

When poetry (some would prefer *verse*) is rigidly bound by conventions such as unvaried meter and rhyme, stock themes, too-familiar metaphors, we say it is conventional and simple. But all poetry—even the most sophisticated—is based on conventions. They are for the poet what notes, measures, and phrases are for the musician.

Our first task as poets, then, is to master the basic conventions of the genre. Only in this way can we achieve freedom as writers, for only when we are at ease with a particular technique are we free to decide whether to use it.

Take, for example, the various systems of creating rhythm. Which is "best," rhythm of stress, meter, or free verse? Best for what? And for whom? Practicing poets base their decisions partly on personal preference and partly on the needs of a particular poem. They can do this only when they are at home with each system.

The first step toward sophisticated work is to master the craft of poetry. The second is learning how to mute that craft so that the technique you use is not obtrusive. This is when you begin to use the language of poetry to reflect what is unique in yourself: your specific insights and reactions. Soon you will find yourself going beyond mere mastery of conventions to develop your own "voice" as a poet.

The following ten chapters will deal with the conventions of verse and with the ways poets use these techniques to create work which is sophisticated and unique.

Chapter **2**

The Sources
of Poetry

The danger of broad *abstractions;* the use of sense of *per-ception:* sight, sound, touch, smell, and taste; the recall of specific *emotions;* the fragmentation and magnification of *experience;* the pleasure of *sound* and *meaning* of words; *getting started.*

When you write an analytical paper, you usually compile a number of objective facts and use them to support an abstract statement. An analysis of the 1960s, for example, might cite newspaper accounts and conclude that the period was one of political dissension. Or a paper on Ezra Pound's "In a Station of the Metro" might focus on the importance of a sudden visual impression.

When you write poetry, however, all that objective and abstract thinking is apt to get in the way. You will find all the material you need in personal experience and in your own emotional responses. Rather than proving a point, your goal is to help the reader share what you yourself have known and felt.

Suppose, for example, you began writing a paper on the plight of the high-school dropout. Your first step would probably be to gather statistics: unemployment figures, crime rates, and the like. If you gathered enough of these impersonal facts you could then draw some abstract conclusion about dropouts in general.

But a poet goes right to the specifics and usually only implies a conclusion. Look how Gwendolyn Brooks does it, using the phrases of street language in a poem called "We Real Cool":

> We real cool. We
> Left School. We
>
> Lurk late. We
> Strike straight. We
>
> Sing sin. We
> Thin gin. We
>
> Jazz June. We
> Die soon.

Those are real people she is writing about. In fact, the poem is normally printed with a subtitle, "The Pool Players. Seven at the Golden Shovel." The poet can't *prove* anything about the life of dropouts from this personal and specific approach, but she can make us *feel* something about them far better than any documented article.

Each type of writing, of course, has its function. But it is important to remember that most of the writing you have done in school has been factual and abstract. Switching to poetry means leaving those broad abstractions and turning to specific feelings, particular people, and personal experiences.

Watch out for words like *love, death, nature, war, peace, brotherhood, hypocrisy, God, beauty, social justice,* and *truth.* They are all important, but treated in the abstract they sound devoid of real feeling. "Love," we are told, "turns the sour taste of life to sweet." A satisfactory slogan, that, but is it rooted in genuine experience? If so, it doesn't show. The pronouncement is still about love as an abstract state. Notice how the same metaphor ("turns the sour taste. . .to sweet") can be plugged into nature, peace, brotherhood, God, beauty, and truth. And with a simple inversion (to "turns the sweetness of our lives to sour"), the metaphor can serve equally well for death, war, and hypocrisy. The poet has thus produced ten different poems without once revealing the smallest hint of personal feeling.

Established poets tend to be more honest. This often requires revealing more of oneself. Here is an example from Adrienne Rich's "Like This Together," the first of six stanzas:

> Wind rocks the car.
> We sit parked by the river,
> silence between our teeth.
> Birds scatter across islands
> of broken ice. Another time
> I'd have said "Canada geese,"

knowing you love them.
A year, ten years from now,
I'll remember this,
this sitting like drugged birds
in a glass case—
not why, only that we
were here like this together.

Miss Rich is not here concerned with Love in the abstract; she is dealing with a specific relationship between two people at a specific moment in time. She recalls the scene through very precise memories—the feel of a car shuddering in the wind, the look of that icy river. And then she develops the *unique* quality of that relationship at that particular stage: the chill of the landscape, the couple sitting "like drugged birds / in a glass case. . ." There is love here, but it is a part of a complex set of emotions and its future is uncertain.

The sources of contemporary poetry tend to be personal and specific. It takes little courage and a good deal of personal honesty to find material which will lend itself to poetic statement. But it is important to remember that we all have in our own lives more than enough experiences with which to work. Here are four areas that are worth exploring.

SENSE PERCEPTION

We make contact with the outside world in five specific ways: seeing, hearing, touching, smelling, and tasting. Some people do remarkably well with one or more senses impaired. Many more were graced with all five but don't fully use them. Poets, as a rule, use them more than most people.

Sight is by far the most frequently used sense in poetry. While writers of fiction look for a sequence of events, poets more often start with a fragmentary vision—faces in a subway crowd, for example. Like photographers, poets are always on the lookout for visual impressions that have the power to evoke complex emotions. They can be found just about anywhere: birch trees bent over from winter storms, a long row of telephone poles, a Yiddish newspaper lying in a gutter, a grassy river bank remembered from childhood, black faces staring out of tenement windows on an oppressive August night, cracks in a concrete playground, patterns of frost on a window, the veins in a maple leaf or an old man's hand, or an abandoned spider web.

Rarely is the poet content to describe the object as an end in itself. The original image is selected because it has certain qualities—feelings, associations, implications, and the like—which develop as the artist expands the initial conception.

Occasionally a city serves as the poet's starting point. Sandburg's use of Chicago and Williams' study of Paterson, New Jersey, are good examples.

Rivers' poem on Harlem appears on page 98 and shows dramatically how bitterness and hope can be rooted in the place where one was raised.

Or poets may turn to specific scenes from their childhood. "Fern Hill" (p. 98) is a fine example. Although the phrasing is dreamlike ("About the lilting house and happy as the grass was green"), the origin is clearly the farm on which the poet was raised. The poem is filled with precise visual details from that scene—wagons, apple trees, daisies, barns, foxes, horses, owls, and the like.

But that is a big scene to work with. More often, poets draw on places that they have visited—specific scenes that have lingered in their memories for some reason. This is the origin of Robley Wilson's "On a Maine Beach" (see p. 97). Written in Iowa, the poem draws on an earlier summer. It doesn't indulge in generalities about the Maine coastline the way travel ads usually do; instead it focuses on specific details, drawing a pattern from them. Almost every line contains a precise visual image which the poet eventually uses to link this scene with broader, more abstract suggestions. I will return to this poem in a later chapter on images, but it would be useful to read it now as an example of how a relatively simple experience can serve as the genesis for a highly sophisticated poem.

Occasionally sounds may also serve as sources for the poet. In "Fern Hill," for example, the boy imagines that the calves "sang" to his horn like a pack of hunting dogs, and he hears the foxes bark "clear and cold," and the sound of distant church bells mingled with that of the brook is described with the phrase, "The sabbath rang slowly"—all this in one stanza!

In using sounds, the poet has to go further than generalities. "The roar of traffic" doesn't give the reader enough to work with; and besides, the metaphor is worn out with overuse. The poet tries to recall those specific elements which created the general effect—the sounds of pneumatic drills, police whistles, car and truck horns, and the like. Or if the scene is in the country, he or she may try to isolate exactly how the wind sounds in a pine grove or through wheat fields.

It is annoying when the sound which actually initiated a poetic sequence is sufficiently overused to be considered a cliché. Brooks babbling, gulls crying, and wind whistling in the rigging have all reached the level of song lyrics. That is the end of the line. If the sound is truly an individual experience, one can include it in the early drafts and decide later whether to delete the image altogether or to revitalize it, as Howard Moss did in "Local Places" where what might have been a babbling brook became "the stream's small talk at dark."

The other senses—touch, smell, and taste—serve less frequently as sources for the poet, but they are worth considering. They may come as mild reactions like the feel of grit on a cafeteria table, the coarse lick of a cow, the smell of a pine grove in August, the taste of potato chips combined with the smell of sweat or the exhaust of a Diesel bus.

Often taste and smell are linked with visual images as in Maya Angelou's "This Winter Day" (p. 92). Right there in her kitchen she describes "green and orange things" which "leak their blood selves in the soup" creating "an odor at my nose" which "starts my tongue to march. . . ." Read that poem when you're hungry!

In addition to simple sensations, there are heavy ones to consider: the sharp pain of a knife wound or of childbirth; or the sounds an injured man makes.

A specific sense impression is called an *image*. Images can be used directly or as a simile, metaphor, or symbol. More about that in Chapter 4. I am concerned here with how you as a poet must not only keep your eyes open but keep your other senses alert and receptive to every stimulus about you.

PERSONAL EMOTIONS

The stress here should be on *personal*. As I pointed out at the beginning of this chapter, only when you are dealing with feelings close to you can you develop the nuances, the overtones, and the ambivalences of the emotion.

Love, as we have seen, is a risky subject when considered in the abstract. But a particular relationship which involves genuine feelings of love—along with other emotions—felt for a specific person might be worth considering. Take another look at Adrienne Rich's "Like This Together" (p. 95). Although the couple are drifting apart, there was love between them once. It is the contrast between that earlier period and the time of writing which gives the poem what we call dramatic tension.

The same applies to hate. In the abstract, it lacks personal conviction. When applied to a person or institution it can become too blunt, even propagandistic. But when it is combined with admiration or envy or even love, it becomes a highly complex emotion which lends itself to sophisticated verse.

In the same way, nostalgia can become sentimental unless tempered with a realistic note. Dylan Thomas' idealized view of childhood, for example, ends with a melancholy recognition of the fact that we are indeed mortal.

There are three questions which help guard against writing poems that are simple or insincere treatments of emotions:

- Did I really feel that?
- Was that all I felt?
- Have I found the specific details which will help my reader to share the same feelings?

Emotions that most naturally generate poetry do not have to be intense, but they do have to be genuine and fairly complex.

THE SWEEP OF EXPERIENCE

Basically, both sense perception and specific emotions are forms of experience. But I am concerned here with those broader portions of one's life, whole episodes including events and dialogue.

These are also the natural materials of fiction. But although we can use the same episodes in either poetry or fiction, we tend to develop them in quite different ways. When we write fiction we concentrate on characterization and events—plot—combining the two in the form of a narrative. To do this, we build from a central incident, adding scenes, characters, and background information.

When we work with poetry, we usually reverse the process by reducing and concentrating the original experience. We seek the most significant emotions and the most effective images to suggest them. Such expression is the very core of the original experience.

Dylan Thomas' "Fern Hill" (p. 98) takes a broad view of his childhood, turning it into a fanciful dream. Maya Angelou has apparently drawn on a single day in her kitchen in "This Winter Day" (p. 92). And Robley Wilson has recalled a single experience on a Maine beach in the poem with that title (p. 97).

One of the most striking uses of personal experience is Anthony Hecht's "Lizards and Snakes" (p. 90). Read it now and examine those characteristics which make it similar to a short story.

It has, first, a vivid setting. Notice the visual details. There are also tactile images ("hot. . .enough to scorch / A buzzard's foot"). Next, there are three main characters clearly designated: Aunt Martha, Joe, and the narrator. And there is a plot which serves as the organizing principle of the piece. Finally, there is a theme which elevates the narration from the level of simple anecdote to a relatively sophisticated poem: Fear of lizards and snakes, the poem suggests, can be funny on one level, but it also can have deep psychological and religious roots which we can't laugh off.

It is, of course, a poem and not a story. Reviewing the characteristics outlined in the first chapter, it is clear that Hecht is making artistic use of the line (it is the basis of his meter and his rhyme scheme). He is also concerned with sound devices (alliteration in addition to rhyme), and compression of statement. Even though the treatment is distinctly poetic, the source of the work is a specific incident—similar to that in most stories.

Now turn to a different treatment of what is apparently personal experience in Adrienne Rich's "Like This Together" (p. 95). Notice how the first stanza has all the ingredients of narrative poetry: a scene, characters, certain events. But she soon moves off into a complex set of metaphors suggesting loss of closeness (razed buildings, misunderstood words, winter, a severed hand), ending with a reaffirmation: "hold fast to the / one thing we know."

Reread the last two stanzas, pretending that they are the entire poem. Notice that the intent would be more difficult to understand, more obscure, but not totally hidden. The first stanza may not be essential, but it leads us into the poem. And it is our clue that this poem, like the other two, had its origins in a segment of personal experience.

DELIGHT IN WORDS

This final source of poetry is perhaps the most significant. If there is any one characteristic which separates poets from writers of fiction, it is their particular fascination with words in themselves. Poetry is normally written more slowly, more painstakingly than fiction, and the finished work is intended for careful, repeated reading. It is natural for the poet to place a special emphasis on the overtones, the rhythmical effect, and the sound of words.

Students who have been taught poetry with a heavy hand sometimes miss the fact that many poems are written with a sleight of hand. The word-play in Shakespeare's sonnets, for example, is often more enjoyable than the theme or "message" of the poem. And how many readers remember that Hamlet was a compulsive punster? John Donne's early poetry may not have won over any more women than his later work won converts, but both continue to dazzle readers with verbal ingenuity.

Lawrence Ferlinghetti's "Dove Sta Amore" (p. 94) is a good example of word play. Why is this a pleasure to read? Certainly not for the theme. The delight comes in the way *dove sta amore* (Italian for "where lies love") can also be read as the English words *dove* and *star;* also because of the repetition of the opening four lines; and mainly because of the way the sounds of the words (more identities than rhymes) echo in almost every line. If there is any statement at all, it is only that love is a "lyrical delight" and comes to us more like a song than a definable idea.

GETTING STARTED

Where should you begin? Keeping a journal is a good first step. A journal differs from a diary in that it is not a simple record of events. A poet's journal is more apt to include the kinds of material I have described in this chapter. Here are some suggestions to start filling those empty pages.

Recall and record the most vivid visual impressions you have had in the past week. Then move back to the past year.

Now turn to what you have heard. Music will come to mind first, but don't forget the voice or laugh of a particular person, mechanical objects like a car, truck, or old refrigerator, or natural sounds like wind or rain. Avoid clichés by restricting yourself to what you really heard.

List the four most memorable sensations of touch in the past year. This includes both pleasurable and painful. Which will you remember ten years from now? Can you add tastes and smells? List them too. Why are some more memorable than others?

Turning to emotions, describe in a phrase the three best moments of the past year and the three worst. Then consider which moments were charged with mixed emotions: love and hate or resentment, desire and fear, revulsion and fascination. These are worth exploring.

How about identifiable personal experiences? A rock pool, a kitchen in winter, a childhood on a farm have been the subjects for three of the poets you have read recently. You must have many such experiences. Which will you remember and why?

When you are in a less introspective mood, try this: Carefully draw these two shapes at the top of a fresh page in your journal:

If each shape had a name, which one would be Kepick and which Oona? Now think of them as a couple. Which is the girl? Assume that one of them is a brand of gasoline and the other a type of oil. Which is which? Suppose one is a melon and the other a lemon? And now listen to them: one is a cymbal and the other a violin. Too easy? One is a saxophone and the other a trumpet; one is the wind and the other a dog's bark. It is an odd and significant fact that nineteen out of twenty people will give identical answers. This is the "language" of association, of connotation, which is the special concern of the poet both consciously and subconsciously.

Thinking of them once again as a couple, give each of them four more nonsense names. Now try a few lines of very free verse describing Oona and Kepick, using their other names as adjectives or verbs. (Surely you think of Oona looking feenly in the shane, but what happens when Kepick kacks his bip and zabots all the lovely leems?)

There is no end to this. It won't lead directly to sophisticated poetry, but it does help to link language with music. The two should not be confused, but poems often have as much to do with sound, rhythm, and overtones as they do with making a pronouncement.

Keep your journal going. Make a point of writing *something* in it every day for a month. It won't produce poetry directly, but it will serve as a reservoir from which to draw material. And it will keep you thinking like a poet.

Chapter 3

The Strength of Fresh Phrasing

The *freedom to choose* your own diction; selecting a *level of usage;* the importance of *fresh language;* the *four primary dangers* in poetic diction: *clichés, hackneyed language, sweeping generalities,* and *archaisms;* the need to *stimulate the reader* through words.

Poets today are as free in their choice of words as are writers of fiction and playwrights. It is an important and valued freedom. But this doesn't mean that poets can be careless in selecting their words. On the contrary, because poems tend to be concentrated and are intended to be read slowly and frequently, phrasing is crucial. Word for word and line by line, poetic composition tends to be more deliberate, more heavily revised than any other type of writing.

LEVELS OF USAGE

When we speak, we adopt different levels of usage without thinking. Giving a talk to a class or other academic group on, say, a literary or scientific topic, our language is formal and the diction may necessarily be more complex than it is ten minutes later speaking to friends in the cafeteria. This isn't dishonest; it is merely a matter of using the type of language which meets the occasion.

Poetry often deals with complex personal feelings and insights, so it frequently uses a vocabulary which is more varied or more complex than what we use in a casual letter to a friend. But this doesn't mean you should use needlessly long words or outdated phrases. That will turn your reader off just as quickly as it would to speak to him or her in language which sounds stuffy or old-fashioned.

The best rule to remember is to find the *right* word, not a fancy word for its own sake. Often this means using fairly straightforward language. Theodore Roethke's "The Waking" (p. 93), for example, deals with the complex subject of how we learn to deal with life while being acutely aware of our own mortality, yet in nineteen stanzas Roethke restricts himself to one- and two-syllable words almost entirely. There is only one three-syllable word and that is "another." How does he suggest so much with such simple diction? By building effective metaphors. That is the subject of the next chapter; my point here is that complex statements can be made with relatively simple words.

Another level of usage is found by adopting the more informal patterns of spoken language. Robert Frost, for example, often echoes the speech of New Englanders so ingeniously that many readers are not aware of the fact that they are reading carefully metered verse. Anthony Hecht in "Lizards and Snakes" (p. 90) draws on the informality of spoken language with phrases like "hot enough to scorch a buzzard's foot" and words like "snoozed."

A third level of usage is street language. Allen Ginsberg described it in "Howl" as "obscene odes on the windows of the skull." Derek Walcott has drawn on the rhythms and diction of the Caribbean. But the greatest and most vivid use of street language comes from black poets writing, frequently, with a clear memory of urban American speech. It is not directly recorded, of course; it is the refashioning of words, phrases, and rhythms used to provide energy to poetic statement. Gwendolyn Brooks' "We Real Cool" (p. 92) and Lucille Clifton's "What the Mirror Said" (p. 99) are fine examples.

One note of warning, however: Don't try street language of any sort unless it comes from your own personal experience. Attempts to echo other people's speech almost always sound patronizing and, at the very least, unconvincing.

Once you have established the level of usage, be consistent. The first three or four lines usually establish the kind of language you will be using throughout.

And, equally important, keep your diction fresh. Whether the poem is formal or colloquial or at some point in between, the words and the phrasing must have impact. One way to achieve this is to guard against the following four dangers which can do real damage to any type of poem.

THE CLICHÉ

We have all been warned against clichés since grade school. Yet they remain a temptation—particularly when we are tired and careless. It is important to understand what a cliché is and why it is so damaging to any kind of writing, especially a poem.

The cliché, as George Orwell pointed out in "Politics and the English Language," is actually a dying metaphor; that is, an expression which was once fresh enough to create a clear picture in the reader's mind but has now lost its vitality. Thus, "sharp as a tack" has become dull; "free as a bird" no longer takes flight; "clean as a whistle" sets readers wondering—if at all—whether they are to picture one of those bright, shiny referee's whistles or the sound of someone whistling; and as Orwell points out, "to toe the line" has drifted so far from the original metaphor that it is now frequently seen in print as "to tow the line."

Yet when these metaphors finally die—that is, become built into the language as single words which no longer appeal to a visual comparison—they occasionally regain respectability as utilitarian words. Thus a "current" of electricity has moved from metaphor to a word in its own right. In the same way, "stereotype" and "cliché" have moved from metaphors based on printers' terms for metal plates of print to abstract meanings. The fact that they no longer work visually as metaphors is shown by the fact that so many people use them without having the slightest idea of their original sense.

As readers, we respond to words like these simply as words. They are a part of the language. But a cliché is midway between a fresh metaphor and an established addition to the language.

Clichés weaken a line of poetry partly because they are a long way of saying something simple. To say that a woman was "brave as a lion" is no more effective than simply saying "brave." And readers tend to skip over phrasing which is that familiar. The cliché, then, is to be avoided not because it is "bad taste" but because it converts intense, compressed, highly suggestive writing into that which is loose and bland.

There are three different ways of dealing with clichés that appear in a first draft. First, one can work hard to find a fresh simile or metaphor which will force the reader to see (hear, taste, and so on) the object being used in the comparison. Or one can drop the comparison completely and deal with the subject directly. Finally, one can twist the cliché around so that it is reborn in some slightly altered form. This technique is often seen in comic verse, but it can be highly effective in serious poetry as well.

For example, if you discover that you have allowed "blood red" to slide into your verse, you can avoid this ancient cliché with such alternatives as "balloon red" or "hot red" or "shouting red" depending on the overtones you wish to establish. If none of these will do, go back to just "red."

A good way to improve one's skill in dealing with clichés is to apply these three techniques to "sea blue," "rosy dawn," "tried and true," "mother nature," and "strong as an ox."

HACKNEYED LANGUAGE

This is a general term which includes not only the cliché but the far more dangerous area of phrases which have simply been overused. Whereas clichés usually consist only of conventionalized similes and are easily identified, hackneyed language also includes direct description which has been seen in print too long to provide impact. A seventh-grader can compile a list of clichés as readily as names of common birds; but only one who has read literature extensively can identify that which is literarily hackneyed. This is one reason why vocabulary lists which are emphasized so heavily in some secondary schools are no substitute for wide and varied reading.

Certain subjects seem to generate hackneyed language like maggots. Take, for example, sunsets. The "dying day" is a true cliché, but perfectly respectable words like "golden," "resplendent," "magnificent," and even "richly scarlet" all become hackneyed when used to describe a sunset. It is not the word itself which should be avoided—one cannot make lists; it is the particular combination which is limp from overuse.

In the same way, smiles are too often "radiant," "infectious," or "glowing." Trees tend to have "arms" and frequently "reach heavenward." The seasons are particularly dangerous: Spring is "young" or "youthful," suggesting virginity, vitality or both; summer is "full blown"; and by autumn many poets slide into a "September Song" with only slight variations on the popular lyrics. Winter, of course, leads the poet to sterility and death, terms which too often describe the quality of the poem as well.

Our judgment of what is hackneyed depends somewhat on the age. That which was fresh and vivid in an earlier period may have become shopworn for us. Protesting "But Pope used it" does not make a metaphor acceptable for our own use. But standards of fresh language are far less tied to period than most students believe. It is difficult to find lines in, say, Shakespeare's sonnets which would even today be considered hackneyed. Conversely, many of the conventions which he attacked as stale and useless have continued in popular use and reappear like tenacious weeds in the verse of college freshmen.

In "Sonnet 130," for example, he protests that

> My mistress' eyes are nothing like the sun;
> Coral is far more red than her lips' red. . . .
> And in some perfumes is there more delight
> Than in the breath that from my mistress reeks.

The poem is directed not so much at his mistress as at those poets of his day who were content to root their work in conventions which were even then thoroughly stale. Yet more than three hundred years later poetry is produced (more often by the greeting card industry than by students) in which eyes sparkle like the sun, lips are either ruby or coral red, and breath is either honeyed or perfumed.

Remember that your task as a poet is to find fresh insights. If you are dealing with seasons, don't tell us that spring is a time for growth. We know that. There are other aspects of spring, however, which are worth considering. Here is what T. S. Eliot saw in that season and described in the opening of "The Waste Land."

> April is the cruellest month, breeding
> Lilacs out of the dead land, mixing
> Memory and desire. . . .
> Winter kept us warm, covering
> Earth in forgetful snow, feeding
> A little life with dried tubers

Not only is he telling us that in some ways winter is "kinder" by keeping the ground covered, he is suggesting that sometimes memory and desire awaken aspects of ourselves which we would rather forget. Both are reversals of the simple sentiments which we see so often in simple verse.

ABSTRACTIONS AND
SWEEPING GENERALITIES

In the chapter on the sources of poems, I warned against beginning with a broad, abstract principle like love, death, nature, and the like. It is equally dangerous to allow a poem which was originally inspired by some genuine experience or personal reaction to slide into generalities. Last stanzas are particularly vulnerable. There is a temptation to "explain" one's poem in a concluding stanza which too easily turns into a truism.

If the origin of a poem is a specific love, try to deal with the details as precisely as possible. There will be, of course, aspects which would mean nothing to another reader without a great deal of background material, and these should be avoided. But if the relationship is dealt with honestly, the reader will be able to draw universals from the specifics you provide.

Adrienne Rich's "Like This Together" (p. 95) is a particularly good example. The relationship she describes is unique, but most of us have at some period felt the desperate need to "hold fast to the / one thing we know." She has defined an aspect of love, but she has done it by sharing with the reader the personal details of an apparently real relationship.

The same is true of death. Treating the subject in the abstract almost always seems empty of real feeling. Before the concept becomes poetically manageable, the poet must find a set of images which will make the familiar abstraction fresh and convincing. John Donne's well-known "Death Be Not Proud" uses personification. In a very different way, so does Anthony Hecht's "Lizards and Snakes" (p. 90). Robley Wilson gets at an aspect of death in his treatment of cycles in "On a Maine Beach"(p. 97). And even Dylan Thomas is concerned with death in "Fern Hill"(p. 98). Notice that in each case the poet has avoided the abstraction and concerned himself either with people or, in the case of Wilson, sea creatures.

Other abstractions like patriotism, liberty, and peace contain the same dangers death does; but in addition they have a special tendency to attract clichés. The mind is so rutted with the language of unimaginative orators that what may have started out on an original course is apt to slip into one of these deep grooves and end, both figuratively and literally, in a political convention.

One solution is to shift the theme and attack rather than support all these concerns. I am convinced that at least some of the violently hostile poetry that appears every year is in part a desperate search for fresh language. But this is no ultimate solution; the anti-convention soon becomes conventional.

A more positive approach is to select a single specific example of the abstraction and concentrate on that. If it is social injustice which concerns you, pick one person you know and one incident which occurred to that individual. If you help us to share your feelings about that event, you will have done more than any generalized statement about Truth and Justice could possibly have done.

If you start out writing "Life is. . ." or "Love is. . .," *stop!* Ask yourself, What made me feel like that? What specific event or experience brought that to my mind? Work with what affected you and you will reach your readers.

ARCHAIC DICTION

This is the last in this list of four threats to fresh language. Quite often it takes the form of time-honored but dated contractions such as "o'er," and "oft" as substitutions for "over" and "often." But there are other words which now have the same musty quality: "lo!" "hark!" "ere," and even "O!" are the most frequently used.

The majority of poets writing today need no such warning, and some may be surprised that it must be included here. Yet the practice is seen repeatedly in college writing classes and is well represented in some of the less distinguished poetry journals.

Sometimes the temptation to use archaic words comes from a determination to write perfectly metered poetry. Meter is the subject of Chapter 6, but I should point out here that the rhythms one creates from a metrical line should never be so regular as to dominate the choice of words. Mature use of meter allows substitutions and variations. There is no need to use "lo!" "hark!" and "ere" just to make the line go "ta-*tum*, ta-*tum*, ta-*tum*" like a piece of machinery.

More often, archaisms slip in because the writer understandably admires poets from former centuries. There is nothing wrong with studying poetry of earlier periods; indeed, for every hour of work on your own composition you really should spend an hour reading the poetry of others. But remember that language changes. You can learn a great deal from studying the sonnets of Shakespeare, the ballad as refined by Coleridge, the lyrics of Wordsworth; but don't forget that they were writing with the language of their day just as you should be doing. One can learn a great deal about the *use* of language without imitating the words themselves.

These, then, are the four practices which most frequently defeat the goal of fresh diction: clichés, hackneyed language, sweeping generalities, and archaisms. They are not absolute taboos. Each may, in certain cases, be used to create a particular effect—especially in verse which echoes daily speech. In most cases, however, stay clear of them all.

Put in more positive terms, the words you choose must hold your reader. Unlike the dramatist, you can't depend on visual impact. In most cases, you don't even have plot as an attraction. So the words themselves and the images they evoke will have to provide impact. Your goal as a poet is to stimulate your reader in some way—intellectually, spiritually, or emotionally. Every line you write should work toward that end.

Chapter 4

Images

The *image* defined; using all your *senses;* images used to create *similes* and *metaphors;* the importance of *vehicle* and *tenor* in every figure of speech; the value of *image clusters;* the image as *symbol; playing* with images in journal writing; *getting serious* with finished work.

In its purest sense, an image in poetry is any significant piece of sense data. Although we tend to think of images as objects seen, the term also covers sounds heard, textures felt, odors smelled, and objects tasted.

As I pointed out in Chapter 2, sense perception is a major source of poetic creation. For this reason alone, the image becomes one of the most significant elements in the construction of a poem. But images are also the foundation of similes, metaphors, puns, hyperbole, and other types of figurative language as well as symbolic suggestion.

Because the term *imagery* is used so frequently in connection with similes and metaphors, it is sometimes used interchangeably with these terms. In this text, however, *image* is used to refer to an object seen or perceived by the other senses regardless of whether that word is used literally or as a part of a figure of speech.

Images, then, tend to be concrete nouns—objects which are specific and have shape and weight. But there is no sharp line between words which are concrete and those which are abstract. It all depends on how vividly we can perceive the object.

"Fury," for example, is not an image. It is an abstract word which is common enough as a concept but cannot be seen or heard in itself. "Bird" is more concrete, though it is still rather general. "A blue jay" is more specific and could serve as an image in a poem. "A screaming blue jay" is more vivid partly because in addition to seeing the object we can hear its distinctive cry. Read over these four words and phrases and notice how an abstract concept becomes clearer and clearer as we provide more material for the senses to work with.

Take another sequence: "Evil" is a simple word but highly abstract. "The devil" presents a picture which has been used for centuries to suggest evil. "The lizard" as described in Anthony Hecht's poem, "Lizards and Snakes" (p. 90), is concrete and made even more so with additional visual details like "a smile in the set of the jaw, a fierce pulse in the throat." The aunt's fear (abstract) is revealed to us through the image of a lizard which she perceives as the devil himself.

USING ALL YOUR SENSES

When we think of images, visual details come to mind first. Poets depend heavily on what they see. In poems like Maxine Kumin's "The Presence" (p. 92) and Robley Wilson's "On a Maine Beach" (p. 97), we assume that the visual impressions—a trail in the snow and a rock pool—were the actual starting points for the poets.

But don't neglect the other senses. Sounds, for example, are well worth considering. Here are six lines from Robert Frost's "Mowing" which make use of a scythe's "whispering."

> There was never a sound beside the wood but one,
> And that was my long scythe whispering to the ground.
> What was it it whispered? I know not well myself;
> Perhaps it was something about the heat of the sun,
> Something, perhaps, about the lack of sound—
> And that was why it whispered and did not speak.

In the next seven lines, not one reference is made to sound—either directly or metaphorically. But the image returns again with this final line:

> My long scythe whispered and left the hay to make.

You have to be careful about the word *sound*, of course. Song lyrics and popular verse have long made use of "sounds in the night," "sounds of the street," and "sounds of the sea." But if you can link the word "sound" with something specific which we can hear—like Frost's "scythe whispering to the ground"—the image will have vitality.

Images of touch, smell, and taste are often used in conjunction with each other and with visual details. The poem "Local Places" by Howard Moss provides a fine example. The following stanza is the first of five, and the italics, mine, have been added to stress the use of sound, sight, and touch.

> The song you *sang* you will not *sing* again,
> Floating in the spring to all your local places,
> Lured by archaic sense to the wood
> To *watch* the frog jump from the mossy rock,
> To *listen* to the stream's small talk at dark,
> Or to *feel* the springy pine-floor where you walk—
> If your green secrecies were such as these,
> The mystery is now in other trees.

The italicized words are not, of course, the images themselves but verbs which introduce and emphasize such images as song, frog jumping, mossy rocks, the sound ("talk") of a stream, and the like. Three of the five senses are used in this single stanza; only taste and smell are missing. The second stanza introduces the desert cactus, which is allowed "To perfume aridness," adding one more dimension of sense experience.

Each stanza of this poem is unified by a dominant visual image: the trees for the first, the desert for the second, the ocean for the third, and the rocks for the fourth. In the final two lines of the poem, Moss recalls each of these visual images and links them with the same sound image used in the first line quoted above:

> The tree, the sand, the water, and the stone,
> What songs they sing they always sing again.

There is, of course, a logical development in this poem; and there is a "theme" or "statement" and something which might be called a "message." But what concerns us here is the degree to which the poet as artist has conceived of his work as the expression of sensation. These images of sight, sound, touch, and smell are not mere turrets and gargoyles added to an otherwise solid piece of logic; they are the bricks and timbers with which the piece is constructed.

IMAGES AS FIGURES OF SPEECH

To this point, I have been describing images used simply as descriptive detail. Images also serve as the heart of any figure of speech.

Figurative language most commonly takes the form of the simile or metaphor. These are both comparisons, the first linking the two elements explicitly with "like" or "as" and the second implying a relationship. Here are three similes from three different poems included in Chapter 11. The italics are mine.

- From Adrienne Rich's "Like This Together":

. . . sitting *like drugged birds*
in a glass case

- From Robley Wilson's "On a Maine Beach":

. . . rocks are *like worn change*

- From Dylan Thomas' "Fern Hill":

Now as I was young and easy under the apple boughs
About the lilting house and happy *as the grass was green*

It should be clear from these examples that similes are not simple comparisons. When we compare, for example, a starling with a grackle, we imply that *in most respects* the two objects are similar. But when Rich compares the couple sitting silently in the car with "drugged birds" in a "glass case," she certainly does not want us to picture them as beaked and feathered. They are alike *only in certain respects*—in this case, their dulled mood and their isolation from the natural world outside the car. As with most similes, the area of similarity is far narrower than the area of differences. Its impact depends on how sharply it can make the reader see a new relationship.

Similarly, when Wilson writes that beach rocks are "like worn change," he is suggesting that only in very specific ways can the two be compared. It is less of a visual comparison than it is a way of describing their value as objects from which we can learn a lot. This is not like saying that the rock pools one finds in Maine are like those one can find on the coast of Oregon. That would be a simple comparison.

A metaphor, one learns in grade school, is a simile that doesn't use *like* or *as*. True, but the difference is far more subtle than that. With a metaphor the comparison is implied. It doesn't make sense literally, but we understand what the intent is. Usually the metaphor demands more of the reader than the simile but it also has greater impact.

In the two lines quoted from "Fern Hill," Thomas used one simile, "happy as the grass was green." But the other three figures of speech are all metaphors. To convert the passage so that it contains all similes requires more than the addition of "like" or "as." It might come out in this awkward fashion:

> Now as I was young and living *as if* all things in
> life were easy and *as if* I spent all my time in the
> orchard looking up through the branches, the house and
> the entire area of my childhood were *like* a merry,
> rhythmical song and I was *as* happy *as* the grass is green.

It should be clear from this brutal translation that a metaphor is not necessarily a simile with "like" or "as" removed. The metaphor is often highly compressed, carrying overtones which require entire phrases or clauses to explain. This is one reason why similes are more common in prose, while metaphors are more frequent in contemporary poetry.

When you begin to write poetry, there is sometimes a tendency to rely on similes as you have in prose. It takes a certain courage to convert these to metaphors. But remember that your poetry is going to be read more carefully (we hope) than a paragraph of prose. And probably more often. Those first two lines from "Fern Hill," for example, are puzzling until you read the poem a second time.

There are two terms which are extremely helpful in analyzing any figure of speech—including one's own. I. A. Richards has suggested *tenor* as the poet's actual subject of concern and *vehicle* as the image by means of which the subject is being presented. "Happiness," then, is the tenor in Thomas' simile and he presents this feeling with the vehicle, "green grass." Grass becomes a vehicle in the sense that it "carries" the subject to the reader.

In the metaphor, the tenor is often left out. Thus, "a house as gay and rhythmical as a lilting song" becomes "the lilting house." Those qualities of joy which Thomas intends the reader to recognize have been implied rather than stated. Sometimes those implications become very complex. Because of this, it is often helpful when revising one's own work to separate tenor from vehicle and to question whether that particular vehicle contains the overtones one has in mind.

Most other figures of speech are forms of the metaphor, and their technical names are more important for critics analyzing literature than for writers in the process of composition. Hyperbole, for example, is commonly defined as extreme exaggeration, but in most cases it is a metaphorical exaggeration. Andrew Marvell's "To His Coy Mistress," is a good illustration.

> My vegetable love should grow
> Vaster than empires and more slow;
> A hundred years should go to praise
> Thine eyes . . . .

Transposing this back to simile, we would begin, "My love would be *like* a vegetable which *like* an empire would grow. . . ."

Even the pun can be seen as a form of metaphor when one is able to separate the tenor from the vehicle. In Thomas' "A Refusal to Mourn . . ." he has a play on "grave":

I shall not murder
The mankind of her going with a grave truth . . . .

The tenor here is "solemn truth," and he has, in effect, added *"as if* spoken at the grave-side." He uses essentially the same device in "Do Not Go Gentle into that Good Night" with the line, "Grave men, near death, who see with blinding sight . . . . " Once again, we have only to convert the pun to a simile in order to see it as a part of metaphorical construction.

BUILDING IMAGE CLUSTERS

Although many metaphors are used only once and then dropped, it is often effective to expand or develop a metaphor. When you read a new poem, look for such clusters or groups of related details even when the central theme is not yet fully clear. Then see if you can apply the same technique to your own work.

In Robley Wilson's "On a Maine Beach" there are two such clusters. That is, in addition to the beach images which one would expect, there are two sets of metaphors which are "clustered" in the sense that their vehicles are similar. Turn to the poem now (p. 97) and read it through carefully, identifying the images and marking the lines on which they appear.

The first of these image clusters is coins. Metaphors in which some form of money is used as the vehicle appear in lines 1, 2, 3, 13, and 14. In some cases these are direct as in "worn change" and "mint-mark." And sometimes they are somewhat indirect as in "miser on them" and "counting them"; but the series runs down through the length of the poem.

The second cluster has to do with circles and spirals. They appear in lines 5, 6, 15, and 16 in direct, unmistakable form like "mainspring" and "pinwheeling." But in a broader sense, circles and spirals are seen in the "small equations" whose "sum" is the end of life, in the shape of the pools, in the shape of the coins, and most significantly in the ebb and flow of the tide. The phrase "beach rhythms" (line 15) becomes the dominant pattern for the entire poem.

As the last line suggests, watching these cycles of living and dying within the rock pool help us to see our own mortality in perspective. In this way, the life and death of the reader is included in the dominant image cluster of circles and cycles.

THE IMAGE AS SYMBOL

Turning now to image as used in symbolic language, we shift to a different emphasis altogether. In brief, the symbol is any detail—an object, action, or state—which has a range of meaning beyond and usually larger than itself. Our language is filled with public symbols, like Madison Avenue (commercial values), the flag (nation), the cross (church), which are widely accepted. But the poet more generally constructs his own private symbols. The process is a form of teaching in which "instructions" are given either in the course of a single poem or in several. Anyone familiar with Dylan Thomas' poetry, for example, has learned that "green" is not just a color but a symbol for youth, vitality, growth, and the like. Thus, the phrase from "Fern Hill" quoted above, "happy as the grass was green," is coupled with other uses of the word in the same poem such as "I was green and carefree," "And fire green as grass," "the whinnying green stable," and "the children green and golden." Once the symbolic association is made, any reference to the word (the vehicle) brings to mind the intended meaning (the tenor).

This private symbol of Thomas' is in sharp contrast, of course, with the public symbol of wealth as seen in the term "greenbacks" developed by Fitzgerald in *The Great Gatsby,* where green lawns and the green light suggest wealth and sophistication.

Symbol is often confused with metaphor. Generally speaking, the symbolic object is itself an important part of the poem. In Hecht's "Lizards and Snakes," for example, a lizard is central to the poem and only toward the end do we realize how it has become a symbol for the devil.

Suppose, on the other hand, we read a poem with the line, "As for charm, she was a green-eyed lizard." Here *she* is the poet's central concern and the lizard has been introduced merely to serve as a figure of speech. In a sense, it exists only for comparison.

Another good example of a symbol is seen in Wilson's "On a Maine Beach." The rock pool with its cycles of high and low tide turns out to be a symbol for the cycles of life and death for humans. By looking at this little world, he is saying, we more fully understand our own life and eventual death. But even if we missed all that symbolic suggestion, the poem would still make sense as a description of a tidal pool.

By way of contrast, imagine reading a poem criticizing a social clique with the line, "They were their own little rock pool." We would know that it is the group which is the concern of the poet and the rock pool is only a figure of speech, the vehicle of a metaphor.

If you review these two pairs of examples, you will see that a symbolic object "makes sense" in a poem even if we don't yet see what it symbolizes. With a metaphor, however, we accept the vehicle as incidental, as something brought into the poem simply to create a figure of speech.

Must a poem have a symbolic suggestion? Certainly not. A great deal of verse is written about a particular place or event (commemorative poetry) or an occasion like a birthday, a coronation, or an election (occasional poetry) or merely for pleasure. The subject of these poems may take on no greater meaning than itself. In general, these are *simple* in the literary sense. But if the subject itself is complex, as in the case of Sandburg's "Chicago," the poem may be relatively sophisticated.

But imagine Wilson's poem if it did nothing but describe an interesting aspect of nature. It might serve to illustrate a book of nature photographs, but by itself it would be too *simple* to hold the interest of anyone who enjoys the sophisticated use of language. In the same way, "Fern Hill" without its symbolic suggestion would seem like a slightly sentimentalized memory of childhood, and "Lizards and Snakes" would be reduced to a humorous anecdote.

Be careful not to tack on a symbol as an afterthought to a poem which is essentially descriptive. The result will probably be unconvincing. Examine carefully just what the subject of your poem has meant to you. If, for example, you are describing some aspect of a person you know, ask yourself why that particular topic came to you. Or if it is a specific place, try to get behind the simple observation that you liked it or hated it. If at that point, the subject of your poem begins to take on symbolic suggestion, the theme will seem genuine and convincing.

PLAYING WITH IMAGES

When you first start working with similes and metaphors and their components, tenors and vehicles, the subject is apt to seem rather forbidding. It's hard to imagine playing games with them. But remember that although writing poetry is ultimately a serious and complex art, practicing in your journal can be just plain fun—as well as valuable.

Here, for a start, is a list of five images. Three of these are visual (two static and one dynamic), one auditory, and one tactile.

1. A fat, lazy cat
2. A city street on a hot summer's day
3. The way a particularly graceful woman walks
4. The sound of good jazz
5. The warmth of an open fire in winter

The simplest sort of conversion is to make each one into a vehicle for a simile. For example: "After winning the Pulitzer Prize, he looked like a fat, lazy cat."

Now that I have used a person as the tenor, try using the image to describe a section of a city or the society. Be careful to avoid clichés.

After composing one simile with each image, try converting them to metaphors. In each case, remember, the item in the list is a vehicle and what you are providing is an appropriate subject, or tenor, such as the man who won the Pulitzer Prize.

Now reverse the process, using each item as the tenor. Try, first, to find an image which would serve as a vivid simile for a fat, lazy cat. Let your mind go free. How about a cat lying in the sun "like a pool of molasses"? Go through each of the others like this.

Next, convert these to metaphors. In some cases, there will be little difference except for the use of "like" or "as." But in other cases there will be a surprising boost of strength. Notice how often the metaphorical version will read more like a line of verse than the simile did.

Here is a different approach: Start with the abstraction and convert it into something we can see, feel, or touch through the creation of a simile or a metaphor. Be careful not to settle for a cliché or hackneyed phrase. As a general rule, if you have seen it in print or heard it in a song lyric, avoid it.

Here are some examples:

- *Beauty:*
  Beautiful as a brook in spring (simile)
  Beautiful as a lioness with cubs (simile)
  She stood there, a lioness protecting her cubs. (metaphor)
- *Anger:*
  Angry as a cornered cougar (simile)
  An avalanche of protest (metaphor)
  The letter was pure acid. (metaphor)

You can continue the process with qualities like *gentle, mean, ugly, lively.* Notice that the same abstraction (tenor) can be seen through quite different objects (vehicles). Just as there are many different kinds of beauty, so each state or quality has variations which can be suggested through vehicles as varied as brooks and lionesses.

For variety, try turning from highly abstract qualities to objects about which you may have strong feelings. See if you can find similes to complete these phrases:

"The city I live in is like . . . . "
"The school I attend (attended) is . . . . "
"Being little in a room full of adults is like . . . . "

When you feel at home with these figures of speech, you might want to try writing some haiku. This is a Japanese verse form which contains no rhyme or meter but is based entirely on line length. Traditionally the poem is three lines long with five syllables in the first line, seven in the second, and five in the third. Occasionally this pattern varies when the poems are translated from the Japanese, but it is helpful to try to maintain it. Haiku often make use of a metaphor, but occasionally they are intended to be more like a quick photograph or painting.

Here are two anonymous samples of the sort you might try in your journal:

> The sax whispering
> Takes me on a distant trip,
> Through lands without time.

> Small town of my birth
> Nurtures its sons and daughters,
> Smothers those it holds.

GETTING SERIOUS

Poets never stop playing with language. But there comes a time when one wants to go beyond the level of one's poetic journal and master what the genre has to offer. Part of this requires reading poetry carefully enough so that you identify the images and see how they are developed as similes, metaphors, or symbolic elements. It helps if you own the book and can mark it with marginal notations. No good poem is ever spoiled by analysis.

It is also important to go beyond the level of images themselves and discover how you can make use of the sound of language. This is the subject of the next chapter.

Chapter **5**

The Sound of Words

The importance of the *spoken word* in poetry; *nonrhyming devices* of sound including *alliteration, assonance,* and *onomatopoeia;* the sound of *true rhyme* and its use in *rhyme schemes;* the need for *subtlety* in using sound; *training your ear.*

Poetry was recited aloud long before it was written down to be read on the page. Today, poetry readings and recordings continue that tradition. It is a great convenience to have poems available in print, but the genre has its roots in the spoken word. Most poets consider the sound of what they write to be an important part of their art.

The use of sound in poetry can be obvious—as in rhyming couplets. But more often it is subtle enough so the casual reader is only aware that it "sounds nice." In order to make use of the great variety of sound devices in your own work, you will have to read poetry closely and analyze just how these effects are achieved. This chapter should help you to identify how words are linked by sound in published poetry and how to use the same techniques in your own work.

NONRHYMING DEVICES OF SOUND

There is a tendency to think of rhyme as the primary method of linking the sound of one word with another. Actually, it is only one of many techniques. To place it in perspective, I shall begin with a sample of prose which is highly lyrical in spite of the fact that it, like all prose, has no regular rhyme scheme.

The selection is from Dylan Thomas' "August Bank Holiday." It describes a summer holiday at the beach not through plot but, in the manner of poetry, through a succession of vivid images. The first paragraph is typical of them all. It is reprinted here with the linking sounds italicized.

> August Bank Holiday.—A tune on an ice-cream cornet. A *s*lap of *s*ea and a tickle of *sand*. A *f*an*f*are of sunshades opening. A *wi*nce and *whi*nny of ba*ther*s *d*ancing into *d*eceptive water. A tuck of dresses. A rolling of trousers. A compromise of paddlers. A sunb*ur*n of g*ir*ls and a lark of boys. A silent hulla*baloo* of *baloo*ns.

There are a number of different ways in which the words in this passage are linked by similar sounds. Some make use of vowels (*a, e, i, o, u,* and sometimes *y*) while others link consonants. It is helpful to be able to identify these by name:

Alliteration is the repetition of consonants, particularly those at the beginning of words. There are three groups of these:

slap—sea—sand
wince—whinny (a similarity, not an identity of sound)
dancing—deceptive

Assonance is the repetition of similar vowel sounds regardless of where they are located in the word. Some good examples are:

W*i*nce—wh*i*nny
sunb*ur*n—g*ir*ls (similarity of sound, not spelling)
hullabal*oo*—ball*oo*ns

Consonance is the repetition of consonantal sounds. Since *alliteration* is used to describe similarity in initial sounds, *consonance* usually refers to sounds within the words. Often the two are used in conjunction. There are three sets of consonance in this passage:

wi*n*ce—whi*nn*y
gir*ls*—*l*ark
si*l*ent—hu*ll*aba*l*oo—ba*ll*oons

Onomatopoeia is often defined as a word which sounds like the object or action which it describes; but in point of fact, most onomatopoetic words suggest a sound only to those who already know what the meaning is. That is, we are not dealing with language which mimics life directly; it is usually just an echo. There are three good examples in Thomas' paragraph:

> slap of sea (the sound of a wave on the beach)
> whinny (an approximation of the horse's sound)
> hullabaloo (the derivation of this coming from "hullo" and "hello" with an echo of "babble")

Analyses like this tend to remain abstract and theoretical until one tries the technique in actual composition. Stop now and think of a scene, a friend, or a piece of music which comes to you with the soft, gentle contours you associated with the Oona figure in Chapter 2. Now try a paragraph of descriptive prose in which you make use of as many sound devices as possible. Remember that this is prose, so there is no need to worry about rhythm or a regular rhyme scheme. It might help to circle the linkages in sound. The point of this exercise is merely to help you find and use sound clusters.

Now, by way of contrast, think of a place, a person, or a piece of music which more closely resembles the Kepick figure. Again, work out one or two prose paragraphs. This is to poetry what preliminary sketches are to a finished painting.

THE SOUND OF RHYME

Here is one sound device which by definition is the exclusive property of poets. Prose may contain scattered rhymes, but only when the composition makes use of prescribed line length can one have a rhyme *scheme* or system.

This is not to suggest, of course, that all poetry makes use of rhyme or even that it should. The choice is up to the poet on the basis of an individual poem. But rhyme is still a primary sound device in a great deal of contemporary verse, so only those poets who have mastered the technique can be sure that they are making a truly free choice. Ignorance in this case is highly limiting.

Definitions of true rhyme can reach levels of incredible complexity. None which I have seen, however, contain more than this three-sentence description: *True rhyme* is an *identity* in *sound* in accented syllables. The identity must begin with the *accented vowel and continue* to the end. The sounds preceding the accented vowel must be *unlike*.

I have italicized the key concepts which seem to give the most trouble. First, we are talking here about true rhyme as opposed to slant rhymes or off rhymes, which are respectable and will be discussed shortly. True rhyme is not a general similarity in sound as are assonance and consonance, but an actual identity. Thus "ru*n*" and "co*m*e" are not true rhymes nor are "see*n*" and "cre*am*."

Second, rhyme is a matter of sound, not spelling. "Girl" and "furl" rhyme, but "to read" and "having read" obviously do not. It is often necessary to repeat the final syllable aloud several times before one is sure whether the rhyme is true or not—as do composers when testing the relationship between chords.

Next, there is the matter of continuing identity which must begin with the accented vowel and run through to the end of each word. This is only a problem with two-syllable rhymes (known as feminine rhymes). In "running," for example, the accented vowel is *u* and the only words which rhyme with it end with *unning* as in "sunning." The word "jumping" has the *u* sound, but the *mp* keeps it from rhyming with "running."

Finally, the sound which comes before that accented vowel must differ from its rhyming partner. Thus, "night" and "fight" rhyme since the accented vowel (*i*) is preceded by *n* in one case and *f* in the other. But "night" and "knight" do not. These are technically known as identities.

Since rhyme is based on the sound of syllables and has nothing to do with the division of words, the same principles apply when more than one word is involved in each rhyming end. "Bind me" and "find me" rhyme (the accented vowel is *i* in each case, and the rhyming sound is *ind me*), but neither rhyme with "kindly" because of the *l*.

Rules like these take on the artificiality of grammar when first met, but like grammar they become absorbed once one is used to working with them. An easy way to check each rhyme (and also review the principles of rhyme) is to ask these three questions of each potential rhyme:

1. What is the accented vowel sound?
2. Is the sound in each word identical from that vowel through to the end of each?
3. Is the consonantal sound preceding that vowel different?

These three questions become automatic; one's eye moves first to that key vowel, then forward to the end of each word, then back to the preceding sound. And in each case the eye is translating what is seen into what would be heard if the word were sounded—a fact which makes it almost impossible to work with rhyme without muttering.

If you have the mechanics of rhyme clearly in mind, study the following table. By placing your hand over the right side of the page, you can test yourself by judging whether the pair of words on the left is a true rhyme or not; and if not, what makes it so.

For a less mechanical examination of rhyme, turn to the Anthony Hecht poem, "Lizards and Snakes" on page 90. You have already studied this poem for its use of image and symbol, but you may not have noticed that

RELATED WORDS	ACCENTED VOWEL SOUND	ACTUAL RELATIONSHIP AND EXPLANATION
1. night fight	*i*	True rhyme (meets all three requirements)
2. night knight	*i*	An identity (preceding consonants are identical)
3. ocean motion	*o*	True rhyme (*cean* and *tion* have the same sound)
4. warring wearing	*or* and *air*	Consonance or off rhyme (accented vowel sounds do not match)
5. lyrical miracle	*y*	Off rhyme (the *i* in "lyrical" does not match the *a* sound in "miracle")
6. track to me back to me	*a*	True rhyme (a triple rhyme used by Hardy)
7. dies remedies	*i* and *em*	Eye rhyme (similarity only in spelling)
8. bear bare	*a*	Identity (preceding consonants are identical)
9. balloon hullabaloo	*oo* and *u*	Consonance and assonance (vowel sounds do not match nor do the endings)
10. then you see us; when you flee us	*e*	Quadruple rhyme—true (rare and usually appears forced—often comic)

it is perfectly rhymed. The rhyme endings don't stand out because they occur on alternate lines—a rhyme scheme referred to as *abab*—and also because the poet has adopted an almost conversational tone. But every line is rhymed and all but two are true rhymes. Can you spot the exceptions? When looking for them, identify the accented syllable in each rhyming word.

THE RHYME SCHEME AS A SYSTEM IN SOUND

Most poets who use rhyme use it regularly in a specific rhyme scheme. *Scheme* implies a recurring cycle. And the basic unit of that cycle is the stanza.

Stanzas in general use today vary from two to eight lines, though they occasionally run even longer as in Adrienne Rich's "Like This Together." It is helpful to be able to refer to the seven more common types by name—couplet, triplet, quatrain, quintet, sestet, septet, and octave. Stanzas are also linked with metrical systems (next chapter), but our concern here is limited to systems of sound.

The rhyming *couplet* is the most obvious of all. Because the rhyming lines are in pairs—*aa, bb, cc*—the reader is very conscious of them. Couplets were popular in the eighteenth century but are rarely used today in serious poetry because of the difficulty of muting the sound of the rhyme. Perhaps too, we associate it with greeting-card verse, which is almost invariably written in rhyming couplets. It is only a matter of taste, but poets in our own century have tended to keep their sound relationships subtle and unobtrusive.

The *triplet* (also called a *tercet*) allows the poet more variety. The most common rhyming pattern is *aba, cdc, efe,* and so forth. This leaves one third of the lines unrhymed, which helps to mute the sound. Only rarely (and usually for comic effect) is the triplet rhymed *aaa, bbb, ccc.*

An effective variation of this stanza form is the *terza rima,* used by Dante, Shelley, and some contemporary poets. In this, each stanza is linked to the next one forming an interlocking rhyme in this fashion: *aba, bcb, cdc,* and so forth.

The *quatrain* is often rhymed in the loose manner of the traditional ballad, *abcb.* Here only two out of four lines are rhymed. It is a relatively simple stanza which lends itself to narrative poetry and to verse which might be set to music.

More demanding but equally common is the *abab* pattern used by Anthony Hecht in "Lizards and Snakes." Notice that he places his quatrains together to form stanzas of eight lines—perhaps to maintain the continuity of an as-if-told story. But the rhyme is regular.

The *quintet* (or *cinquain*) is an odd-numbered stanza which is sometimes rhymed with a couplet at the end, *ababb.* Although Swinburne's "Hertha" is a fine example, the quintet has not been popular in rhymed verse.

The *sestet* (or *sextet*) is often thought of in connection with the second portion of a sonnet, which I will come to in Chapter 9. Notice that as the length of the stanza grows, the number of possible rhyme schemes increases at a rapid rate—particularly if you include systems which leave certain lines unrhymed.

The *septet* is famous for the *rhyme royal* which is *ababbcc.* And the *octave* develops this further with the *ottava rima, abababcc.*

KEEPING SOUND DEVICES
SUBTLE

In simple verse, like nursery rhymes and street chants, rhyme is often blatant. In sophisticated poetry, however, the uses of sound are usually kept subtle so that they won't dominate the poem. This is not necessarily achieved by using fewer sound combinations; often it has to do with placement.

As I have already pointed out, rhyming couplets are far more obvious than lines which alternate the rhyme endings. Here, for example, is an altered version of the first four lines of Masefield's "The Lemmings":

> Once in a hundred years the Lemmings come,
> Westward until the salt sea drowns them dumb.
>
> Westward in search of food over the snow;
> Westward till all are drowned, those Lemmings go.

This, let me repeat, is not how he wrote it. I have recast the lines so that they are rhyming couplets—*aa bb.* I have also altered the punctuation so that each line ends with a comma, a semicolon, or a period. These are called *end-stopped* lines. They are opposed to *run-on lines,* in which the grammatical flow and the sense continue to the next line. When rhymes fall on end-stopped lines, they are far more noticeable.

Here is how Masefield actually wrote those opening four lines:

> Once in a hundred years the Lemmings come
> Westward, in search of food, over the snow,
> Westward, until the salt sea drowns them dumb,
> Westward, till all are drowned, those Lemmings go.

His rhyming lines alternate, *abab.* And notice how his punctuation tends to draw the reader on to the next line—particularly from the first to the second. This reduces the emphasis we place on the final word in the line.

Alliteration can also be softened by increasing the distance between the alliterative words. "Salt sea" in the passage quoted above is particularly noticeable and appears to the modern ear to be overused (the poem was published in 1920). But "drowns them dumb" is subtler because the pair of words are separated.

Robley Wilson's "On a Maine Beach" mutes both rhyme and alliteration still further. Turn to it now (p. 97) and read it again, marking all the sound combinations you can find—including rhyme, slant rhyme, alliteration, assonance, and consonance.

At first reading, one is apt to miss the fact that there is a rhyme scheme at all. To see the pattern, it helps to divide the poem into four groups of four lines each. These "stanzas" are for analysis only.

The rhyme scheme is best seen in the final "stanza" of four lines: "sky," "slow," "flow," "die,"—a perfect *abba..*

The next-to-last "stanza" runs as follows: "stone," "weed," "bleed," "gone." The middle pair is made up of true rhymes, but "stone" and "gone" are just slightly off in sound, making them slant rhymes. Like most slant rhymes, they are also examples of assonance.

The general rhyming pattern, then, seems to be *abba.* But when we apply that to the first two "stanzas" we see that it is not complete. There is only one pair of rhymes in each of those units.

Rhyme, then, is highly muted in this poem. But assonance and alliteration are found on almost every line. There are three pairs just in the first two lines:

Look, in these pools, how rocks are like worn change
Keeping the ocean's mint-mark; barnacles

Here, then, are two approaches to the use of sound: Masefield's poem is a sonnet with a traditional rhyme scheme which he employs while muting the rhymed endings; Wilson's poem is still rhymed, but the scheme is more irregular, and he makes far greater use of the other sound devices.

Dylan Thomas' "Fern Hill" is a third approach, one which is still less structured. What little rhyme there is cannot be detected without careful study; instead, the poet relies on alliteration, assonance, and consonance in much the same way he did in the prose passage quoted at the beginning of this chapter. The only trace of a rhyme is seen (if you look hard) linking the third and the eighth lines in all but one stanza. These are slant rhymes and the gap is far too great to hear on first reading, but when they are added to the heavy use of other sound devices, they contribute to what we sense as the "musical tone" of the poem as a whole.

The number of sound connections is astonishing. Almost every line contains two or more words which are linked by sound. Yet the connections are muted enough so that we sense the general effect long before we see the mechanics of how he achieves it.

It is true that some poems rely more heavily on images than on the sound of language. Adrienne Rich's "Like This Together" (p. 95) is an example. But the great majority make full use of the spoken aspect of the genre whether it be through a regular rhyme scheme, partial rhymes, or that array of nonrhyming techniques.

TRAINING YOUR EAR

It is hard to imagine a musical composer who doesn't spend a good deal of time listening to music. Yet some beginning poets are reluctant to read too much published poetry for fear of being influenced. Actually there is no danger of becoming imitative if one reads a wide variety of works; and only by reading—preferably aloud—can one begin to appreciate the ways in which poetry is written for the ear.

The best way to hear poetry is to read it slowly and aloud. But you can also "hear" a poem by mouthing the lines—a necessity if you are working in the library.

Another method is listening to records of poets reading their own work. Most large libraries have collections. If you have a cassette recorder, you may be able to make tapes for your own personal use. Repeated listening is valuable as well as pleasurable.

If you are going to make use of sound devices in your own writing, however, you have to go one step further: It is essential to analyze just how these effects are achieved in the works of poets you admire. This means marking your own copy (or photocopy) of a poem and identifying the sound linkages. After you have done this, read or listen to the poem again, internalizing your analysis.

Finally, practice sound combinations in your poetry journal. Don't limit yourself to those lines which might develop into finished poems. Let yourself go. Experiment with assonance, with alliterative runs, with light verse in rhyme. Try a few imitations of poets with pronounced styles.

Sound in poetry is partly a matter of knowing what you are doing—technique. But it is also a matter of hearing what you are writing—a sensitivity to spoken language. Good poetry requires both.

Chapter 6

Rhythms of Stress

Rhythm as a psychological need in humans; *stress* as one method of achieving rhythm in language; *meter* as a development of stress with the addition of metrical *feet* and metered *lines;* the value of *staying loose* with metrics; the reasons for the *continuing popularity* of meter.

Rhythm is a surprisingly basic need in human beings. Some babies thump their cribs rhythmically long before they are introduced to language. Children throughout the world learn and enjoy schoolyard chants long before they are introduced to sophisticated poetry. And even adults who have not come to enjoy the subtleties of poetry take pleasure in the strong rhythms of bands, dance, and dramatic oratory.

Almost all poetry is rhythmical in some way. This is partly due to the close affinity between poetry and music. It is significant that the word *lyric* has its roots in *lyre* and that even today the word *verse* is used interchangeably for metered poetry and lines to be sung. This is no mere historical accident. Poetry makes fuller use of verbal rhythms than fiction or prose drama mainly because poets are able to maintain control over the length of the lines they write. As we shall see, all meter is based on the length of the line, and most free verse systems of rhythm also rely heavily upon this control.

The study of rhythm should never be thought of as a constricting or limiting aspect of writing any more than it is in music. It is a part of the art form. There are six widely used methods of creating rhythmical patterns in

English and an infinite number of variations possible within each. Some are fairly simple to master, and others (like meter) require learning certain terms. But those who have at least tried all approaches are then free to choose their own individual style, and this freedom is for most poets extremely important.

RHYTHM OF STRESS

English is a language of stress. That is, most words in our language are pronounced with a heavier emphasis on one syllable than on the others. So important are these stresses that in some cases an error in stress alone makes the word incomprehensible—much to the frustration of foreign students.

This is in sharp contrast with French. Take the words *animal* and *nation,* for example. Although they are spelled the same way in each language, English places a special stress on the first syllable of each word, *animal* and *nation.* In French, on the other hand, there is a tendency to place more nearly even weight on each syllable, particularly in verse.

Partly because of this factor, French poets began early with a complex set of rhythmical systems based on the division of syllables, while the Old English poets merely counted the number of stresses in a line. *Beowulf,* for example, is based on a line containing two stressed syllables, a pause, and two more stresses. No attention was paid to the number of unstressed syllables. By French standards, this was a rather crude system of composing verse.

Here is a passage where Beowulf pursues the sea monster down into her underwater lair. Read the selection a couple of times and underline the stresses.

> Then bore this brine-wolf, when bottom she touched,
> the lord of rings to the lair she haunted,
> whiles vainly he strove, though his valor held,
> weapon to wield against wondrous monster
> that sore beset him; sea-beasts many
> tried with fierce tusks to tear his mail

It is obvious that the poet never counted syllables. He was concerned only with having four stresses in each line. He concentrated on this simple beat, and in *Beowulf* it is so clear that one can pound on the table while the song is chanted or sung—which is probably just what the ancients did.

This is a simple system of rhythm. A much more subtle (and literarily *sophisticated*) use of stress was developed by Gerard Manley Hopkins. Like the poet of *Beowulf,* he based his rhythms on the spoken language, usually with a given number of stresses per line. He often paid no attention to the number of unstressed syllables, calling his method "sprung rhythm" in the sense of "freed rhythm."

Turn to his "Pied Beauty" on page 97. For a comparison with the *Beowulf* passage, underline what you feel are the four stressed words in each line. The first line is clear enough, but others are not as pronounced. Stress is being used more subtly here.

FROM SIMPLE STRESS TO METER

Historically, meter came to English verse when the French language was imposed on the Anglo-Saxons after the Norman invasion. And it has been in use ever since. It has provided poets with a great variety of rhythmical techniques.

Before we turn to the terminology, here is how a metrical rhythm is created. Read this sentence out loud: "I wake to sleep, and take my waking slow." Now read it again, this time stressing the syllables which are naturally stressed and only whispering the others. If italics are used, the emphasized words would appear as follows: "I *wake* to *sleep,* and *take* my *waking slow.*" Notice that we are not forcing anything on the language; we are only emphasizing a rhythm which was already there in the spoken language.

If we want to describe that rhythm without using technical terms we might say that it goes ta-*tum,* ta-*tum,* ta-*tum,* ta-*tum,* ta-*tum.* There are five pairs of unstressed and stressed syllables here.

How might we convert that to a line which reverses each pair of syllables? That is, how can we create a pattern of *tum*-ta, *tum*-ta? Read this aloud: "Waking gently, taking living slowly." Never mind about the sense of it yet; just concentrate on the rhythm. The way English is spoken requires that we read this "*Wak*ing, *gent*ly, *tak*ing *liv*ing *slow*ly."

This little example demonstrates two important aspects of meter. First, that it is based on the natural sounds of the spoken language. Second, that the patterns we perceive (in this case pairs of stressed and unstressed syllables) depend on how we begin a line of verse. This is why you can't have meter in the usual sense with prose.

There are a few basic terms which are necessary if we are going to describe what can be done with metrics. The unit of stressed and unstressed syllables, for example, is called a *foot.* Although many varieties of feet have been used, you can analyze metrical verse and write it as well by knowing just four basic types.

The *iamb* is the most popular foot in English. The first example I gave, ta-*tum* in "I wake"—is an iambic foot. Many two-syllable words fall naturally into this pattern: ex*cept,* al*low,* dis*rupt,* a*dore.* There is a tendency for sentences and lines of verse to begin with an unstressed syllable and to be perceived as an iamb. Notice in the selection from *Beowulf*, which is not written to any meter, that most lines begin with an unstressed syllable: "Then bore. . .," "the lord. . .," "that sore. . . ."

The *trochee* is simply the reverse of the iamb, *tum*-ta. Since the metrical system is determined from the beginning of each line, position is all-important. Remember how the iambs in "I *wake* to *sleep*. . ." were converted to trochees as soon as the line was rewritten to begin with a stressed syllable: "*Wak*ing *gen*tly. . . ." Here is another example: "the lord of rings" is clearly two iambic feet (ta-*tum* ta-*tum*); but we can shift these to trochees by starting the line with a stressed syllable: "Lord of rings and master" (*tum*-ta *tum*-ta *tum*-ta).

Trochees can be used as the basic foot for an entire poem. But more often they are used as a substitution for an iambic foot in an iambic poem. As we shall see, this can give a special emphasis to a word or phrase, particularly if it is done at the beginning of a line.

The other two feet each consist of three syllables. The *anapest* has two unstressed syllables followed by a stressed syllable, as in "disap*point*" and "lower *down*." The *dactyl* is the reverse of this, as seen in "*hap*pily," "*mer*rily," and "*sing* to me."

These basic four feet are common enough so that familiarity with them is sufficient to scan (analyze and classify) almost any sample of metered verse in English and related languages. And they will provide you with enough flexibility to write metered verse skillfully without studying some thirty other combinations used by classical poets.

Conscientious scanning occasionally requires familiarity with the *spondee*—two equally stressed syllables, as in "heartbreak"—and the *pyrrhic foot*—two equally unstressed syllables, such as "in the" or "and the"; but the practicing poet often reads these as softened versions of iambs or trochees.

As review, the following table shows the four basic metrical feet, with the stress pattern and examples of each.

In addition to the types of feet, there is the matter of how many feet are used in each line. By far the most popular length in English is five feet, known as pentameter. Unrhymed iambic pentameter, known as blank verse, was used by Shakespeare in his plays; pentameter is also the line used in the sonnet which will be described in the next chapter. In our own century

TYPE OF FOOT	ADJECTIVE	STRESS PATTERN	EXAMPLES
iamb	iambic	ta-*tum*	except; she might
trochee	trochaic	*tum*-ta	Midas; lost it
anapest	anapestic	ta-ta-*tum*	disappoint; lower down
dactyl	dactylic	*tum*-ta-ta	happily; sing to me

such poets as Robert Frost, Richard Wilbur, and X. J. Kennedy have made extensive use of this line. The clearest example in this text is Theodore Roethke's "The Waking" on page 93.

The four-footed line, tetrameter, is a close second. And trimeter is also used widely. Lines which are longer than pentameter and shorter than trimeter are used far less frequently, but for the purpose of clarity, here is a list of types:

One foot to each line (very rare)	*monometer*
Two feet to each line (rare and usually comic)	*dimeter*
Three feet to each line (fairly common)	*trimeter*
Four feet (sometimes combined with trimeter)	*tetrameter*
Five feet (most common in English)	*pentameter*
Six feet (less used in this century)	*hexameter*
Seven feet (rare)	*heptameter*
Eight feet (a heavy, very rare line)	*octometer*

Don't let the terms put you off. They are intended for your use. At this point, it would be helpful to try three lines of iambic tetrameter. Take some simple topic as if you were about to write a haiku and follow the iambic pattern: ta-*tum*, ta-*tum*, ta-*tum*, ta-*tum*. Don't worry about rhyme and don't feel you have to be profound. This is just to help you feel the rhythm.

Now try shifting those lines so that they are trochaic: *tum*-ta, *tum*-ta, and so on. Once you get the line started, the rest should follow somewhat more easily.

Next, shift the topic to something lighter and try a few lines of anapests, ta-ta-*tum*, ta-ta-*tum*. For example: "In a leap and a bound, the gazelle in delight welcomes spring!"

Most writers find the iamb the easiest to work with. The trochee has added punch, thanks to that initial stress in each line. The anapest usually has a lilting quality. And the dactyl, least used of the three, tends to have some of the heavy quality of a trochee and the length of an anapest.

Iambs and anapests are similar in that they both end on a stressed syllable. This is called *rising* (or *ascending*) meter. Trochees and dactyls, on the other hand, end on unstressed syllables and therefore are *falling* (or *descending*) meters. This distinction becomes important when one begins to use substitutions for variety and special effects.

STAYING LOOSE WITH METRICS

Until now, I have been working only with skeletal outlines. They may appear to be as far from the actual creation of lyrical poetry as the study of notes and clefs appears to be from musical composition. But the process of absorption is similar in these two cases. What appears at first to be a set of arbitrary rules eventually becomes—even for those who may then depart from them—an internalized influence.

When you first begin working with meter, there is a natural tendency to make it as perfect and blatant as possible. The result is apt to be like the dancer who is still counting out each step. As soon as possible, try to mute your meter—not by careless construction but by adopting the methods of poets you admire.

There are four ways of keeping your metrical rhythm from taking over a poem, and often you will find three or all four used in a single work.

The first and most commonly used method is to make sure that at least some of your words bridge two metrical feet. "I wake to sleep," for example, is rather bluntly metered since each foot contains two complete words. But the end of that line, ". . .and take my waking slow," divides "waking" between two feet: "my *wak*/ing *slow*." This is a subtle but effective method of softening your metrical impact. If your meter strikes you as too regular, too monotonous, make sure that you haven't hit too many of those stressed beats with one-syllable words.

A second method of muting your meter is to use *run-on lines*. A run-on line, described briefly in the previous chapter, is one in which both the grammatical construction and the sense are continued into the next line. It is opposed to the *end-stopped line* in which there is a natural pause—usually with a comma or a period. Some end-stopped lines are more abrupt than others, of course; and the more pronounced such a line is, the more it will emphasize the meter.

Run-on lines help to soften the impact of meter just as they mute rhyme. The example we looked at in the previous chapter on rhyme applies equally well. Notice how the metrical beat remains regular but is made less pronounced when the meaning continues into the next line:

> Once in a hundred years the Lemmings come
> Westward, in search of food, over the snow

The same sort of run-on pattern is seen frequently in Wilson's "On a Maine Beach." Here are the concluding two lines:

> Round lifetimes half-awake. Beach rhythms flow
> In circles. Perfections teach us to die.

Another technique of softening the impact of meter is rarely used but well illustrated in Anthony Hecht's "Lizards and Snakes" (p. 90). Instead of writing consistently in lines of pentameter or tetrameter, he alternates between these two. The first line has five feet and the next has four. A few of his lines even have six feet.

This is a risky approach since the reader is apt—at least un-consciously—to expect greater regularity. One reason it seems natural here is that the poet has consciously adopted an informal, conversational tone.

The fourth and by far the most frequently used method is called *substi-tution*. That is, the poet occasionally substitutes a different foot from the one which has been adopted for the poem as a whole.

In iambic verse, for example, it is often effective to place a trochaic foot at the beginning of the line to stress a particular word or phrase. Here is how Masefield does it:

> Westward, in search of food, over the snow

Notice how that first word is highlighted. He repeats that particular substi-tution in five different lines, making it into a kind of refrain.

There is another substitution in that same line. "*Over*" is trochaic. This has no clear function in terms of emphasis, but it helps to mute the meter.

Robley Wilson's "On a Maine Beach" (p. 97) is even more loosely me-tered. Essentially, the poem is iambic pentameter, but notice the substitu-tions in those first two lines:

> Look, in/these pools,/how rocks/are like/worn change
> Keeping/the o/cean's mint-/mark; barn/acles

He uses trochaic substitutions at the beginning of each line and several words are split between different feet.

Anapests have a different effect. Often that three-beat measure (ta-ta-*tum*) seems to lighten the tone of a poem. Returning to Masefield's "The Lemmings," the notion of all those little creatures running into the sea be-cause of some strange imprinting of instinct is essentially comic. The poem doesn't turn serious until the last six lines which suggest that perhaps hu-mans move in the same sort of quest. Masefield keeps the tone of the poem from growing serious too quickly with anapestic substitutions in the seventh and eighth lines:

> And memory of the place has burnt its brand
> In the little brains of all the Lemming Kings.

Much of the tone, of course, is created by word choice—the picture of those lemming kings is almost like a cartoon. But some of the lightness also stems from those anapestic substitutions, especially the one which takes the first three syllables of the second line: "In the *lit/le brains*. . . ."

How much substitution can a poem absorb? Anthony Hecht's "Lizards and Snakes" comes close to the limit. The poem is essentially iambic, but here is a line in which three of the five feet are non-iambic substitutions. Can you scan it and spot the variations?

> In the set of the jaw, a fierce pulse in the throat

The most logical way to scan this is to read the opening six words as two anapests. The other substitution is the trochee in "pulse in."

With so many variations, why do we call the poem iambic? Because *most* of the lines are largely iambic with no more than one or occasionally two substitutions. When we come to a line like the one just quoted, we retain the memory of that iambic beat and assume that the poem will return to it. As indeed it does. If the poem contained very many lines with so few iambs, we would begin to conclude that it was unmetered.

THE VALUE OF METRICS

There are, of course, other ways of creating rhythm in poetry. One can use typography (the arrangement of words on the page), syntactical rhythms (using grammatical units), syllabics, and breath units. These will be discussed in Chapter 7, "Rhythms of Free Verse."

In spite of all these free-verse alternatives, a large number of poets in our own century prefer the structure which meter provides. Robert Frost is widely quoted as having said that writing poetry without meter is "like playing tennis with the net down." In varying degrees poets like Auden, Anthony Hecht, X. J. Kennedy, Theodore Roethke, Robert Lowell, Richard Wilbur, and many others agree.

Why? Tastes vary just as they do in any art; but here are four reasons often given by poets themselves.

Some simply prefer to establish the rhythmical base in advance, seeing meter as a flexible structure which saves them from devising new rhythmical cues with each line. In addition, the very process of revising so as to create a metrical pattern often leads to word choice and arrangement which one didn't consider at first. In this way meter can push a poet into exploring possibilities which might not have been tried with less structured systems.

Third, many like the opportunity of emphasizing or highlighting a word or phrase through the natural stress of a metrical foot or—stronger still—through substitution. We have already seen how trochaic substitution emphasizes words at the beginnings of lines. And sometimes it is used to give a whimsical lilt, as in Masefield's "The Lemmings." The result is almost like underlining a word or telling a reader what the poet's mood is at a particular point in a poem. It is a delicate control of language which prose can't match.

Finally, meter provides an identifiable rhythm from which one may depart and return again, a pleasure in itself which is somewhat like a jazz player who feels free to improvise around an established melody. Because metrical rhythms are regular, the poet can, in a sense, play with them. For some, this is an important aspect of writing poetry.

In any case, meter should not be thought of as some external system added to a poem for decoration. It is for many a basic part of the creative art, a way of making the poem do more than it could have otherwise.

Chapter 7

Rhythms
of Free Verse

Using *typography* to establish rhythms; *syntactical rhythms* of Whitman and others; *syllabics,* the counting of syllables; *breath units;* methods of *developing a facility* in the full range of rhythmical techniques.

Free verse abandons meter for other rhythmical devices, and it avoids regular rhyme in favor of looser sound systems. But it is not a revolution in poetry. It is not even new. It is a continuing traditon with some of its roots reaching back to the verse of the Bible.

Essentially, it refers to all those methods of creating rhythmical patterns which are *not* based on stress and meter. In no way, however, does *free verse* suggest an absence of rhythm. Much of it is highly rhythmical, but the methods are nonmetrical.

There are at least four different ways of creating free-verse rhythms: typography, syntax, syllabics, and breath units. Varied as these are, they do not represent separate, unrelated systems. They are often used in conjunction with each other.

There is sometimes a temptation to establish a personal "style" by adopting a single rhythmical system and repeating it in poem after poem. This is limiting. Most accomplished poets vary their methods, particularly early in their careers. This helps one to grow. Dylan Thomas, for example, was equally at home with the rhyme and meter of a sonnet as he was with the syllabics and breath units of free verse. Once again, being familiar with a wide range of methods will give you the artistic freedom to choose what is best for a particular poem.

THE VISUAL PATTERNS OF TYPOGRAPHY

This method of creating rhythmical effects is not strictly a matter of sound. Since it depends heavily on how the poem looks on the printed page, it is often called visual rhythm. But actually there is no clear separation between visual and auditory rhythms. The way a poem is arranged on the page is going to affect a reading in some way. *Typography,* then, refers to the arrangement of words on the page, but it is linked closely with the sound of a poem.

Turn now to Denise Levertov's free-verse poem, "Merritt Parkway" on page 91. Read it a couple of times just for the sense of motion.

The Merritt Parkway is one of the nation's early multilane highways, but the sense of continuing motion and the ceaseless shifting of lanes applies to any section of the interstate system. The typography of the lines are clearly designed to suggest both the motion and our mood as we drive.

Although the structure is not formal as it is in the stanzas of metered verse, there are cues which establish form. Notice, for example, the phrase "keep moving—" which appears in the third line and again a little more than halfway through. In each case the words are used to introduce a new block of images—the first indented to the right and the second brought out to the left.

The images tend to be linked visually more than by the sound of the words, but notice how at the end the poet employs not only alliteration but onomatopoeia in the echo of cars sliding by on the highway:

> . . .gliding
> north & south, speeding with
> a slurred sound—

E. E. Cummings' poem, "Buffalo Bill's" (p. 94) is an even more dramatic example of typography. Turn to it now and read it over several times for the pleasure of it. Then study it carefully, looking for the ways in which he controls the speed of your reading and provides elements of surprise.

There are two ways in which Cummings appears to speed up your reading of this poem: by running words together and by using long, fairly uncluttered lines which can be read as fast as prose. In some cases, however, this may only be an illusion of speed—particularly in the first reading. It often takes longer to puzzle out lines which are printed without spaces. But once one is used to the poem, these lines seem to ripple by as if they were moving.

and break onetwothreefourfive pigeonsjustlikethat

                                                                            Jesus

he was a handsome man

Here the word "Jesus" appears to be linked syntactically with Buffalo Bill's shooting ability; but then it leaps forward to become linked with how handsome he was. It is essentially a visual trick, tripping our expectations through an unexpected shift in rhythm. Of course, the same device of syntactical ambiguity can be used in metered verse, but the effect is heightened here by hanging the word between the two lines.

Notice, too, the way he uses line length. In many cases it is clear that he has kept a line short to highlight a certain phrase or even a word. But remember that one cannot find a rational explanation for every typographical element. Like the brush strokes of a painter, a majority of decisions which go into a poem are intuitive.

One extreme form of typography is the "shaped poem" which molds the shape of the work into the object it is describing. This was particularly popular in the seventeenth century and is well illustrated by Herbert's "The Altar" and "Easter Wings," as well as by Herrick's "The Pillar of Flame," each of which resembles the object suggested in its title. More recently, contemporaries like Allen Ginsberg have published poems in the shape of atomic clouds and, with the aid of punctuation, rockets. And certain painters have moved in from the other end, arranging the letters in a single word like *LOVE* as their composition. Here, of course, the written word becomes painting just as, in the case of the chant, it becomes a form of music.

Shaped poetry—sometimes called *concrete poetry*—does have certain limitations, however. As a poem begins to rely more and more on visual shape, it generally becomes less and less concerned with sound devices, rhythmical systems, and even metaphorical language. It is as if concern for the visual composition drains all other aspects. The most extreme experiments in shaped poetry are remembered for their curiosity value rather than their literary worth.

Even nonpictorial use of typography has its internal limitations. Sophisticated poetry depends at least in part on maintaining unity and flow—concerns which I will return to in Chapter 9. As one increases the rearrangement of words and lines on the page, the poem becomes proportionally fragmented and, as a result, less of an organically unified work.

The use of typography, therefore, continues to be a part of the poetic tradition, but it has its own set of limitations.

SYNTACTICAL RHYTHMS

In essence, syntactical rhythm is merely the patterning which one achieves through the sentence structure itself. It is one device which poetry shares with prose. Here elements of the sentence—grammatical units—are arranged to create relationships. This is not strictly visual rhythm—one can respond to it without seeing the work on the page; but it is not rhythm of sound either—unlike meter it cannot be detected by one who does not know the language. This last sentence, by the way, is an example of syntactical rhythm in prose which can be described as: "statement—amplification; but second statement—amplification." Note that this involves both meaning and grammatical sequence.

Walt Whitman made full and varied use of syntactical rhythms. Here is a sample from his "Passage to India":

> Ah who shall soothe these feverish children?
> Who justify these restless explorations?
> Who speak the secret of impassive earth?
> Who bind it to us? what is this separate Nature so unnatural?
> What is this earth to our affections? . . .

This is rhythm by syntactical repetition. The repetition of the word "who" is only a cue; the full interrelationship among these quoted lines has to do with the echo of each question with the one which precedes it. The key verbs are "soothe," "justify," "speak," "bind," and "is." One can see from these highly varied verbs that the *statement* is not repetitious; it is only the *form*. Whitman has replaced rhythm of metrical units with rhythm of grammatical units.

Allen Ginsberg wrote "Howl" in 1959, one hundred and four years after Whitman first published "Leaves of Grass," and his indebtedness is clear. Here is a sample:

> who broke down crying in white gymnasiums naked and trembling before the machinery of other skeletons,
> who bit detectives in the neck and shrieked with delight in police-cars for committing no crime but their own wild cooking pederasty and intoxication,
> who howled on their knees in the subways and were dragged off the roof waving genitals and manuscripts
> who let themselves be . . . in the . . . by saintly motorcyclists, and screamed with joy. . . .

Ginsberg is clearly influenced by Whitman, but both of them drew on a still earlier source, the Bible. Although Whitman's version was in English, the King James translation, and Ginsberg's was in the original Hebrew, both men were strongly influenced by the rhythmical patterns found there. Compare, for example, the selections quoted from these two poets with this passage from *Job* 38: 34:

> Canst thou lift up thy voice to the clouds,
>   that abundance of waters may cover thee?
> Canst thou send lightnings, that they may go
>   and say unto thee, Here we are?
> Who hath put wisdom in the inward parts?
>   or who hath given understanding to the heart?
> Who can number the clouds in wisdom?
>   or who can stay the bottles of heaven,

Here too, it is the entire syntactical unit which is repeated to achieve the rhythm. The repeated words are merely cues which signal the repeated form. For further examples, read over the rest of the *Book of Job* and review *The Psalms*. Then go back and study the complex system of syntactical rhythms in *Genesis*. Doing this makes one far more open to the rhythms not only of Whitman and Ginsberg but Ferlinghetti, Gregory Corso, John Ashbery, Amiri Baraka (LeRoi Jones), and many others writing today.

Syntactical repetitions do not have to be blatant. Turn to Lucille Clifton's "What the Mirror Said" (p. 99). Notice how she has organized that poem around the word *listen*. She repeats it three times, providing a structure as distinct as stanzas are in metered verse.

After one has absorbed a variety of samples—ancient, nineteenth century, and contemporary—one is ready to try the form. It may help to select some topic about which one feels strongly since the chant-like aspect seems to lend itself to moods of indignation, rage, exultation, and derision.

Start with a strong line which has some complexity and length. Then try to match the syntactical form in the second and third lines. At this point, shift the sentence pattern and repeat this one or two more times. The poem might then be rounded out with a seventh line which returns to the pattern of the first. The variations, of course, are endless. One is bounded only by these two extremes: a lack of rhythm which is so complete that the piece becomes fragmentary (and therefore *simple*) prose; and on the other hand a regularity of rhythm which becomes monotonous and sounds like a childish (and literarily *simple*) chant.

SYLLABICS AND BREATH UNITS

The two systems of creating rhythm which were discussed in the previous chapter, stress and meter, are closely related. Meter is both a refinement and an elaboration of stress. And the two rhythmical systems already discussed in this chapter, typography and syntax, are also closely linked. They

are often used in conjunction with each other. These next two systems, however, are in no way related to each other. They are the "et cetera" in this list
of six methods of creating verbal rhythms.

Syllabics, quite simply, involves counting syllables. A haiku, discussed
briefly in Chapter 4, is one form of syllabics. It is an unrhymed and
unmetered poem in which the first line has five syllables, the second has
seven, and the third has five. Here are two samples which have been translated from the Japanese.

> After spring sunset
> Mist rises from the river
> Spreading like a flood
>   (Chora)

> Even with insects . . .
> Some are hatched out musical . . .
> Some, alas, tone-deaf
>   (Issa)

Like all types of syllabics, this form is partially visual and only faintly auditory. When we look at a haiku we recognize the shape even before we count
syllables—just as we do the fourteen-line form of the sonnet. The shape creates certain expectations if we have read other haiku. We assume that probably there will be a single image (often from nature) and that the central concern may be merely a visual impression rather than a philosophical
statement.

As for the sound, the predetermined pattern of line length does not affect our way of reading the poem out loud as in the case of meter, but it does
make our reading more deliberate. Often each line is a single visual unit or,
as in the second poem, a single suggestion.

In general, however, the value of the form is not strictly visual or auditory. For many it is merely a recognizable way of concentrating a single impression or insight. The formal requirements are simple, yet the varieties of
treatment are infinite. In Japan where many nonpoets enjoy writing and
reading haiku, it has been estimated that a million new haiku are published
each year.

Syllabics for the practiced poet can become a far more complex form
of expression. Dylan Thomas' "Fern Hill" is a fine example.

It is clear that the poem is not metered. The lines do not scan and they
are far too varied in length to fit any traditional stanza pattern. But you can
read the poem many times (as I did) without realizing that it is meticulously
composed in stanzas which have the same pattern of syllables.

To be specific, the first line of every stanza has fourteen syllables and
so do all the second lines. The third line of every stanza has nine syllables,
the fourth line regularly has six syllables, and the fifth line always has nine.
Up to this point the system is absolutely regular.

The sixth line has fourteen syllables in every stanza but the first (which has fifteen); the seventh line also has fourteen in every stanza but—you guessed it—the last (which again has fifteen). The eighth lines are either seven or nine syllables, and the final lines are either nine or six.

This is a highly complex system. Even his variations take on a certain order. And this in a poem which on first reading appears to be a free, lilting lyric without form.

Why should Thomas bother if we aren't going to notice it after the first reading? Presumably he felt that even if we never analyzed the intricacies of the pattern, we would respond at least unconsciously to the patterns.

Although we have been concentrating on syllables, the poet has linked the stanzas in other ways as well. The second lines of most stanzas are not only the same length but serve to announce the scene for that stanza: the "lilting house," the "happy yard," the "fields," and so forth. In this way the form is wedded to content. As for sound, there are so many samples of assonance, consonance, and alliteration within almost every line that it is easy to miss the trace of a rhyme scheme. There is a slant rhyme linking the third and the eighth lines in four stanzas and a slight variation of this in the other two. No one is going to hear this consciously, but like the syllabic count it adds to the total effect of what we think of as "musical" poetry.

Breath units are the loosest form of rhythm in poetry today. Essentially, the poet breaks the line at that point where the reader might be expected to take a breath. Poets like Charles Olson, who defended this approach, argue that it emphasizes the oral aspect of verse and provides greater freedom for the poet. A good example of a poem which appears to have been composed in breath units is Maxine Kumin's "The Presence" (p. 92). The lines are often unified by a visual image; but they also serve as a cue to oral delivery.

DEVELOPING A FACILITY IN RHYTHM

These methods of creating rhythm in free verse are closely related to the metrical rhythms discussed in the last chapter. The goal is essentially the same. To see the relationship, it is helpful to take a single work and convert it into various rhythmical systems, both metrical and free.

Here, for example, is a sample of iambic pentameter, the first four lines from Shakespeare's "Sonnet 2":

When forty winters shall besiege thy brow
And dig deep trenches in thy beauty's field,
Thy youth's proud livery so gazed on now,
Will be a tattered weed of small worth held.

It is an unusual passage because there is not a single substitution. For this reason, it serves as a good base for rhythmical doodling. One might begin, for example, by converting it to iambic trimeter. There are many ways of handling this, but here is one:

When forty winters shall
Besiege thy brow and dig
Deep trenches in thy face
Thy youth's proud livery
Will be a worthless weed.

The point of this exercise is not to improve on Shakespeare but to improve one's own ability to work with meter and one's inner *sense* of pentameter and trimeter. Line-length conversions are easy; shifting from iambic to trochaic requires a little more effort. It might come out like this:

Forty winters shall besiege thy lovely
Brow and dig deep trenches in thy beauty's
Field and youth's proud livery loved so fully
Soon will be a tattered weed of little worth.

The perceptive reader will notice that I have slurred "livery," a three-syllable word, to "liv'ry," two syllables; I also allowed an extra stressed syllable at the end of the fourth line. Keeping in mind that there is no one way to handle meter, you may be able to devise a more perfect rendering.

Moving from meter to visual rhythm, any number of possibilities might be tried. Here is one sample:

When forty winters shall
    besiege
        starve
            torment
The rounded beauty of your brow,
                        then
Your light step will
    limp
      pause
        trembling before the last descent.

When we turn from typography to syntactical rhythms our attention shifts from the purely visual arrangement of lines on the page to the dramatic use of sentence structure. Remember the impact of rhetorical questions and repeated words and phrases as often seen in Biblical verse and the work of Whitman and Ginsberg. Freely rendered, our Shakespearean passage might come out like this:

Forty winters shall besiege thy brow
Winters that will dig deep trenches in thy beauty's field
Winters that will wither that proud young livery
Winters that will leave you but a tattered weed of little worth

All this is doodling for your journal. You could continue with, say, the last four lines of Wilson's "On a Maine Beach" (p. 97) or any stanza from Roethke's "The Waking" (p. 93). It should be fun. But if you apply some of the specific approaches described in this and the previous chapter, it should be useful as well.

In addition to composing in your journal, spend some time each day examining the rhythms of published poetry. Since almost all poetry contains rhythmical patterns of some sort, every anthology and literary quarterly can serve as a source for study. By combining exercises in your journal and extensive, careful reading, the varieties of rhythm will soon become a part of you.

Chapter **8**

Tone

Tone as *the poet's attitude* toward the subject; examples such as *comic, somber, angry, neutral;* the identity of the *narrator* or *persona;* the value of *contrasts* in attitude and *ambivalence;* the use of *irony, satire; revising* your tone.

"I want that."

This looks like a clear statement. How could we mistake its meaning? But if someone said that to us, would we respond just to the words or to other factors, such as who the speaker is and what is the tone of voice?

Suppose, for example, the speaker is a stranger on a dark street and he is holding a gun. That's going to evoke one set of responses. But suppose those same words were the joking comment of a friend on first seeing Fort Knox. The whole meaning shifts.

Now imagine a situation in which there is no threat and no humor involved: the same words are said by a sobbing child in a supermarket, pointing to a sugar-coated breakfast cereal you detest. And what happens to the statement when it is the retort of someone who has just discovered her tax rate has been doubled—"I want that like a hole in the head"?

In spoken language we respond not only to the literal meaning of words, the *denotation*, but almost always to an array of *connotations* which we gather from who is speaking and with what tone of voice.

Tone is equally important in poetry. It consists of all the cues by which the reader judges the attitude of the poet toward the reader and toward the subject of the poem.

TONE AS ATTITUDE TOWARD THE SUBJECT

Tone on its simplest level informs the reader whether a poem is intended to be comic, serious, somber, angry, or merely neutral. Tone also suggests the degree of formality or informality.

There are no sharp divisions between these categories, of course, any more than there are clear divisions between differing tones of voice. And it is important to remember that they can be combined in interesting ways—which will be discussed later in this chapter. I am concerned here with tone on its most accessible level—what we mean when we say "that's a funny poem" or "it has a dark tone."

Comic verse is often looked on as being unworthy of serious effort. Much of it, of course, is *simple* in the sense that it is written for special occasions or for a chuckle and is not intended for the kind of attention we give sophisticated poetry. Remember, however, that sophisticated poetry can have humorous or comic elements and still have the range of suggestion we associate with sophisticated work.

"Lizards and Snakes" (p. 90) is a good example. In some respects it is a humorous anecdote about a boy and his friend Joe who used to slip lizards into the knitting box of a spinster aunt. If that were all, we would be amused and leave it at that. The fact that we go on to deal with the lizard as suggesting the devil and representing a genuine nightmare for the old woman does not mean that we should discount the humor.

The same applies to Gwendolyn Brooks' "We Real Cool" (p.92). The echo of street language gives the poem a light-verse tone at first. But there is nothing light about the ending: "We / Die soon."

One effective way of combining comic situations with serious themes is to give the impression of lightheartedness at first and then present a darker implication at the end. This is essentially the pattern in both of these poems. And while the body of "Fern Hill" (p. 98) is not really comic, it is certainly joyful. The somber recognition of mortality is prepared for in the middle of the last stanza with the words "forever fled from the childless land" and completed in those last two lines:

> Time held me green and dying
> Though I sang in my chains like the sea.

Somber tones often dominate student poems. This may stem from the fact that it is easy to confuse the phrase *serious verse* with *gloomy poetry*. In most cases, *serious verse* refers to work which is sophisticated—that is, intricate in implication and suggestion though not necessarily in technique.

As we have seen, a light touch can make one's approach to a serious subject more effective. It is also possible to express somber issues with a sustained good humor. Roethke's "The Waking" (p. 93) is such a poem. When he writes "I wake to sleep," he is suggesting that one is born only to die. But what a difference in tone between his wording and the blunt paraphrase! Although he is acutely aware of the fact that life ends with death, he describes his life as a dance: "I hear my being dance from ear to ear." A poem like this is a good reminder of the fact that the tone is not determined by the subject matter; the tone is how the poet feels about the subject.

Anger and *protest* have long been expressed in poetry. Some of the strongest examples come from the Hebrew prophets. They tended to stand outside the mainstream of their own cultures, and they were highly critical of the societies of their day. Their language was blunt and direct. Take this brief example from *Isaiah* 3:24:

> And it shall come to pass, that instead of sweet smell
> here shall be stink; and instead of a girdle, a rent;
> And instead of well set hair, baldness; and instead of
> a stomacher, a girding of sackcloth;
> And burning instead of beauty.
> Thy men shall fall by the sword,
> and thy mighty in the war.

The following (*Isaiah* 33:1) is an attack on those in power. It is not far in spirit and to some degree in technique from the attacks made in the 1960s by poets like Allen Ginsberg, Gregory Corso, and others.

> Woe to thee that spoilest, and thou wast not spoiled;
> and dealest treacherously, and they dealt not treacherously with thee!
> When thou shalt cease to spoil, thou shalt be spoiled;
> And when thou shalt make an end to deal treacherously,
> they shall deal treacherously with thee.

In this country, black Americans have struck the same note. For generations, slaves in this country identified themselves with the oppressed Jews of the Old Testament and this link is reflected in the spirituals. The protest poetry of today, however, is released from the sense of resignation which characterized most of the spirituals. In many respects, these are closer to the bitter sense of outrage which is so much a part of the works of Isaiah, Jeremiah, and Ezekiel.

Turn now to Conrad Kent Rivers' "The Still Voice of Harlem" (p. 98) and study the pattern of tensions there. Notice how the harshness of life for black Americans is contrasted with the sense of serenity within the "gar dens" of Harlem. Obviously this is not intended to suggest literally that life in Harlem is easy; the "hope" is the sense of identity found there. This poem has many parallels in Biblical verse where the Jews looked to Israel as a source of identity—the brutality of the world pitted against the solidarity of the group. The tone is a complex mix of bitterness and hope.

When examining the tone in one of your own poems, be sure to ask yourself this crucial question: Is this what I *really* feel about the subject of this poem? If you are even unconsciously trying to sweeten the tone, you may reduce it to sentimentality. And, in the other direction, if you dramatize it beyond your real feelings, you may end up with melodrama. If the subject matter interests you, it is quite possible to adopt what is sometimes called a neutral tone. Robley Wilson's "On a Maine Beach" (p. 97) is generally neutral in tone and so is Maxine Kumin's "The Presence"(p. 92). Yet each is effective and highly sophisticated.

WHO IS SPEAKING?

In the example with which I opened this chapter, the identity of the speaker was very important. The actual meaning of the phrase "I want that" changed on the basis of who was making the statement.

Some poems are written with no hint of a speaker or narrator, but in others the identity of the fictitious narrator is central to the meaning of the poem.

John Masefield's "The Lemmings" (p. 93) is an example of a poem with no trace of a narrator. Written in the third person, it presents the analogy between lemmings and ourselves in essentially neutral tones. One might think that Wilson's "On a Maine Beach" is written in the same way, but review the opening and closing lines. "Look, in these pools . . . " he begins. At the end he writes "Perfections teach us to die." There is the faint trace of a speaker here, someone who is urging us to look and to consider the implications of this little scene.

There are two poems included in Chapter 11 which are cast in the first person plural—*we*. Denise Levertov's "Merritt Parkway," for one, includes us at the very outset of the poem with the phrase, "we keep moving." Turn to it now (p. 91) and try to imagine the subtle shift which would occur if there were no references to "we," only "they." It would not make a radical difference, but the poem might seem more critical of those people who are forever on the move. Now read the poem in the first person: "I keep moving" and "my dreamlike continuum" and "the people—myself . . . . " Notice how dramatically the presence of a single, identifiable speaker makes the poem a personal statement. Suddenly we sense that we are listening to an individual who is harried and upset at this constant motion.

Gwendolyn Brooks also uses "we" in "We Real Cool." Here, however, the identity of the speaker is clearly removed from the poet herself. We do not for a minute think that Gwendolyn Brooks left school and spends her time drinking gin, nor do we think that she has included herself in that harsh last line. From the start we see the poem as if it were lines in a play intended to suggest a character—in this case a group of them.

The first person, *I*, is used often in poetry—sometimes to express feelings close to the poet and just as frequently to create a fictitious *persona*. Adrienne Rich's "Like This Together" is written as if these are the persona's thoughts while sitting in that car by the river on a winter's day.

> . . . . Another time
> I'd have said "Canada Geese",
> knowing you love them.

She does not say this out loud, but her thoughts are shaped as if the person with her were her audience.

T. S. Eliot in "The Love Song of J. Alfred Prufrock," to which I will return later in this chapter, writes as if the poem were a monologue, but the poem is intended as a satirical criticism of the speaker who reveals himself through his own words. The poet achieves in the first person what Gwendolyn Brooks does in the first person plural.

When you begin a new poem, your narrator may occur to you almost without conscious thought as a part of your original conception. But when you look over that first draft, try to imagine the poem presented through a different speaker or persona. Sometimes a personal experience is more easily told from the point of view of another individual; occasionally the feelings or experiences of another are best presented as if they were your own.

Although we normally turn to the first person or to the third, remember that occasionally a poem is best presented as direct address to the audience or a character within the poem, "you," or as a group, "we," or even "they." If you consider these various ways of adjusting the tone of your poem and return to your original version, you will be sure that you have adopted the best approach. In some cases, however, the reexamination may send you in a direction you hadn't originally considered.

CONTRASTING TONES CREATE POETIC TENSION

If you study a sophisticated poem carefully, you will almost always find some sort of contrast, mixed emotion, or apparent contradiction in tone. These are the crosscurrents which help to keep a poem from becoming static. They are ways of creating poetic tension.

Contrasts in attitude are common and fairly easy to identify. We have already touched on a few: Roethke's delight in the process of living contrasted with his resignation in the face of death ("The Waking"); Brooks' easygoing use of street language contrasted with the jolting prophesy at the end ("We Real Cool"); and Hecht's merry anecdote played against the dramatic and dark image of the devil ("Lizards and Snakes").

Such shifts in mood have a long history in poetry. You will find them frequently, for example, in Shakespeare's sonnets. Often the first eight lines, the octave, take one "side" and the remaining six lines, the sestet, present the alternative. Although this sort of division between octave and sestet is more generally associated with the Italian sonnet (described in the next chapter), it appears in a surprising number of Shakespeare's as well. In fact, thirteen of his sonnets begin the sestet with "but" or "yet." Here, for example, are the opening lines from "Sonnet 29" clearly cast in a tone of near despair.

> When in disgrace with fortune and men's eyes
> I all alone beweep my outcast state,
> And trouble deaf heaven with my bootless cries,

And here is the shift in tone starting with "Yet" on the ninth line—the beginning of the sestet:

> Yet in these thoughts myself almost despairing,
> Haply I think on thee, and then my state,
> Like to the lark at break of day arising
> From sullen earth, sings hymns at heaven's gate;

Ambivalence is an important concept in all three genres. It refers to the conflicting emotions which we sometimes have toward a person or object—not alternating but at the same time. We may, for example, love and hate an individual simultaneously; we may be fond of a particular place and long to get away at the same time. It is possible, too, to feel anger and compassion for someone, resentment and envy, even scorn and admiration.

The reason ambivalence in tone is so important is that it is one of the characteristics which distinguishes sophisticated verse from simple. Who has ever seen a birthday card verse to a mother who is at the same time solicitous and a tyrant? Or, to be fair, a get-well card to dear old Dad, admitting the fact that it gives some satisfaction to see him flat on his back? Ambivalence in tone does not guarantee sophistication in a poem, but the lack of it may suggest that you have not probed your own feelings deeply enough.

Ambivalence is particularly appropriate when dealing with individuals who are close to you. Adrienne Rich, for example, develops a highly complex set of emotions in "Like This Together." It is a relationship which is both loving and distant, close yet separated like the houses which are being torn down and "cut in half. . .flayed."

IRONIC TONE

All forms of irony are based on a reversal of some sort. We expect a logical order in our world and are jolted when, say, the fire truck catches fire or the Olympic swimming champion drowns in his backyard pool. Since these involve our assumptions about the world around us, they are called examples of *cosmic irony*.

Or irony can appear in the form of a statement which unwittingly suggests future events either directly or indirectly. "I bring good news" the messenger in *Oedipus Rex* says, and the audience shudders, knowing that disaster is at hand. Since this is most closely associated with plays, it is called *dramatic irony*. More will be said about this in the chapters on drama.

The type of irony most frequently found in contemporary poetry is *verbal* or *conscious* irony. The terms are used interchangeably. *Verbal* differentiates it from a turn of *events* which characterize cosmic irony. Verbal irony is usually based on a turn of a phrase or on tone. *Conscious* differentiates this type of irony from statements given by innocent speakers as is the case in dramatic irony.

Often poetic irony can be achieved with a single word or brief phrase. Anne Sexton, for example, when writing of her mother's death in "Division of Parts" plays outward appearance against reality with these lines:

> . . .I trip
> on your death and Jesus, *my stranger*
> floats up over
> my Christian home. . . .

The italics here are hers, thrusting the irony at the reader blatantly. Actually there are two samples of verbal irony in these lines. The phrase "Jesus, my stranger" is a jarringly effective reversal of the conventional "Jesus, my savior." She relies on the reader's familiarity with the conventional phrase just as Eliot relies on the reader's knowledge of the Lord's Prayer in "The Hollow Men" with the lines:

> For thine is
> Life is
> For Thine is the
>   This is the way the world ends

Both these examples are based on the way our expectations are twisted by the intent of the lines. Almost all verbal irony can be seen as creating a tension between what we expect (the literal meaning) and the intended meaning.

These two cases are fairly clear, but often irony in poetry is more subtle and sometimes easy to miss. Take, for example, these lines from Denise Levertov's "A Solitude" in which she is describing a blind man in a subway:

> . . . He doesn't care
> that he looks strange, showing
> his thoughts on his face like designs of light
>
> flickering on water, for he doesn't know
> what *look* is.
> I see that he has never seen.

There is a clear ironic contrast in the last line in which she *sees* his lack of sight. More subtle, however, is the example earlier which works as a kind of a faint pre-echo: The face of a man whose world is total blackness is described as "designs of light."

Poets do not usually add irony to a poem the way a cook adds seasoning to a bland recipe—though the results may be similar. Instead, ironies suggest themselves to the poet either in the original conception or in the revisions.

But of course you can't be passive either. You should be willing to probe your own ambivalences honestly, looking for elements of hate in love, hidden longings in hatred, or subtle desires buried in fears. You should consider potential reversals in each image you use. Just as April is in some ways cruel and old age is in some ways beautiful, so also a love for the good life can be deadly, a war might be soothing, a serene dawn could be a deadly threat, and the roar of a jet a lullaby.

Closely related to the reversal of expectations in irony are the apparent contradictions and ambiguous meanings in the *paradox* and the *pun*. A paradox is a statement which at first appears to be a contradiction but which on a second level makes a specific point by implication.

John Donne, for example, in his sonnet "Death Be Not Proud" ends with these lines:

> One short sleep past, we wake eternally,
> And death shall be no more; Death, thou shalt die.

The core of the paradox lies in the last clause. It is illogical to state that death can die; yet if we think about it, the statement makes sense. In this respect a paradox is a little like a metaphor which is literally untrue but on the level of suggestion makes sense to us.

Even more dramatic is the paradox in Donne's Sonnet 14, "Batter My Heart." At the end of this poem God is pictured as a violent suitor and the poet himself as the woman. Speaking directly to God, Donne ends the poem with these three extraordinary lines:

> Take me to you, imprison me, for I
> Except you enthrall me, never shall be free
> Nor ever chaste, except you ravish me.

There are actually two paradoxes here, both charged with high voltage. The first suggests that he cannot be "free" unless he is "enthralled," a word which was then synonymous with "enslaved." Stronger yet is the final suggestion that he cannot be "chaste" unless he is "ravished."

Paradox is really a form of irony in that there is an apparent or literal meaning on the one hand and an intended meaning on the other. There is a tension set up between them which adds vitality to poetry.

The *pun* has a bad reputation these days. We tend to groan rather than laugh at them. But Shakespeare didn't hesitate to use puns in both his plays and his sonnets. In contemporary poetry there is a tendency to use them sparingly—if at all—since they can become obtrusive and take over the entire line.

Dylan Thomas, however, uses the same pun in two major poems: "I shall not murder / The mankind of her going with a grave truth" in "A Refusal to Mourn. . ." and "Grave men, near death, who see with blinding sight" in "Do Not Go Gentle into that Good Night." This particular pun was also used by Shakespeare in *Romeo and Juliet* when Mercutio, a wit even while dying, says "Ask for me tomorrow and you shall find me a grave man."

Quite frequently the pun is not made up of perfect equivalents but approximations in sound, like this opening of Anne Sexton's "The Farmer's Wife":

> From the hodge porridge
> of their country lust

The pun here, which links their married life with a hodgepodge and a bland bowl of porridge, is particularly interesting because of the fact that "hodgepodge" comes from the Walloon "hosepot," which literally meant "housepot" or the daily stew eaten by simple farming people such as those described in the quoted poem. Whether Sexton was aware of this is of no importance; the point is that the much maligned pun can be made to reverberate with echoes of etymology and suggestive overtones.

THE CAUSTIC TONE OF SATIRE

Satire criticizes or ridicules through some form of exaggeration. In the mild satire the exaggeration may be only a matter of selecting some characteristics and neglecting others. The tone may be a gentle kidding. Or, at the other extreme, it may be wildly exaggerated and the tone vitriolic.

Satire and irony can, of course, be used independently from each other. All the examples of irony above are nonsatiric, and the first example of satire below does not use irony. But ridicule is particularly effective when it is presented "with a straight face." That is, the cutting edge of satire is sharpest when the poet gives the illusion of presenting an unbiased view. It is the tension between the poet's apparent honesty and the actual intent which makes satire almost invariably ironic. In fact, when satire is presented without irony the result often appears rather crude. Such is the case with Kingsley Amis' "A Tribute to the Founder." In this first of four stanzas, the intent to ridicule is clear, but because the material is presented directly rather than ironically the attack lacks subtlety:

> By bluster, graft, and doing people down
> Sam Baines got rich, but mellowing at last,
> Felt that by giving something to the town
> He might undo the evils of his past.

There is, of course, irony in the title since "tribute" is not intended literally. But the first line destroys all chance of sustaining subtlety. As soon as we see the words "bluster, graft, and doing people down" we know exactly where the poet stands, which is no sin in itself unless one asks more of poetry than one does of a good newspaper editorial.

William Jay Smith describes essentially the same sort of individual in his poem "American Primitive," and he also is satiric. But notice how different the effect is when irony is sustained.

> Look at him there in his stovepipe hat,
> His high-top shoes, and his handsome collar;
> Only my Daddy could look like that,
> And I love my Daddy like he loves his Dollar.

The lines flow like the ripple which runs silently down the length of a bull whip; and with his final word comes the "snap" which is sharp enough to make the most sophisticated reader jump. This is still fairly light verse, but the satire, sharpened with irony, draws blood. The tension here lies in the contrast between the *apparent* tone of sentimental tribute and the *actual* tone of cutting protest.

Moving further—much further—in the direction of subtlety and complexity, we have a third example of satire in Eliot's "The Love Song of J. Alfred Prufrock." The poem is an entire course in satire and deserves much more careful scrutiny than I can give it here. One brief selection from 131 lines will have to serve as appetizer.

Like the other two poems, this one aims its attack at an individual who represents a general type. Unlike the other two, the attack comes not from the poet directly but from the character himself. As in the case of Browning's "My Last Duchess," the narrator damns himself. But unlike Browning's characters, Prufrock recognizes at least some of his weaknesses. He veers constantly from self-deprecation to self-defense, employing both in a pattern of self-deceit which almost deceives us, the readers, until we notice that in even a brief description of the man the word "self" is constantly repeated.

Take, for example, these lines in which Prufrock reflects on his own worth:

> Should I, after tea and cakes and ices,
> Have the strength to force the moment to its crisis?
> But though I have wept and fasted, wept and prayed,
> Though I have seen my head (grown slightly bald) brought in
>   upon a platter,
> I am no prophet—and here's no great matter;
> I have seen the moment of my greatness flicker,
> And I have seen the eternal Footman hold my coat, and snicker,
> And in short, I was afraid.

The tension here is established in the strain between his apparent modesty and his extraordinary egotism; a more subtle form of tension is seen in the satiric irony of a man who reveals his conceit through the very phrases which he intends to be self-deprecating.

Specifically, we are tempted to see him as he sees himself: a man who recognizes the superficiality of his own society ("tea and cakes and ices"), a man who has tried to rise above it ("wept and fasted"), a man who is aware of his failure ("I have seen. . .my greatness flicker") and is, finally, uneasy about death ("I was afraid").

In the context of the entire poem, however, these lines expose an outrageous egotist. He is quick to blame the superficiality of his society ("tea and cakes and ices") when clearly he has himself selected that society by his own choice. The question he asks ("Should I . . . Have the strength . . .?") implies a choice when in fact he clearly does not have the strength. His description of his efforts to achieve greatness ("wept and fasted, wept and prayed") are such an absurd hyperbole that we cannot believe him. His confession ("I am no prophet") disguises the fact that he is not even a whole man as does the line above ("I have seen my head . . .") in which he actually compares himself with John the Baptist. And the last phrase ("I was afraid") is the technique of a man who hides terror by confessing to uneasiness.

Notice that this satire is not based simply on one or two exaggerated characteristics. It is developed from the maze of a man's ironic observations about himself.

One can learn a good deal about poetic satire from these three examples. First, you can achieve greater subtlety and effectiveness if you use irony. Second, remember the impact you can achieve with some degree of surprise. The "snap" may come at the end of a phrase, a line, or a stanza; but no matter where it is placed, it can serve as a kind of jolt for the reader.

Finally, if your satire seems simple, make sure that it doesn't limit itself to a single aspect of your subject. Sophisticated satire touches on several characteristics of the person, object, or institution being ridiculed.

REVISING YOUR TONE

When you are writing the first draft of a poem, tone may not be your primary concern. It will seem reasonable to address your subject with whatever attitude strikes you first. But as you begin to revise, consider the tone carefully. Slight shifts may be made fairly easily, and many times they will improve the poem dramatically.

In some cases you may find that your attitude is too serious. Look with particular care at poems which describe your feelings about those close to you.

Ask yourself, too, whether the poem in a sense plays only one note. That is, does it present only one side of your feelings? Would it be worth countering that feeling with a bit of its opposite? This may come in the form of an alternation—this side, but that side too—or simultaneously as the mixed emotions of ambivalence. This may require looking closely and honestly at your own feelings.

Irony and satire are often avoided because they tend to stress the intellectual portion of the poem—less feeling and more opinion. But if you find yourself writing a poem which criticizes a person or an institution, an ironic or satiric tone may be appropriate.

Although we have been examining tone as if it were a separate element, it is interwoven with the theme or statement of a poem. In the examples of how we might respond to the statement "I want that," the meaning was ambiguous until we knew what the tone was. In other words, tone was really a part of the meaning. In the same way, the meaning of a poem is often shaped by the signals you give to the reader regarding your attitude toward the subject. Your poem is not complete until you have established just the right tone.

Chapter 9

From Units to Unity

The structure of thoughts and feelings developed through *key images, comparisons, contrasts,* and *narrative;* creating unity through *visual patterns* including *stanzas, typography;* the use of traditional *verse forms* including *haiku, ballad, sonnet,* and *villanelle;* techniques of *revision* for unity.

Until this point we have been examining aspects of poetry as if they were separate elements. This is necessary for analysis. But a poem, like any art object, is a single, unified creation. This chapter deals with the ways in which the various elements of a poem are brought together to form such a unity.

THE STRUCTURE OF THOUGHTS AND FEELINGS

When we write prose, it seems reasonable to outline our ideas in advance: we decide whether to begin with the major point or to work toward it, whether to present the paper as an argument or a set of alternatives, and the like. With poetry, however, there is an understandable reluctance to be so concerned with structure. The work is often personal, after all, and usually much shorter than an analytical essay. We like to trust our natural feelings, our "poetic instinct."

As indeed we should—up to a point. But remember that even when we write with total disregard for structure, we will unconsciously follow some sort of organizational scheme. The question we should ask ourselves at some point in the development of a poem is whether our initial ordering is the most effective for this particular work.

A sequence of *key images* is often used to focus the attention of the reader and to provide a sense of order. This is particularly evident in Maxine Kumin's "The Presence." Turn to it now (p. 92) and circle each image which seems to dominate and define a unit of about two to four lines.

Most of these images are animals. There is the opening picture of a trail in the snow made by a creature which went "crabwise." Then she speculates on a series of specific animals—the raccoon, porcupine, fox, and woodcock. To this point, both the organization and the content have been kept simple. Here, however, the concern and the tone shift. The next four lines are unified by "those bones" down in the burrow—bones, that will serve the fox which did the killing. The final four lines balance this with "snowshoes" that the narrator wears, possessions which came from "the skin and sinews" of some creature which had been killed for the purpose.

When we look back on the earlier lines, we then see how a raccoon that takes a knapsack and a porcupine that steals a tennis racket (to subsist, we assume, on the wood and gut strings) are further examples of how all creatures including humans benefit by what "went before."

Although this poem is not divided into stanzas, the organization is clearly based on four-line units. Each of those units is unified by a single dominant image and the punctuation further highlights the divisions.

Robley Wilson's "On a Maine Beach" is also written without stanza divisions, but as we have already seen (Chapter 5), the rhyme scheme is based on a four-line unit as if the poem were written in quatrains. If you look closely, you will see that those units are also defined by certain key images. The pattern is not as pronounced as in the Kumin poem, but it is there.

We begin with the phrase, "Look, in these pools" and the four lines focus on just that. The fifth line begins with "Salt logics rust like a mainspring" and the mainspring image is continued with "pinwheeling." "Tides" dominate the next four lines. And "old coins" become the unifying image for the concluding four lines.

The organizational structure, then, is established by key images and is reinforced by the rhyme scheme without a division of stanzas. These various parts are unified by the final two lines in which the roundness of pools and mainsprings are fused in the phrase "round lifetimes," and the motion of the tide is repeated in "beach rhythms."

A second method of organizing the content of a poem is through *comparisons*. Masefield's "The Lemmings" is a vivid example. As we have already seen, the poem describes the strange suicidal quest of the lemmings in the first eight lines—the octave. The final six lines, the sestet, make a comparison with the human quest.

I will have more to say about the sonnet later in this chapter, but it is worth noting that Masefield's comparison (his theme) is augmented by both the structure of the sonnet and the punctuation (form). The unity of the poem is created not just by the basic comparison but by the form as well. We discuss them as separate elements simply for analysis; in fact, they are a part of the same process.

The technique of comparison is also used in "The Presence" (p. 92) (animals and humans) and Ezra Pound's "In a Station of the Metro" (p. 93) (faces in a crowd and petals on a wet bough).

One might think that contrasts would not provide unity for a poem, but remember that one does not contrast elements which have no relation to each other. In some significant way, they are similar. In Brooks' "We Real Cool," for example, the easygoing, couldn't-care-less individuals who are describing themselves in the first lines are the same ones who jarringly admit at the end that they will "die soon." There is a dramatic contrast between these two views, but they are part of a single picture. For all the tension between the two elements in that poem, it is unified.

Another popular method of drawing together a poem is *narrative*. Story telling was, after all, one of the original purposes of poetry. Epics like the *Iliad* and the *Odyssey* were long stories set in verse primarily to aid memorization. Unwritten epics have been recorded in black Africa, India, Yugoslavia, and elsewhere. What we call the *literary ballads* of the nineteenth and twentieth centuries have their roots in poetry intended to be sung and often presented by individuals who could not read. Narrative sequence, like meter and rhyme, made the works easier to remember.

Anthony Hecht's "Lizards and Snakes" makes effective use of narrative sequence. It tells a story. It does other things also, of course; but its primary organizational technique is to keep the reader wondering what will happen next.

In addition to plot, narrative poems often have a speaker who helps to unify the work. In the Hecht poem the identity of the narrator is not clearly defined. We know only that he and his friend, Joe, were a part of the action and he is now looking back after what appears to be a number of years.

In other poems the speaker is used as a more clearly defined character who can be a major source of unity. Coleridge's "The Rime of the Ancient Mariner," for example, is a literary ballad which is unified not only by a dramatic plot but by the unmistakable presence of the narrator, a mariner who insists on telling his story to a stranger, holding the listener "with his glittering eye." Robert Browning's much-anthologized poem, "My Last Duchess," is another example in which the narrator is as important as the story he tells. In this case, he damns himself as a coldblooded murderer while maintaining an air of chilly self-righteousness. Unity in that poem is as much a matter of tone as it is of narrative.

Notice that in all these cases the unity, which was established through the use of key images, comparisons, contrasts, and narrative sequences, is often strengthened by aspects of form—rhyme, meter, the conventions of a sonnet, and the like.

UNITY THROUGH VISUAL PATTERNS

Both metered poetry and free verse often make use of the visual pattern the lines form on the page. In the case of metered poems, it is the division of stanzas which catches the eye. In Chapter 5 the various stanza forms as they applied to rhyme schemes were discussed. Stanzas are equally important as basic organizational units.

As we have seen, it is possible to write metered as well as unmetered verse without any stanzaic divisions. Robley Wilson's "On a Maine Beach" is an example even though the rhyme scheme suggests quatrains. Most poets, however, prefer to use some form of stanza division (often highly irregular in free verse) since the divisions provide some of the same benefits in verse which paragraphs offer in prose.

Stanza lengths in metered poetry tend to remain fixed in any one work. Each stanza length has its own set of advantages and disadvantages which are worth considering when you begin a new poem.

Couplets, as I pointed out in Chapter 5, are less popular today than they were in the past because if they are rhymed they can become too noticeable. In addition, the units of thought are so brief that one begins to long for a lengthier stanza.

Yet look once more at "We Real Cool" by Gwendolyn Brooks (p. 92). It is not only written in couplets, it is welded together with three feminine rhymed pairs: *aa bb cc de*. Described this way, it seems hard to imagine how the poem could be made to echo informal speech patterns. Who speaks in rhyming couplets? Yet the impression we get *echoes* common speech because the units are short and the phrasing seems natural.

The triplet offers a larger unit. Maya Angelou's "This Winter Day" is essentially unmetered, but it opens and closes with a triplet. Review it now (p. 92) and notice how each of those three stanzas (triplet, quatrain, triplet) is a complete sentence and, in addition, is unified by the key image at the very opening: "The kitchen," "Ritual sacrifice," and "The day."

The quatrain, often associated with ballads, allows an entire scene to be developed. For this reason it is popular with narrative poetry. It also serves as a "form within a form" in the sonnet which I will describe later in this chapter.

The longer forms—quintet, sestet, septet, and octave—all share the advantage of providing a solid block of writing in which entire sets of images or extended metaphors can be developed within its borders. The variety of rhyme schemes and random rhyme endings in these long stanzas is practically limitless.

Remember, however, that the longer the stanza the more careful one has to be to provide some sort of coherence within that unit. In the final analysis, this is the only limit to the length of a stanza or stanza-like divisions.

It is helpful at this point to make a distinction between *recurrent* and *nonrecurrent stanzas.*Strictly speaking, the term *stanza* applies only to recurrent units. That is, in metered and rhymed verse, the metrical and rhyme schemes of one stanza are repeated in the others. Monotony is avoided by muting the metrical scheme and the sound devices within each stanza rather than changing the system as one moves from one stanza to the next. Hecht's "Lizards and Snakes" is a good example of octaves, though the rhyme scheme divides the poem as if it were made up of quatrains.

Although we associate recurrent stanzas of identical length with metered poetry, they are also found in poems written in syllabics, a form of free verse. Dylan Thomas' "Fern Hill" is a good example. As I pointed out in Chapter 7, each stanza repeats with precise regularity the same syllable count, line by line, as the others. The very definition of syllabics calls for such recurrence—even though the result may appear to be remarkably free.

Adrienne Rich's "Like This Together" seems at first reading to be written in regular stanzas, but the degree of recurrence is actually far less than in "Fern Hill." There are six stanzas, but even the length of these units varies from twelve to fifteen lines. They do resemble each other visually, but they are not matched in meter or rhyme (it is not metered or rhymed) nor do the lines match in numbers of syllables. Her lines seem to be broken more or less into breath units and the stanzas are unified not by form but by a dominant visual image which in all but the third stanza appears in the first couple of lines. When one considers all these factors, it is clear that her stanzas resemble in some respects the nonrecurrent paragraphs of prose. Like paragraphs, her stanzas vary in length and are unified more by content than by form.

It is only one step from this to the loose typographical divisions in such poems as "Buffalo Bill's" by E. E. Cummings and "Merritt Parkway" by Denise Levertov. In such verse the word "stanza" is used rather freely to describe any group of lines which are set off by extra spacing. These are truly nonrecurrent in that they, like the prose paragraph, are not intended to echo each other in length or internal structure. They are merely divisions of thought, feeling, tone, or topic.

The *canto* is a longer division which is found in both metered and free verse. It usually consists of several stanzas, and the divisions are often signaled by printing numerals at the head of each. It serves somewhat the same function as the chapter does in fiction. The canto can be very helpful in longer poems to suggest a new setting, a new mood, or a new aspect of the theme. Sometimes it is possible to signal such shifts in the first lines in the same way that Adrienne Rich does in her stanzas.

The *refrain* is closely associated with lyrics written for singing. All but the simplest stanza forms depend on the written page for their identification, and so do cantos. But the refrain can be detected easily by ear alone.

Refrains in ballads are a simple example. There, a line or two is repeated either after each verse (stanza) or at regular intervals such as every three verses. In contemporary popular music the refrain may dominate the lyrics, taking well over half of the playing time.

In sophisticated verse, the refrain is used sparingly if at all. As a device, it has less of a place in works intended primarily for the written page. The tendency is to use the visually effective division bewteen stanzas and the variety of typographical arrangements available in free verse.

TRADITIONAL VERSE FORMS

There are many verse forms which provide the poet with a certain pattern of meter, rhyme, syllables, refrains, or other structural elements. These are sometimes called fixed forms. While some poets find them restrictive, others find them a pleasure and even liberating in that the demands of the form may, like metered verse, suggest new directions in thought and phrasing.

Traditional verse forms need not be complex or demanding. The *haiku,* discussed in Chapter 7, is a simple system of syllabics in which the first line has five syllables, the second has seven, and the third has five. There is no meter involved and generally no rhyme.

Like many fixed verse forms, the haiku has a *convention* associated with it which one can make use of or ignore. The classical haiku dating from the eighteenth century in Japan often makes use of an image from nature and suggests one of the four seasons. But these conventions are not a part of the form which specifies only the pattern of syllables in each line.

The *ballad* is a longer, looser form associated with narrative poetry and verse to be sung. The ballad stanza is a quatrain which alternates lines of iambic tetrameter with iambic trimeter. The rhyme scheme is *abcb.* Early ballads tended to be simple in plot with lively action reported by someone outside the story. Ballads today often follow those conventions.

Coleridge adapted the ballad form to develop a highly sophisticated poem in "The Rime of the Ancient Mariner." Although he allowed himself occasional variations in traditional ballad meter, here is a dramatic stanza which follows the form faithfully:

> The selfsame moment I could pray;
> And from my neck so free
> The Albatross fell off, and sank
> Like lead into the sea.

Although Coleridge used the ballad form to create an extraordinarily complex work, we still tend to think of ballads as entertaining stories set to verse, often with musical accompaniment. When selecting a verse form, it is generally a good idea to use one which harmonizes with the tone and subject matter you have in mind.

The sonnet is more often associated with inner feelings and thoughts. It is not long enough for a rambling story, yet it has sufficient length to develop far more intricate statements than are possible in a haiku.

The sonnet is a metered and rhymed poem of fourteen lines usually in iambic pentameter.

There are two basic rhyme schemes, and these are important because they usually result in somewhat different ways of organizing the material. The first is the *Italian sonnet* which can be thought of as two quatrains and two triplets: *abba, abba; cde, cde.* Another version substitutes a sestet of *cdc, dcd.* The *Elizabethan sonnet,* on the other hand, is often thought of as three quatrains and a final rhyming couplet: *abab, cdcd, efef, gg.*

One can't talk about the organization of a sonnet without reference to the rhyme scheme. Shifts in mood, tone, or even concern may come after any of the quatrains or—in both types of sonnets—after the octave. The rhyming couplet of an Elizabethan sonnet provides an opportunity to sum up the statement or present a countering view.

John Masefield's "The Lemmings" is a good example of an Elizabethan sonnet. As I have already pointed out, the concern shifts after the octave. And the final couplet is really a summary of the sestet—which is also the theme of the poem. You may want to turn to it now (p. 93) and draw a line between the octave and the sestet and mark the rhymed endings with letters: *abab, cdcd,* and so forth. This will clearly demonstrate how the form (rhyme and meter) is blended with statement to create the unity of the poem.

The villanelle is the most complex verse form I will discuss in this text, but it is no mere trick or stunt. Beginning poets have often found its requirements rewarding as well as a pleasure to work with.

The poem has nineteen lines divided into five triplets and a final quatrain. Like the sonnet, it is usually written in iambic pentameter. Unlike the sonnet, there are only two rhymes. The pattern is *aba, aba, aba, aba, aba, abaa.* In addition, the first line is used as a refrain and repeated in its entirety to form lines six, twelve, and eighteen; and the third line is also a refrain which is repeated entirely to form lines nine, fifteen, and nineteen.

It is not as cumbersome as the description makes it appear. Turn to "The Waking" by Theodore Roethke (p. 93) and mark the first refrain (line one) with an *A* and the second refrain (line three) with a *B.* Then identify the refrains with *A* or *B.* The rest is simply iambic pentameter with an *aba* rhyme scheme.

Yet perhaps the villanelle is not quite that simple. One of your goals will be to use those refrains so that they have slightly different meanings in different stanzas. Another will be to build the poem so that when we come to the final two lines we will have a new or greater insight than we did halfway through.

You will notice that Roethke takes certain minor liberties with the form. Some of the rhymes, for example, are slant rhymes and one of the refrains is subtly altered (without giving up the pentameter). But he is essentially faithful to the form, and if you enjoy this kind of challenge you will want to match his fidelity.

REVISING FOR UNITY

Even a tentative rough draft of a new poem will have some kind of unity. At some point, however, it is wise to assess just what holds the poem together. There may be key images, or the structure may be based on comparison or contrast. Or is it essentially a narrative sequence?

Next, look at the formal elements: What kind of visual cues have you given the reader? And if it is a traditional verse form, have you made full use of the form you have selected?

After you have identified what you have, it is time to consider what to cut, what to add, and what to rearrange.

Remember that the poem as a whole is a true joining of form and content. Whether you are working with a comparison in the precise pattern of the sonnet or the sensation of constant motion through scattered typography, the arrangement of words on the page is a part of the statement. In a successful poem, each unit contributes to an overall unity.

Chapter 10

Developing as A Poet

Evaluating your own work through the reactions of other readers and your own; the *six critical questions* which lead to effective revision; the importance of *learning from other poets* and the sense of *fellowship* among practicing poets.

Developing as a poet is a continuing process. Although poetry is unlikely to become your sole source of income, it can become and remain an important part of your life. Like all sophisticated art forms, it is self-reinforcing: the more you do to expand your abilities, the more it does to expand your life.

How do you continue developing? There are two aspects of the process and each is absolutely necessary. If either one is ignored, there will be no growth and, eventually, not enough satisfaction to continue. First, you have to be able to evaluate your own work with some objectivity and be willing to revise. Second, you must learn how to learn from other poets.

Evaluating your own work starts with asking the right questions. It is often helpful to have the reactions of a fellow poet or a group, but make sure that you are turning to individuals who read poetry. Well-meaning friends may not know what questions to ask or how to advise. As a result, they tend to respond subjectively. "I like it," one may say. "It doesn't do much for me," another says. "Well," a third says, "it works for me. Sort of." Reactions like these will tell you more about the speaker than about your poem.

The kind of criticism which will be the most help to you as a practicing poet will be primarily descriptive and only secondarily evaluative. Such criticism will also be very specific. What you need to find out is precisely what came through to the reader. In the process you may learn what didn't come through as well.

A helpful critic might say something like this: "Your three opening images are really dramatic and got me into the poem, but I lost track of them later. I don't see what you are doing with them. And I can't hear any sound devices in this poem." You may be tempted to use the well-worn defense, "that's the way I intended it." But resist that impulse! Ask yourself whether it might be possible to develop those opening images and whether it might be possible to do more with the sounds of the poem.

There is a distinct advantage of having your poem discussed by a group rather than evaluated by a single reader. No matter how specific and articulate your reader is, personal feelings may affect the critique. With a group you can weigh what is a chance misreading against what is a general impression. If several readers feel your poem is too static and needs some kind of tension in tone or attitude, that is worth more careful consideration than if only one had that feeling. This is not to say that you should follow majority rule. But it is important to understand how your work is being perceived by a number of careful readers.

Important as group reaction is, the final decisions are yours alone. You have to be able and willing to ask yourself the kind of critical questions which will lead to improvement.

SIX CRITICAL QUESTIONS

Here are six questions which are often asked in writing classes and by individual readers who know how to help a poet. They are also questions which you will find helpful in analyzing your own work. I present them not as a simple checklist but as a description of the range of concerns which will be important to you as you revise. Eventually they will become internalized.

Each of these topics has been the subject of at least one chapter, though the order here has been changed slightly. The discussion of every poem will vary with the work and with the inclination of the group, but it is often helpful to begin with those aspects which strike the reader first—key images, for example. The more complex concerns such as tone, unity, and theme are sometimes best postponed until later in the discussion.

First, *are the images effective?* In a difficult poem, isolated images may be all that reaches the reader the first time through. These may be vivid visual details used for their own sake, or they may be vehicles for metaphors; but the poet needs to know what has really made an impression. It is mainly by listening to the reactions of others that you will be able to judge for yourself what is a fresh image and what is bland, flat, or too familiar.

Second, *is the diction fresh?* The concern here shifts to individual words and phrases. It is very important to make sure that all your readers have a copy of your work in front of them. They will be looking not only for clichés but for familiar phrasing, echoes from song lyrics, and conventional adjectives which are either unnecessary or poorly selected. If a reader says, "Some of your phrases seem sort of hackneyed," don't get sulky or defensive, ask "Which ones?"

Occasionally critics will tell you that your poem or a part of it seems "prosaic" or "prosy." This may come from using too much abstract language (references to "love" and "trust" when what you had in mind was a particular person); or you may be telling a story without focusing on key images. In either case, encourage your critic to identify specific lines so you can decide whether the problem lies in images, diction, or the degree of compression.

If you are working alone—as you probably will much of the time—you will have to serve as your own critic. These same questions become the basis of your own analysis.

Third, *are there sound devices?* True, some poems depend heavily on sharpness of image and do not make use of such techniques as rhyme, assonance, alliteration, consonance, and onomatopoeia. But such poems are rare. In student-written poems, lack of sound devices is more often a matter of forgetfulness than intention.

Occasionally the problem may be just the reverse: sound devices which are obtrusive. As was pointed out in Chapter 5, rhyming couplets can do this, particularly when they are emphasized with regular, end-stopped lines. Contiguous alliteration can also become blatant. Just how much is too much obviously is a matter of individual opinion, but if several readers make the same complaint, the line certainly deserves reconsideration.

Fourth, *does the poem make use of rhythm?* Here again it is important to urge your critics to be as specific as possible. If the poem is metered, where does the meter become monotonous and where, on the other hand, do the metrical substitutions become so numerous that the flow of reading is interrupted? Even if your critic is unable to scan metered poetry, he or she should be able to detect awkwardness in the rhythm. And if the poem is free verse, what rhythmical systems are being used? Don't instruct your critics, let them tell you what they have perceived in their reading.

Rhythm, of course, is closely connected with the sound linkages—rhyme, assonance, alliteration, and the like. You may find it valuable to read your work out loud to your group or, if you are working alone, to yourself. Some poets use cassette recorders for their own work. But it is still important to have copies to look at. As we saw in Chapter 7, some rhythms—particularly in free verse—depend on seeing as well as hearing the work.

Fifth, *what is the tone?* This may surprise you. Those choice samples of wit may have eluded your readers. And what you took most seriously may not have had the impact you intended.

Equally important, you will want to determine whether the tone has developed some kind of tension—one attitude or reaction played against another. If it does not, have you considered all the aspects of your subject? Did you honestly have such a clearly defined attitude? Is there really only one way of looking at the subject? Sometimes, what you thought was a finished poem ends up being a portion of a longer, more complex poem involving some kind of contrast or ambivalence.

Sixth, *how is the poem constructed and how do those various parts achieve unity?* Frequently this will turn into a discussion of the poem's theme or central concern. This is important, of course, but it shouldn't obscure the question of how the elements of the poem are put together.

Unity, you remember, can be achieved by the way thoughts or feelings are arranged; it can be augmented by the visual patterns of the stanzas or free-verse typography. Or the poem may be drawn together through a traditional verse form. When we ask the familiar question, "What does this poem mean?" we run the risk of implying that a poem is a philosophical statement with a lot of verbal decoration. When examining a poem —especially your own—try to see the arrangement of elements and the unity of the whole.

There are times when a poem may shift from one mood or set of suggestions to another in the course of revisions. There is no harm in this, but make sure that each line and every image in the new version really belongs there. This is particularly important when your attitude toward your subject has changed between, say, the third and fourth draft. Make sure that your original approach doesn't "show through" as an inconsistency in the later draft.

LEARNING FROM OTHER POETS

This book is *about* poetry. It suggests ways of reading poetry and approaches to writing it. From here on, you should be reading books which *are* poetry. No matter how far you may be from a classroom or even a fellow poet, there are volumes of poetry available, and those poets will become your teachers through their works.

When students tell me that they are "very serious" about poetry, I don't ask how much they have written; I ask what was the last volume of poetry they read and what poetry journal they subscribe to.

How do you find out what to read? If you live in a large city or near a college or university, you have an advantage. Attend poetry readings and find out which poets you admire. And buy their books. Don't do so as an act of charity; do so because these poets can teach you about the genre and help you to develop your own abilities.

If you are not near such resources, buy an anthology of contemporary poetry and browse. (*A Geography of Poets*, a Bantam paperback edited by Edward Field, is good for a starter.) Pick out three poets whose work you respect and order their books through your local bookstore. The library is also a possibility, but owning the book and being willing to make marginal comments is far more valuable. This is your best way to share the work of a poet.

And then there are the poetry journals and quarterlies. Poets who write and submit work without reading what others have published are involved in a self-centered game which has little to do with poetry. Poetry journals are the way poets stay in touch with each other. If you are serious about poetry, such journals will not only give you pleasure but they will help you to grow.

Again, browse in your library to find out which periodicals publish work you find enjoyable and meaningful. Then subscribe. As for the cost, a year's subscription, like a volume of verse, will be less than one trip to the supermarket.

There is a fellowship of poets in this country and they are connected across great distances through quarterlies, journals, and slim volumes of poetry. If they speak and you do not listen, what right have you to ask them to hear your own work? If you isolate yourself, how will you grow? Developing as a poet does not mean grinding out more lines and chalking up publications; it means joining that fellowship of practicing poets and sharing their values.

Chapter 11

Poems for Study

Lizards and Snakes

ANTHONY HECHT

On the summer road that ran by our front porch
    Lizards and snakes came out to sun.
It was hot as a stove out there, enough to scorch
    A buzzard's foot. Still, it was fun
To lie in the dust and spy on them. Near but remote,   5
    They snoozed in the carriage ruts, a smile
In the set of the jaw, a fierce pulse in the throat
Working away like Jack Doyle's after he'd run the mile.

Aunt Martha had an unfair prejudice
    Against them (as well as being cold   10
Toward bats.) She was pretty inflexible in this,
    Being a spinster and all, and old.
So we used to slip them into her knitting box.
    In the evening she'd bring in things to mend
And a nice surprise would slide out from under the socks.   15
It broadened her life, as Joe said. Joe was my friend.

But we never did it again after the day
    Of the big wind when you could hear the trees
Creak like rockingchairs. She was looking away
    Off, and kept saying, "Sweet Jesus, please   20
Don't let him hear me. He's as like as twins.
    He can crack us like lice with his fingernail.
I can see him plain as a pikestaff. Look how he grins
And swinges the scaly horror of his folded tail."

Merritt Parkway

DENISE LEVERTOV

    As if it were
forever that they move, that we
    keep moving—

        Under a wan sky where
        as the lights went on a star   5
           pierced the haze & now
        follows steadily
              a constant
        above our six lanes
        the dreamlike continuum . . .   10

And the people—ourselves!
    the humans from inside the
    cars, apparent
    only at gasoline stops   15
            unsure,
      eyeing each other

           drink coffee hastily at the
        slot machines & hurry
    back to the cars
        vanish   20
        into them forever, to
        keep moving—

Houses now & then beyond the
sealed road, the trees / trees, bushes
passing by, passing   25
    the cars that
        keep moving ahead of
    us, past us, pressing behind us
             and
          over left, those that come   30
        toward us shining too brightly
moving relentlessly

      in six lanes, gliding
    north & south, speeding with
    a slurred sound—   35

The Presence

MAXINE KUMIN

Something went crabwise
across the snow this morning.
Something went hard and slow
over our hayfield.
It could have been a raccoon   5
lugging a knapsack,
it could have been a porcupine
carrying a tennis racket,
it could have been something
supple as a red fox   10
dragging the squawk and spatter
of a crippled woodcock.
Ten knuckles underground
those bones are seeds now
pure as baby teeth   15
lined up in the burrow.

I cross on snowshoes
cunningly woven from
the skin and sinews of
something else that went before.   20

This Winter Day

MAYA ANGELOU

The kitchen is its readiness
white green and orange things
leak their blood selves in the soup.

Ritual sacrifice that snaps
an odor at my nose and starts   5
my tongue to march
slipping in the liquid of it drip.

The day, silver striped
in rain, is balked against
my window and the soup.   10

We Real Cool

GWENDOLYN BROOKS

**The Pool Players.
Seven at the Golden Shovel.**

We real cool. We
Left school. We

Lurk late. We
Strike straight. We

Sing sin. We
Thin gin. We   5

Jazz June. We
Die soon.

The Waking

THEODORE ROETHKE

I wake to sleep, and take my waking slow.
I feel my fate in what I cannot fear.
I learn by going where I have to go.

We think by feeling. What is there to know?
I hear my being dance from ear to ear.   5
I wake to sleep, and take my waking slow.

Of those so close beside me, which are you?
God bless the Ground! I shall walk softly there,
And learn by going where I have to go.

Light takes the Tree; but who can tell us how?   10
The lowly worm climbs up a winding stair;
I wake to sleep, and take my waking slow.

Great Nature has another thing to do
To you and me; so take the lively air,
And, lovely, learn by going where to go.   15

This shaking keeps me steady. I should know.
What falls away is always. And is near.
I wake to sleep, and take my waking slow.
I learn by going where I have to go.

In a Station of the Metro

EZRA POUND

The apparition of these faces in the crowd;
Petals on a wet, black bough.

The Lemmings

JOHN MASEFIELD

Once in a hundred years the Lemmings come
Westward, in search of food, over the snow,
Westward, until the salt sea drowns them dumb,
Westward, till all are drowned, those Lemmings go.
Once, it is thought, there was a westward land   5

(Now drowned) where there was food for those starved
    things,
And memory of the place has burnt its brand
In the little brains of all the Lemming Kings.
Perhaps, long since, there was a land beyond
Westward from death, some city, some calm place,   10
Where one could taste God's quiet and be fond
With the little beauty of a human face;
But now the land is drowned, yet still we press
Westward, in search, to death, to nothingness.

"Buffalo Bill's"

E. E. CUMMINGS

Buffalo Bill's
defunct
        who used to
        ride a watersmooth-silver
                    stallion   5
and break onetwothreefourfive pigeonsjustlikethat
                    Jesus
he was a handsome man
            and what i want to know is
how do you like your blueeyed boy   10
Mister Death

"Dove Sta Amore"

LAWRENCE FERLINGHETTI

    Dove sta amore
    Where lies love
    Dove sta amore
    Here lies love
The ring dove love   5
    In lyrical delight
Hear love's hillsong
Love's true willsong
Love's low plainsong
    Too sweet painsong   10
In passages of night
    Dove sta amore
    Here lies love
The ring dove love
    Dove sta amore   15
    Here lies love

Like This Together

ADRIENNE RICH

1.
Wind rocks the car.
We sit parked by the river,
silence between our teeth.
Birds scatter across islands
of broken ice. Another time   5
I'd have said "Canada geese,"
knowing you love them.
A year, ten years from now,
I'll remember this —
this sitting like drugged birds   10
in a glass case—
not why, only that we
were here like this together.

2.
They're tearing down, tearing up
this city, block by block.   15
Rooms, cut in half,
hand like flayed carcasses,
their old roses in rags,
famous streets have forgotten
where they were going. Only   20
a fact could be so dreamlike.
They're tearing down the houses
we met and lived in,
soon our two bodies will be all   25
left standing from that era.

3.
We have, as they say,
certain things in common.
I mean: a view
from a bathroom window
over slate to stiff pigeons   30
huddled every morning; the way
water tastes from our tap,
which you marvel at, letting
it splash into the glass.
Because of you I notice   35
the taste of water,
a luxury I might
otherwise have missed.

4.
Our words misunderstand us.
Sometimes at night   40
you are my mother:
old detailed griefs
twitch at my dreams, and I
crawl against you, fighting
for shelter, making you   45
my cave. Sometimes
you're the wave of birth
that drowns me in my first
nightmare. I suck the air.
Miscarried knowledge twists us   50
like hot sheets thrown askew.

5.
Dead winter doesn't die.
It wears away, a piece of carrion
picked clean at last,
rained away or burnt dry.   55
Our desiring does this,
make no mistake, I'm speaking
of fact: through mere indifference
we could prevent it.
Only our fierce attention   60
gets hyacinths out of those
hard cerebral lumps,
unwraps the wet buds down
the whole length of a stem.

6.
A severed hand   65
keeps tingling, air still suffers
beyond the stump. But new
life? How do we bear it
(or you, huge tree)
when fresh flames start spurting   70
out through our old sealed skins,
nerve-endings ours and not yet ours?
Susceptibilities we still
can't use, sucking
blind power from our roots—   75
what else to do but
hold fast to the
one thing we know,
grip earth and let burn.

Pied Beauty

GERARD MANLEY HOPKINS

Glory be to God for dappled things—
   For skies of couple-colour as a brinded cow;
     For rose-moles all in stipple upon trout that swim;

Fresh-firecoal chestnut-falls; finches' wings;
   Landscape plotted and pieced—fold, fallow, and plough;   5
     And áll trádes, their gear and tackle and trim.

All things counter, original, spare, strange;
   Whatever is fickle, freckled (who knows how?)
     With swift, slow; sweet, sour; adazzle, dim;
He fathers-forth whose beauty is past change: 10
            Praise him.

On a Maine Beach

ROBLEY WILSON

Look, in these pools, how rocks are like worn change
Keeping the ocean's mint-mark; barnacles
Miser on them; societies of snails
Hunch on their rims and think small thoughts whose strange
Salt logics rust like a mainspring, small dreams   5
Pinwheeling to a point and going dumb,
Small equations whose euphemistic sum
Stands for mortality. A thousand times
Tides swallow up such pools, shellfish and stone
Show green and yellow shade in groves of weed;   10
Rocks shrink, barnacles drink, snails think they bleed
In their trapped world. Here, when the sea is gone,
We find old coins glowing under the sky,
Barnacles counting them, snails spending slow
Round lifetimes half-awake. Beach rhythms flow   15
In circles. Perfections teach us to die.

The Still Voice of Harlem

CONRAD KENT RIVERS

Come to me broken dreams and all
    bring me the glory of fruitless souls,
I shall find a place for them in my gardens.

Weep not for the golden sun of California,
    think not of the fertile soil of Alabama. . .   5
nor your father's eyes, your mother's body twisted
    by the washing board.

I am the hope of your unborn,
    truly, when there is no more of me. . .
there shall be no more of you. . . .   10

Fern Hill

DYLAN THOMAS

Now as I was young and easy under the apple boughs
About the lilting house and happy as the grass was green,
    The night above the dingle starry,
      Time let me hail and climb
    Golden in the heydays of his eyes,   5
And honoured among wagons I was prince of the apple towns
And once below a time I lordly had the trees and leaves
    Trail with daisies and barley
    Down the rivers of the windfall light.

And as I was green and carefree, famous among the barns   10
About the happy yard and singing as the farm was home,
    In the sun that is young once only,
      Time let me play and be
    Golden in the mercy of his means,
And green and golden I was huntsman and herdsman, the calves   15
Sang to my horn, the foxes on the hills barked clear and cold,
    And the sabbath rang slowly
    In the pebbles of the holy streams.

All the sun long it was running, it was lovely, the hay
Fields high as the house, the tunes from the chimneys, it was air   20
    And playing, lovely and watery
      And fire green as grass.
    And nightly under the simple stars
As I rode to sleep the owls were bearing the farm away,
All the moon long I heard, blessed among stables, the nightjars   25
    Flying with the ricks, and the horses
    Flashing into the dark.

And then to awake, and the farm, like a wanderer white
With the dew, come back, the cock on his shoulder: it was all
        Shining, it was Adam and maiden,   30
            The sky gathered again
        And the sun grew round that very day.
So it must have been after the birth of the simple light
In the first, spinning place, the spellbound horses walking warm
        Out of the whinnying green stable   35
            On to the fields of praise.

And honoured among foxes and pheasants by the gay house
Under the new made clouds and happy as the heart was long
        In the sun born over and over,
          I ran my heedless ways,   40
        My wishes raced through the house-high hay
And nothing I cared, at my sky blue trades, that time allows
In all his tuneful turning so few and such morning songs
        Before the children green and golden
          Follow him out of grace,   45

Nothing I cared, in the lamb white days, that time would take me
Up to the swallow thronged loft by the shadow of my hand,
        In the moon that is always rising,
          Nor that riding to sleep
        I should hear him fly with the high fields   50
And wake to the farm forever fled from the childless land.
Oh as I was young and easy in the mercy of his means,
        Time held me green and dying
        Though I sang in my chains like the sea.

What the Mirror Said

LUCILLE CLIFTON

listen,
you a wonder.
you a city
of a woman.
you got a geography   5
of your own.
listen,
somebody need a map
to understand you.
somebody need directions   10
to move around you.
listen,
woman,
you not a noplace   15

anonymous
girl;
mister with his hands on you
he got his hands on
some
damn   20
body!

After Spring

CHORA

After spring sunset
Mist rises from the river
Spreading like a flood

Even with Insects

ISSA

Even with insects . . .
Some are hatched out musical . . .
Some, alas, tone-deaf

Part 2

The Writing of Fiction

Chapter **12**

The Dynamics of Fiction

Fiction as a mix of *experience* and *invention;* fiction contrasted with *descriptive writing; simple vs. sophisticated* as seen in *plot, character,* and the *five narrative modes;* the *motives* for writing and how they affect the results.

Fiction tells an untrue story in prose. This brief statement is a reminder of just how broad the scope of this genre is. It also defines where its limits are: When a story is told in lines of verse, it becomes narrative poetry. When it is intended to be acted out on the stage it is drama. And when it is purported to be factually true—that is, openly and consistently based on actual characters and events—we call it nonfiction and classify it under headings like biography, autobiography, and historical analysis.

EXPERIENCE AND INVENTION

Fiction is "untrue" in the sense that it is not dependent on actual people and events. Stories which ask the reader to assume the existence of ghosts, dragons, or unicorns are good indications of just how free the genre is. But fiction is also rooted in the actual world—and frequently in the life experiences of the author. Fictional characters who "come alive" in a story are often the ones based on real people the writer has known. And in the same way, descriptions of places which readers describe as "vivid" are frequently close to scenes from the writer's own life.

As a result, fiction is usually a dynamic mixture of personal experience and invention. The blend will vary from story to story and with different elements in the same work. One character may be an exact likeness of the author's brother and another an almost complete invention. Or the basic incident may be autobiographical while the setting and characters are devised.

It is, of course, possible to write a good story which is based literally event by event on experience. Life occasionally takes on the pattern of fiction, and that is when one is tempted to report it directly. The danger is that the author may be tempted to include irrelevant material and may hesitate to revise and reshape the pattern of events. Too often, such stories read like journal entries which are of interest only to the writer.

On the other hand, it is possible to do the reverse: to avoid the personal element either intentionally or from a kind of psychic modesty. Slick fiction, for example, is usually constructed by revising old conventions of plot and situation. Good science fiction is apt to be more sophisticated, but the concern for plot and social statement often eliminates the use of details from the author's own life.

Sometimes beginning writers are tempted to stick with western scenes, fantasy situations, or conventionalized plots because they are reluctant to reveal aspects of their own lives. If you find yourself so drawn, remember that you know your own life better than anyone else. The external events may not have high drama, but good fiction is not dependent on high drama. Your life is populated with complicated people and your experiences have been intricate. In addition to what has happened to you, there are episodes you have heard about. If you learn how to draw on the more interesting events from your own experience and to shape them through fictional invention, you will have discovered one of the essential dynamics of fiction.

FICTION VS. DESCRIPTIVE WRITING

The border between fiction and descriptive or factual writing is forever in dispute. In libel cases, it is argued in court. For the writer, however, it is not a legal distinction but one which is at the heart of the creative process.

Once again, it is helpful to recall Northrop Frye's distinction between literary writing and descriptive writing which was discussed in Chapter 1. Descriptive writing, you will remember, has as its primary function the task of describing or interpreting some aspect of the world about us. Newspaper articles, for example, must answer the questions of *Who? When? What? Where?* and *How?* Each question refers to the incident being reported. We judge the article by how accurate and how insightful it is. The same applies to a doctor's records on a patient or a social worker's report on a client. And even a journal, though a personal document, is essentially descriptive writing, for its function is to record the thoughts and emotions of its author. In each of these cases, the writing is tied to events in the actual world and is judged by how effectively it does this.

Literary writing, as defined by Northrop Frye, is fundamentally different in its approach. Each work is a self-contained world and is judged on that basis, as a painting or a symphony is judged. Poetry and drama as well as fiction are forms of literary writing in this sense; but of the three genres, it is fiction which most frequently is confused with forms of descriptive writing.

If you do not see your fiction as literary in this sense, you may begin writing something which is really a segment from a journal. One clear indication that you are moving in this direction is defending a story with the excuse, "But it really happened that way."

The reason this is limiting is that as soon as you begin to feel that your first responsibility is to record the events as they happened, you have given up your ability to shape them into a work of art. That is, if your primary loyalty is to the actual events, you are no longer free to reshape the material into the best possible story. You will not be writing fiction.

The writer of fiction may draw heavily on personal experience or that of others, but in the process of creating fiction, that raw material will be revised and reshaped to make the most effective story.

The division between fiction, as literary writing, and descriptive or factual writing has been blurred—especially in the 1970s and '80s. Truman Capote suggested the term "nonfiction fiction" to describe his novel, *In Cold Blood,* because although it is written like a novel (with dialogue and thoughts included), it is based literally and openly on actual events. The term has been applied to E. L. Doctorow's *Ragtime* and a number of other works, though they tend to be novels with historical figures added.

The distinction in each case is based on whether the work is *primarily* a record of real events or whether it is essentially an artistic creation which stands on its own no matter how much it may make use of characters and events from life. We can never criticize fiction for being "untrue"; we can only concern ourselves with whether it *seems* true.

SIMPLE VS. SOPHISTICATED FICTION

This distinction has already been made in the poetry section. It is equally important in fiction. Essentially, sophisticated works "do" more in the sense that they suggest more, imply a greater range of suggestions, develop more subtle shadings of meaning. This text is concerned with sophisticated writing, but this does not mean that such work is "better." It is simply "other" in the sense that the biologically simple jellyfish is different from the far more sophisticated porpoise.

The span between the most simple and relatively sophisticated fiction is enormous. Compare a comic strip about adolescents like *Archie, The Jackson Twins,* or *Gil Thorpe* with a novel about adolescents like Knowles' *A Separate Peace* or Salinger's *Catcher in the Rye.* They are similar in that they are both samples of fiction as I have been defining it—they both tell untrue stories in prose. Further, they both have plot, characters, setting, and themes. And they share certain basic techniques: dialogue, thoughts, action, description, and exposition. They even use the same subject matter: that highly charged period between childhood and adulthood. And before one brands one as "good" and the other as "bad," remember that many intelligent adults read the comics in the morning paper, and *Catcher in the Rye* is still barred from many secondary schools as immoral and unacceptable.

But obviously they are utterly different forms of fiction. Archie as a fictional character is *simple* and so are the stories in which he appears. There are only a limited number of suggestions or implications which can be made from the highly conventional, monotonously repetitive types of situations in which he is placed. On the other hand Holden is a sophisticated character as is the novel in which we come to know him. It is important here to distinguish this literary use of *sophisticated* from its popular use which describes merely personal characteristics. Mark Twain's Huck Finn, for exmple, is certainly unsophisticated as an individual, but the complexity and intricacy with which the author presents him is unmistakably sophisticated.

Since this text is primarily concerned with writing which is sophisticated, we should examine the term carefully. There are two ways of doing this. First, one can analyze the *content* of a story, the basic elements such as plot, characters, and the like. Second—and equally important to the practicing writer—one can examine the *process* by which the story is presented as seen in the five *narrative modes* available to the writer of fiction: dialogue, thoughts, action, description, and exposition.

Starting with plot, it is obvious that all fiction, whether simple or sophisticated, is developed through a sequence of actions. Simple fiction, however, not only reduces the complexity of the plot, but it usually avoids originality as well. Simple plots tend to be based on well-used conventions known in the magazine field as "formulas." The pleasure some people derive from, say, husband-tempted-by-widow-next-door-but-finally-returns-to-wife is not the excitement of a fresh experience but, rather, the anesthesia of the safely familiar.

Chapter 15 is devoted entirely to structure, from individual scenes to the construction of plot. The point to remember here, however, is that sophistication in plot does not necessarily mean complexity. What one aims for is a situation and a sequence of actions which are fresh and which subtly suggest a great deal to the reader. The determining factor is how much the reader discovers, not how many twists and turns the synopsis may take.

The same is true with characters. In simple fiction, the characters do a lot, but you never get to know much about them. It is possible to read, as some adults have, the adventures of Little Orphan Annie over a period of twenty years and still not know her as a character the way one comes to know the character Joanna in "The Nightingales Sing," which appears in this book as Chapter 18.

All fiction has setting, but in simple fiction it is often all too familiar: New York City pieces make use of Madison Avenue or 42nd Street, San Francisco scenes are "in the shadow of the Golden Gate," and Paris stories have a vista looking out onto the Eiffel Tower. "Originality" frequently takes the form of the exotic: a ski resort high in the Andes, a spy headquarters four hundred feet beneath the House of Parliament, a royal palace constructed entirely in glowing lucite on the planet Octo.

Sophisticated fiction, on the other hand, tends to avoid both the hackneyed and the bizarre. The setting is used as a way of increasing credibility and placing the reader in the center of the story—regardless of whether it is based on an actual place or upon the dreamscape of the author.

Theme is another aspect of fiction which varies with the degree of sophistication. Simple themes suggest truisms which make no more impact on us than the background music in a restaurant. So-called detective magazines and their television counterparts reiterate endlessly, "Crime doesn't pay, but it's exciting to try." Many of television's situation comedies suggest repeatedly that "Nice girls eventually end up with nice boys, but only after being hurt." The fact that we know nice girls who have ended up with rotten boys and nice boys who never got married at all doesn't seem to weaken the popularity of this simple thematic concern. There are others which will be discussed in the next chapter.

Sophisticated fiction tends to have thematic concerns which suggest mixed feelings. Often this takes the form of ambivalence, a blending of love and hate for the same person at the same time. Further complexity is sometimes achieved with irony, a reversal of one's normal expectations.

Whenever you read fiction you evaluate the level of sophistication on the basis of elements like these either consciously or unconsciously. And when you write, they are concerns which will hold your attention at every stage.

In addition to the content of a story, you will want to examine the way the material is presented. For purposes of analysis, it is helpful to see every sentence in a story as presented in one of five different ways or *narrative modes:* dialogue, thoughts, action, description, or exposition.

I will develop the idea of narrative modes further in Chapter 23 because they are a helpful method of looking at a writer's style. I am concerned here, however, mainly with the matter of literary sophistication.

Dialogue and thoughts are two effective ways of suggesting character, and often they are used in tandem so that one sees a contrast between the inner and the outer person. In simple fiction, however, they are often stereotyped—predictable lines for predictable characters.

Action is the dominant mode for simple fiction—particularly adventure stories. But as we will see in the examples included in this text, sophisticated fiction makes significant use of action too. The difference is that as the story begins to gain a greater range of suggestion, the action necessarily must take on a more subtle role of implication. Put another way, action shifts from being an end in itself to being a means of suggestion.

The same is true of description. In a sophisticated story, almost every phrase devoted to describing characters, places, possessions, and the like contributes to the theme or to some aspect of characterization.

The last of these five narrative modes, exposition, is perhaps the most dangerous. In simple fiction it is used to point up the theme as one progresses through the story and, often, to sum it up directly at the end. "Down deep," we are told periodically, "Old Karl had a warm spot in his heart." And in case we missed it, we are given the clincher at the end: "Though his parting words were gruff, there was an undertone of kindness in the old prospector's voice. It was clear that he still knew the meaning of love."

Those who are used to sophisticated fiction, grimace at this because it is a familiar convention. It is also close to the technique of the essay. A sophisticated story may use just as much exposition, but it will rarely label the theme that way. This is not because authors want to be evasive, but because the success of literarily sophisticated fiction depends on the degree to which readers have the feeling that they themselves have discovered the thematic suggestions in a story. It is similar to the way we make judgments about people and situations in actual life. We listen to what people say and watch what they do and then we come to conclusions. In fiction, of course, those lines of dialogue and actions are carefully selected by an author, but when we read we like the illusion of discovering significances on our own.

MOTIVES OF THE WRITER

Both in the poetry section and at the beginning of this chapter I have stressed the fact that sophisticated writing is not "better" than simple works. We have all read well-respected literature—poetry and fiction—which we didn't enjoy; and we have all had times when a simple story, comic strip, or jingle was enjoyable. In this respect, "better" is a personal opinion.

But it should be clear by now that the concern of this book is for writing which is literarily sophisticated. Since this is a skill which takes a good deal of study and practice and does not promise early financial reward, it is important to ask yourself just why you are making the effort. Your motives will significantly affect how you develop as a writer.

There are many reasons for writing fiction, but they tend to fall into three distinct groups. Each has a different set of assumptions and results in a different kind of work.

First, there is the *private motive*. This is what leads to writing merely for the personal pleasure of the act without any regard for another reader. Often it takes the form of journal entries. Spontaneous and usually unrevised, writing like this is essentially a private act.

Many writers find it helpful to keep a journal regularly or to write from time to time "off the top of one's head." It is for the writer what sketching often is for the painter. But it is a mistake to ask a friend or a writing class to evaluate such work. There is really no way to judge it as "good" or "bad" or even "sophisticated" or "simple." It may be valuable as practice or enjoyable as a release, but it shouldn't be passed off as anything more than that.

Second is the *commercial motive*. In its pure form, commercial writing is the opposite of private writing since it is motivated entirely by outer rather than inner demands. It is writing for others. It is producing a product.

Commercial writers usually define their work as a craft rather than an art, and their primary goal is monetary reward. They produce entertainment. They study the market carefully and invest their time and energies in those areas which seem to have potential profit. Many spend more of their time writing nonfiction than they do fiction since the demand is greater.

The fiction produced by commercial writers tends to be conservative and conventional mainly because that is what readers of large-circulation magazines pay for. Like businesspeople, their work consists of supplying a demand. Although there is a tendency for literarily minded individuals to be scornful of these writers for selling to the so-called pulps and the dwindling field of women's magazines, it is an honest profession that fills a need.

Third is the *literary motive*. Writers in this area are moved in part by what I have called the private motive. But they are not content to leave their work at that stage. Fiction for them involves reaching readers—a highly sophisticated form of communication.

Like commercial writers, they would also like to be paid for their efforts, but this is not their primary goal. For every nationally-known novelist like John Updike, Saul Bellow, or E. L. Doctorow, there are hundreds who continue to write fiction without a major following. What keeps them going? Like sculptors, painters, and composers, they value the quality of the artistic objects they are able to create. Having some kind of audience is obviously important for all literarily inclined writers—an unread manuscript is like an unplayed symphony. But unlike commercial writers, they do not generally tailor their work to meet the whims of the public. Their revisions are largely inner-directed rather than outer-directed.

Because literary writers require sophisticated readers, they must often (though not always) be content with a relatively small audience. Their novels may not be best sellers, and their short stories frequently appear in "little magazines" which have small circulations and do not pay their authors lavishly. Many have to do something else for their major income. But they have a special satisfaction in knowing that they are reaching readers who will spend time with their work and will react to it with some sensitivity. More than that, they are working in one of the few areas where one does not have to compromise. For many, this is very important.

Every literary writer has different drives and goals, and one can see what variety there is by reading any of the four volumes published by Penguin under the general title of *Writers at Work* (George Plimpton, ed.). What I am concerned with here, however, is not the variety but that which is shared by all literary writers: a common respect for literature as something of value in itself. Without this, and without extensive reading to support it, no text can help an individual to create new literature.

The dynamics of fiction lie in the fact that it is an instable mix of personal experience and invention, of private feelings and literary conventions like plot and character. The more sophisticated your skills become, the more you can do with these dynamic forces.

Chapter 13

The Sources of Fiction

Sterile sources: the "seven deadly sins"; fruitful sources: *drawing on experience* including family relationships, other interpersonal relationships, and moments of intensity; the technique of *metamorphosis* to sharpen material, to mute thematic patterns, and to gain control over personal experience.

When a short story seems hackneyed, trite, or lacking in credibility, the fault often rests with the source from which it was developed. It is essential to start with material which is fresh. It is for this reason that this chapter begins with what will be for some a rather discouraging set of prohibitions.

As I pointed out in the previous chapter, a story is a blend of personal experience and invention. The danger comes when what one thinks of as invention is merely a borrowing from a familiar convention. Like clichés, these overused plot patterns automatically reduce a piece of writing to the simplest level. As soon as readers recognize the familiar ruts, they slip into that glazed half-attention with which they watch the average television drama or listen to the monotony of background music at a restaurant.

The following, then, are seven deadly sins of fiction which, because of their associations, usually corrupt any attempt at sophisticated writing.

The Shootin' and Killin' Rerun. The source is television. Television took it from Hollywood budget films. And Hollywood's source was the five-cent adventure magazines of the 1920s and 30s.

It comes in two basic forms, the abbreviated Western and the war story. It is extraordinary how many well-read, articulate students revert to these standard plots, somewhat disguised but still complete with their stylized, almost ritualized representations of such virtues as manliness and courage as well as their antonyms, weakness and cowardice. The result is almost always failure.

The frequency and the strength of this temptation is due partly to the fact that there are many intelligent individuals who have, by the time they reach twenty, absorbed more television drama than they have literary works. If, for example, you have watched five television dramas a week for four years, you have absorbed 1,040 separate (but similar) plots, at least 3,120 attempts at characterization, more than 4,160 separate dramatic scenes, and the equivalent of 20,800 pages of dialogue. It is true that not much of this material was studied carefully, but the repetition of plot types, stock characters, and highly formal patterns of diction and syntax are presented in a day-to-day sequence which outdoes the most scientific presentation of programmed learning yet devised by educators.

The danger is not due to the subject matter. Good novels have, after all, used nineteenth-century western United States as a setting, and several great novels have made use of war. The reason these shows prove to be so disastrous as source material is that they have almost nothing to do with the complexity of genuine human experience or even genuine human beings. The original script writers were not writing from experience or even first-hand knowledge. They had as their source nothing but a set of stylized conventions involving situations, characters, and the use of language.

Most writers consider themselves beyond or "above" such influence. Many are. But one should always be on guard. When a plot begins to have a familiar sound to it, hunt down the source ruthlessly.

The Adolescent Tragedy.   The adolescent period is an excellent one for sophisticated fiction as long as you keep your material genuine and fresh in detail. But there are three dangerous pitfalls: lack of perspective, unconscious borrowing from slick and conventionalized fiction, and sentimentality.

Lack of perspective occurs when the experience is too fresh. In such cases, you find yourself *in* the story rather than *above* it. You cannot control it. This may well be your problem if you find yourself calling your fictional characters by the names of their nonfictional counterparts. Another sign is when you find yourself reluctant to change the plot because "that's not the way it happened."

To avoid this lack of perspective, make sure that enough time has elapsed between the event and your attempt to convert it into fiction. The more emotional the experience, the more time will be required to gain some measure of detachment.

Unconscious borrowing from slick fiction is sometimes as difficult to spot as influences from television. But it does happen. Those who do not read stories in the women's magazines may find themselves reaching back to conventionalized plots half-remembered from comics. Whenever one detects the slightest borrowing from such sources, it is important to ask, "Where did the rest of this come from?" Not only the plot but types of characters, lines of dialogue, and even descriptive details may be contaminated.

Sentimentality, the third danger in writing about adolescents, may come from secondary sources like magazines and television or it may just as easily come from the simple desire to move the reader. The difference between the sentimental story and one which is genuinely moving is a matter of sophistication. When a story is simple and rigged to short-circuit the emotions of the reader, we say it is sentimental. These are the stories in which the lonely, misunderstood little boy, the plain little girl with glasses, the cripple, the blind girl, the son of alcoholics are placed in some pitiable situation—any cold street corner will do, but a bombed-out village is better—simply to evoke tears.

But what if you really were the plain little girl with glasses or the son of alcoholics? The fact that the background is from life is never an excuse for fiction which *seems* like a sentimentalized treatment. Your job will be to find those unusual details or to explore ambivalences which will break the mold and convince the reader that this is a genuine experience.

The O. Henry Twist.   This is, I hope, almost self-explanatory. The formula of the trick ending has been so popular that it is imitated by many who have never read O. Henry. The transmission often comes through television. O. Henry's fiction was never very sophisticated to begin with, and it doesn't improve when converted into a television script.

True, his stories were entertaining. But his method was not that of fiction in the contemporary sense. O. Henry's stories were more like charming, well-constructed, well-told, after-dinner anecdotes. When this technique is imitated, the result is usually a slow moving unconvincing build-up to a single punch line. It is simple and it is apt to be dull. Student writers who are interested in working with sustained irony do much better by studying contemporary authors like Cheever, Roth, Updike, and Bellow.

Mock Faulkner.   No writer can help being influenced by his or her favorite modern author, but the attempt to imitate (either consciously or unconsciously) often results in unintended satire. Hemingway and Salinger are frequently borrowed from, but Faulkner is truly contagious. My favorite example is an early attempt at fiction by a college sophomore who managed to pack into a single story one seduction, one rape, one case of incest, and a suicide—all in 2,000 words. Grim as the subject matter and the author's intention were, the end result was a hilarious burlesque.

The origin of that story was not, of course, Faulkner's work but a corrupted memory of selected passages. There was no awareness of the intricate structure of a Faulknerian novel in which violence, which does often appear, becomes woven into the fabric of the entire work. In *Sanctuary*, for example, the scene which is so frequently branded as objectionable is in fact so obliquely presented that many readers are not aware of just what happened until later in the novel—or even until they have turned to the critics for help.

In addition, the imitative story showed no awareness of the relationship between the length of a story and the degree of violence which it can contain without spilling over into the area of melodrama. If one thinks of violence as electrical voltage, it is easy to see that what is successfully sent through a heavy-gauge woven cable will burn out if sent through a single strand of light wire.

By way of specific example, it is worth noting Faulkner's "Dry September" and J. F. Powers' "The Eye." Both stories involve a brutal lynching. Both stories mute the degree of violence by refusing to describe directly the actual lynching scene. Neither author can be accused of literary cowardice. Inclusion of the lynch scenes in these two stories would have overloaded the circuit and the result would have been melodrama; exclusion, in these cases, allows for the maximum possible impact.

The Gray Flannel Sermon   is one of the most common patterns in college writing courses. The protagonist is a hard-driving businessman. He doesn't have time for his wife or children. The story usually begins with a sample of his ruthless drive to the top. The setting is often his luxurious office on the eighty-eighth floor looking out over the twinkling lights of Manhattan or San Francisco Bay. On his desk there are three telephones and a picture of his long-suffering wife. The plot builds toward his realization that Man-does-not-live-by-Success-alone and ends as he puts a bullet through his head. Or sometimes he jumps. Perhaps we will now see a woman in a tailored suit who sacrifices her family for a career. The shift will be no great improvement for fiction.

It would be nice to think that such plots were influenced by novels like Dreiser's *American Tragedy* or short stories like Fitzgerald's "Winter Dreams," but usually they are not. The tradition seems to have been sustained through the scriptwriters of such shows as "Rich Man, Poor Man" and "Dallas." How else could so many beginning authors all describe the same mahogany desk with its identical set of three telephones, the same long-suffering wife, and the same "understanding" secretary who in almost every case has the same shade of blond hair?

The Poe Gimmick.   One does not have to abandon one's respect or even admiration for Poe's inventiveness in order to scorn the wellworn and essentially boring imitations of his work. There are three reasons why warmed-over Poe is generally unsuccessful. The first is an historical consideration: Poe was working in a period when the short story as an independent genre was just being born. His tricks were fresh and truly surprised readers who were, in this area, naive. Since then, our expectations have increased. We are no longer content with pure melodrama such as we find in "The Pit and the Pendulum" or "Ms. Found in a Bottle." We now expect fiction to contain more elaborate characterization, more complexity of theme, and greater variety of tone. Even that last bastion of melodrama, the horror film, could make no more use of Poe's material in the film called *The Raven* than to treat it as fodder for the lowest sort of satire.

Another reason for the collapse of the Poe market as a source for good fiction is that most of his gimmicks were one-shot affairs. That is, once the trick has been used, we can no longer be truly surprised by it. And when almost the entire impact of the story is based on the melodramatic elements, the contemporary writer cannot borrow without being obviously imitative.

Essentially, however, the problem is the same as in the other types: the imitation lacks both originality and sophistication. It becomes so far removed from genuine human experience and reactions to that experience that it no longer suggests an insight into anything.

The Free-Flying Fantasy is the last of these seven fictional sins. Although it is not derived from the traditions of commercial writing or television, it has a long and tired history and is perhaps the most dangerous item on our list.

In the 1920s it was called "automatic writing." Writers simply typed whatever came into their heads for three hours and saved the final fifteen pages as a "story." Occasionally they were published, but no one has republished them. They tended to be rather boring.

There was another flurry of interest in the late 1960s when it was defended as "literary tripping," an hallucinogenic voyage on paper. Again, it was generally more fun to write than to read.

This technique of aimless composition is not to be confused with *stream-of-consciousness* writing. The latter, made famous by James Joyce, is designed to give the illusion of entering the mind of a fictional character. It is presented as a part of a story, not as a display of the author's own psyche. It is a literary device.

Automatic writing, on the other hand, is very much a private act. It may be therapeutic and it may later suggest the beginnings of a short story, but by itself it belongs in your journal.

These, then, are seven of the most common causes for failure in short stories. They shouldn't discourage you. One of the primary functions of this text is to reduce the difficult period of trial and error in the creative process and to help you move on to the aspects of writing which are more intricate and individual. If you keep in mind how important it is to start with fresh and honest material, you will be ready to examine more fruitful sources.

DRAWING ON EXPERIENCE

There are usually two phases in the genesis of a successful story. The first is selecting the experience or some aspect of an experience; the second is a process of reshaping this material in fundamental ways, a technique called *metamorphosis*.

This selection of a significant or meaningful incident may come easily without conscious searching. But often it does not. Even experienced writers have "dry periods" in which their search for material becomes deliberate. Here are some of the areas which they probe.

Family relationships are natural subjects for fiction. Everyone has had either parents or foster parents; everyone has experienced in some proportion that mixture of love and resentment which is a natural part of that relationship. And that instable balance is normally in constant flux. In very general terms, it is apt to be a progression from idealization through disillusionment to a new acceptance usually based on a fairly realistic evaluation. But this is a vast oversimplification, and stories which are based on a simple thematic statement of "The day I discovered my father was no saint" are apt to turn out thin and unconvincing. The writer has to probe deeper in order to discover and dramatize those unique shifts in attitude. Often it is some *specific* characteristic of, say, the father that is altered in some slight but significant way which lends itself to good fiction.

In addition to child-parent relationships, there are a variety of other intrafamily attitudes which also shift significantly: brother and sister, two sisters and a maiden aunt, two brothers and their cousin, a daughter dealing with a stepfather, the reactions of three brothers to their uncle. Relationships like these keep shifting in real life and the shifts are remembered because something was done (action) or said (dialogue) or thought in such a way as to dramatize the change. To some degree, you can use such relationships directly, but often you will have to metamorphose experience into something related but different—a process which I will explain shortly.

Relationships between girls and boys and men and women are used repeatedly in fiction, and there are hackneyed situations which you should avoid. But in most cases you can find a safe path by asking these two essential questions: What *really* happened? And what was there about the action, the thoughts, the outcome which was truly unique? Of course there are those situations which at first glance seem too close to clichés to be credible or interesting. Occasionally lovers really do patch up quarrels while standing on the shore of Lake Placid under a full moon in June. But not often. You may have to douse the moon, change the name of the lake, and give the characters some uneasiness about that reconciliation if the story is to take on a sense of authenticity.

Some of the best relationships to examine are those with individuals who are much younger or older. The greater the gap in age, the more difficult it may be to enter the mind of the other individual. But you can always write the story from the point of view of the character who is about your own age.

A different way of stimulating your memory is to recall moments of intensity. Often these involve some kind of discovery about yourself or another person. As you examine the event (a good use for a journal), you may not really understand why the experience has remained so vivid in your memory. But you can be sure that if it is still clear there must have been some special meaning in it for you.

Such a memory may be fragmentary. Settings like a particular shopping plaza, a playing field or vacant lot where you used to play, a view from a car window, or a kitchen seen only once often stand out with extraordinary sharpness. They have remained for a reason.

Characters (not to be confused with "characters" who are held to be "unforgettable" by the *Reader's Digest*) may remain in your mind only from an overheard conversation or a quick glimpse: a subway attendant, a store clerk, a hitchhiker, or an auto mechanic. And incidents do not even have to be directly connected with the observer. They may involve an argument overheard in a supermarket; the smashing of a window; an automobile accident; or the playful flirtation of a girl and three boys on a beach, a park, or a parking lot.

One of the first things to do with such a memory-fragment is to recall every possible detail: the visual minutiae, the sounds, and the intricacies of your own feelings. From these you may discover why that particular experience remained in your memory while so many others drifted beyond recall. The final story may or may not include you as a character, and it will probably be far removed from the facts of the original episode, but it will have the advantage of being rooted in a genuine and personally significant experience.

METAMORPHOSIS
OF EXPERIENCE

Important as experience is in the writing of fiction, it is only a starting point. You may find it necessary to consider major changes in plot, character, or setting even before you begin to write. Such radical transformations of personal experience are called metamorphosing.

Metamorphosis often occurs unconsciously. You may begin writing without knowing how dependent your story idea is on some disguised aspect of your own life. What concerns us here, however, is the conscious decision to reshape your material.

The most common reason for doing this is to clarify either the theme or character development. Experience, after all, is apt to be a clutter. One of the functions of fiction is to transform that confusion into patterns which seem to the reader orderly and meaningful yet at the same time credible. This often requires weeding out unnecessary events and characters—sometimes even yourself!

Revisions, of course, will come later. Metamorphosing is usually done at the outset. It is a part of the initial organizing of material. Few authors outline stories down to every detail, but it helps to settle on the basic elements: the plot, the theme, and the characters.

Suppose, for example, the original experience took place on a hot August day on which plans for a family picnic in the country were ruined when the car boiled over in the heart of the city's slums. The thematic elements which have kept the experience itself vivid in the writer's mind may consist of such varied details as a boy's first awareness of his father as a man hopeless in a crisis, a surprising insight into the instability of his parents' relationship, a recognition of a special bond between mother and daughter, the beginnings of social consciousness in the face of an economically repressed community, an introduction to racial distinctions, and an ironic contrast between the narrator's sense of high adventure and his parents' sense of disaster.

A good story can echo all of these themes. But the writer will probably want to focus on just one or two. Here is the first stage of the metamorphosis. If the father and the son are the focus, is there a need for the mother and the sister? Or if the important relationship is between daughter and mother, which of the other characters are really necessary? If social issues are the primary concern, is it necessary to include the tensions which went on between the two adults? This is partly a matter of selecting an aspect of the event and deciding which characters to use.

More radical, the final story may end with no children involved—this would swing the attention directly to the parents. Or the entire family might be dropped in order to build from some minor sequence of events observed while waiting for the car to be repaired. Occasionally all one retains is the flavor of the setting and a few individual details, such as a man's conversation with a woman leaning out of a fifth floor window or an impatient cab driver waiting for his car to be repaired at the garage.

The first and primary reason for metamorphosing experience, then, is to sharpen the focus and to clarify the literary concerns such as theme, characterization, motivation, tone, and the like.

The second function of literary metamorphosis is the reverse in that occasionally the patterns of experience are too neat, too contrived for fiction. When the theme of a story is blatant, we are acutely aware of an author at work and no longer enter into the story as if it were an extension of experience. It becomes only a trick. And there is nothing to be gained by telling the reader that "it really happened that way." If, for example, the father in the story outlined above really was consistently irascible or without exception dependent on his wife's suggestions, he would become a "flat" character, a cliché of fiction. Variation and further insight would be needed not to clarify characterization but to make it more convincing. Or if the story ended up so obviously in the category of "The day I discovered father was not perfect," the author might be well advised to add other thematic elements so that we no longer have the feeling that it has become an extended anecdote.

The third and final justification for these basic transformations is the experience which has not yet been emotionally digested. In most cases it takes a year or more for an author to look on a personal experience with some objectivity and perspective. True, some experiences turn into fiction without much change. But this is far rarer than most people realize. And when one is still very much involved in an experience, one has little control over it.

In these cases, it is sometimes helpful to break the mold set by the experience itself. This is usually done through an initial metamorphosis of the story. Childhood experiences are sometimes converted in this way by dropping the child and seeing the story through the eyes of an adult; the original setting can be shifted to some completely different place; ages can be changed; even the sex of a character can be shifted (as in the extraordinary source of Proust's Albertine), and, most basic of all, what originally came to mind as a minor or secondary theme can be developed as the primary theme of a story. Through this technique, the author can often re-establish control over a story which might otherwise have been only a journal entry.

Occasionally a story idea will come to you which needs no analysis and no radical overhaul. It may be fairly close to experience or it may have been metamorphosed unconsciously. When this happens, move ahead before you lose it!

But whenever you find it difficult to start a story, review the relationships you have had with members of your own family, classmates, people with whom you have worked—any vivid experience. When you have settled on an episode, see if it needs some kind of basic transformation. Decide which characters are important and what we are going to discover about them. Don't let the original experience limit you. Feel free to metamorphose the material from the very start.

When you consider the extraordinary variety of experiences stored in your mind and add to that the infinite number of variations you can devise for each, you can see how each new story is unique. This is the true meaning of *creative* writing.

Chapter 14

A Story by Stephen Minot

Sausage and Beer

I kept quiet for most of the trip. It was too cold for talk. The car, a 1929 Dodge, was still fairly new, but it had no heater, and I knew from experience that no matter how carefully I tucked the black bearskin robe about me, the cold would seep through the door cracks and, starting with a dull ache in my ankles, would work up my legs. There was nothing to do but sit still and wonder what Uncle Theodore would be like.

"Is it very far?" I asked at last. My words puffed vapor.

"We're about halfway now," he said.

That was all. Not enough, of course, but I hadn't expected much more. My father kept to his own world, and he didn't invite children to share it. Nor did he impose himself on us. My twin sister and I were allowed to live our own lives, and our parents led theirs, and there was a mutual respect for the border. In fact, when we were younger Tina and I had assumed that we would eventually marry each other, and while those plans were soon revised, the family continued to exist as two distinct couples.

But this particular January day was different, because Tina hadn't been invited—nor had Mother. I was twelve that winter, and I believe it was the first time I had ever gone anywhere alone with my father.

The whole business of visiting Uncle Theodore had come up in the most unconvincingly offhand manner.

"Thought I'd visit your Uncle Theodore," he had said that day after Sunday dinner. "Wondered if you'd like to meet him."

He spoke with his eyes on a crack in the ceiling as if the idea had just popped into his head, but that didn't fool me. It was quite obvious that he had waited until both Tina and my mother were in the kitchen washing the dishes, that he had rehearsed it, and that I wasn't really being given a choice.

"Is Tina going?" I asked.

"No, she isn't feeling well."

I knew what that meant. But I also knew that my father was just using it as an excuse. So I got my coat.

The name Uncle Theodore had a familiar ring, but it was just a name. And I had learned early that you just do not ask about relatives who don't come up in adult conversation naturally. At least, you didn't in my family. You can never tell —Like my Uncle Harry. He was another one of my father's brothers. My parents never said anything about Uncle Harry, but some of my best friends at school told me he'd taken a big nail, a spike really, and driven it into his heart with a ball peen hammer. I didn't believe it, so they took me to the library and we found the article on the front page of the *Herald* for the previous Saturday, so it must have been true.

I thought a lot about that. It seemed to me that a grown-up ought to be able to *shove* it between his ribs. And even if he couldn't, what was the point of the ball peen hammer? I used to put myself to sleep feeling the soft spaces between my ribs and wondering just which one was directly over my heart.

But no one at school told me about Uncle Theodore because they didn't know he existed. Even I hadn't any real proof until that day. I knew that my father had a brother named Theodore in the same way I knew the earth was round without anyone ever taking me to the library to prove it. But then, there were many brothers I had never met—like Freddie, who had jointed a Theosophist colony somewhere in California and wore robes like a priest, and Uncle Herb, who was once in jail for leading a strike in New York.

We were well out in the New England countryside now, passing dark, snow-patched farm fields and scrubby woodlands where saplings choked and stunted each other. I tried to visualize this Uncle Theodore as a farmer: blue overalls, straw hat, chewing a long stem of alfalfa, and misquoting the Bible. But it was a highly unsatisfactory conjecture. Next I tried to conjure up a mystic living in—didn't St. Francis live in a cave? But it wasn't the sort of question I could ask my father. All I had to go on was what he had told me, which was nothing. And I knew without thinking that he didn't want me to ask him directly.

After a while I indulged in my old trick of fixing my eyes on the big radiator thermometer mounted like a figurehead on the front end of the hood. If you do that long enough the blur of the road just beyond will lull you nicely and pass the time. It had begun to take effect when I felt the car slow down and turn abruptly. Two great gates flashed by, and we were inside a kind of walled city.

Prison, I thought. That's it. That's why they kept him quiet. A murderer, maybe. "My Uncle Theodore," I rehearsed silently, "he's the cop killer."

The place went on forever, row after row of identical buildings, four stories, brick, slate roofs, narrow windows with wire mesh. There wasn't a bright color anywhere. The brick had aged to gray, and so had the snow patches along the road. We passed a group of three old men lethargically shoveling ice and crusted snow into a two-wheeled horse cart; men and horse were the same hue. It was the sort of setting you have in dreams which are not nightmares but still manage to leave a clinging aftertaste. At least, *I* have dreams like that.

"This is a kind of hospital," my father said flatly as we drove between the staring brick fronts. There was a slow whine to second gear which sang harmony to something in me. I had based my courage on the romance of a prison, but even this slim hold on assurance was lost with the word "hospital."

"It's big," I said.

"It's enormous," he said, and then turned his whole attention to studying the numbers over each door. There was something in his tone that suggested that he didn't like the place either, and that did a lot to sustain me.

Uncle Theodore's building was 13-M, but aside from the number, it resembled the others. The door had been painted a dark green for many years, and the layers of paint over chipped and blistered paint gave it a mottled look. We had to wait quite a while before someone responded to the push bell.

A man let us in, not a nurse. And the man was clearly no doctor either. He wore a gray shirt which was clean but unpressed, and dark-green work pants with a huge ring of keys hanging from his belt. But for the keys he might have been a W.P.A. worker.

"Hello there, Mr. Bates," he said in a round Irish voice to match his round face. "You brought the boy?"

"I brought the boy." My father's voice was reedy by comparison. "How's Ted?"

"Same as when you called. A little gloomy, maybe, but calm. Those boils have just about gone."

"Good," my father said.

"Funny about those boils. I don't remember a year but what he's had trouble. Funny."

My father agreed it was funny, and then we went into the visiting room to await Uncle Theodore.

The room was large, and it seemed even larger for the lack of furniture. There were benches around all four walls, and in the middle there was a long table flanked with two more benches. The rest was space. And through that space old men shuffled, younger men wheeled carts of linen, a woman visitor walked slowly up and down with her restless husband—or brother, or uncle. Or was *she* the patient? I couldn't decide which might be the face of madness, his troubled and shifting eyes or her deadened look. Beyond, a bleak couple counseled an ancient patient. I strained to hear, wanting to know the language of the place, but I could only make out mumbles.

The smell was oddly familiar. I cast about; this was no home smell. And then I remembered trips with my mother to a place called the Refuge, where the lucky brought old clothes, old furniture, old magazines, and old kitchenware to be bought by the unlucky. My training in Christian charity was to bring my chipped and dented toys and dump them into a great bin, where they were pored over by dead-faced mothers and children.

"Smells like the Refuge," I said very softly, not wanting to hurt anyone's feelings. My father nodded with an almost smile.

We went over to the corner where the benches met, though there was space to sit almost anywhere. And there we waited.

A couple of times I glanced cautiously at my father's face, hoping for some sort of guide. He could have been waiting for a train or listening to a sermon, and I felt a surge of respect. He had a long face with a nose so straight it looked as if it had been leveled with a rule. I guess he would have been handsome if he hadn't seemed so sad or tired much of the time. He worked for a paint wholesaler which had big, dusty offices in a commercial section of Dorchester. When I was younger I used to think the dirt of that place had rubbed off on him permanently.

I began to study the patients with the hope of preparing myself for Uncle Theodore. The old man beside us was stretched out on the bench full length, feet toward us, one arm over his eyes, as if he were lying on the beach, the other resting over his crotch. He had a kind of squeak to his snore. There was nothing in him I could not accept as my Uncle Theodore. Another patient was persistently scratching his back on the dark-varnished door frame. If this were Uncle Theodore, I wondered, would I be expected to scratch his back for him? It wasn't a very rational speculation, but there was nothing about the place that encouraged clear reasoning.

Then my father stood up, and when I did too, I could see that Uncle Theodore was being led in by a Negro who wore the same kind of key ring at his waist that the Irishman had. The Negro nodded to my father, pointing him out to Uncle Theodore, and then set him free with a little nudge as if he were about to pin the tail on the donkey.

Surprisingly, Uncle Theodore was heavy. I don't mean fat, because he wasn't solid. He was a great, sagging man. His jowls hung loose, his shoulders were massive but rounded like a dome, his hands were attached like brass weights on the ends of swinging pendulums. He wore a clean white shirt open at the neck and blue serge suit pants hung on suspenders which had been patched with a length of twine. It looked as if his pants had once been five sizes too large and that somehow, with the infinite patience of the infirm, he had managed to stretch the lower half of his stomach to fill them.

I would have assumed that he was far older than my father from his stance and his shuffling walk (he wore scuffs, which he slid across the floor without once lifting them), but his face was a baby pink, which made him look adolescent.

"Hello, Ted," my father said. "How have you been?"

Uncle Theodore just said "Hello," without a touch of enthusiasm, or even gratitude for our coming to see him. We stood there, the three of us, for an awkward moment.

Then: "I brought the boy."

"Who?"

"My boy, Will."

Uncle Theodore looked down at me with red-rimmed, blue eyes. Then he looked at my father, puzzled. "But *you're* Will."

"Right, but we've named our boy William too. Tried to call him Billy, but he insists on Will. Very confusing."

Uncle Theodore smiled for the first time. The smile made everything much easier; I relaxed. He was going to be like any other relative on a Sunday afternoon visit.

"Well, now," he said in an almost jovial manner, "there's one on me. I'd forgotten I even *had* a boy."

My face tingled the way it does when you open the furnace door. Somehow he had joined himself with my father as a married couple, and done it with a smile. No instruction could have prepared me for this quiet sound of madness.

But my father had, it seemed, learned how to handle it. He simply asked Uncle Theodore if he had enjoyed the magazines he had brought last time. We subscribed to the old version of *Life*, and my mother used to buy *Judge* on the newsstand fairly regularly. It was the right subject to bring up, because Uncle Theodore promptly forgot about who had produced what child and told us about how all his copies of *Life* had been stolen. He even pointed out the thief.

"The little one with the hook nose there," he said with irritation but no rage. "Stuffs them in his pants to make him look bigger. He's a problem, he is."

"I'll send you more," my father said. "Perhaps the attendant will keep them for you."

"Hennesy? He's a good one. Plays checkers like a pro."

"I'll bet he has a hard time beating you."

"Hasn't yet. Not once."

"I'm not surprised. You were always the winner." And then to me: "We used to play up in the cupola for hours at a stretch."

This jolted me. It hadn't occurred to me that the two of them had spent a childhood together. I even let some of their conversation slip by thinking of how they had grown up in the same old rambling house before I was born, had perhaps planned the future while sitting up there in the attic room, looking down on the world, had gone to school together, and then at some point—But what point? And how? It was as incomprehensible to me looking back as it must have been for them looking forward.

"So they started banging on their plates," Uncle Theodore was saying, "and shouting for more heat. Those metal plates sure make a racket, I can tell you."

"That's no way to get heat," Father said, sounding paternal.

"Guess not. They put Schwartz and Cooper in the pit. That's what Hennesy said. And there's a bunch of them that's gone to different levels. They send them down when they act like that, you know. The doctors, they take a vote and send the troublemakers down." And then his voice lowered. Instinctively we both bent toward him for some confidence. "And I've found out—God's truth—that one of these nights they're going to shut down the heat *all the way. Freeze us!*"

There was a touch of panic in this which coursed through me. I could feel just how it would be, this great room black as midnight, the whine of wind outside, and then all those hissing radiators turning silent, and the aching cold seeping through the door cracks—

"Nonsense," my father said quietly, and I knew at once that it was nonsense. "They wouldn't do that. Hennesy's a friend of mine. I'll speak to him before I go."

"You do that," Uncle Theodore said with genuine gratitude, putting his hand on my father's knee. "You do that for us. I don't believe there would be a soul of us"—he swept his hand about expansively—"not a soul of us alive if it weren't for your influence."

My father nodded and then turned the conversation to milder topics. He talked about how the sills were rotting under the house, how a neighborhood gang had broken two windows one night, how there was talk of replacing the trolley with a bus line, how Imperial Paint, where my father worked, had laid off fifty percent of its employees, how business was so bad it couldn't get worse. But Uncle Theodore didn't seem very concerned. He was much more bothered about how a man named Altman was losing his eyesight because of the steam heat and how stern and unfair Hennesy was. At one point he moved back in time to describe a fishing trip by canoe through the Rangeley Lakes. It was like opening a great window, flooding the place with light and color and the smells of summer.

"Nothing finer," he said, his eyes half shut, "than frying those trout at the end of the day with the water so still you'd think you could walk on it."

He was interrupted by the sleeper on the bench beside us, who woke, stood, and stared down at us. Uncle Theodore told him to "Go blow," and when he had gone so were the Rangeley Lakes.

"Rangeley?" he asked, when my father tried to open that window again by suggestion. "He must be one of our cousins. Can't keep 'em straight."

And we were back to Mr. Altman's deafness and how seriously it hindered him and how the doctors paid no attention.

It was with relief that I smelled sauerkraut. That plus attendants gliding through with carts of food in dented steel containers seemed to suggest supper, and supper promised that the end was near.

"About suppertime," my father said after a particularly long silence.

Uncle Theodore took in a long, deep breath. He held it for a moment. Then he let it go with the slowest, saddest sigh I have ever heard.

"About suppertime," he said at the end of it.

There were mumbled farewells and nods of agreement. We were thanked for copies of *Judge* which we hadn't brought; he was told he was looking fine, just fine.

We were only inches from escape when Uncle Theodore suddenly discovered me again.

"Tell me son," he said, bending down with a smile which on anyone else would have been friendly, "what d'you think of your Uncle Ted?"

I was overwhelmed. I stood there looking up at him, waiting for my father to save me. But he said nothing.

"It's been very nice meeting you," I said to the frozen pink smile, dredging the phrase up from my sparse catechism of social responses, assuming that what would do for maiden aunts would do for Uncle Theodore.

But it did not. He laughed. It was a loud and bitter laugh, derisive, and perfectly sane. He had seen my statement for the lie it was, had caught sight of himself, of all of us.

"Well," he said when the laugh withered, "say hi to Dad for me. Tell him to drop by."

Father said he would, and we left, grateful that the moment of sanity had been so brief.

It was dark when we got back into the car, and it was just beginning to snow. I nestled into the seat, soothed by the familiar whine of second gear.

We had been on the road about a half hour when my father said quite abruptly, "I could do with a drink." It was so spontaneous, so perfectly confidential that I wanted to reply, to keep some sort of exchange going. But I couldn't suggest a place to go—I couldn't even throw back an easy "So could I."

"It's OK with me," I said, without any of the casual air I tried hard to achieve.

There was a long pause. He flipped the manual windshield wiper. Then he said, "I don't suppose you like sausage."

"I love sausage," I said, though I had never had any at home.

"Well," he said slowly, "there's a place I go—but it might be better to tell your mother we went to a Dutchland Farms for supper."

"Sure," I said, and reached up to flip the windshield wiper for him.

When we got to the city we traveled on roads I had never been on. He finally parked on a dark street and began what turned out to be a three-block hike. It ended at an unlit door, and after some mumbled consultations through an apartment phone we were ushered into a warm, bubbling, sparkling, humming, soothing, exciting bit of cheerful chaos. There was a bar to our right, marble tables ahead, booths beyond, just as I had pictured from the cartoons in *Life* magazine. My father nodded at a waiter and said hi to a group at a table, then headed toward the booths with a sure step.

We hadn't got halfway before a fat man in a double-breasted suit came steaming up to us, furious.

"Whatcha doing," he said even before he reached us, "corruptin' the youth?"

I held my breath. But when the big man reached my father they broke out in easy laughter.

"So this is the boy?" he said. "Will, Junior—right?" We nodded. "Well, there's a good part of you in the boy, I can see that—it's in the eyes. Now, there's a girl too, isn't there? Younger?"

"She's my twin," I said. "Not identical."

The men laughed. Then the fat one said, "Jesus, twins sure run in your family, don't they!"

This surprised me. I knew of no other twins except some cousins from Maine. I looked up at my father, puzzled.

"Me and Ted," he said to me. "We're twins. Nonidentical."

We were ushered to a booth, and the fat man hovered over us, waiting for the order.

"Got sausage tonight?" my father asked.

"Sure. American or some nice hot Italian?"

"Italian."

"Drinks?"

"Well"—My father turned to me. "I guess you rate beer," he said. And then, to the fat man, "Two beers."

The man relayed the order to a passing waiter. Then he asked my father, "Been out to see Ted?"

"You guessed it."

"I figured." He paused, his smile gone. "You too?" he asked me.

"Yes," I said. "It was my first time."

"Oh," he said, with a series of silent nods which assured me that somehow he knew exactly what my afternoon had been like. "Ted was quite a boy. A great tackle. A pleasure to watch him. But no dope either. Used to win meals here playing chess. Never saw him lose. Why, he sat right over there."

He pointed to the corner booth, which had a round table. All three of us looked; a waiter with a tray full of dirty glasses stopped, turned, and also looked at the empty booth as if an apparition had just been sighted.

"And you know why he's locked up?"

"No," I whispered, appalled at the question.

"It's just the number he drew. Simple as that. Your Dad, me, you—any of us could draw the wrong number tomorrow. There's something to think about."

I nodded. All three of us nodded. Then the waiter brought a tray with the order, and the fat man left us with a quick, benedictory smile. We ate and drank quietly, lost in a kind of communion.

Chapter **15**

Structure:
From Scenes to Plot

Episodes in experience related to *scenes* in fiction; *plot* described as a succession of scenes; *nonchronological* patterns of plot; *controlling the pace* by revising the plot; building a story toward an *epiphany*.

Clocks move at a steady rate. And in one sense, so do our lives. Awake or asleep, we progress from birth to death at a steady pace.

But now take a moment to review what you did yesterday from the time you got up to the end of the day.

Notice how naturally that chronology turned into a list of identifiable events or episodes: getting dressed, eating breakfast, and, for students, attending classes, a coffee break with friends in the cafeteria, a conversation in the hall, and lunch. For nonstudents, the events would be different, but the rhythm from one unit of activity to the next is essentially the same. The point is that while the *clock* moves perfectly regularly, our *life* as we look back is recalled as a sequence of episodes.

These episodes have certain characteristics which every writer of fiction should consider. First, we often identify them by where they occurred—the setting. Second, we recall who was there—the characters. Third, such episodes remain clear long after we have forgotten what came just before and just afterward. Those unstructured periods of time which merely link one episode with the next (walking, waiting, driving, watching television, sleeping) tend to blend together and blur quickly.

Finally, we don't always remember these events in the order in which they occurred. Students complaining about bad teachers are not necessarily going to start with kindergarten; football fans recalling dramatic games they have watched are not going to begin with the first one they attended; and a man recalling his love for a woman is not necessarily going to begin with the day he met her.

Fiction tends to imitate these patterns. What we call *episodes* in life become *scenes* in fiction. These are the basic units. And their arrangement is what we call *plot*.

SCENE CONSTRUCTION
IN "SAUSAGE AND BEER"

A scene in a short story is not as clearly defined as in drama, but generally speaking it consists of an episode which is identifiable either because of the setting or the characters involved. The reader senses a transition from one scene to the next whenever the author changes the setting or alters the "cast of characters" by having one leave or arrive.

If you examine the scenes in "Sausage and Beer," you will see that there are six of them. The story opens with the boy being driven by his father on a cold January day. Although there is a flashback which tells us about the father inviting his son to visit the mysterious Uncle Theodore, the opening scene really continues until they arrive at the hospital grounds.

There is a short scene outside the hospital buildings which focuses on young Will's reactions, but the story quickly shifts to the waiting room, the third scene.

Uncle Theodore's arrival signals the beginning of the fourth scene. Although the setting is the same, there is a decided psychological shift as soon as he appears.

After the father and son leave the hospital, there is a brief scene in the car and then a longer, more important one in the bar.

Why six scenes? In blocking out the general pattern of the story, this is what emerged. But don't feel bound by the pattern or even the number of scenes in early drafts. In this particular story, a two-page flashback was cut before the story was published in the *Atlantic* and another page was cut from the version which appeared in the second edition of this textbook. It would be possible, of course, to cut the story down to a single scene—the one in which father and son talk with Uncle Theodore in the hospital. But too much would be lost. The earlier scenes provide suspense, and the concluding scenes shift the story from a simple initiation (the boy introduced to the disturbing reality of mental illness) to a kind of first communion in which a young man is welcomed into the fellowship of adult life with all its distressing ironies.

The answer to the question of why the story is in six scenes is not a simple matter of rules. It is judgment. More scenes would weigh the story down, and less would begin to make it too sketchy, too simple. It is very helpful to have a rough idea of the scene pattern in advance—even a tentative outline. But it is equally important to be willing to make adjustments after the first draft, adding or cutting scenes where needed.

VARIETIES OF PLOT PATTERNS

The three stories included in this volume which have clearly defined plots move chronologically from scene to scene. A majority of stories do—particularly those which are relatively short. But even in those cases, the writer is not bound to move relentlessly forward in time. The author—like the scriptwriter—is free to include glimpses of past action.

The flashback is a simple method of inserting an episode which occurred previous to the main flow (or *base time*) of the plot. The term "flashback," first used by film writers, describes more than a simple reference to the past seen through a character's thoughts or dialogue. A true flashback consists of a whole scene which took place previous to the main action of the story and which is presented with setting and often dialogue.

Take, for example, the flashback which occurs in the opening scene of "Sausage and Beer." The father and son, you remember, are driving in silence, and the earlier incident is dropped in almost as if in brackets:

> The whole business of visiting Uncle Theodore had come up in the most unconvincingly offhand manner.
> "Thought I'd visit your Uncle Theodore," he had said that day after Sunday dinner. "Wondered if you'd like to meet him."
> He spoke with his eyes on a crack in the ceiling as if the idea had just popped into his head, but that didn't fool me.

Notice that the reader is informed of the fact that the story is moving back to an earlier time by the brief use of the past perfect: "*had* come up" and "he *had* said that day." This is a standard method of entering a flashback even though many readers are not consciously aware that they are being signaled by a shift in tense. In fact, many *writers* have used the technique without knowing that the *had* form is called the past perfect. Never mind the terminology, *had* is the cue for your reader. After one or two sentences, shift back to the simple past: "It was quite obvious" and "asked."

How do you come out of a flashback? The most obvious way is to identify the transition directly: "But that was hours ago" or "But that was when he was much younger." More often, authors simply make sure that the new paragraph starts with a bit of action or a line of dialogue which clearly indicates to the reader that the story has returned to base time, the events and setting of the primary plot line. In this particular flashback the reader should be set straight by the paragraph which begins: "We were well out in the New England countryside now."

Multiple flashbacks are sometimes used when the author wants to suggest a complicated set of clues leading to a symbolic or a literal trial. Joseph Conrad's *Lord Jim* is in this form and so is William Faulkner's well-known, "A Rose for Emily." Such an approach tends to fragment the story line, of course, and it may be for this reason that it is usually found in longer works and ones which have a type of mystery or trial which maintains the story's unity and the reader's interest.

The frame story traditionally refers to a tale told by a character appearing in a larger work such as the separate narrations within Chaucer's *The Canterbury Tales*. But by common usage it also refers to any story in which the bulk of the material is presented as a single, long flashback. It is possible to do this in the third person; but often a frame is achieved through the device of a narrator who recalls an incident which happened some time in the past.

"Sausage and Beer," for example, could have opened with the narrator looking back like this:

> As I stood with my wife waiting for the funeral to begin, I realized how little I had really seen of my father. It was as if he were a stranger until I was twelve. The turning point came one day when he took me to visit my Uncle Theodore.
> As I remember it, I had kept quiet for most of the trip. It was too cold for talk.

Notice the traditional use of the past perfect for a single sentence and then the simple past. And if the story were to have a complete frame, the ending might be rounded out with a return to the opening scene.

> Sitting there in the chapel, listening to the service intended to honor my father, I couldn't help feeling that he and I had years ago experienced a more meaningful ritual there in that most secular bar years ago.

Such an ending seems wooden to me—a bit too obvious. But it does indicate how any story can be surrounded in a frame. Or, as an alternative, the frame can be left incomplete simply to avoid the danger of a needless summing up.

The use of the frame is well justified if there is a good reason for contrasting the attitude of the narrator at the time of the narration with that back when the event took place. Conrad's "Youth" is a particularly interesting example because it is actually a double frame: an unnamed narrator recalls a number of men sitting around a mahogany table and remembers how one of them, Marlow, narrated a lengthy story about his early sailing experiences. At the close of the story Marlow finishes and the original narrator describes the faces of the listeners sitting around the table. The elaborate frame is justified because so much of the story focuses on the contrast between youthful romanticism and the gentle cynicism of age.

Be careful, however, not to weigh down a simple story with too many flashbacks or a needless frame approach. If the story will do well without such devices, it is best not to add what may seem like mere clutter.

CONTROLLING THE PACE
BY REVISING THE PLOT

Every reader is aware that some sections in a story "move slowly" or "drag," while others "move quickly." A writer, however, has to know *why* this has happened.

In part, the pace of fiction is controlled by the style—particularly the length and complexity of the sentence structure. This is discussed in Chapter 23. By far the greatest factor, however, is the *rate of revelation.* That is, a story seems to move rapidly when a great deal is being revealed to the reader; and, conversely, it slows down when the author turns to digression, speculation, description, or any type of exposition.

One can, of course, maintain a high rate of revelation simply by concentrating on what reviewers like to call an "action-packed plot." This is one of the recurring characteristics of many best sellers, adventure stories, and stories of "true romance." Extreme examples are seen in television drama series and the comics. What these stories sacrifice is the richness of suggestion and the range of implication which one finds in sophisticated fiction.

When you write sophisticated fiction you have to be on guard against two dangers: If you maintain a consistently high rate of revelation, entertaining your readers with a lively plot, you may bore them for lack of significance. They will find your work superficial. But if you become philosophically discursive or heavily symbolic, you may also bore your readers for lack of drama. Because of this, most successfully sophisticated stories shift the pace throughout the work.

Openings are frequently given a high rate of revelation. It helps to plunge the reader into an ongoing situation or to present some kind of dramatic question. "Sausage and Beer" begins with the narrator driving with his father and wondering what his Uncle Theodore will be like. "The Windmill Man," which appears as Chapter 16, begins with the question: "What was the premonition?" and hooks the reader with the information that it began "the day Old Clayton Hobbs fell off the mill and killed himself." In Chapter 18, "The Nightingales Sing" opens with the protagonist being driven to a strange place in the fog.

All three of these stories, however, indulge in description and in background information within the first two pages. Exposition, remember, is like the connective links between what is going on and what led up to the situation. Description helps to place the reader in the situation.

When you shift the setting you will find yourself facing a situation somewhat similar to that at the beginning of the story. You want to give enough physical detail to place the reader in that new location, but description is static so you also have to provide action or new information to maintain the rate of revelation.

In "Sausage and Beer," for example, it was necessary to describe the hospital and later the bar, which because of Prohibition was a speak-easy. When you read "The Nightingales Sing" you will notice that the house the main character enters has to be described in some detail. But in all of these cases, the description is to some degree broken up and woven into the action and often enlivened with the introduction of new characters.

As you read over your first draft, try to feel where the story loses momentum. If it is only slight, you have no problem. The motion of a story is like a skater—after each forward thrust you can afford to glide a bit. But not too long. Very short stories are sometimes constructed with a single scene and move at a steady pace right through to the end. In most cases, however, you will need more than one scene to achieve what you have in mind and with such a story you should examine the pace throughout. Remember that you as author have complete control over the pace through the rate of revelation.

BUILDING TOWARD
AN EPIPHANY

A major difference between a journal entry and a finished, sophisticated short story is the fact that the latter usually builds toward what James Joyce called an *epiphany*. In brief, it is a moment of recognition or a discovery. It usually comes in one of two forms: either the reader learns something significant from the events of the story or the reader and the central characters share the discovery.

In "Sausage and Beer," there are, I think, two such moments—one recognized by the boy and the other an insight perceived only by the reader. The first is given through the fat man at the speak-easy who, in a serious moment almost at the end of the story, poses the question of why one of two brothers should live a normal life and the other should end up in a mental hospital. His answer is that it is just chance. We all run that risk. The boy understands this and perhaps is more struck with it than others might be since he too is a twin.

The final sentence, however, suggests a parallel which the reader (it is hoped) understands but which is too complicated for the boy to understand.

The father and son, having shared this difficult experience, now share something like a communion—not a religious experience but a partaking of life itself.

The building of scenes and their arrangement as plot becomes more intuitive after writing several stories. But there are ways you can speed this process. First, examine the scene construction of short stories in print. Mark in the margin where they begin and end. Study the transitions and the shifts in pace and in mood.

Second, study and question your own scene construction. Be on guard against two problem areas: the scattering of scenes which cover too broad a spectrum of time for the length of the story and, on the other hand, those long, talky or highly descriptive scenes which sag for lack of development.

If the story seems too brief or thin or lacking in development, don't start "padding" the existing scenes with more explanation and longer sentences. Carefully consider whether the reader needs to know more about the characters or the situation through the addition of entire scenes. Conversely, if the story seems to ramble, don't think that the only solution is to remove a sentence here and a phrase there. Consider cutting or combining entire scenes.

Finally, ask yourself just what it is that the reader learns from going through this experience. This shouldn't be a simple "moral" which the reader can shrug off as a truism, nor must it be a far-reaching philosophical or psychological truth. What most authors aim for is a subtle sense of having achieved some insight either with the protagonist or independently.

This chapter corresponds roughly to the one entitled "From Units to Unity" in the section on poetry. The type of unit in fiction is different from that in verse, and the methods of creating an artistic whole vary as well. But the story resembles the poem (and the play as well) in that it is a construction of units; and like all art forms, the whole is greater than the sum of its parts.

Chapter 16

A Story by
Tim McCarthy

The Windmill Man

What was the premonition? It had been with him at least since the day old
Clayton Hobbs fell off the mill and killed himself. Nearly a month ago now.
Clayton had been astride the tail pouring fresh oil into that gear case. The
simplest of jobs. But Clayton was over seventy years old and had vowed
never to climb another windmill tower. "Hang it all. I ain't going to drag
Justus across forty miles of desert just to pour a few quarts of oil into a gear
case." Those might have been his words, talking to himself in the way of the
lonely, tobacco juice bubbling at his lip, bursting, staining his mustache. The
simplest of jobs, yet something went wrong. The old man lost his balance, or
his heart kicked up on him—something! He fell sixty feet to the ground. No
one found him for three days, after the ravens and the coyotes had got to
him, an oil can crushed in his fist. Justus sent flowers: "Condolences. Justus
Knight." And that night he crept out of bed while his wife slept, went out
and leaned against the windmill down by the corral, and cried.

For fifty years Clayton had been a windmill man in that part of the state and clear over into Arizona. He had been one of many to begin with. But gradually the others had died off or been killed or crippled, and no one had showed up to fill their shoes. Clayton was alone. In those last years he taught Justus everything he knew about windmills—including how to fear and love them, if such things can indeed be taught. Justus had the ten sections his father left him but they were mostly sand and creosote bush and they wouldn't carry fifty head without feeding extra. He also had two daughters and a wife who wanted her slice of the American pie, so he had to find some other way to earn money. The neighbors laughed at him when he finally went into the windmill business on his own. Windmills were on the way out; he would never make a living. That was six years ago. Clayton had referred his dwindling trade to Justus and now the younger man had more work than he could handle. Six years had brought changes that were astonishing to most people. Gas was short, electricity threatened or curtailed. You couldn't buy anything when you wanted it, and what you did get hold of cost twice what it was worth. The country was going to pot, and some of its people were turning back to the things they could more or less rely upon. Things like the windmill, a machine as simple as it was old upon the earth. And the wind to drive it, which for all its capriciousness was free and full of power. Now Clayton was dead, and Justus was the only good windmill man for a long way around.

He should have been content, and he supposed that for the most part he was. Until a month ago at least. He was keeping his wife happy. She had a new pickup, and they had recently moved from the adobe ranch house his father had built into a shiny, air-conditioned mobile home that had arrived in two sections and was designed to look like a house. It almost succeeded, too, when it was set on a concrete foundation and surrounded by a trim lawn. A year of work and watering had turned the place into a regular oasis, with the towering antenna for the colored television filling in for a palm tree. Justus was glad that his wife liked the place, and he always felt cool and clean there himself. But there were days when he still preferred the corral and pens and old adobes down across the arroyo to the rear. Usually such things didn't trouble him one way or the other. He was on the road most of the time. He had his work and he liked it. There was a solid, straightforward satisfaction in building a windmill from the ground up—lowering the drop pipe, cylinder, and sucker rod two, three, or even four hundred feet toward the bowels of the earth, cementing the anchor posts, and coaxing the tower up stage by stage until the stub tower clamped into its peak and you could set the gin pole to haul the mill up. Then before long he could throw the furl lever and watch that towering creation groan to life. Those first strokes never failed to pump up an edge of tension, of anticipation, that drew his belly a little tight. For after all those years, all those windmills, he had not overcome the wonder, the sudden thrill he felt every time that first jet of water spurted from the lead pipe. That was the kind of satisfaction a man could stand upon, could build his life upon from the ground up.

If anyone had ever succeeded in getting Justus to talk seriously about his work, he probably would have told him something of the sort. Yet even that much was unlikely. Justus was a reserved man, a little shy in his ways. He thought he knew himself pretty well. He was small and trim, with light brown eyes and a straight look. His round chin bulged from a squarish face and he kept his sandy hair cropped so close that from a distance he appeared bald. On the ground his manner was tight, even stiff at times. He didn't smoke, swear, or drink. His voice was an even drawl, subdued, almost a hush, as if there were something deep within himself that he feared to awaken. But once up on a windmill tower his whole body and bearing seemed to relax, to run with life. He swung out free as a wild thing, silent and sure, and often those who watched from below clamped their awe-hung jaws for fear of giving themselves away. What most men found dangerous Justus experienced as a kind of liberation.

That was his secret. He was hardly conscious of it himself, but even if he had been able to articulate it down to its last wind-torn detail, he never would have done so. Justus was not the kind of man to give so precious a thing away. He kept what was his to himself and let others think what they would. There was a kind of sideways satisfaction even in that. Anyway it all held for him until the day Clayton Hobbs fell off the mill. What was the premonition? At first it was only a shadow, a certain darkness that he could all but feel in his chest, as if a cloud had come between him and his heart. Then he got the job of erecting what he had come to call the Royal Don windmill, and the shadow began to take shape. It was as if that windmill were the voice of his premonition, an articulation of it shaping itself girt by girt, angle brace by angle brace into the sky.

The Royal Don windmill fought him from the start. Clayton had warned him that might happen. "Cussed things can get so ornery they might as well as be human," he said. The mill was to pump a domestic well on a newly purchased piece of land up off the old Royal Don Mine road. Once you left the shade of the giant cottonwoods along the Mimbres there was nothing up there but rocks and hills, rugged arroyo-slashed rangeland, flood-heaved, wind-dried, and sun-cracked. Oak, juniper, mesquite. No one had ever lived on it before—no white man at any rate—then along came Jesse Pruit and drilled a well on an impossible hill. Why in God's name would anyone ever want to live out here? That was Justus's first reaction as he turned off the mine road onto Pruit's track. But the place had its pull. Even Justus felt it, and he was a man who usually saw land only in terms of wind, water, and grazing potential. There was a subdued, even subtle grandeur to it, if you can imagine such a thing. It stretched north to the brooding Black Range, west and south along the coppery Santa Rita hills, then past the granite jut of Cooke's Peak and clear into Mexico. A long, lonely landscape that could tumble your heart and in the next breath ache low in your belly with the spirit of a half-forgotten place, an old memory you could not quite catch and conquer. Justus hopped out of his pickup, turned a quick circle, then let his gaze come to rest on the rough, raw pyramid called Cooke's Peak, monumental, anchoring the Mimbres Range to the plain. "Nice place you got here," he said. Jesse Pruit seemed to ponder this. He looked sideways at the ground, shoved his hands in his jeans with his thumbs thrusting free, hunched his hulking sholders, spit, shifted his plug, lurched Justus a straight look, and said, "Yup." Jesse had come over from Texas, but Justus didn't hold that against him. He liked the man from the start. Though Jesse was over fifty, you could tell at a glance that he was still a working fool. He looked to have been carved from oak, the whole of him, from his salted sideburns to his down-at-the-heel boots. Solid. You would have had to roast him an hour to get an ounce of fat off of him. His cap was the only whimsical touch. He favored the same floppy, polka-dotted affair that Justus liked to wear on the job. Justus had a sign reading "I work alone" taped to the toolbox in the back of his truck. But when Jesse offered to give him a hand, he did not hesitate to accept. Good thing he did, too! He needed all the help he could get with the Royal Don windmill.

It wasn't just the windmill, either. The land itself seemed to resent the intrusion. It offered them about a foot of stony topsoil, then crumbled to a rock-ribbed grainy substance that looked more like ashes than dirt. It was like digging into the record of some primordial conflagration deep as the earth. The more you dug, the more there was to dig; the hole never got any deeper. They finally had to drench it with river water so they could take the anchor holes down to four feet. From there the first two sections of the ʹower went up easily. Justus began to feel better. But the ground around the well sloped two ways, and they had a devil of a time squaring and leveling those sections so they could cement them down. They'd get one leg right only to throw another one off. Round and round they wrestled it through an afternoon of ninety-degree heat, a vicious circle that brought them both to the edge of cursing. They kept looking to the west for wind but none came, and they counted themselves lucky on that score. At five they got it leveled and went down to Jesse's trailer for a drink of cold water. Suddenly—out of a sky so calm that even the ravens had forsaken it—a fierce wind gusted up, rocked into the hill, snapped sotol stalks, swooshed like sixty through the juniper, and died. In the silence that whirled like a second, soundless wind into its wake both men turned to face the hill, knowing full well what they would see. For a moment, neither could draw a breath. There was no air! Up there on the hill the tower lay on its side like the skeleton of some prehistoric beast. Jesse spit and looked sideways at the ground. Justus yanked off his polka-dotted cap and swabbed his glistening pate.

And that's the way it went with the Royal Don windmill. Two anchor posts were bent beyond use. Parts were hard to find. There was a delay of three days before they could heave the tower back into place. Then they took it up, section by section, girt by girt, fighting, it seemed, for every bolt and nut they could punch or hammer home. After what seemed a month of Sundays, Justus pried the ill-fitted stub tower close enough to clamp, then worked the wooden platform down over it. The tower was up! Justus looked down at the other man and almost smiled. Jesse had been watching every move, shading his eyes with a big brown hand, one cheek bulging with tobacco. Now he looked aslant and rotated his shoulders, the way a boxer does sometimes to loosen up, spat, then knelt by one corner post to chain a block into place. With luck they would haul the mill up before quitting time. But the first time Justus swung up onto the platform he knocked a wrench off. "Watch it!" The shout was too late. Jesse's forearm was gashed to the bone, the wrench bloody by his knee. Justus had to drive him into Silver for stitches. Another day shot. He began to hate that windmill the way he would never have allowed himself to hate another man. He'd already lost money on it. Now it had cost him his helper. Next thing he knew he would be losing his temper—something no windmill man could safely allow himself to do.

The next day they got the tailbone, vane, and motor assembled and the whole works onto the tower—Justus handling the tackle and a somewhat wan Jesse backing the pickup with one hand. But of course the wind had gusted up at the very moment Justus was anchoring the block on top of the gin pole. He rocked there forty feet in the air, fighting for balance, clinging like a lover to that wavering plastic pole, his heart punching into his throat. And then the motor wouldn't slip blumb onto the mill pipe. Justus wrestled it every which way until his belly burned with anger and the blood surged hot into his head. He could barely see for the sweat smarting his eyes. Finally he gripped the rim of the gear case, braced both feet against the motor and wrenched his whole weight into it, time after time, hunched parallel to the ground like some lesser primate raging at the mesh of his cage, heaving, twisting, until Jesse heard him screech something that sounded like shhee-at! and the motor clunked home. Jesse smiled, looked sideways at the ground, and spat.

The wheel went on without undue trouble, arm after arm, tediously but true, which for this windmill was something of a small miracle. By sunset the sucker rod was bolted to the pump pole, the connection made between the towering mill and the short brass cylinder three hundred feet into the earth. The wind was still up. Justus threw the furl lever, but for the first time that he could remember he did not keep watch for that first jet of water. He put his ear to the drop pipe, and as soon as he heard that both check valves were working properly, he turned his back on the clicking, clanking mill, hopped into his pickup and began to make out Jesse's bill. For all he cared that windmill could spin itself off the face of the earth—even if he would have to replace it under his usual guarantee.

What was the premonition? It weighed heavy in him again as he crossed the divide into Silver City that afternoon. Jesse had caught up with him by phone at the Carlton ranch outside of Lordsburg: "That windmill of yours has gone crazy. Furl wire's broken, storm's coming, tank's full, and the water's wasting all over the ground."

My windmill. The protest rose in Justus's throat but he forced it down. His heart fell, quaked. In a small, quiet voice he said, "I'm real busy right now. Can't you climb up there and brake it?"

There was a long silence. For a moment he thought Jesse had hung up. Then he pictured him looking slantwise at the floor, one hand holding the phone, the other stuffed in his pocket, thumb thrusting free. He waited, fought to gird his heart for what he knew he was about to hear. Finally Jesse spoke: "I could . . . but I'm not about to. Not the way that thing's turning . . . You *do* guarantee your work, don't you?"

"I'll be there directly."

Now he had crossed the Santa Ritas and was heading down the valley. He drove mechanically, watching the road but not really seeing it. He tried not to think, to imagine. The few thoughts that forced themselves upon him seemed to come from somewhere outside his head. Echoes. But always it was there. The premonition. Towering into a roiling sky. A runaway windmill. He hadn't realized until that afternoon how hard he had been fighting to put the Royal Don windmill behind him. Now it was there. A runaway. A premonition.

It hadn't rained for nearly a year. The grass was burned beyond feeding, the ground cracked like a dead skin. Today the first rain of the season was brewing over the Black Range. A runaway windmill was bad enough. But a runaway with lightning, a shifting wind . . . Justus shrugged and felt a little better. It would be, *had* to be that way with the Royal Don windmill.

He was almost through the village before he realized where he was. Haphazard adobes, most of them unplastered, rusted tin roofs, mud walls bellying above crumbling stone foundations, a rickety store with a single gas pump in front, a squat bar, its one small window bright with a neon beer sign. Only two miles to the turn. Not a soul in sight. Newspapers blowing down a dirt street. An election poster on a fence post, half the candidate's head flapping in the wind. A dying place. Yet up there in the hills a few miles above the valley Jesse Pruit was staking a claim on life. With a pick and shovel, some rocks and mud, he was starting the whole circle all over again. A man ought to take hope from that. Justus could not. His belly turned with dread.

Water was running in the Mimbres. First time in months. Justus took note as he crossed the bridge. Must have been raining in the mountains for hours. As he crossed the first cattle guard up from the valley the wind nearly tore the steering wheel from his hand, jolting him from his daze. He had to pull himself together. Get this job done. Go home and watch TV from a big chair, with the first rain clicking on the trailer roof. The image settled him somewhat. And then he caught sight of it. The Royal Don windmill. About a mile to the west across that humping time-slashed land. Barely visible against the lowering day, the roiling blackness of the sky. He looked away, his stomach tightening again, as he turned onto Jesse's track.

Jesse was waiting at the foot of the tower, beneath the whir of the great wheel, in the swift four-beat click-click-clank-click of the mill, the wind beating his yellow slicker about his legs. The moment Justus hopped from the pickup it begain to rain. Cooke's Peak had vanished in the storm. Lightning jagged in a sudden simultaneous row of four across the Black Range. All the land—the hills, the canyons, the arroyos, and the valley—between the Emory Pass and Caballo Blanco in the Santa Rita range was wind-rocked and thundered, heaving with sound. The wind tore at Jesse's hill, wrenched the junipers nearly flat to the rocks. Justus was soaked in the ten steps it took him to reach the tower. "Where's it broke at?" he shouted in response to Jesse's nod.

Jesse spat, the wind smearing his tobacco spit against the storage tank behind. He seemed to consider the question for a moment then shouted his response. "Right at the furl lever. Only way you can hitch it is from the platform."

"We'll see," said Justus setting his jaw. But as he spoke the wind shifted, gusted south, violently. The great wheel heaved round, its tail thrashing, wind-whipped, as if the mill were some monstrous sea creature beached in the storm. Justus stared at it, rain drilling his face, and he realized that what he felt swelling into his heart from the very pit of him was fear.

With a quick, slashing motion he turned and stepped to the pickup, dug a short iron bar from the jumble in back. Maybe he could pry the furl lever home from below the platform, brake the wheel. Supporting the bar like a stubby lance against his hip, he advanced on the tower. "We'll get her," he said with a glance toward Jesse. But the wind snatched his words, smashed them back past his own ear, and Jesse, unhearing, spat and looked aslant. Justus's polka-dotted cap was smeared to his head and pulled so far down over his ears that nothing could blow it off. He tugged at it one last time, then shoved the heavy bar into his belt and scampered up the corner post ladder.

The wind seemed to redound, redouble as he climbed the shuddering tower. The upper cross braces hummed and rattled. The four-beat rhythm of the mill, louder, more immediate, click-click-clank-click. And the wheel, always the wheel, whirring louder, fiercer, until those whirling arms cleaved just above his head. He wrapped his legs around the stub tower and hitched himself around beneath the platform until he could arch the bar up over and probe for a hold on the furl lever. The bar, the tower, everything was slick and slippery in his hands. There! He'd almost had it. Again. Again. But no. It was no good. The wheel was going too fast. He'd never be able to brake it with the bar. Damn this windmill anyway. Damn it all to hell. He would have to attach the furl wire then have Jesse brake the mill from below. Lightning thundered onto the valley, blazing, blinding deep behind his eyes—a cold, white heat. *Rising.* Damn you! Damn you! He heaved himself up and beat at the furl lever with the bar. Beat at it. Beat at it. Damn you! Damn you! But nothing. He could barely hear the iron strike home. He was breathless, exhausted, trembling. He hurled the useless bar out into the blackness of the storm and inched back to the ladder. For a few moments he clung there, motionless, feeling foolish and afraid, despising himself to the edge of tears, breathless, gathering strength. He would have to go up.

His breath was returning. He raised his head above the platform, so close to the raging wheel that its breath felt more powerful than the wind itself. He gauged his move, concentrating so hard that for a moment both the windmill and the storm faded to the recesses of his hearing. If the wind didn't decide to shift he would be all right. He turned his attention to the wind, gauging it, feeling it out. But that voice howling out of the black was dumb, deep as madness, and he could not hear its intent. Now, Justus! He heaved himself onto the platform and in almost the same motion caught the furl lever with one boot and from that foothold swung up onto the tail. At first he merely held on for dear life, straddling that cold, ribbed giant as if it were some towering, insensible mutation of the horse. Then he gradually got his bearings. The wind clubbed and ripped at him, rain stung his face, but he felt he had firm hold. The wheel couldn't touch him here. He was on top! He had been there before, a thousand times, wind or no wind. Here the wheel's whir was a fiercesome roar. Its twelve-foot span whirled so fast that the curving, cleaving blades were one. No. Faster yet! There was a tail of speed, of motion, an aureole of velocity ringing the wheel, making it appear larger than life. But suddenly he was not afraid. His cap was planted firmly, safely upon his ears. He felt light, almost happy—the way he used to feel in the old days, when Clayton was alive. He glanced confidently down at Jesse. The other man's face was in shadow, his slicker a yellow blur. Only his hands stood forth. They looked huge and very white on the corner post. Even from that height Justus could see that their grip was hard, immovable, as if Jesse alone were holding up the tower. Justus clucked his tongue and twisted his upper body down toward the furl lever, the toe of one boot snagged in the ribbing for support. His heart thrilled to the whir and race of the wind. He had been here before! He had the wire hitched in a jiffy. "Brake the wheel!" he shouted as he arched himself back onto the tail. Then a blast of lightning, thunderous blaze. For a blink of time Justus felt himself burned black against the jagging light. His arms were already flailing, as if he sensed the shift before it came. It came. A clubbing crosswind out of the black. Whipping the tail round, flipping the man off like so much jetsam. He turned once in the air, his body loosely awry, as if it were already limp and lifeless. Yet he landed on his hands and knees—at the last trying to rise even as he fell. The shock was tremendous. His insides seemed to explode against his spine, then collapse into his belly in a mush. Only the polka-dotted cap held true.

What was the premonition? He felt it looming there in the descending black, heard it above the storm in the four-beat rhythm of the mill, in the great wheel whirring as if it would turn forever. He had been there before. He puked a blackish gob, smearing his mouth, the darkening earth, dying, dying out, the windmill man.

Chapter 17

Viewpoint:
The Means
of Perception

The *means of perception* defined; *variations* in the means
of perception; *first vs. third person* and the *spectrum*
which they represent; the *focus* of a story; *reviewing your
options* in viewpoint, person, and focus.

THE MEANS OF PERCEPTION

This term refers to the agent through whose eyes a piece of fiction appears
to be presented. For example: "He looked at his grandfather, wondering if
the old man had understood." Here the means of perception is clearly the
boy. We know his thoughts and hopes. We don't know the grandfather's reaction and will not until he speaks or makes some gesture to the boy. Our
view of the scene, then, is not the author's but the boy's.

The means of perception is often used synonymously with *point of view* and
viewpoint. They all refer to the character whose thoughts are revealed. Be
careful not to confuse these terms with *mood* and *tone* which refer, as in
poetry, to the author's attitude toward the work. They will be considered as
aspects of style in Chapter 23.

Most fiction—particularly the short story—limits the means of perception to a single character, regardless of whether the first or third person is
being used. This means that as readers we enter the mind of only one character, we do not know factual material that he doesn't know, and we are not

addressed directly by the author. In the example given, for instance, we would be surprised to have the next sentence read, "Actually Grandfather did agree, but he knew that he could never tell the boy." We would be even more surprised to read, "Little did either of them realize that on the very next day Grandfather would take a trip to the hospital." Here we not only moved out of the boy's world, we moved out of the story altogether. We have the sense of the author talking to us which, although possible, is a sharp break in the convention, similar to that when the playwright jumps to the stage and describes the next act.

The primary advantage to limiting the means of perception to a single character is that the reader is more readily drawn into the story. This is partly due to the sense of identification with that character—a feeling which should not be confused with sympathy, respect, or even approval. Another advantage, closely related, is that it allows the author to withhold information.

In "Sausage and Beer," for example, the means of perception is the first-person narrator, young Will. As the boy sits there in the car wondering where they are going and who his Uncle Theodore is, the reader also wonders. We identify with the boy because we are given the same information he is—and also because information which is withheld from him is also withheld from us as readers. It would not have helped to have provided the missing information at the outset or to enter the mind of the father.

It seems natural to limit the means of perception in first-person stories. But frequently there is a tendency when starting to write fiction to move from mind to mind when working in the third person. This is possible, of course, but few authors do. A majority of short stories limit the means of perception to a single character.

"The Windmill Man" follows this pattern. What we learn is limited to what the protagonist, Justus, knows. We come to understand what kind of man Jesse Pruit is but only through what he does and says, not from what he thinks.

When Justus first meets the solitary rancher he says "Nice place you got here." Here is the response:

> Jesse Pruit seemed to ponder this. He looked sideways at the ground, shoved his hands in his jeans with his thumbs thrusting free, hunched his hulking shoulders, spit, shifted his plug, lurched Justus a straight look and said, "Yup."

That tells us a good deal about Jesse Pruit! And we receive the information as Justus did. We as readers remain psychologically in the story.

Consider the alternatives. The author could have given us an analysis through exposition: "Jesse Pruit was a man of few words who didn't confide in strangers." Or the means of perception could have been shifted: "Jesse Pruit pondered this, trying to judge this windmill builder, wondering if he could be trusted to do a good job."

The author's decision to stay in Justus' mind and describe only what he sees, hears, and feels is cued by writing "Jesse . . . *seemed* to ponder this." This is all our observer knows for sure.

When you read the next story, "The Nightingales Sing," notice how important the strictly limited means of perception is. The protagonist, a young woman named Joanna who has led a rather sheltered life, is introduced briefly to a more worldly group, and every aspect of this other world is brought to us through what Joanna sees and hears. In that story, however, you should end up understanding more about the situation than the protagonist does.

VARIATIONS IN THE MEANS OF PERCEPTION

Although a majority of short stories limit the means of perception to a single character, there are other approaches.

One variation is the reportorial style in which the author does not enter the mind of any character. Normally this has a limiting effect and makes the fiction read like a newspaper account. But it is highly sucessful in Shirley Jackson's "The Lottery." That story is told objectively as if a feature writer were on the scene. The reason this approach does not usually succeed in student writing (and the reason it is rarely found in published work) is that it eliminates the opportunity of identifying with any one character. The reader is always kept outside the action. It succeeds in Miss Jackson's story partly because the subject of concern is not an individual but an entire community. Another factor is the degree of dramatic impact. With such a strong story, the reportorial style is a method of control.

Another variation—and a more common one—is the use of multiple viewpoints. Since this approach is usually reserved for longer short stories and novels, it is not represented in this text. One of the more famous examples, however, is "The Short Happy Life of Francis Macomber" by Ernest Hemingway. The plot involves a triangle: Mr. and Mrs. Macomber who are on a safari in Africa and their guide, Wilson. Through hunting, Macomber is able to redefine himself; but this discovery also leads to his death.

The bulk of this story is told alternately from the point of view of the husband and Wilson, the guide. A few brief insights are given into the private mental world of Mrs. Macomber, and two solid blocks of thought and feelings are given to the wounded lion.

This is sometimes described as the *omniscient point of view* although the author does not move rapidly from one mind to another. Long sections of the story are given to first one and then another character.

William Faulkner has experimented a good deal with point of view. One of the most interesting is in the novel *As I Lay Dying*. Here he uses the first person exclusively, but he shifts the means of perception from chapter to chapter. In a sense he shifts the fictional world, leading us to view one situation in several different ways. This, of course, lends itself better to a long work. Each chapter becomes a short story in itself with its own individual style.

In his story "A Rose for Emily," Faulkner adopts a means of perception which seems at first to be omniscient but in fact is quite different. It is the view of the townspeople generally—not based on inner thoughts but on various reports such as might be exchanged by members of a small, rural community.

Stories and novels such as these deserve careful study. But there are good reasons why the single and clearly defined means of perception is preferred so often.

FIRST VS. THIRD PERSON

When children first start telling stories they often devise a mixture of autobiography and fantasy. Without thinking of technique they tend to select the first person.

"And I went down behind Mr. Syke's house where the woods are and I saw a little pond and right next that pond lying down was a blue lion and I *ran*."

Everything is here: a setting, a sequence of action, a climax with a protagonist pitted against a beast (at the age of five, stories are apt to be epic and archetypal), an emotional response, and a resolution. But the decision to use "I" rather than "she" or "he" has been made unconsciously. This makes sense for a child of five, but it is too random a choice for someone who is trying to write a literary short story for adult readers.

Fiction which is based on one's own personal experience is not necessarily going to develop most successfully in the first person. And in the same way, an event which happened to someone else should not automatically be handled in the third person. The decision should be made not on the basis of where the story came from but what the story as a literary work is to become.

One use of the first person, for example, is not to reveal the most personal feelings of the author but to satirize the speaker. When Swift decided to write *Gulliver's Travels* from the point of view of Gulliver speaking in the first person, it was not to reveal Swift's own views directly through his protagonist. Some of the finest satire in that book comes from the author's subtle ridicule of conventional middle-class views as seen in Gulliver's reactions.

Exactly the same technique was used by Sherwood Anderson in the short story "I'm a Fool." Again, we have the first person used by the protagonist. A fine irony is drawn from the fact that this poor boy is a far greater fool than he ever suspects, not because of what he has done but because of the melodramatic way in which he tells it. Here again, the author has not selected the first person to reveal his inner convictions or secret life but to gain a new dimension by allowing the reader to learn more about the character than the character understands. This fictional technique is similar to the poetic irony in T. S. Eliot's poem, "The Love Song of J. Alfred Prufrock," which I discussed in Chapter 8.

Another use of the first person is seen in stories of reminiscence. "Sausage and Beer" has some of that flavor. It is clear that the narrator is looking back to his childhood—though in fact the story was placed earlier than the event on which it was based in order to make the bar a speak-easy. In any case, the story has the illusion of an adult recalling an experience which occurred when he was twelve.

Stories of reminiscence are fairly common because they give the author a kind of double viewpoint—the older narrator and the younger self going through the experience. As I have pointed out earlier, Conrad's long story, "Youth," is an excellent example. He alternates between the seasoned attitude of the aging narrator and the naive enthusiasm which characterized his younger self. All the advantages of the single means of perception are preserved, yet a different viewpoint is offered as well.

Another use of the first person is to give the illusion of a storyteller speaking out loud. This as-if-spoken style is achieved by phrasing that echoes the spoken language. If Tim McCarthy had decided to write "The Windmill Man" in as-if-spoken style from Jesse Pruit's point of view, it might have started something like this:

> From what I hear, that there windmill builder had some kind of premonition. He'd learned his trade from old Clayton Hobbs—the fellow who got himself killed a while back.

Twentieth-century authors rarely suggest the spoken language through phonetic spelling. The illusion can be effectively achieved with informal word order and phrases like "From what I hear" and "got himself killed."

If this form interests you, look up Sherwood Anderson's frequently anthologized "I'm a Fool," Faulkner's "Spotted Horses," or Eudora Welty's "Why I Live at the P. O." Although these are all fine stories, the technique they employ is not widely used. Some feel that it is awkward maintaining the illusion of a nonstop talker. In addition, it depends as much on a good ear for dialogue as music depends on a good ear for tone.

Remember that the first person is not necessarily limited to the protagonist. In devising a first-person variation of "The Windmill Man," for example, I turned to a secondary character since the protagonist dies in the end. In other cases, there may be an advantage in presenting the story from the point of view of a character who does not know all the facts about the protagonist. The means of perception then becomes a handy means of with-holding information.

F. Scott Fitzgerald's novel, *The Great Gatsby,* is a good example of this approach. The protagonist, Gatsby, cannot be given the means of percep-tion because so much of the novel depends on the mystery of his past. And it would be awkward giving it to his love, Daisy, because she has never been able to understand Gatsby's values. So the "I" of the story is a secondary character who is related to each of the other two in his values and back-ground. He never views impartially, but he does provide the reader with equal insights into two different worlds.

The advantages of the third person are not as easy to categorize. There are, of course, some very simple considerations: It is the form to use if the story is to have more than one means of perception. It is clearly the form to use if the protagonist dies at the end of the work. And it has a certain advan-tage if the protagonist is the sort most readers would have difficulty identi-fying with. But these are not enough to explain the popularity of the third person.

The most persuasive defense for the third person is its flexibility. Whereas the first person sets the author squarely within the mind of a single character, the third person can fluctuate between a kind of neutral style and that which is truly an echo of first-person narration. In the following passage, for example, the means of perception remains with the boy, but there is a shift away from the neutral view toward the boy's own speech.

> He had been kept after school again. It was a simple matter of writing "Good boys do not cheat" fifty times and then cleaning up the classroom, but it took the length of the afternoon. Now he was in a hurry to get home because the shadows were long and it would be dark and scary soon. The short cut was through crazy old Mr. Syke's back lot—"Old Mr. Syke is higher than a kite" they used to chant, though no one had ever seen him actually drunk. He slipped through the hedge, down across the corner of the lawn, and under the trees. The air was still. He walked fast and held his breath. A few more feet and he would be past the pond where . . . . But there it was again, the enormous blue lion. It lay calmly by the edge of the pond, its paw dangling in the water. "Run" he thought, and he was running.

This is no longer a story written by a child. We have some factual material at the very beginning which, though known by the character (and therefore in harmony with the means of perception), is told in neutral terms. Then the passage begins to echo the phrasing of what might be the boy's own telling. The first hint of this is the word "scary" which is borrowed from his own vo-cabulary. And we are then prepared to accept Mr. Syke as "crazy." All this leads us to a quick and natural acceptance of the blue lion.

Here the third person borrows some of the objectivity of the clinical re-port and some of the subjectivity of first-person narration. It avoids the cold detachment of a psychologist's statement which would humorlessly place "crazy old Mr. Syke" and "blue lion" in quotation marks to indicate that these are not the "truth." And it avoids a slavish adherence to a child's vocabulary which, particularly in longer pieces, becomes difficult to maintain.

The popular argument that the first person lends to a story "immediacy" or "realism" which cannot be achieved in the third person doesn't hold true. If there were that kind of advantage to first-person writing, most writers would use that form most of the time. In point of fact, third-person stories predominate. The decision for each story should be made on the basis of that story's own needs.

How does one decide? One way is to try different versions in rough draft. The decision will be made partly by literary judgment and partly from the "feel" of the story. This is a subtle factor which you can best learn by making conversions from first to third person and the reverse.

One highly effective way to develop a sensitivity to the difference between first and third person is to study the first page of a published short story and then write out a version in which only the person is changed—first to third or third to first. Using this volume, for example, you can learn a good deal by converting a part of "Sausage and Beer" to third person and then sections of "The Windmill Man" and "The Nightingales Sing" to first person. Work like this is often far more effective as a learning process than is abstract critical analysis.

THE SPECTRUM FROM FIRST TO THIRD PERSON

It is helpful to talk about the selection of first or third person as if it were a simple choice between two alternatives. But this is also a simplification. The fact is that you have much more choice than that. Just as it is easier for the artist to speak of "blue" and "green" as clearly defined entities, it is convenient for the writer to speak of "first person" and "third person." But as soon as you study a number of published stories, you will discover that there are many more approaches available to you for your own fiction.

These gradations run from the most inward, limited, and personal to the most external and impersonal. I list them here as separate entities, but in practice each blends with the next.

1. *Stream of consciousness* is the most subjective form of writing. In a sense it is the purest form of the first person. The writer creates the illusion of listening to a character's thoughts without interruption from the outside world. The result is wandering, disjointed, highly personal. The connections are by association rather than by logic or narrative sequence.
    This approach has both assets and liabilities. If done carefully, it is a vivid insight into a character. (Don't confuse this with journal writing which may provide insights into your own feelings but which will not be of

value to others.) But the liability is that stream-of-consciousness writing cuts you off from such valuable devices as action, dialogue, setting, and even exposition. Because of this limitation, it is rarely used as the sole medium for a story. The most famous example, the last fifty pages of Joyce's *Ulysses,* is only a small portion of that novel. Short stories often limit it to a paragraph or two.

2. *First person as-if-spoken* allows you to describe the action and dialogue of other characters just as if you were speaking out loud. And you can arrange the events in chronological order more successfully than when limited to the random patterns of thought. But you may find that colloquial speech is hard to sustain for very long.

3. *First person in neutral style* is the approach taken in "Sausage and Beer." It is particularly useful when the story depends on withholding a good deal of important information until the end.

4. *Third person* is the most flexible approach to fiction, though normally it is limited to a single means of perception.

5. *First person plural* ("we") is a very rare and difficult form to be tried, if at all, only by those who have been writing for some time. One example is seen in Faulkner's "That Evening Sun" which begins in the first person but soon shifts to "we" and remains so. As I have already described, Faulkner's "Rose for Emily," is told as if by the townspeople and so uses "we." And in Conrad's novel, *The Nigger of the Narcissus,* the "we" refers generally to the crew. This approach is not often used because it is apt to be too far removed from the inner life of any one character.

6. *Objective reporting* or the *reportorial style* is at the opposite end of the spectrum from stream-of-consciousness writing. Instead of being totally immersed in the mind of a character, your material is presented as if by an outside observer. You are writing like a reporter.

   Normally this is out of the area of fiction as defined in Chapter 12. But occasionally it is borrowed as a literary form when an author wants to create the *illusion* of objective reporting while in fact writing a self-contained piece of fiction. European short-story writers have been more inclined to use this approach than British and American authors. But Shirley Jackson's "The Lottery" is as fine an example as can be found anywhere.

THE FOCUS OF A STORY

The focus of a story answers the question, "Whose story is it?" In "The Windmill Man," for example, the focus is clearly placed on Justus Knight. The title places the spotlight on him, and he is also the means of perception. It is his sense of a premonition which concerns us at the outset and his death which moves us at the end. The focus in that story is unmistakable.

But a different story might be written with essentially the same situation in which the focus was shifted to the rancher, Jesse Pruit. To do this you would have to concentrate on how the death of a windmill builder might affect a dour, inward man. Suppose, for example, Jesse kept insisting that anyone foolish enough to go into the windmill business deserved whatever problems he might run into, yet as he watched the final desperate efforts of Justus, Jesse suddenly saw this dedication as heroic and at the same time felt a wave of guilt for having insisted that the windmill be repaired in the height of the storm. The final death, then would be a sudden revelation of Jesse Pruit's own values. And perhaps he would realize that he had underestimated the young windmill man.

This is a different story, of course. But it is worth considering because it illustrates how the same material can be used for two stories which focus on different characters.

In that particular case, it would have been almost essential to change the means of perception in order to shift the focus. It would be just about impossible to show a new attitude on the part of Jesse down there on the ground while remaining in the mind of the windmill man.

Another revision would seem appropriate. In the published version, Jesse is not introduced until after a good deal of background information has been presented. In our metamorphosed version, it would be natural to start out with Jesse. There is no absolute rule, of course; but readers assume that the character introduced first or at least close to the beginning is going to be the focus or main concern of the story.

In some stories the focus may be placed on two characters almost equally. This is rare, however. Even when it is the relationship which dominates a story, one side of that relationship is usually treated in greater depth. In "Sausage and Beer," for example, the developing bond between son and father is important; but essentially the focus is on the son who also serves as the means of perception.

It might have been possible in that story to have shifted the focus without changing the means of perception. In such a story, the speculations on the part of the boy would be reduced to a minimum. And the dialogue of the father would have to be increased considerably so that we could learn much more about his innermost feelings.

Such a story, for example, might begin by having the father talk to his son about duty and responsibility and how it was time for the boy to learn that relatives had to be visited no matter how unpleasant the experience. He might give examples of how illness—even the insanity of close friends—never bothered him. In that final scene, however, the father might reveal himself as utterly shaken by the experience of seeing his brother once again. The story would then focus not on the boy (though still told by him) but on the contrast between what the father said he felt and what his true feelings were.

REVIEWING YOUR OPTIONS

The means of perception, person, and focus are three options which will radically affect your story. It is a good idea to consider at least briefly why you made the decisions you did early in the first draft. Metamorphosing a story at the outset may save you hours of rewriting later.

After the first draft is completed, the sections which should be reviewed most carefully are the opening and the closing. And of the two, it is the ending which seems to give the most trouble. It is sometimes a temptation to add a final paragraph which sums up the theme of the story. At the worst, it comes out as a moral: "She learned once and for all that . . . " or, "From then on, Tom was careful about what he said when the old man was around; and never again did he bring up the touchy business of World War II."

Notice that in both of these examples, the means of perception has been abandoned and the author has spoken to the reader directly. Most successful stories end with some sort of significant action or a line of dialogue. Endings can be dramatic—a windmill man dying; or they can be very quiet—a son and a father eat and drink, "lost in a kind of communion." But they usually maintain the means of perception.

Occasionally there are stories in which the author makes some kind of observation. But this is rare because generally a story reveals its theme in action and dialogue—the end included. If you find yourself tacking on a summary ending, you may find that it can simply be cut. If the story doesn't explain itself without that final analytical statement, there may well be some problems in the way you presented the earlier material.

Some of the same problems occur with openings. "It was a beautiful August day on Lake Placid, and there was little to suggest that before sunset Laura and Harry would learn much about the vicissitudes of weather and perhaps a bit about themselves as well." Notice that the means of perception has not been established. The opening is essentially the author's view. Perhaps no one does quite this badly, but the principle is worth considering: the reader will have the feeling that the story has begun when a particular character is doing something, thinking something, or saying something.

In reviewing your means of perception, remember that most stories are told from a single point of view. It is almost always possible to suggest the thoughts of other characters through what they say or do—or don't say and don't do. The single means of perception is particularly valuable in stories of less than twenty manuscript pages since unity is so important in works of that length.

Finally, resist the temptation to play with bizarre points of view just for effect: the adventure story which assures us that the hero will live because it is presented in the first person, until we discover at the end that it is a note written in a bottle; the first person account of an outrageously over-supervised little girl who turns out to be a happy little dog; the brother-sister story which turns out in the last sentence to concern two robots.

Such a warning should not be necessary, but it is. The fact that certain authors such as Poe and Kafka have used plots which are clever, even tricky, does not justify a story whose single purpose is to surprise the reader. Such work is bound to be simple.

As I pointed out in earlier chapters, the success of a story is heavily dependent on its source—the raw material—and the formation of plot. But selecting the right viewpoint is just as important. In fact, of the three concerns, this last is the most frequently neglected. Many students who feel free to metamorphose experience and experiment with plot continue to leave the viewpoint unchanged and unquestioned in draft after draft.

You are not fully in control of your craft until you can imagine and truly *feel* what changes you can create in a particular story by altering the means of perception.

Chapter 18

A Story by
Elizabeth Parsons

The Nightingales Sing

Through the fog the car went up the hill, whining in second gear, up the sandy road that ran between the highest and broadest stone walls that Joanna had ever seen. There were no trees at all, only the bright-green, cattle-cropped pastures sometimes visible above the walls, and sweetfern and juniper bushes, all dim in the opaque air and the wan light of an early summer evening. Phil, driving the creaking station wagon with dexterous recklessness, said to her, "I hope it's the right road. Nothing looks familiar in this fog and I've only been here once before."

"It was nice of him to ask us—me especially," said Joanna, who was young and shy and grateful for favors.

"Oh, he loves company," Phil said, "I wish we could have got away sooner to be here to help him unload the horses, though. Still, Chris will be there."

"Is Chris the girl who got thrown today?" Joanna asked, remembering the slight figure in the black coat going down in a spectacular fall with a big bay horse. Phil nodded, and brought the car so smartly around a bend that the two tack boxes in the back of it skidded across the floor. Then he stopped, at last on the level, at a five-barred gate that suddenly appeared out of the mist.

"I'll do the gate," said Joanna, and jumped out. It opened easily and she swung it back against the fence and held it while Phil drove through; then the engine stalled, and in the silence she stood for a moment, her head raised, sniffing the damp, clean air. There was no sound—not the sound of a bird, or a lamb, or the running of water over stones, or of wind in leaves; there was only a great stillness and a sense of height and strangeness and the smell of grass and dried dung. This was the top of the world, this lost hillside, green and bare, ruled across by enormous old walls—the work, so it seemed, of giants. In the air there was a faint movement as of a great wind far away, breathing through the fog. Joanna pulled the gate shut and got in again with Phil and they drove on along the smooth crest of the hill, the windshield wipers swinging slowly to and fro and Phil's sharp, red-headed profile drawn clearly against the gray background. She was grateful to him for taking her to the horse show that afternoon, but she was timid about the invitation to supper that it had led to. Still, there was no getting out of it now. Phil was the elder brother of a school friend of hers, Carol Watson—he was so old he might as well have been of another generation and there was about him, still incredibly unmarried at the age of thirty-one, the mysterious aura that bachelor elder brothers always possess. Carol was supposed to have come with them but she had developed chickenpox the day before. However, Phil had kindly offered to take Joanna just the same, since he had had to ride, and he had kept a fatherly eye on her whenever he could. Then a friend of his named Sandy Sheldon, a breeder of polo ponies, had asked him to stop at his farm for supper on the way home. Phil had asked Joanna if she wanted to go and she had said yes, knowing that he wanted to.

Being a good child, she had telephoned her family to tell them she would not be home until late.

"*Whose* place?" her mother's faraway voice had asked, doubtfully. "Well, don't be late, will you, dear? And call me up when you're leaving, won't you? It's a miserable night to be driving."

"I can't call you," Joanna had said. "There's no telephone."

"Couldn't you call up from somewhere after you've left?" the faint voice had said. "You know how Father worries, and Phil's such a fast driver."

"I'll try to." Exasperation had made Joanna's voice stiff. What earthly good was *telephoning*? She hung up the receiver with a bang, showing a temper she would not have dared display in the presence of her parents.

Now, suddenly, out of the fog great buildings loomed close, and they drove through an open gate into a farmyard with gray wooden barns on two sides of it and stone walls on the other two sides. A few white hens rushed away across the dusty ground, and a gray cat sitting on the pole of a blue dump cart stared coldly at the car as Phil stopped it beside a battered horse van. The instant he stopped, a springer ran barking out of one of the barn doors, and a man appeared behind him and came quickly out to them, up to Joanna's side of the car, where he put both hands on the door and bent his head a little to look in at them.

"Sandy, this is Joanna Gibbs," said Phil.

Sandy looked at her without smiling, but not at all with unfriendliness, only with calm consideration. "Hello, Joanna," he said, and opened the door for her.

"Hello," she said, and then forgot to be shy, for, instead of uttering the kind of asinine, polite remarks she was accustomed to hearing from strangers, he did not treat her as a stranger at all, but said immediately, "You're just in time to help put the horses away. Chris keeled over the minute we got here and I had to send her to bed, and Jake's gone after one of the cows that's strayed off." He spoke in a light, slow, Western voice. He was a small man about Phil's age, with a flat freckled face, light-brown, intelligent eyes, and faded brown hair cut short all over his round head. He looked very sturdy and stocky, walking toward the van beside Phil's thin New England elegance, and he had a self-confidence that sprang simply from his own good nature.

"Quite a fog you greet us with," said Phil, taking off his coat and hanging it on the latch of the open door of the van. Inside in the gloom four long, shining heads were turned toward them, and one of the horses gave a gentle, anxious whinny.

"Yes, we get them once in a while," said Sandy. "I like 'em."

"So do I," said Joanna.

He turned to her and said, "Look, there's really no need in your staying out here. Run in the house, where it's warm, and see if the invalid's all right. You go through that gate." He pointed to a small sagging gate at a gap in the wall.

"All right, I will," she answered, and she started off across the yard toward the end gable of a house she could see rising dimly above some apple trees, the spaniel going with her.

"Joanna!" Sandy called after her, just as she reached the gate.

"Yes?" She turned back. The two men were standing by the runway of the van. They both looked at her, seeing a tall young girl in a blue dress and sweater, with her hair drawn straight back over her head and tied at the back of her neck in a chignon with a black bow, and made more beautiful and airy than she actually was by the watery air.

"Put some wood on the kitchen fire as you go in, will you?" Sandy shouted to her. "The woodbox is right by the stove."

"All right," she answered again, and she and the spaniel went through the little gate in the wall.

A path led from the gate, under the apple trees where the grass was cut short and neat, to a door in the ell of the house. The house itself was big and old and plain, almost square, with a great chimney settled firmly across the ridgepole, and presumably it faced down the hill toward the sea. It was conventional and unimposing, with white painted trim and covered with gray old shingles. There was a lilac bush by the front door and a bed of unbudded red lilies around one of the apple trees, but except for these there was neither shrubbery nor flowers. It looked austere and pleasing to Joanna, and she went in through the door in the ell and saw the woodbox beside the black stove. As she poked some pieces of birch wood down into the snapping fire, a girl's voice called from upstairs, "Sandy?"

Joanna put the lid on the stove and went through a tiny hallway into a living room. An enclosed staircase went up out of one corner and she went to it and called up it, "Sandy's in the barn. Are you all right?"

"Oh, I'm fine," the voice answered, hard and clear. "Just a little shaky when I move around. Come on up."

Joanna climbed up. Immediately at the top of the stairs was a big square bedroom, papered in a beautiful faded paper with scrolls and wheat sheaves. On a four-posted bed lay a girl not many years older than Joanna, covered to the chin with a dark patchwork quilt. Her short black hair stood out against the pillow, and her face was colorless and expressionless and at the same time likeable and amusing. She did not sit up when Joanna came in; she clasped her hands behind her head and looked at her with blue eyes under lowered black lashes.

"You came with Phil, didn't you?" she asked.

"Yes," said Joanna, moving hesitantly up to the bed and leaning against one of the footposts. "They're putting the horses away and they thought I'd better come in and see how you were."

"Oh, I'm fine," said Chris again. "I'll be O.K. in a few minutes. I lit on my head, I guess, by the way it feels, but I don't remember a thing."

Joanna remembered. It had not seemed possible that that black figure could emerge, apparently from directly underneath the bay horse and, after sitting a minute on the grass with hanging head, could get up and walk grimly away, ignoring the animal who had made such a clumsy error and was being led out by an attendant in a long tan coat.

She also remembered that when people were ill or in pain you brought them weak tea and aspirin and hot water bottles, and that they were usually in bed, wishing to suffer behind partly lowered shades, not just lying under a quilt with the fog pressing against darkening windows. But there was something here that did not belong in the land of tea and hot water bottles—a land that, indeed, now seemed on another planet. Joanna knew this, though she did not know what alternatives to offer, so she made no suggestions but just stood there, looking with shy politeness around the room. It was a cold, sparsely furnished place and it looked very bare to Joanna, most of whose life so far had been spent in comfortable, chintz-warmed interiors, with carpets that went from wall to wall. In this room, so obviously untouched for the past hundred years or more, was only the bed, a tall chest of drawers, a wash-stand with a gold and white bowl and pitcher, two plain painted chairs, and a threadbare oval braided rug beside the bed. There were no curtains at the four windows, and practically no paint left on the uneven old floor. The fireplace was black and damp-smelling and filled with ashes and charred paper that rose high about the feet of the andirons. Joanna could not make out whether it was a guest room, or whose room it was; here and there were scattered possessions that might have been male or female—a bootjack, some framed snapshots, a comb, a dirty towel, some socks, a magazine on the floor. Chris's black coat was lying on a chair, and her bowler stood on the bureau. It was a blank room, bleak in the failing light.

Chris watched her from under her half-closed lids, waiting for her to speak, and presently Joanna said, "That was really an awful spill you had."

Chris moved her head on the pillow and said, "He's a brute of a horse. He'll never be fit to ride. I've schooled him for Mrs. Whittaker for a year now and ridden him in three shows and I thought he was pretty well over his troubles." She shrugged, and wrapped herself tighter in the quilt. "She's sunk so much money in him it's a crime, but he's just a brute and I don't think I can do anything more with him. Of course, if she wants to go on paying me to ride him, O.K., and her other horses are tops, so I haven't any kick, really. You can't have them all perfect."

"What does she bother with him for?" asked Joanna.

"Well, she's cracked, like most horse-show people," said Chris. "They can't resist being spectacular—exhibitionists, or whatever they call it. Got to have something startling, and then more startling, and so on. And I must say this horse is something to see. He's beautiful." Her somewhat bored little voice died away.

Joanna contemplated all this seriously. It seemed to her an arduous yet dramatic way of earning one's living; she did not notice that there was nothing in the least dramatic about the girl on the bed beside her. Chris, for her part, was speculating more directly about Joanna, watching her, appreciating her looks, wondering what she was doing with Phil. Then, because she was not unkind and sensed that Joanna was at loose ends in the strange house, she said to her, suddenly leaving the world of horses for the domestic scene where women cozily collaborate over the comforts of their men, "Is there a fire in the living room? I was too queasy to notice when I came in. If there isn't one why don't you light it so it'll be warm when they come in?"

"I'll look," said Joanna. "I didn't notice either. Can I get you anything?"

"No, I'll be down pretty soon," Chris said. "I've got to start supper."

Joanna went back down the little stairs. There was no fire in the living room, but a broken basket beside the fireplace was half full of logs, and she carefully laid these on the andirons and stuffed in some twigs and old comics and lit them. The tall flames sprang up into the black chimney, shiny with creosote. As they roared up, she sat on the floor and looked around the room. It was the same size as the bedroom above it, but it was comfortable and snug, with plain gray walls and white woodwork. A fat sofa, covered with dirty flowered linen, stood in front of the fire. There were some big wicker chairs and four little carved Victorian chairs and a round table with big bowed legs, covered with a red tablecloth; a high, handsome secretary stood against the long wall opposite the fire—its veneer was peeling, and it was filled with tarnished silver cups and ribbon rosettes. A guitar lay on a chair. There were dog hairs on the sofa and the floor was dirty, and outside the windows there was nothingness. Joanna got up to look at the kitchen fire, put more wood on it, and returned to the living room. Overhead she heard Chris moving around quietly, and she pictured her walking about the barren, dusty bedroom, combing her short black hair, tying her necktie, folding up the quilt, looking in the gloom for a lipstick, and suddenly a dreadful, lonely sadness and longing came over her. The living room was growing dark too, and she would have lit the big nickel lamp standing on the table but she did not know how to, so she sat there dreaming in the hot golden firelight. Presently she heard the men's voices outside and they came into the kitchen and stopped there to talk, one of them rattling the stove lids. Sandy came to the door and, seeing Joanna, said to her, "Is Chris all right?"

"Yes, I think so," Joanna said. "She said she was, anyway."

"Guess I'll just see," he said, and went running up the stairs. The spaniel came in to the fire. Joanna stroked his back. His wavy coat was damp with fog and he smelled very strongly of dog; he sat down on the hearth facing the fire, raised his muzzle, and closed his eyes and gave a great sigh of comfort. Then all of a sudden he trotted away and went leaping up the stairs to the bedroom, and Joanna could hear his feet overhead.

Phil came in next, his hair sticking to his forehead. He hung his coat on a chair-back and said to Joanna, "How do you like it here?"

"It's wonderful," she said earnestly.

"It seems to me a queer place," he said, lifting the white fluted china shade off the lamp and striking a match. "Very queer—so far off. We're marooned. I don't feel there's any other place anywhere, do you?"

Joanna shook her head and watched him touch the match to the wick and stoop to settle the chimney on its base. When he put on the shade the soft yellow light caught becomingly on his red head and his narrow face with the sharp cheekbones and the small, deep-set blue eyes. Joanna had known him for years but she realized, looking at him in the yellow light, that she knew almost nothing about him. Before this, he had been Carol's elder brother, but here in the unfamiliar surroundings he was somebody real. She looked away from his lighted face, surprised and wondering. He took his pipe out of his coat pocket and came to the sofa and sat down with a sigh of comfort exactly like the dog's, sticking his long thin booted feet out to the fire, banishing the dark, making the fog retreat.

Sandy came down the stairs and went toward the kitchen, and Phil called after him, "Chris all right?"

"Yes," Sandy said, going out.

"She's a little crazy," Phil said. "Too much courage and no sense. But she's young. She'll settle down, maybe."

"Are she and Sandy engaged?" Joanna asked.

"Well, no," said Phil. "Sandy's got a wife. She stays in Texas." He paused to light his pipe, and then he said, "That's where he raises his horses, you know—this place is only sort of a salesroom. But he and Chris know each other pretty well."

This seemed obvious to Joanna, who said, "Yes, I know." Phil smoked in silence.

"Doesn't his wife *ever* come here?" Joanna asked after a moment.

"I don't think so," Phil answered.

They could hear Sandy in the kitchen, whistling, and occasionally rattling pans. They heard the pump squeak as he worked the handle and the water splashed down into the black iron sink. Then he too came in to the fire and said to Joanna, smiling down at her, "Are you comfy, and all?"

"Oh, *yes*," she said and flushed with pleasure. "I love your house," she managed to say.

"I'm glad you do. It's kind of a barn of a place, but fine for the little I'm in it." He walked away, pulled the flowered curtains across the windows, and came back to stand before the fire. He looked very solid, small, and cheerful, with his shirt-sleeves rolled up and his collar unbuttoned with the gay printed tie loosened. He seemed to Joanna so smug and kind, so, somehow, sympathetic, that she could have leaned forward and hugged him round the knees—but at the idea of doing any such thing she blushed again and bent to pat the dog. Sandy took up the guitar and tuned it lazily.

As he began playing absent-mindedly, his stubby fingers straying across the strings as he stared into the fire, Chris came down the stairs. Instead of her long black boots she had a pair of dilapidated Indian moccasins with a few beads remaining on the toes, and between these and the ends of her breeches legs were gay blue socks. The breeches were fawn-colored, and she had on a fresh white shirt with the sleeves rolled up. Her curly hair, cropped nearly as short as a boy's, was brushed and shining, and her hard, sallow little face was carefully made up and completely blank. Whether she was happy or disturbed, well or ill, Joanna could see no stranger would be able to tell.

"What about supper?" she asked Sandy.

"Calm yourself," he said. "I'm cook tonight. It's all started," He took her hand to draw her down on the sofa, but she moved away and pulled a cushion off a chair and lay down on the floor, her feet toward the fire and her hands folded like a child's on her stomach. Phil had gone into the next room and now he came back carrying a lighted lamp; it dipped wildly in his hand as he set it on the round table beside the other one. The room shone in the low, beneficent light. Sandy, leaning his head against the high, carved back of the sofa, humming and strumming, now sang aloud in a light, sweet voice.

> "For I'd rather hear your fiddle
> And the tone of one string
> Than watch the waters a-gliding,
> Hear the nightingales sing."

The soft strumming went on, and the soft voice, accompanied by Chris's gentle crooning. The fire snapped. Phil handed round some glasses and then went round with a bottle of whisky he had found in the kitchen. He paused at Joanna's glass, smiled at her, and poured her a very small portion.

> "If I ever return,
> It will be in the spring
> To watch the waters a-gliding,
> Hear the nightingales sing."
> The old air died on a trailing chord.

"That's a lovely song," said Joanna, and then shrank at her sentimentality.

But Sandy said, "Yes, it's nice. My mother used to sing it. She knew an awful lot of old songs." He picked out the last bars again on the guitar. Joanna, sitting beside him on the floor, was swept with warmth and comfort.

"My God, the peas!" Sandy said suddenly in horror, as a loud sound of hissing came from the kitchen. Throwing the guitar down on the sofa, he rushed to rescue the supper.

Joanna and Chris picked their way toward the privy that adjoined the end of the barn nearer the house. They moved in a little circle of light from the kerosene lantern that Chris carried, the batteries of Sandy's big flashlight having turned out to be dead. They were both very full of food, and sleepy, and just a little tipsy. Chris had taken off her socks and moccasins and Joanna her leather sandals, and the soaking grass was cold indeed to their feet that had so lately been stretched out to the fire. Joanna had never been in a privy in her life and when Chris opened the door she was astonished at the four neatly covered holes, two large and—on a lower level—two small. Everything was whitewashed; there were pegs to hang things on, and a very strong smell of disinfectant. A few flies woke up and buzzed. Chris set the lantern down on the path and partly closed the door behind them.

There was something cozy about the privy, and they were in no particular hurry to go back to the house. Chris lit a cigarette, and they sat there comfortably in the semi-darkness, and Chris talked. She told Joanna about her two years in college, to which she had been made to go by her family. But Chris's love was horses, not gaining an education, and finally she had left and begun to support herself as a professional rider.

"I'd known Sandy ever since I was little," she said. "I used to hang around him when I was a kid, and he let me ride his horses and everything, and when I left college he got me jobs and sort of looked after me."

"He's a darling, isn't he?" Joanna said dreamily, watching the dim slice of light from the open door and the mist that drifted past it.

"Well, sometimes he is," said Chris. "And sometimes I wish I'd never seen him."

"Oh, *no!*" cried Joanna. "Why?"

"Because he's got so he takes charge too much of the time—you know?" Chris said. "At first I was so crazy about him I didn't care, but now it's gone on so long I'm beginning to see I'm handicapped in a way—or that's what I think, anyway. Everybody just assumes I'm his girl. And he's got a wife, you know, and he won't leave her, ever. And then he's not here a lot of the time. But the worst of all is that he's spoiled me—everybody else seems kind of tame and young. So you see it's a mixed pleasure."

Joanna pondered, a little fuzzily. She was not at all sure what it was that Chris was telling her, but she felt she was being talked to as by one worldly soul to another. Now Chris was saying, "He said that would happen and I didn't care then. He said, 'I'm too *old* for you, Chris, even if I was single, and this way it's hopeless for you.' But I didn't care. I didn't want anybody or anything else and I just plain chased him. And now I don't want anything else either. So it *is* hopeless. . . .I hope you don't ever love anybody more than he loves you," said Chris.

"I've never really been in love," said Joanna bravely.

"Well, you will be," Chris said, lighting a second cigarette. The little white interior and their two young, drowsy faces shone for a second in the flash of the match. "First I thought you were coming here because you were Phil's girl, but I soon saw you weren't."

"Oh, *no!*" cried Joanna again. "He's just the brother of a friend of mine, that's all."

"Yes," said Chris, "he always picks racier types than you."

Racy, thought Joanna. I wish *I* was racy, but I'm too scared.

"I've seen some of his girls, and not one of them was as good-looking as you are," Chris went on. "But they were all very dizzy. He has to have that, I guess—he's so sort of restrained himself, with that family and all. I went to a cocktail party at his house once, and it was terrible. Jeepers!" She began to laugh.

Vulgarity is what he likes, then, said Joanna to herself. Perhaps I like it myself, though I don't know that I know what it is. Perhaps my mother would say Chris and Sandy were vulgar, but they don't seem vulgar to me, though I'm glad Mother isn't here to hear their language and some of Sandy's songs.

She gave it up, as Chris said with a yawn, "We'd better get back."

As they went toward the house it loomed up above them, twice its size, the kitchen windows throwing low beams of light out into the fog. Still there was no wind. In the heavy night air nothing was real, not even Chris and the lantern and the corner of a great wall near the house. Joanna was disembodied, moving through a dream on her bare, numb feet to a house of no substance.

"Let's walk around to the front," she said. "I love the fog."

"O.K.," said Chris, and they went around the corner and stopped by the lilac bushes to listen to the stillness.

But suddenly the dampness reached their bones, and they shivered and screeched and ran back to the back door, with the bobbing lantern smoking and smelling in Chris's hand.

When they came in, Phil looked at them fondly. "Dear little Joanna," he said. "She's all dripping and watery and vaporous, like Undine. What in God's name have your girls been doing?"

"Oh, talking," said Chris.

"Pull up to the fire," Sandy said. "What did you talk about? Us?"

"Yes, dear," said Chris. "We talked about you every single second."

"Joanna's very subdued," remarked Phil. "Did you talk her into a stupor, or what?"

"Joanna doesn't have to talk if she doesn't want to," said Sandy, "I like a quiet woman, myself."

"Do you now?" said Phil, laughing at Chris, who made a face at him and sat down beside Sandy and gave him a violent hug.

Joanna, blinking, sat on the floor with her wet feet tucked under her, and listened vaguely to the talk that ran to and fro above her. Her head was swimming, and she felt sleepy and wise, in the warm lamplight and with the sound of the bantering voices which she did not have to join unless she wanted to. Suddenly she heard Phil saying, "You know, Joanna, we've got to start along. It seems to me you made a rash promise to your family that you'd be home early and it's nearly ten now and we've got thirty miles to go." He yawned, stretched, and bent to knock out his pipe on the side of the fireplace.

"I don't want to go," said Joanna.

"Then stay," said Sandy. "There's plenty of room."

But Phil said, getting up, "No, we've got to go. They'd have the police out if we didn't come soon. Joanna's very carefully raised, you know."

"I *love* Joanna," said Chris, hugging Sandy again until he grunted. "I don't care how carefully she was raised, I love her."

"We all love her," Sandy said. "You haven't got a monopoly on her. Come again and stay longer, will you, Joanna? We love you, and you look so nice here in this horrible old house."

They really do like me, thought Joanna, pulling on her sandals. But not as much as I like them. They have a lot of fun all the time, so it doesn't mean as much to them to find somebody they like. But I'll remember this evening as long as I live.

Sadly she went out with them to the station wagon, following the lantern, and climbed in and sat on the clammy leather seat beside Phil. Calling back, and being called to, they drove away, bumping slowly over the little road, and in a second Chris and Sandy and the lantern were gone in the fog.

Joanna let herself in the front door and turned to wave to Phil, who waved back and drove off down the leafy street, misty in the midnight silence. Inland, the fog was not as bad as it had been near the sea; but the trees dripped with the wetness and the sidewalk shone under the street light. She listened to the faraway, sucking sound of Phil's tires die away; then she sighed and closed the door and moved sleepily into the still house, dropping her key into the brass bowl on the hall table. The house was cool, and dark downstairs except for the hall light, and it smelled of the earth in her mother's little conservatory.

Joanna started up the stairs, slowly unfastening the belt of the old trench coat she had borrowed from Phil. The drive back had been a meaningless interval swinging in the night, with nothing to remember but the glow of the headlights blanketed by the fog so that they had had to creep around the curves and down the hills, peering out until their eyes ached. Soon after they had left the farm they had stopped in a small town while Joanna telephoned her family; through the open door of the phone booth she had watched Phil sitting on a spindly stool at the little marble counter next to the shelves full of Westerns, drinking a Coke—she had a Coke herself and sipped it as the telephone rang far away in her parents' house, while back of the counter a radio played dance music. And twice after that Phil had pulled off the road, once to light his pipe, and once for Joanna to put on his coat. But now, moving up the shallow, carpeted stairs, she was back in the great, cold, dusty house with the sound of Sandy's guitar and the smell of the oil lamps, and the night, the real night, wide and black and empty, only a step away outside.

Upstairs, there was a light in her own room and one in her mother's dressing room. It was a family custom that when she came in late she should put out her mother's light, so now she went into the small, bright room. With her hand on the light-chain she looked around her, at the chintz-covered chaise longue, the chintz-skirted dressing table with family snapshots, both old and recent, arranged under its glass top, at the polished furniture, the long mirror, the agreeable clutter of many years of satisfactory married life.

On the walls were more family pictures covering quite a long period of time—enlargements of picnic photographs, of boats, of a few pets. There was Joanna at the age of twelve on a cowpony in Wyoming, her father and uncle in snow goggles and climbing boots on the lower slopes of Mont Blanc heaven knows how long ago, her sister and brother-in-law looking very young and carefree with their bicycles outside Salisbury Cathedral sometime in the early thirties, judging by her sister's clothes. The world of the pictures was as fresh and good and simple as a May morning; the sun shone and everyone was happy. She stared at the familiar little scenes on the walls with love—and with a sympathy for them she had never felt before—and then she put out the light and went back along the hall.

In her own room she kicked off her sandals and dropped Phil's coat on a chair. A drawn window shade moved inward and fell back again in the night breeze that rustled the thick, wet trees close outside; her pajamas lay on the turned-down bed with its tall, fluted posts. Joanna did not stop to brush her teeth or braid her hair; she was in bed in less than two minutes.

In the darkness she heard the wind rising around Sandy's house, breathing over the open hill, whistling softly in the wet, rusted window screens, stirring in the apple trees. She heard the last burning log in the fireplace tumble apart, and a horse kick at his stall out in the barn. If I'd stayed all night, she thought, in the morning when the fog burned off I'd have known how far you could see from the top of the hill.

For in the morning the hot sun would shine from a mild blue sky, the roofs would steam, the horses would gallop and squeal in the pastures between the great walls, and all the nightingales would rise singing out of the short, tough grass.

Chapter 19

Characterization

Characterization as *illusion* based on three elements: *consistency* of behavior and attitudes, *complexity*, and *individuality;* techniques of developing these elements including *direct analysis,* the use of significant *action, dialogue, thoughts,* and *physical details; blending* these various techniques.

Characterization, like all aspects of fiction, is illusion. When we as readers feel that a fictional character is "convincing," "vivid," or "realistic," it is not because that character resembles someone familiar; the illusion we have is of meeting and coming to know someone new.

It is not necessary, for example, to have known a professional horse trainer to appreciate and understand Chris in "The Nightingales Sing." We don't have to know the first thing about windmills to see how someone like Justus in "The Windmill Man" could push pride in his work to the ultimate. Nor is it necessary to have known mental patients to have the illusion of having just met one in "Sausage and Beer." In each case, our sense of having been introduced to a person as if in real life is based not on familiarity but on the way that character is revealed in the fiction.

Consider for a moment the full range of characters you feel that you have "met" through fiction. The list may include such varied types as Faulkner's Snopeses and Tolstoi's aristocratic Anna Karenina. Fiction has induced you to cross the barriers of age, class, sex, race, and national identity. Our sense of credibility is in no way dependent upon having lived in

Mississippi or in Russia during the nineteenth century. And our compassion for Gregor in Kafka's "The Metamorphosis" certainly is not dependent on knowing from experience what it is like to wake up one morning as a six-foot cockroach.

This "willing suspension of disbelief" has enormous power. How is it achieved? There are three elements involved: consistency, complexity, and individuality.

In practice, of course, making a character "come alive" on the page is not at all this mechanical. Most writers borrow heavily from people they have known and then metamorphose the details in a variety of ways, both consciously and unconsciously. This is the way they find those hundreds of minute details which go into a finely drawn character. But the reason for this dependence on experience is that it is the most natural way to develop consistency, complexity, and individuality.

CONSISTENCY

In real life we come to expect a certain consistency in our friends—patterns of behavior, outlook, dress, and the like. In spite of variations, some people tend to be naturally generous or constitutionally sloppy or ambitious.

In addition, these characteristics tend to be interlocked. If a man is an insurance executive, we don't expect him to be politically radical or to have a long black beard or to speak in incomplete sentences prefaced with "like," or to race his Honda on Sunday afternoons. It might be nice if he did, of course; and making such a contradiction plausible could be the start of a story. But that comes under the heading of *complexity,* which I shall turn to shortly. The point here is that consistency of character is one of the basic assumptions we make about people in real life and it is also the fundamental assumption upon which fictional characterization is built.

In simple fiction, consistency is pushed to the point of predictability—and monotony. We know, for example, that Dick Tracy will never under any circumstances take a bribe or punch a sweet little old lady in the nose. It is most unlikely that little orphan Annie will turn junkie. And Tarzan is not going to start wearing a suit. For many readers, these rigid conventions destroy the illusion of credibility; yet for others it is so effective that they send letters and presents to these fictional characters in care of their local paper, utterly confusing art and life.

In sophisticated fiction, the major characters are usually complex. Pure consistency is limited to minor characters. The heavyset host of the speak-easy in "Sausage and Beer" has an important role and significant speaking lines, but he is what E. M. Forster calls a "flat character," one who is there merely to serve a function and so is not developed. He is all consistency, as is Jesse Pruit in "The Windmill Man." Satiric characters and comic figures also tend to be entirely consistent.

COMPLEXITY

To achieve complex characterization, you have to develop more than one aspect of a character. You can do this by establishing a pattern, countering it in some way, and then showing how both elements are a part of the whole character.

You will have to go beyond the stereotypes of film and television, of course. We are all familiar with the hard-driving businessman who has a secret longing for simple pleasures and the man-hating woman who turns out to be secretly in love. To achieve real complexity don't settle for the formula of the character who is "this but secretly that."

Take Joanna in "The Nightingales Sing," for example. In some respects she is a romantic young woman looking forward to new experiences and what she imagines to be the excitement of adulthood. She sees Chris' life as an "arduous yet dramatic way of earning one's living" even though *we* see Chris as a woman who has not only been thrown by a horse but who is forlornly involved with a married man, a relationship which clearly has no future. Joanna would like to be "racy" like Phil's other girls and in the final scene she wistfully wonders what it would have been like to have spent the night there.

Yet on the other hand, she is also cautious. Although she is exasperated with her mother on the telephone, she does go back to the familiar security of her house and her room with those photographs from her childhood. She has taken one step toward adulthood and then retreated—though we know from her dreamy vision at the end of the story that she will soon enter the adult world.

The story, then, is not about a naive girl in a circle of older, more sophisticated people. It deals with a protagonist who is at the same time a girl who has led a sheltered life and a young woman looking forward eagerly to what she believes will be the excitement of adult life. We see this pattern in the vacillation of her attitude. Most readers of either sex and any age will recognize this ambivalence even if they have never known people like this.

Chris is also presented in a fairly complex manner even though the focus of the story is not placed on her. In part, she is a tomboy who loves horses and riding. She values her independence highly. Yet on the other hand she is very fond of a married man who has told her that there is no future in their relationship. We assume that she will go on loving Sandy just as she loves riding spirited horses who will, from time to time, throw her.

Developing one or two characters in a complex manner is about all you can do in a short story. Secondary characters tend to be presented more simply. For instance, the two men in this story are credible, but they are not presented in detail.

In "Sausage and Beer," the complexity in Uncle Theodore takes the form of alternation: He appears at first to be quite sane and then reveals himself to be hopelessly out of contact with the real world. When, at the end of the visit, the boy assumes that a polite lie will do as well for a mad uncle as it does for other relatives, Theodore has an unnerving moment of lucidity.

More basic to the development of the story, however, is the complexity which I hope is apparent in the father. Before the visit, he is austere and distant. He is not the kind of man who confides anything. But visiting the hospital is an ordeal for both of them and after that he reveals a different side of himself. He draws his son (and the reader) into an almost secret world of sociability and in doing so he reveals his own love for his son.

Complexity, then, involves adding at least one other aspect to a character's original pattern. If the variation is too slight, the character may seem hackneyed and dull or inconsequential. But if the change is too great or is unconvincing, readers will feel that the character lacks consistency. "I just don't believe anyone would behave like that," they say, and the story has failed. Balancing complexity of character development with consistency is often a major concern as one revises.

INDIVIDUALITY

Some characters are memorable and some are not. Occasionally we recall a particular character long after the plot has been forgotten. In other cases we have to ask questions like, "Wasn't there a father in the story somewhere?" or, "I remember the fight, but what was it all about?" The characters who stick in our memory are those that have a high degree of individuality.

To some degree, individuality is simply a function of complexity. A many-sided character who remains credible is apt to seem individual or unique. But there is another factor as well and this is the element of the unusual.

In specific terms, it is more difficult to develop sharp, convincing characters when their names are Bill and Frank and they are college roommates than it is to develop an Uncle Theodore living in an insane asylum. The unusual setting, the unlikely occupation, the striking deformity all serve to make a character vivid and memorable.

But these same devices can also be pitfalls. When used as an artificial stimulant to an otherwise dull story, the result is failure. An inconsequential tale about two college roommates is not going to be saved by being metamorphosed into an inconsequential tale about two hunchbacks living in an abandoned fun house.

It is possible, however, to stress the unusual aspects of unusual people one has known. It is helpful to find incidents which dramatize aspects of characters in a fresh way. And it is essential to avoid those standardized, middle-class fathers and mothers and brothers and sisters and dogs which appear with such regularity both in television dramas and in commercials.

How far can you push a character in the direction of the unusual? There is no easy answer to that, but many writers find it helps to keep a lingering connection between the fictional character and someone real. In "The Windmill Man," for example, we can assume that the author did not personally experience what it is to die while repairing one's handiwork, but it is clear that he is familiar with the construction of windmills. It would appear that Justus Knight as a character is the magnification of someone known to the author, a magnification which created a figure who seems not only heroic but mythic.

"The Nightingales Sing" is a far more modulated story, but Chris' situation and life style are not patterns you see every day. Imagine how bland that story would be if Chris and Sandy were happily married and living in a house like every other house and raised dogs for a living!

In the case of "Sausage and Beer," I can be more explicit. Uncle Theodore is autobiographical and the hospital really exists. But the physical description of Uncle Theodore is based on a man I once saw for about ten seconds in a hotel lobby, and the bench in the waiting room is taken from Grand Central Station, New York, as is the man lying on it. The father in the story is based on an uncle of mine, and the twin sister is fictional.

The story had its origin in actual visits to my uncle and these were chosen mainly because they seemed to have "fictional potential"—an almost unconscious feeling for what is memorable. The many visits were reduced to one and treated as a kind of initiation. The final sharing or "communion" with the father is fictional, unfortunately. And so is the historical period. In an early draft, the final scene took place in a restaurant; but by moving the time back to the end of the Prohibition days, I could let father and son share a quietly illegal pastime, eating and drinking in a speak-easy. Since the ending needed a slight increase in voltage to compete with the asylum scene, and because I wanted to dramatize the almost religious sharing of food and drink (the sausage and beer), the speak-easy helped to individualize both the father and the final scene itself.

DIRECT ANALYSIS OF CHARACTER

Consistency, complexity, and individuality are the goals one works for in creating fictional characters. The techniques which one uses to achieve these goals are more numerous. In addition to direct exposition, one can use a character's action, dialogue, thoughts, and physical details. Each of these deserves a close look.

The direct approach is tempting because through exposition you can include a great deal of material very quickly. Suppose, for example, "The Nightingales Sing" had begun this way:

> Joanna was young and shy but growing restless with her safe, protected life. The future looked exciting and romantic to her though just a bit scary too. It seemed to her that Chris and Sandy held the key to a wonderful life.

This little paragraph unfolds a great deal of information which the reader of the original version has to gather over the course of several pages. But what appears to be an advantage also has liabilities which you should consider.

First, an opening like this is apt to deprive the reader of the sense of discovery. The language of exposition, remember, is closer to that of the case history and newspaper article than it is to fiction. If you review the actual opening of the story you will see how carefully the element of mystery is created: "Through the fog the car went up the hill . . . up the sandy road that ran between the highest and broadest stone walls that Joanna had ever seen." Where are they going and what will it be like? Both Joanna and the reader wonder.

Exposition also tends to slow the pace no matter where it appears. Joanna's character is occasionally commented upon through exposition, but these passages are brief and scattered throughout the story. In this way the plot is kept moving by action and dialogue.

The greatest danger of using too much exposition, however, is the risk of laying out the theme. In stories like "The Nightingales Sing," theme and character are merged and if the author analyzes her protagonist in detail she will be explaining the theme itself. If this happened the story would begin to resemble a case history or feature article and the reader would lose that sense of discovery which is so necessary in good fiction.

This is not to say that direct analysis of character is to be avoided at all cost. It is often valuable to reveal some aspect of character which simply isn't worth the space it would take to imply through action or dialogue. And direct analysis is frequently used to describe minor characters who are only presented in sketchy form.

THE USE OF
SIGNIFICANT ACTION

Some novice writers tend to avoid action. Their stories turn inward on the character, stressing thoughts and long, moody descriptions. This is partly a reaction against the simple plots of television and the comics. The point to remember is that it is not action alone which makes a story simple, it is the absence of any significance to the action.

"The Windmill Man" is an excellent example. There is a lot of action there. Essentially the same plot could appear in some adventure magazine or a half-hour, action-packed television drama. What makes the story a sophisticated piece of fiction is the way that action is used to create a character who develops from a man of simple tastes into a kind of hero. He is not one of the familiar heroes we are used to seeing in dramas about soldiers, police officers and fire fighters, but a solitary hero who pits his will against an ornery piece of machinery and, finally, against nature itself.

"The Nightingales Sing" is at the opposite end of the scale in terms of action. Nothing dramatic happens. At the conclusion, the protagonist decides *not* to stay. Yet the story is packed with examples of subtle action which reveal character.

We see something of Joanna's exasperation with her parents through the way she hangs up the receiver; we see her desire to help and be a part of this new world from the way she lays and lights the fire—significantly burning old comics. When she feels an impulse to hug Sandy, we see her turn and pat the dog instead. And when she returns to the familiarity and comfort of her family, she follows the old custom of putting out her mother's light.

These are minor touches, but they work together to create a portrait of Joanna. And our view of Phil, while sketchy, also comes to us in part through action. The author devotes an entire paragraph to describing the spaniel—coming in, sitting by the hearth, giving a sigh of comfort, then suddenly trotting away. This might seem like needless action until soon afterward we see Phil sit down "with a sigh of comfort exactly like the dog's . . . making the fog retreat." Phil's ability to "make the fog retreat"—making the strange seem less threatening for Joanna— is seen toward the end when he lends her his coat.

Fiction, then, does not have to be highly dramatic to reveal character through action. The slightest movement or gesture can tell us a good deal. And as we have seen in Joanna's case, even a decision not to do something is a decision and may help us to understand a character in depth.

THE USE OF DIALOGUE AND THOUGHTS

The most obvious use of dialogue is to unfold plot. A boy, driving with his father, asks how far they are from their destination; a man telephones and reports that a windmill has gone out of control; a girl asks if someone named Chris was the one who was thrown by a horse. In each of these cases, dialogue has nudged the plot ahead.

But dialogue is also one of the best methods of revealing character. In fact, every line should be "in character," which is to say it should appear appropriate for that speaker.

Some stories, like "The Windmill Man," use very little dialogue, depending more heavily on action. But "The Nightingales Sing" is more typical in that the dialogue is used in almost every scene to reveal both major and minor aspects of character.

Take a close look at how Joanna reveals her rather naive and romantic notions about this house and those who use it.

"It's wonderful," she says to Phil who replies that to him it seems like a "queer place." Undaunted, she tells Sandy, "I love your house." This pleases him but he then describes it as "a barn of a place." Later Joanna responds to the song which Sandy sings with "That's a lovely song"—though by this time she has begun to understand the tone of these people and she is described as shrinking at her own sentimentality.

These little exchanges seem to the casual reader to be snatches of routine conversation such as a hidden tape recorder might have picked up; yet actually they have been designed by the author to give readers not only insights into Joanna's attitude but further understanding of Phil and Sandy as well.

Chris is a secondary character, but she is developed in considerable detail. Almost all we learn about her is revealed through what she says. Here, for example, is the passage in which she describes her feelings about the horse which threw her:

> "He's a brute of a horse. He'll never be fit to ride . . . . he's just a brute and I don't think I can do anything more with him."

She goes on to admit that she probably will go on riding him and adds, "He's beautiful."

This is a fine example of *ambivalence* which I described in the section on poetry: a simultaneous blending of two opposing feelings. This quotation alone would tell us a good deal about Chris and why she continues in a vocation which has already done her damage. But add to that the dialogue in which she describes her feelings about Sandy:

> "Sometimes I wish I'd never seen him. . . . He's got so he takes charge too much of the time. . . . But the worst of all is that he's spoiled me—everybody else seems kind of tame and young. So you see it's a mixed pleasure."

Now she has revealed two "mixed pleasures" and while Joanna is not able to make much of what she has heard, we as readers are able to see the complication of Chris' life and her needs. None of this has been stated by the author through exposition; it has all been revealed through dialogue.

Thoughts are merely internalized lines of dialogue. Normally they are presented without quotation marks. Quite often they counter or amend what a character has just said. Or they may simply be a reaction which is not stated out loud. When Joanna hears about the kind of women Phil usually goes out with, here are her thoughts.

> Vulgarity is what he likes, then, said Joanna to herself. Perhaps I like it myself, though I don't know that I know what it is.

Notice how close it is to spoken dialogue. It even seems natural to describe it as something she "said to herself."

Another passage appears as the next-to-last paragraph and draws the story together in ways which Joanna herself doesn't yet understand:

> If I'd stayed all night, she thought, in the morning when the fog burned off I'd have known how far you could see from the top of the hill.

There are, incidentally, five conventions connected with dialogue which readers generally expect. If you are going to create the illusion of a real character through your use of dialogue, it helps to handle the mechanics smoothly so that they don't become distracting.

First, most stories use quotation marks about that which is said out loud and none around thoughts. You will find occasional exceptions, but such stories run the risk of confusing readers. Second, most writers indent the first line of speech of each new speaker. This may appear to waste paper, but readers are used to it both in fiction and in drama. In exchanges between two characters, the reader does not have to be told each time which one spoke. It is a convenient signal.

Third, "she said," "he said," and "I said" are used more like punctuation marks than phrases and for this reason are repeated frequently. The prohibition agaist redundancy just doesn't apply to them. And trying to find substitutions like "she retorted," "he sneered," "she questioned," "he hissed" is obtrusive and sounds amateurish. In general, keep these identification tags simple. There is usually no reason for adding adverbs like "said angrily" or "said excitedly." Let the phrasing itself suggest the mood.

Finally, as I have suggested earlier, dialogue is rarely aided by phonetic spelling. If you are trying to catch the flavor of spoken language, try to find appropriate phrasing rather than tinkering with conventional spelling.

In addition to the direct use of dialogue and thoughts, there is also the indirect use of each. A fine example of indirect discourse appears in the opening of J. D. Salinger's "Uncle Wiggily in Connecticut." It begins with a one-sentence statement about the situation and then moves directly into an echo of their conversation.

> It was almost three o'clock when Mary Jane finally found Eloise's house. She explained to Eloise, who had come out of the driveway to meet her, that everything had been absolutely *perfect*, that she had remembered the way *exactly*, until she had turned off the Merrick Parkway. Eloise said "*Merritt* Parkway, baby," and reminded Mary Jane that she had found the house twice before, but Mary Jane just wailed something ambiguous, something about her box of Kleenex, and rushed back to her convertible.

Notice how the sound of their speech is simulated both by the choice of words and by the stress which he achieves through italics (indicated in a typed manuscript by underlining). The story then moves into a conventional pattern, but with heavy use of dialogue.

This opening section could also have been presented as dialogue directly quoted, of course, but his treatment has given the scene a kind of breathless quality.

There are occasions, of course, when conventional bits of dialogue are simply referred to without even the echo of the spoken language. "They greeted her warmly," for example. And "They lingered at the door, saying their goodbyes." Notice, however, that these are the occasions when character is *not* going to be revealed by either direct or indirect dialogue. In general, try to make every line of dialogue contribute to characterization and —the other side of the coin—come from character. If you can't do that, skip over the communication with a passing reference.

THE USE OF PHYSICAL DETAILS

We almost always have a visual impression of a character who is presented in detail. Sometimes this comes from direct description, but quite often we construct it in our imagination on the basis of other information.

In "Sausage and Beer," Uncle Theodore is described as heavy but not fat:

> He was a great, sagging man. His jowls hung loose, his shoulders were massive but rounded like a dome, his hands were attached like brass weights on the ends of swinging pendulums.

The real uncle was actually tall, lean, and rather distinguished looking. But the father in the story had been described in essentially those terms, and it was important to have these twins strikingly dissimilar in appearance as they were in their fates. The physical description of Uncle Theodore was for that reason developed from the memory of a perfect stranger, someone I had seen only for an instant.

Direct description rarely comes at the beginning of a story because it is a slow opening. More often it is buried farther along after the narrative has begun. In "The Windmill Man," for example, the author waits two pages before telling us:

> He was small and trim, with light brown eyes and a straight look. His round chin bulged from a squarish face and he kept his sandy hair cropped so close that from a distance he appeared bald.

Joanna is described in a highly unorthodox switch in the means of perception (the kind I have urged you to avoid!) to the two men:

> They both looked at her, seeing a tall young girl in a blue dress and sweater, with her hair drawn straight back over her head and tied at the back of her neck in a chignon with a black bow. . . .

Helpful as these descriptions are, not one of them is essential. The stories would not be badly damaged without them. Keep that in mind before you load a short story down with a page of physical description.

Of equal importance—greater in some cases—are all the surrounding details: what a character wears, the house she or he lives in, the furnishings, the car, the cigarette or pipe, the ring. Every possession from the largest to the smallest can contribute to characterization.

When we think of Chris and Sandy, for example, we think of that house which is as sparse and cut off from society as they are. Our impression of Phil is influenced by our associations with men who smoke pipes and also from the comparison with the carefully described spaniel. To create an individualized character it helps to link that character with individualizing physical objects.

BLENDING THE TECHNIQUES

When we analyze how characters are revealed in fiction, the process seems enormously complex. The same is true when we explain any artistic technique in abstract terms whether it be dance, music, or some aspect of painting. Actual practice requires a blend of unconscious decision making along with conscious knowledge of craftsmanship.

The best way to develop what we think of as an "intuitive" ability to create believable characters in fiction is to read as much as possible. After an initial reading of a story for pleasure, go back over it and examine as a fellow writer just what the balance is between consistency and complexity. How is the character individualized? And how is the character revealed? Can you find samples of direct analysis on the part of the author? Could they have been avoided? How much has action contributed to your understanding? Or were dialogue and thoughts employed to a great extent? Exactly how much of a description were you given and how much is your impression based on the objects associated with that character? This is *active reading*—not for course credit but for your own development.

When you turn to the actual process of starting to write a new story, consider your characters carefully before you even outline the plot. Do you really know them? If you keep a journal, you may want to use it to record significant facts about the major characters in a new story: What kind of childhoods did they have? What kinds of parents? Where do they live and how do they spend their days—school? job? waiting for something to happen? What kind of music do they like and what kinds of people do they enjoy? You should be able to write a page or so about the protagonist of any new story. You may not use more than half of the details you devise, but it helps if you have far more information about a character than is needed. Conversely, there is no kind of action, dialogue, or thoughts which can successfully reveal a character who is not yet fully formed in your own mind.

Finally, after having completed your first draft, you may wish to review your work from the point of view of craft to make sure that your characters are consistent yet complex, and that they have individuality. It is at this point that you may wish to adjust the ways in which you have revealed your characters. Try to be as objective with your own work as you were when examining published stories.

In many cases the literary sophistication of a story is developed more from characterization than from complexity of plot. For this reason, those goals of consistency, complexity, and individuality will continue to be major concerns for as long as you write fiction.

Chapter 20

Narrative Tension

Tension created through *dramatic conflict* between individuals, between an individual and society, or within a character; *curiosity* as developed through a *dramatic question; suspense* and *shock; irony* and *satire* as additional methods of establishing tension.

(A) Joanna went with a brother of a friend of hers to visit a couple who lived in the country. She had dinner with them, enjoyed the talk and companionship, and then was driven home at a reasonable hour.

(B) As soon as she entered that strangely stark house, Joanna found herself plunged into an entirely different life style. It seemed inviting, yet a bit unsettling too. Should she spend the night?

It is easy enough to *feel* the difference between these two passages. But stop for a moment and see if you can analyze precisely what it is that makes passage *A* so different from passage *B* even though they describe the same story. Here is another pair of descriptions:

(A) Justus Knight, a local windmill distributor and installer, was killed yesterday afternoon when he was struck by lightning while trying to repair the furl wire on a windmill he had recently constructed on the ranch of Jesse Pruit.

(B) Justus Knight thought that in building windmills he was escaping the problems of society and working instead with a product which was solid and reliable. But there came a time when his stubbornness went out of control, and he met his match battling nature and a machine gone crazy.

There are various ways to describe the differences between each pair. The first version in each case seems flat, factual, undramatic. The second seems somewhat more dynamic and charged with dramatic interest.

An inclusive term which covers all of those distinctions is *tension*. The first version in each pair lacks tension and the second generates it.

You can create tension in fiction by providing some kind of conflict or by arousing your reader's sense of curiosity. You can also generate suspense or jolt your reader with shock. Or you can develop tension through irony and satire. Since it is tension which provides the energy and sense of vitality in fiction, each of these approaches deserves a close look.

DRAMATIC CONFLICT

Conflict is found in all narrative forms. We call it "dramatic" partly because we associate it with plays, but mainly because the term suggests direct confrontation between major forces—"dramatic" in the sense of vivid or striking.

On its simplest level, dramatic conflict is the mainspring of simple fiction. Some stories, television scripts, and films are reduced to the point where there is almost nothing but conflict. Man against man, for example, (and just occasionally heroic woman against man) is the core of almost every Western. The struggle between the hero and the antagonist is formalized in dress (color of hats), in ethics (clean vs. dirty fighting), and ritualized in action (a physical fight in which many bottles, two chairs, and at least one mirror will be shattered).

The same applies to other forms of dramatic conflict. Man against an aspect of himself is repeated over and over in juvenile fiction (usually a boy's conscience against the temptation to cheat or lie—an essentially moralistic pattern). Man against the group is a pattern in adventure fiction (the detective tangling with the Mafia, "Chaos" agents, spy rings; the American hero pitted against the Oriental foe-of-the-year—"Japs," Koreans, Chinese, Vietnamese). Man against nature brings to mind Tarzan and his eyeball-to-eyeball confrontations with giant spiders and short-tempered crocodiles. And even that most modern type of inverted conflict, alienation, is seen in fiction for the very young: the little switch engine who was sneered at by all the locomotives, the little reindeer who was laughed at by those on Santa's regular team, the ugly duckling who was actually a beautiful swan, and the archetypal Cinderella—duckling to swan again.

In recent years there have been a good number of film and television plots which give active, sometimes heroic roles to women protagonists. Some scripts have been sophisticated treatments, but others have merely created a new set of stereotypes.

With associations like these, it is no wonder that some novice writers unconciously avoid all forms of conflict and keep their characters passive or isolated, thinking deep thoughts through pages of only partially disguised exposition.

Actually there is no need to avoid conflict. It will serve you well and will provide vitality in your fiction as long as you make the conflict subtle, suggestive, and as sophisticated as your characterization.

"The Windmill Man" is a good example of high drama which is integrated with the story as a whole. A simple adventure story (or script) might pit Justus Knight against the elements and leave it at that—a thriller which we respond to in the reading but soon forget. But the author is concerned with more than that.

The difference is rooted partly in characterization. We are told that Justus "thought he knew himself pretty well." He thought his attraction to the windmill business was straightforward:

> The country was going to pot, and some of its people were turning back to the things they could more or less rely upon. Things like the windmill, a machine as simple as it was old upon the earth.

He thought of the windmill as "free and full of power." Indeed, he thought of *himself* as free and full of power.

But then he has to deal with the Royal Don windmill, the type described by the former windmill man as "so ornery they might as well be human."

As the story heads for its climax, the conflict is not merely a man against the windmill but a man's discovery that windmills and nature are not as simple as he had thought, and that he is not as "free and full of power" as he thought. Not only that, but the runaway windmill (which "might as well be human") becomes a metaphor for Justus' own runaway and "ornery" determination to make the machine work as it should. Both man and machine have lost control and the result is disaster.

While we often think of conflict as pitting an individual against another individual or some aspect of nature, occasionally the opponent is society. This pattern is not represented here, but it appears in a number of well-anthologized works. In Shirley Jackson's "The Lottery," for example, the individual who is finally selected as the town's scapegoat faces the entire community in an almost archetypal confrontation. In "The Ox-Bow Incident" by Walter Van Tilburg Clark, three innocent men face the wrath of a mob and on the basis of circumstantial evidence are hanged. This has become the basis of an endless series of simple imitations, but the story still maintains some degree of literary sophistication. Another example is seen in Faulkner's "Dry September." This also deals with a lynching, but the story is primarily concerned with a sexually charged bigot and his motivation.

One has to be careful in stories like this to avoid stereotypes. As I have pointed out before, western scenes—particularly if set in the nineteenth century—are risky at best. Racial conflicts are charged with tension, but the writers who can make use of them are those who have lived through some version of racial strife. If you are writing as a total outsider, you will have to borrow details from what you have read or seen in films and the result will not be convincing.

Be careful, too, about the danger of melodrama. Simple characterization and excessive concentration on conflict will turn any good, dramatic story into a melodrama.

Conflicts between the individual and society take many forms since almost any kind of group can represent the whole society. Racial barriers, for example, wall off blacks and other minorities from the white society; national prejudices work against the foreign born; snobberies of various sorts are exercised by social classes against the individual. "Society" may be as simple a group as a fifth-grade class seen through the eyes of the unfortunate student who has been selected as the scapegoat.

Very often, conflict is internal. It is described as part of the individual struggling with another. This is clearly the pattern in "The Nightingales Sing." As we have already seen, part of Joanna is being drawn forward into a world which seems exciting and rewarding; yet another part is cautious and content to return, at least for the present, to the protective and sheltering life her family has provided. If we were given the feeling that this was her one bid for escape, her return might seem like a defeat. But the ending indicates that she is eagerly looking forward to entering the adult world even though she may eventually share some of Chris' mixed feelings.

When working with internal conflict, be careful not to rely too heavily on your protagonist's thoughts. They can begin to sound like a little explanatory essay. Look instead for those events and decisions which will dramatize that conflict of attitude. Even physical objects can help the reader to sense the division. Notice the contrast between that stark, unadorned house Joanna visits and her home, which is described as "comfortable, chintz-warmed" and at the end of the story those photos in her room in which "the sun shone and everyone was happy."

AROUSING CURIOSITY

It takes time to develop conflict in a story. But you can arouse the reader's curiosity in the very first paragraph. Both "Sausage and Beer" and "The Nightingales Sing" open with the protagonist being driven to some unknown spot. In the second story the sense of mystery is increased with the fog, the high stone walls, and the "dim . . . wan light" of early evening. Phil is not even sure they are on the right road.

"The Windmill Man" also arouses curiosity at the outset. The first sentence is a question: "What was the premonition?" Even before we come to know the protagonist we learn that someone named Clayton Hobbs was killed working on a windmill. As in a Greek tragedy (and several of

Shakespeare's), the hint of impending disaster is given almost before the action begins.

This element which arouses our curiosity is called the *dramatic question* (also the *hook*). Occasionally it is sustained until the very end. A detective story, for example, is one long dramatic question with the answer as a conclusion. Literary short stories, however, usually shift from one dramatic question to another to keep the technique from turning the work into a suspense thriller.

In "Sausage and Beer," for example, the initial question is "Where are they going?" This is partially explained and is replaced by the larger question. "Who is Uncle Theodore?" In the last third of the story, there is once again the question of where they are going.

There is also a series of quietly dramatic questions in "The Nightingales Sing." Once we learn that Phil and Joanna are about to visit Chris and Sandy, there are a number of questions which arouse our curiosity just as they do Joanna's: Why does this couple live like this, and why does Chris keep on riding when obviously there are dangers involved? These questions are somewhat diffuse, but they are the elements which keep the reader in the story.

Suspense is simply a heightened form of curiosity. "The Windmill Man" makes use of suspense once we learn that Justus will go back in the height of a storm and try to repair the windmill. Notice how carefully the author sustains that suspense with the description of the landscape, the newspapers blowing down the street, and the "roiling blackness of the sky." It takes careful judgment to determine how long you can do this without having the reader feel impatient or, worse, manipulated. Much will depend on whether the element of suspense is used as an end in itself or whether, as in this case, it is being used to highlight or dramatize some aspect of character or theme.

Shock is also used to create tension, but it cannot be sustained. It is generally a single flash. If you use it as the climax of the story, be sure you have led up to it carefully. If you hit readers with a shocking conclusion for which they were not prepared at least unconsciously, they will shrug off the whole story as a piece of sensationalism. Try instead to create the sense of inevitability—without predicting the exact outcome. The death of the windmill man, for example, provides shock. It is not a pleasant description. But some kind of strong outcome has been predicted from the very opening of that story and has been repeated with little hints throughout.

It is also possible to use more muted forms of shock within a story. In a sense they are more like jolts. In "Sausage and Beer," for example, there is the moment when the boy has just made a polite but absurdly untrue statement, "It's been very nice meeting you," and the uncle reacts with "a loud and bitter laugh, derisive, and perfectly sane." The jolt here is coupled with irony because the uncle has appeared most threatening in his one moment of lucidity.

IRONY AND SATIRE

Both irony and satire provide tension in quite a different way. Occasionally they are merely tonal devices, but they can be created from the plot as well.

There are three very different kinds of irony, and it is helpful to be able to distinguish between them. *Verbal irony* is a statement in which the literal meaning is different or even the opposite of the intended meaning. It can take the form of understatement as when someone describes a hurricane as "quite a blow." Stronger irony would be phrased as a full reversal as if he had said, while watching his house being washed away, "Great day for a sail!"

When verbal irony is sustained throughout an entire work, it is usually a vehicle for satire. That is, the author continually reverses his or her actual feeling in order to make the ridiculed more ridiculous. In nonfiction, Swift's "A Modest Proposal" is perhaps the best-known example. His proposal to solve the overpopulation problem in famine-ridden Ireland by eating small children is presented with such restraint, such logic, that every year a few students read it as a serious proposal, turning Swift from an ironic humanitarian into an outrageous sadist.

In fiction, verbal irony is often the base for satire—treating a character or institution with mock seriousness.

Dramatic irony is similar except that the character making the statement does not understand that it is ironic. The classic example is in Sophocles' *Oedipus Rex.* When the messenger comes on stage saying "Good news!" those in the audience who know the story wince with the realization that the news will actually be catastrophic. For the others, the impact of the irony will be delayed until later in the play, as it will be for the characters themselves. Note that the reversal here turns on outcome. If, by way of contrast, the messenger had already given information known by him and the others to be disastrous and then added with bitter sarcasm, "Now *there's* a piece of good news," we would have verbal irony.

Dramatic irony could be called unconscious irony in that the characters are not aware of its presence. It is often used in comedy by having characters say things which have a significance they don't yet understand.

A more serious example is seen in a story by Peter Taylor called "A Spinster's Tale." The title informs the reader that the first-person narrator has become a spinster, but even in her own telling she doesn't understand how clearly she is revealing her life-long fear of men and sex.

The third type of irony is sometimes called *cosmic* or the *irony of fate*, though it may take the form of a very minor event. In general terms, it is any outcome which turns out the opposite of normal expectations. It is, however, more complicated than a simple reversal. It is not enough to have a normally brave character turn cowardly. The characteristic must be firmly identified with the agent, and the reversal must be a clear denial. For a person who has spent a lifetime being a firefighter to die from smoking in bed, for example, is ironic enough for a news item—though it would make rather clumsy and obvious fiction.

There is a subtle sample of the irony of fate in "The Windmill Man," though it is carefully buried. In a passage already quoted, Justus is described as setting up windmills partly because he felt that the country was "going to pot" and that it made sense to turn back to the things they could "more or less rely upon." That is, with aspects of society seeming to become unreliable, people like Justus turn to more natural things like the windmill which gives "solid, straightforward satisfaction." Yet eventually the very object which was thought of as reliable, natural, and straightforward, turns out to be perverse and, ultimately, the agent of his death.

The tension created by this kind of irony runs like an undercurrent below the more obvious conflict between man and windmill. It provides a kind of resonance which you don't find in stories based on the simpler forms of conflict.

Satire creates tension by playing an exaggerated view of characters or institutions against the reasonable view. Many readers are introduced to simple satire through magazines such as *Mad* and, later, *National Lampoon.* Neither these nor the satiric sketches one often sees on television are very subtle. In fiction there is a greater range from the light satire in the works of J. P. Marquand to the heavier but still ingenious and insightful works of Peter DeVries. And the tone can also approach the bitter and corrosive as in sections of Joseph Heller's *Catch-22.*

There are two dangers in the writing of satire. The first is a lack of focus. Decide in advance just what kind of person or what type of institution it is which you wish to ridicule. Keep your satiric attack precise and detailed.

The other danger is one of simple excess. If you let it run away with you, the result may be comic but simple and quickly forgotten.

Satire is often avoided on the unfounded assumption that a story must be either wholly satiric or strictly literal. This is unfortunate. Frequently a story can be intensified or enlivened by turning the satiric ridicule on a secondary character, an aspect of the society, or some institution involved in the plot. If the level of satire is kept light, there is not apt to be any damaging break in the tone of an otherwise nonsatiric story.

Casual readers often sense the lack of tension without being able to identify it or suggest a remedy. "It doesn't grab me," they say; or, "It seems kind of flat." These are not literarily precise statements, but they are worth taking seriously. Better yet, try to evaluate your own first draft before anyone else reads it. Does it have the energy, the vitality needed to hold a reader who might have other things to do?

If not, see if there is the potential for at least implied conflict between two individuals or between one and a group. Or is the story better suited for an internal conflict within a single character? Check to make sure that you have aroused the reader's curiosity early in the story and have provided a few dramatic questions to maintain interest. And if you have made use of suspense or shock, make sure you haven't overdone it.

If the story is critical of particular types of people or institutions or traditions, could this best be described with irony or even pushed into satire? Remember that in doing this, the story will become less penetrating in character development since satiric characterization stresses surface appearance; but it may create the result you want.

When starting a new story, tension will not be your first concern. Plot, character, and theme are quite enough to deal with at that stage. But once you have the basic famework clearly in mind, make sure you have provided enough tension to give your story a sense of vitality and life.

Chapter **21**

Orientation: Place and Time

Establishing the *geographic setting;* the tone of a *specific place;* time as *historical period, season* and *hour* of the day; *revising* the orientation—metamorphosing, heightening, and muting of details.

Orientation is the sense of being somewhere specific. This includes not only an awareness of what country one is in, but what kind of city or town and what sort of house or room. In terms of time, it may involve the historical period, the season, or the time of day.

Stories vary in the degree to which they stress orientation and in which aspects are emphasized, but even the most dreamlike fantasies provide, as do dreams themselves, details which help readers to place themselves. Without such details the characters tend to remain detached and unconvincing. And the story itself may not provide that sense of authenticity which readers need if they are to become absorbed in the work. Setting is a major factor in creating the illusion of reality.

ESTABLISHING THE GEOGRAPHIC SETTING

"Where am I?" is the stereotyped response for those who are regaining consciousness. It is also an instinctive question on the part of a reader who has begun a new story.

One of the most common questions concerning geographic setting is whether to use and label cities from real life or to create one's own area. But there is a fallacy in the question itself. Since all fiction is only an illusion, you don't have a choice between a "real" location and one of your own creation. All fictional settings are imaginary, and everyone's fictional use of, say, New York or Los Angeles, is going to be a product of imagination.

Your true choice is not, then, "Shall I set this story in a real city?" but "Shall I use the name and certain characteristics of a real city in the exercise of my imagination? Will it help readers see what I want them to see?"

There are two good reasons for drawing on a known city and naming it. First, it can serve as a geographic shorthand for the reader. There are aspects of our larger cities like New York, San Francisco, and Chicago which are known even by those who do not live there. In addition, using a real city can be a convenience for you as a writer *if* you know the area well. It will save you the trouble of making up your own map.

But there are a couple of dangers as well. Unless you are really familiar with the city you are using, you may begin to depend on scenes and details you have unconsciously absorbed from other stories and from television. Students who have never been to New York, for example, are apt to fall back on such standard conventions as a rainy night on Forty-Second Street, poodles on Park Avenue, hysteria on Madison Avenue, rumbles on either the lower East Side or the upper West Side, and general perversion in the Village.

The same is true for Paris. If in blind ignorance the author spices a story with shots of the Eiffel Tower, cancan dancers, and prostitutes with hearts of gold, the fiction is bound to reflect the television programs and musical comedies from which this material was taken.

To avoid this, make sure that you know the city well if you are going to name it, and try to focus your attention not on the most obvious aspects of the city but on districts and details which will seem authentic to your readers without being reminders of hackneyed stories and films.

Another problem with using a specific place is that you may find it difficult to metamorphose your material. That is, your fiction may become locked into the town or city. This is particularly common when the events have been taken from recent experience.

Perhaps for this reason, a majority of published stories are set in towns or cities which are linked to but not identified directly with real-life locations. John Updike describes this in his foreword to *Olinger Stories:*

> The name Olinger is audibly a shadow of "Shillington," the real name of my home town, yet the two towns, however similar, are not at all the same. Shillington is a place on the map and belongs to the world; Olinger is a state of mind, of my mind, and belongs entirely to me.

In this spirit, John Updike has used Olinger, Pennsylvania, in eleven short stories. The names and ages of the protagonists vary, but essentially they are the same boy. The approach is similar to that of Sherwood Anderson's in *Winesburg, Ohio*. On a broader scale, Faulkner blended historical and fictional elements this way in his stories and novels set in his imaginary Yoknapatawpha County, Mississippi.

None of the three stories you have read here are linked with a specific town or even a state, but two of them are placed geographically in general terms. In "Sausage and Beer," we learn that they were driving "well out in the New England countryside," and in "The Windmill Man," we are told that Clayton "had been a windmill man in that part of the state and clear over into Arizona."

Neither of these quotations come from the opening paragraph. Setting is static and is not as effective for an opening as action or dialogue. But both have been placed within the first few pages in order to "ground the action"—that is, provide a sense of orientation. Both stories, of course, draw heavily on a geographic area, but neither is locked into a specific town or state.

The other extreme is emphasizing the locale at the expense of plot, theme, or characterization. At best, this turns into what is known as *local color* writing. Bret Harte, Mark Twain, and Sarah Orne Jewett were all in this tradition, each working with a different section of America. But stories which become too concerned with the regional surroundings often become dull. Worse, they can appear to be patronizing. This happens if you try to write about a culture or society which you have seen only from the outside. If you spend some time in New Mexico as a tourist, for example, you may gather some excellent material for a story about tourists in New Mexico, but that does not mean that you are ready to depict the life of a Navaho living on the reservation.

THE TONE OF A SPECIFIC PLACE

In addition to geographic setting, each story has a very specific local setting: a house, a room in that house, a neighborhood, a forest, a section of ranch land. Often the tone of a story or of a particular scene will be established largely through the way that place is described. It is extraordinary how the very same spot can be described in ways which create dramatically different moods.

The following examples have been taken from the three stories you have already read. When you have finished each passage, stop for a moment and ask yourself what the story would be like if all such details were removed. Then see if you can analyze how the description has, in addition to placing the reader in a particular setting, established a tone for the entire scene.

(A) The room was large, and it seemed even larger for the lack of furniture. There were benches around all four walls, and in the middle there was a long table flanked with two more benches. The rest was space. And through that space old men shuffled, younger men wheeled carts of linen, a woman visitor walked slowly up and down with her restless husband. . . .Or was she the patient?

(B) Haphazard adobes, most of them unplastered, rusted tin roofs, mud walls bellying above crumbling stone foundations, a rickety store with a single gas pump. . . . Not a soul in sight. Newspapers blowing down a dirt street. An election poster on a fence post, half the candidate's head flapping in the wind. A dying place.

(C) In this room, so obviously untouched for the past hundred years or more, was only the bed, a tall chest of drawers, a washstand with a gold and white bowl and pitcher, two plain painted chairs, and a threadbare oval braided rug beside the bed. There were no curtains. . . . and practically no paint left on the uneven old floor. The fireplace was black and damp-smelling and filled with ashes. . . .

The *plot* of each story would not be altered in any way if we were to cut these descriptive passages. But the *tone* would become less distinct.

In the selection from "Sausage and Beer," the size of the room, the open space, and the slow motion of old men who "shuffle" and a woman who "walks slowly up and down" should provide a reader with some sense of what it is like to spend day after monotonous day in such an institution. This could have been stated in exposition (as I have just done here), but the story should work as illusion, permitting the reader to make discoveries through the setting as well as through action and dialogue.

You will recognize the passage from "The Windmill Man" as coming from the scene in which Justus heads for the runaway windmill. Those newspapers blowing and the torn poster flapping begin to set the mood for the storm which is to come. And referring to this little town as a "dying place" is one more way of suggesting that tragedy is in the offing.

The final quotation is one of several descriptions aimed at showing the stark simplicity of that house and, specifically, Chris' room. She has not made curtains as she might have if she were married to Sandy. They have made no effort to make the place homey. Yet, later, Joanna feels very much at home when the fire warms the living room and she feels welcomed by these new friends. As readers we are able to sense through the stark descriptions of the house that the life Chris and Sandy lead is not ideal; yet we can also appreciate Joanna's rather romanticized view of this life style. The contrast between the unadorned, stark furnishings and the warmth which is created mainly by the people themselves is central to the story as a whole.

TIME AS HISTORY

Orientation involves more than place. The reader also wants to know about time. The historical period, the season, and the hour of day are all aspects of this concern, and it is entirely up to the author whether any of these should be emphasized in a particular story.

Most stories are set in the same historical period in which they are written. It is simply easier and more natural that way. The author is using settings, customs, speech patterns, and incidents which are familiar. It requires a great deal of reading to be sufficiently familiar with an earlier period to use it as a fictional base.

There is an even more compelling reason for novice writers to avoid earlier periods. The tendency is to move back to the nineteenth century, borrowing not from real events but from that great backlog of televised dramas and historical novels which themselves, on the whole, were rooted in the convention rather than in life. It is essential that the writer ask, Where did I get that idea? On what am I basing that scene? What made me name that character "Lulubelle" and put her in that saloon?

There are, I think, two justifications for using an historical period other than one's own. First, some writers have a special interest in some period of history and have been reading material about it over the course of many years. This concern may be a part of one's cultural or racial tradition. Even in these cases, of course, the writer has to be careful to avoid those over-used scenes and situations which will reduce even the most sincere work to the level of hackneyed fiction.

The second justification is in the case of those who are old enough so that their childhood has become "history." Occasionally it is possible to push back a decade or so to avoid that "dead period" which editors object to on nonliterary grounds. Their prejudice springs from the fact that a story which takes place noticeably in the historical past but less than twenty years before the time of the writing looks like a manuscript which has been circulating a long time.

As I have explained, "Sausage and Beer" was moved back from the early 40s to the early 30s primarily for the dramatic effect of the speakeasy. But having made the decision, I was then able to draw on other details from that period—the incredible cold of cars before there were heaters, the titles of such magazines as the old *Life* and *Judge,* and the W.P.A. But the story is also an example of how careful a writer has to be when moving even slightly out of his or her experience: old-car experts were quick to point out that 1929 Dodges did not have those round radiator thermometers "mounted like a figurehead on the front end of the hood."

If you are careful, you may be able to draw on specific memories of a parent or grandparent. It helps if your informant is willing to provide a great deal of background, however. Mere plots are not enough. You will have to have enough information to fill in little details if the story is to be convincing.

With these exceptions, it is probably wiser to draw on the historical period you know best—your own lifetime.

TIME OF THE YEAR

If the season has no real significance in a story, you can ignore it without the reader even noticing. But occasionally it helps to fix a story in a specific season and make use of it. "Sausage and Beer," for example, makes use of winter. The opening paragraph starts the story with the fact that "It was too cold for talk." The car had no heater. And at the hospital Uncle Theodore tells about his nightmarish theory that some night the hospital will shut off the heat and freeze the patients to death. It is not until the end of the story that this pattern of cold is broken. When father and son enter the speak-easy together the boy discovers a "warm, bubbling, sparkling, humming. . .bit of cheerful chaos." In that case, the cold of a New England winter served as a contrast with the warmth of friendship and, particularly, the new-found relationship between father and son.

Season can also be used as a method of metamorphosing a personal experience into something which is manageable. An episode which occurred in the heat of midsummer can sometimes be shifted to January merely to remove it from the confines of experience. Or an event which happened to take place in autumn might lend itself to spring and at the same time give you some sense of freshness and objectivity over your material. You must, of course, be on guard against the clichés of season. A first love which ends with a paragraph about the spring buds on the apple tree is as hackneyed as the story about an old couple which ends with the fallen leaves of November. Seasons can be enormously valuable—but only when they are used with subtlety and originality.

THE TIME OF DAY

There is the danger of clichés in the hour of the day as well. A surprising number of stories begin with waking and wondering where one is. Fewer—but still too many—use the stock film ending: hand in hand in the sunset, "looking forward to another day."

In spite of these problems, the time of the day can often serve to orient the reader and to provide the writer with a system to organize the plot. "The Nightingales Sing," for example, starts with the "wan light of an early summer evening" (season as well as time), and continues to the late evening with her parents asleep and Joanna musing sleepily what it would have been like if she had stayed. The mystery of that foggy evening and the vision of the next day help to suggest her sense of uneasiness in the face of a new experience and her naive but sincere view of what the future will hold. References to evening and morning, then, are not either casual or incidental; they have symbolic suggestion.

Even if you are not making specific use of the time of day, keep track of it in your own mind. This will help you to avoid careless errors in which a character refers to the morning coffee break one moment and quitting time five minutes later.

Carelessness in time sense can lead to another type of error as well. It often takes this form: Two characters meet, sit down and talk for what in fact is only two minutes of dialogue, and then they part saying, "It's been great to be able to talk this over with you." Since serious conversations are rarely that brief, be sure to provide some reference to the rest of their talk with a phrase like, "She kept on arguing, but her heart was not in it," or "The conversation turned to milder topics."

Whether you make direct use of the time of day depends on whether it is useful to the story. But remember that whatever scene you develop exists in the fictional time of the story and the reader will expect it to be consistent.

REVISING THE ORIENTATION

Most often, revising aspects of place and time comes early in the development of a story. It may, as I have pointed out, take the form of fundamental metamorphosing of the original experience. As the story develops, however, such sweeping changes become more and more difficult. A basic sense of geographic and seasonal setting tends to permeate a story so that revisions become much more elaborate than, say, changing a Nebraska farmhouse into a Chicago apartment or replacing the references to a winter scene with details about summer. If one has used place and season prominently, they become a part of the "feel" of the story. For this reason, it is best to make sure that the place and the season of a story are right before one has invested many hours of work.

There is, however, a great deal of heightening and muting of these details which go on through successive drafts. Heightening often is the result of chance. One selects a season, perhaps, because that is when the experience took place; and then various implications and suggestions come from the material and demand development. The use of cold as a vehicle to suggest separation and isolation in "Sausage and Beer" evolved in just this way.

In more serious cases, sharpening the visual details of a story is demanded because the action has gone on in a non-place. A surprising number of unsuccessful stories are placed in some ill-defined urban area which conveniently allows the protagonist to dodge city traffic one minute and, when the plot demands it, to be wandering "in the outskirts of town" the next. If you find yourself doing this, shift the story to a specific town or city which you know even if you do not use the name.

Muting aspects of setting may be necessary if you feel your use of place or season has become hackneyed. The kinds of clichés which damage fiction have already been described, but I should stress here that it is easy even for experienced writers to borrow from overworked conventions. Sometimes it is due to the fact that the experience has, infuriatingly, echoed a fictional cliché. There is no cosmic law which forbids life from imitating the worst in fiction. Occasionally a beautiful woman and a handsome man really do fall in love while strolling by the Eiffel Tower in Paris on a lovely June day. They may even live happily ever after. But who is going to believe it? Leave that plot to the musical comedy writers. If you really have had such a marvelous experience, find aspects of it which are further from the conventional pattern. This may involve moving the story to another setting or another season or both.

Occasionally the setting has to be revised because it has begun to resemble a literary convention. Stories about migrant workers tend to sound like John Steinbeck; hitchhiking stories often pick up the smells and sounds of Jack Kerouac's *On the Road* or the many motorcycle films which have been produced in the past ten years; scenes involving city gangs often use the standard details including switch blades and leather jackets. One often has to mute these details and stress ones which the reader will see as if for the first time. Once again, be careful not to assume that details from your own life will necessarily be convincing as fiction. If you present a setting which your reader will associate with another author or a film or song lyric or television commercial or musical comedy, your story will be damaged by the association. Muting those details and highlighting other elements will be necessary, and usually you can do this without losing your original conception.

It is important to understand that a sense of place, historical period, season, and time of day are not adornments to a story. They are part of what you see and feel as you write; they are also the primary means by which your readers are going to enter your story and experience it as if they were physically present. It is this sense of being there that makes fiction an "as-if-real" experience.

Chapter 22

A Prose Narrative
by Jamaica Kincaid

Girl

Wash the white clothes on Monday and put them on the stone heap; wash the color clothes on Tuesday and put them on the clothesline to dry; don't walk barehead in the hot sun; cook pumpkin fritters in very hot sweet oil; soak your little cloths right after you take them off; when buying cotton to make yourself a nice blouse, be sure that it doesn't have gum in it, because that way it won't hold up well after a wash; soak salt fish overnight before you cook it; is it true that you sing benna* in Sunday school?; always eat your food in such a way that it won't turn someone else's stomach; on Sundays try to walk like a lady and not like the slut you are so bent on becoming; don't sing benna in Sunday school; you mustn't speak to wharf-rat boys, not even to give directions; don't eat fruits on the street—flies will follow you; *but I don't sing benna on Sundays at all and never in Sunday school*; this is how to sew

---

*Caribbean English for calypso and, more recently, rock-and-roll or any music that is not religious.

on a button; this is how to make a buttonhole for the button you have just sewed on; this is how to hem a dress when you see the hem coming down and so to prevent yourself from looking like the slut I know you are so bent on becoming; this is how you iron your father's khaki shirt so that it doesn't have a crease; this is how you iron your father's khaki pants so that they don't have a crease; this is how you grow okra—far from the house, because okra tree harbors red ants; when you are growing dasheen, make sure it gets plenty of water or else it makes your throat itch when you are eating it; this is how you sweep a corner; this is how you sweep a whole house; this is how you sweep a yard; this is how you smile to someone you don't like too much; this is how you smile to someone you don't like at all; this is how you smile to someone you like completely; this is how you set a table for tea; this is how you set a table for dinner; this is how you set a table for dinner with an important guest; this is how you set a table for lunch; this is how you set a table for breakfast; this is how to behave in the presence of men who don't know you very well, and this way they won't recognize immediately the slut I have warned you against becoming; be sure to wash every day, even if it is with your own spit; don't squat down to play marbles—you are not a boy, you know; don't pick people's flowers—you might catch something; don't throw stones at blackbirds, because it might not be a blackbird at all; this is how to make a bread pudding; this is how to make doukona; this is how to make pepper pot; this is how to make a good medicine for a cold; this is how to make a good medicine to throw away a child before it even becomes a child; this is how to catch a fish; this is how to throw back a fish you don't like, and that way something bad won't fall on you; this is how to bully a man; this is how a man bullies you; this is how to love a man, and if this doesn't work there are other ways, and if they don't work don't feel too bad about giving up; this is how to spit up in the air if you feel like it, and this is how to move quick so that it doesn't fall on you; this is how to make ends meet; always squeeze bread to make sure it's fresh; *but what if the baker won't let me feel the bread?*; you mean to say that after all you are really going to be the kind of woman who the baker won't let near the bread?

Chapter 23

Literary Concerns: Theme, Tone, Symbol, and Style

Theme described as the *central concern* of a story; *tone* seen as a variable regardless of the subject matter; *suggestive* and *symbolic* details presented as methods of increasing the "resonance" of fiction; *style* analyzed as a product of *diction, syntax,* and the balance of *narrative modes.*

In a broad sense, of course, this entire text deals with literature. But the title of this chapter refers to four abstract concepts which are at the heart of literary composition.

On a simple level, each of these is used quite unconsciously. All fiction except the freest sort of journal entry has a theme of some sort. And it is always written with some kind of tone—usually reflecting the emotion of the writer at the time of the experience or shortly thereafter. Symbolic details can be stumbled upon accidentally, and style is present in every line of writing whether the author is aware of it or not.

On a more sophisticated level, however, these are four concerns with which experienced writers grapple all their lives. These are not concepts to be learned; these are continuing concerns.

THE THEME

As I pointed out in the poetry section, theme is often overemphasized. Certain stories—like certain poems—can't be summed up neatly in a single, complete sentence. Others may be primarily studies in character. But some type of theme is essential in every kind of story.

It is theme that distinguishes fiction from an aimless journal entry or a pointless fantasy. If you do not provide a degree of thematic unity, your readers are apt to respond with questions like, "But what's the point?" or "What are you getting at?"

There are usually several themes, one of which can be called primary. Because of this, some critics prefer the *central concern*, a term which I will use interchangeably with *theme*. *Central concern* serves as a reminder that we are not dealing with something as logically specific as a thesis or as ethically concerned as a moral. It is also a reminder of why some type of theme is nonetheless important. After all, what is a story which has no concern at all?

Like almost every other aspect of literature, the theme can be simple or highly sophisticated. Fiction for the very young repeats such themes as "It's terrible being the littlest (ugliest, weakest, stupidest), but with luck you can be the hero of the day." This is no more demanding than the themes which still appear with fair regularity in women's magazines and on television: "Nice girls win out eventually," "Crotchety old grandfathers are sometimes just lonely old men," and "Newly marrieds face problems which we mature readers solved two and three years ago."

Sophisticated fiction often has a cluster of related concerns. This can be true even when a story is particularly short and apparently simple. Jamaica Kincaid's "Girl" is a case in point. Written mainly in the form of a monologue in the rhythms of the West Indies where she was born and raised, this piece is perhaps more fairly called a prose narrative than a story in the traditional sense. It has no plot and no identified character. But the primary speaker does emerge and a theme does develop.

What we hear are fragments of what a girl hears from her mother. The details are rooted in the author's own island, Antigua, but the repetition of "do this" and "don't do that" is universal. Much of the advice is practical, shaping a young person in the pattern seen appropriate for girls—sharply delineated, we assume, from the rules for boys. The daughter protests once (the first section in italics), but the admonishment continues as if she had not spoken.

There are a number of concerns here: West Indian traditions, the way girls are molded to conform to a particular role pattern, the way subservience to men can become a part of that pattern, the inability of children to speak back and defend themselves against unjust accusations, the way firmness and kindness can be merged in the same parent.

Which is the central concern? Were this published fifteen years ago, readers might have seen it as primarily a story about West Indian life as recalled by one who was raised there. But the story appeared in *The New Yorker* in 1978, and most readers see the piece as essentially what the title implies: the careful shaping of behavior which leads to the concept of "girl"—not just in the Caribbean but in the United States as well.

"The Windmill Man" is in many ways at the opposite end of the spectrum of fiction: it stresses plot and achieves its goals through symbolic action rather than dialogue. But complexity of theme is important in this story too. In fact, without such nuances, the story would be a simple adventure story.

If we describe the theme of "The Windmill Man" in terms of a cluster of concerns, we can start with the one announced in the very first sentence: "What was the premonition?" That question is repeated midway in the story and again at the end like a refrain. That sense of foreboding, of overriding fate, is one important concern.

But it is more than a story about an individual who is swept up in a course of events which leads finally to his death. He is, after all, a windmill man. As in "Girl," the title turns our attention to a particular thematic concern. The protagonist has taken up his work with the hope of "turning back to the things [he] could more or less rely upon." But at the very end he is described as "dying, dying out, the windmill man." That's not just Justus Knight who is dying, it is an independent way of life which is "dying out." Seen this way, the central concern becomes a social statement—and a dark one at that.

Turning now to "Sausage and Beer," I should point out that an author is not necessarily the best judge of his own work. (Faulkner's analysis of his own novel, *Sanctuary*, for example, is entirely unjustified.) But it is sometimes helpful for writers to learn what was in the mind of fellow writers as they wrote. The first thematic concern of "Sausage and Beer" was the suggestion that when one discovers just how much of life is run by pure chance, one is initiated into adulthood. Thus, the boy and his twin sister could think of themselves as a couple, but they would never be able to marry each other. They had no control over this. In the same way, the boy's father and Uncle Theodore were born twins, but by chance their lives took utterly different routes. The waiter at the end of the story highlights this aspect of the story.

But in the development of the story, a second major concern began to grow and may have to some degree taken over as the central concern. This might be described as the need to reach others and the difficulty we all have in this effort. In the case of Uncle Theodore, contact with the real world is sporadic—like a light with a bad electrical connection. In the case of father and son, however, the progression is from polite distance to a kind of communion.

It helps to have a fairly clear idea of your central concern before starting to write a story. But it is also important to stay flexible and to allow shifts in emphasis to occur as you write. This is one reason why it is so important to review early drafts as objectively as possible. Often you will find passages or even entire scenes which are left over from when you had a different notion of what your central concern would be.

Revisions will also be necessary to avoid having so subtle a theme that no one can understand what the story is about. It helps, of course, if you have a conscientious reader or, better yet, a group which will discuss your work. But often you will have to make judgments on your own. If highlighting an obscure theme seems wise, think twice before you do so with a paragraph of exposition. Try instead to find a line of dialogue, a specific action, or perhaps even a new scene which will help your readers to see for themselves what you had in mind.

Occasionally, the theme of your story may strike you as too obvious or lacking in depth. It will not help simply to "fuzz it up." Try instead to amplify and broaden the thematic suggestions. It may be possible, for example, to have a second or third character demonstrate other aspects of the same theme. Or an additional scene may provide a broader perspective.

The point to remember is that any sophisticated story generates a number of concerns only one of which is seen as the core of the work. Your task is to develop that central concern without becoming blatant. It is this type of "fine tuning" which usually makes the revisions take far more time than the first draft.

TONE

We remember experiences with the coloring of the emotion we felt at the time. We remain embarrassed at awkward moments which occurred years before; we continue to smile at comic events; and we remain bitter toward those who hurt us. If you are writing a story which is at least partially based on personal experience, it will seem natural to present it with the emotional response you still feel.

This is reasonable, but remember that what you are writing is fiction and you should be able to shift the tone if you feel that such a change would improve the story. Most of the time such changes take the form of light touches to stories which have become too heavy, too close to melodrama.

Be on the alert when working with a personal experience which you recall with strong emotions—deep sorrow, strong anger, and the like. It may be that what are sincere emotions will appear sentimental or superficial in a short story if presented without relief. The same applies to experiences which were charged with excitement and fear. If you are not careful, they can become conventional thrillers. Remember that a story—particularly a relatively short one—is a rather delicate art form. Think of it as an electrical wire which cannot take too heavy a surge of voltage without burning out. By "burning out" I simply mean appearing ridiculous. It is not a pleasant experience to have readers respond to a scene which you thought was moving or dramatic with chuckles and comments like, "Oh, come on now!"

The solution may be to back off from the material a bit. Look at your protagonist with a slightly detached attitude. See if there aren't some aspects of the situation which could be treated either lightly or at least with a hint of a smile. When you do this, you are establishing *distance* between you and your material.

In my own story, for example, I made a conscious effort to keep the asylum scene from turning excessively dark by working in some of the simple, humdrum complaints which the mad share with anyone living within an institution. Uncle Theodore's little worries about fellow patients were invented for this purpose. This is one of those cases in which the actual experience had to be softened to keep the scene from becoming melodramatic.

In "The Nightingales Sing" what might have been a heavy-handed, earnest talk between Joanna and Chris is given a light, near comic twist by having it take place in a privy. And in "The Windmill Man," a strongly dramatic story, there are light touches associated with Jesse Pruit, who occasionally is almost a parody of a taciturn rancher.

Sometimes the entire subject of a story can be treated as a comedy. Presenting normally serious topics like death, despair, and sadism as high comedy is known as *black humor* (not to be confused with black literature) and usually leaves the reader caught between shock and laughter. In most cases, however, you will not find it necessary to alter the tone more than to add light touches to material which seems to have become oppressive.

Occasionally you may have to shift the tone in the opposite direction—from light to dark or from superficial to penetrating. This may be necessary if your early draft seems trivial or inconsequential. Look carefully at your characters and see if you can present other aspects of their personalities. You may have to provide dialogue or perhaps a whole new scene to develop such a character more fully.

Finally, there is the technique of intentionally shifting the tone within the story. If this is done carelessly, it will seem to make the work fall apart. Readers tend to predict what the tone of a story is going to be from the first paragraph, and they can be put off by an abrupt shift. But a change is possible if you prepare for it carefully enough. If your story is going to begin on a light note and end more seriously, provide some hint of what is in store fairly early. If, on the other hand, you open with a serious situation which you plan to resolve happily at the end, think of a phrase or two in a lighter vein which will assure the reader of the direction the story will take.

SUGGESTIVE AND SYMBOLIC DETAILS

A symbol, as defined in the poetry section of this text, is any detail, such as an object, action, or state, which takes on a range of meaning beyond and larger than itself. Most frequently it is a visual image. I use the term "suggestive detail" to refer to items which don't have the impact of true symbols but which do have overtones and implications.

The major object in a story often takes on symbolic importance. That stark house in "The Nightingales Sing" which is warmed not by furnishings but by the people themselves (and by the fire which Joanna lights) suggests the kind of life Chris led—none of the comforts of more conventional lives, but punctuated with periods of warmth and companionship. Look closely at the windmill called the Royal Don which a character named Justus Knight fights. Sound familiar? There are echoes here of Don Quixote, a self-proclaimed knight, who battles windmills thinking they are giants, in the novel by Cervantes. The parallel is more than quixotic. Both characters revere the values of a former age and both are defeated. This is not to say that "The Windmill Man" is a retelling of the Don Quixote plot. The author has simply provided details which will help the reader link this story with one which is widely known. As a result, the Royal Don windmill takes on the symbolic overtone of a giant which one cannot defeat.

Little details can also be presented in a way to take on symbolic suggestion. As I mentioned earlier, it is no accident that Joanna in "The Nightingales Sing" burns the comics, an element of childhood, when she lights the fire and brings warmth to the room. And if you read the story carefully you will recall that the only flowers by the front door consisted of "a bed of unbudded red lilies around one of the apple trees"—a significant detail for a young protagonist who is just about to enter womanhood. Out of context it may seem blatant, but the detail is buried in a descriptive paragraph.

"Sausage and Beer" as a title directs the reader's attention to the end of the story when the waiter brings the tray and leaves them with a "benedictory smile." Father and son are then "lost in a kind of communion"—a parallel with the wafer and wine used in certain Christian services. Recognizing this central symbol is not essential to an understanding of the story, but it should add another range of overtones or *resonance* for those who make the connection.

One word of warning about symbols, however: If they are too obvious, they can turn a good story into something contrived and artificial. It is very risky (I'm tempted to say *disastrous*) to start with some symbolic notions and try to make them convincing. Stories which are rooted in the Adam and Eve myth (complete with a junkie named Snake-eyes) are a kind of original sin in writing classes. The symbol is too blunt, too obvious. And Noah has already been done.

The use of symbols in short stories is usually more successful if it is done subtly. You can be sure you are on the right track if the symbol you devise does not in any way defeat characterization. Some authors go further and try to mute symbolic details to the point where the story still is meaningful for those who may fail to identify the device.

This is not to suggest that you should avoid symbolic details. They can keep a story from resembling a piano melody played with one finger. They can provide resonance. The goal, however, is to have them serve the story, not dominate it.

STYLE

All fiction has style. You can't compose without it any more than you can write your name without revealing—for better or for worse—your hand-writing. But it is important to examine just what your style is and then to judge whether it is the best possible approach for a particular story.

Essentially, there are three factors which determine your prose style in fiction: *diction* (word choice), *syntax* (sentence structure), and the *balance of narrative modes*.

Diction, the words you select, is a more significant factor in English than in most other languages because there is such a radical difference in sound and tone between those words which came to us from the Norse and Anglo-Saxon and those which are from the Greek or Latin. To cite an extreme example, contrast your reaction to these two samples:

> Edgar got in the boat and gripped the seat, sweating like an ox. He hated the sea.
>
> Julius entered the vessel and embraced the cushions, perspiring profusely. He detested the ocean.

In the first, the nouns and verbs are without exception of Anglo-Saxon or Old Norse origin. In the second, every noun and verb is of Latin origin. Except for the articles and the conjunctions, these could be two different languages, each with its distinctive sound, and each with its own tone. Past generations were taught that words of Latin and Greek derivations were "elegant" and "refined," and some of that prejudice remains. You should feel free to use whatever the language has to offer, but remember that your choices will affect your style.

Needless to say, you can't look up the derivation of every word you use. But we all have a built-in awareness of the distinction between these two verbal heritages: one dominated by short, abrupt sounds which imply simplicity, roughness, and in some cases obscenity; the other characterized by longer words, smoother sounds and imbued with a sense of elegance or even pomposity.

Aside from the derivations, there are the subtle distinctions between short words and long ones, harsh ones and smooth ones, crude ones and those which sound elegant. As with nonfiction writing, you will want to choose an appropriate *level of usage*. If the story is being narrated by a city-dweller who is street wise, your choice of words is going to be dramatically different than it would be if you were writing a third-person story in what is sometimes called a neutral style. And of course the diction of each line of dialogue should be appropriate to the character who is speaking.

Fiction is not written word by word, however. When it is going well, let it flow. The time to take a close look at your diction is when you read over the completed first draft. Decide what effect you want and revise carefully.

Syntax is the second factor which determines style. Long, elaborate constructions have a distinct effect not only on the feel of the passage but even on the pace at which one's eye moves over the page. Read the following two passages quickly and try to identify your different reactions:

> When Nick opened the door and went into the room he saw Ole Anderson, a former heavyweight prizefighter, lying on the bed with all his clothes on. He was too long for the bed and lay without looking at Nick, his head on two pillows.

> Nick opened the door and went into the room. Ole Anderson was lying on the bed with all his clothes on. He had been a heavyweight prizefighter and he was too long for the bed. He lay with his head on two pillows. He did not look at Nick.

The first has two sentences. The second has five. The first might be criticized by some as containing a run-on sentence and the second for having what is often called "baby sentences." But writers of fiction, fortunately, have more latitude than students in their weekly themes, and in this case Ernest Hemingway chose the second as his highly individual style. The selection is from "The Killers."

At the opposite end of the stylistic scale are authors like Marcel Proust, Henry James, Thomas Wolfe, and William Faulkner. These highly varied novelists were all fascinated with the long sentence, and each of them occasionally strung one out for almost the length of an entire page.

But length is not the only variable. The construction itself can be simple or complex; the punctuation can be strict or loose; the phrasing can be rhythmic or nonrhythmic. Whenever one of these variables is pushed to an extreme, the author is a pronounced stylist.

Having a clearly identifiable style, however, is in no way a necessity. In fact, a majority of stories in print are closer to what is sometimes called a neutral style. Every author varies, of course, but the differences are not pronounced. In the three full-length stories in this volume, for example, the differences are minor and have less to do with diction and syntax than they do with mode, which I will turn to shortly.

Jamaica Kincaid's "Girl," on the other hand, is stylistically distinctive. The most noticeable device is the use of semicolons instead of periods. Strictly speaking, this is one long sentence. The effect is to run the material together like an uninterrupted monologue. The units are fragments recalled from different days over the course of several years; but the punctuation blends them as if they were running through the mind of the young woman whose own voice is heard only twice.

Less noticeable than punctuation but just as important is the fact that these "sentences" are almost all simple rather than complex or compound. Even "as-if-spoken" passages can use fairly complex grammatical units if the speaker is that kind of person; but the effect Kincaid wants to achieve is the kind of offhand, casual conversation which is apt to go on between mother and daughter while performing chores around the house.

Notice that for all the syntactical individuality, the author has done very little to the words themselves. There are a few specific details which suggest the West Indies—singing benna, growing dasheen and okra—but there is not one sample of phonetic spelling. This is writing which comes from a region rather than being regional. Her concerns are far larger than the geographic area she is drawing upon.

"Girl" is unusual in that the syntactical units are fairly regular in length. This has, as I pointed out, helped to suggest the rhythms of casual conversation and is effective in a short piece. Longer, more fully developed stories usually vary the length of sentences. Uniform length can become monotonous, particularly if you are using simple sentences which bounce along with subject-verb, subject-verb regularity. An occasional very short sentence or, on the other hand, a long and complex one may help to provide variety and vitality.

The third method of influencing your style in fiction is the balance of *narrative modes.* I am using *mode* here in the special sense introduced in Chapter 12: dialogue, thoughts, action, description, and exposition.

The first two, dialogue and thoughts, are closely related in that they quote either directly or indirectly the words of a character. The last three are in a sense external to the character and are as a result closer to an authorial voice.

Needless to say, any one sentence may involve more than one mode. A statement like "I hate the way you use that green eyeshadow" is basically dialogue, but it also implies the speaker's thoughts, a description of the woman, and exposition about her habits. In spite of these various functions, one mode is usually dominant in each sentence. And occasionally one mode may become dominant in the entire story. This can be effective, but make sure that you have done it intentionally and for a good reason.

"Sausage and Beer" and "The Nightingales Sing" contain a fairly even distribution of the five modes. If you skim over these stories you can see that some pages have more dialogue, while others might have more action or exposition. But no one mode is stressed in the course of either story.

"The Windmill Man," on the other hand, relies on action, description, and exposition in that order and almost eliminates dialogue and thoughts. Look at how McCarthy describes the moment in which his two characters see that the tower they have just constructed with such difficulty has just been blown over.

> Jesse spit and looked sideways at the ground. Justus yanked off his polka-dotted cap and swabbed his glistening pate.

Neither of them utters a word. Their thoughts are not reported. But in the context of the story, we know exactly how they feel.

This style lends itself to the character of both men. They are not talkers. It also adds to that mythic quality of the story—the sense that we are witnessing a kind of ritual between a man with a strong idea of what kind of life he wants to lead and a piece of machinery which seems as strong as the will of the gods in Greek mythology.

Kincaid's style in "Girl" is equally distinctive but relies on a different mode: dialogue which is almost a monologue. A mother speaks all the lines except for two brief responses from the daughter. No description except by implication. No thoughts directly reported—though we can fill in the gaps. The effect is entirely different yet it seems appropriate for this piece. We rely here on the illusion of hearing someone's voice, just as in the McCarthy story we had the sense of watching a ritual drama being peformed almost without words.

It is important to examine the balance of the five modes in your own writing because occasionally you may favor one over another for the wrong reasons. It is a mistake, for example, to avoid dialogue merely because you don't feel at home with it. And conversely you may find that a talkative character has taken over a story for no good reason just as such people occasionally do at social gatherings. Remember that in writing fiction, the choice of who talks and for how long is entirely up to you.

The balance of narrative modes will also affect the pace of your story. As I pointed out in Chapter 15, pace is the rate at which a story reveals information and so is largely controlled by how you handle the plot. But the pace of a story can also be increased by adding action or dialogue, and it can be effectively slowed by inserting a paragraph of description or exposition. There is a good example of this in McCarthy's "The Windmill Man." After Justus agrees to repair the runaway windmill the author slows the pace with four paragraphs—a full page of writing which is essentially descriptive and reflective. He may be writing about a runaway windmill and nature gone wild, but he maintains careful control of his narrative pace.

If you study the nature of literary elements such as theme, tone, symbol, and style in abstract terms very long, the task of actually employing them in a short story may seem overwhelming. To avoid this, move from abstract concerns to actual published stories and then to your own writing. This will help to keep you from being self-consciously literary in the act of writing.

There are, of course, no absolute rules when it comes to style, but here is an approach which many writers find helpful: Trust your literary instinct in your first draft and let the story find its own style; then trust your critical judgment as you review your work and be willing to revise.

Chapter **24**

Developing as a Writer of Fiction

The importance of revision; six critical questions to be asked about a work of fiction regarding characterization, plot construction, tensions, theme, setting, and tone; *learning from published fiction* in story collections and magazines.

If you are going to develop as a writer of fiction, you will have to spend a great deal of your time revising. You will also have to study published fiction carefully enough and regularly enough so that the authors become your teachers in a process of growth which will never stop.

You will find that the more time you spend writing fiction the more emphasis you will place on revision. It is true that this is difficult when taking a writing course. An academic term is relatively short, and the effectiveness of a course requires a high output of new material. Rewriting cannot in most cases be given as much credit as new writing. But when you are working on your own or as a member of an informal writing group, you will not have that kind of pressure and you will find that a far greater percentage of your time will go into the revisions than was spent on the original draft.

As with poetry, it is very helpful to receive a critical reaction from those who are familiar with the genre. But unless you are taking a course, it will be difficult to find qualified individuals who have the time. Writers of fiction are thrown on their own rather abruptly. For this reason, it is all the more important to acquire an ability to criticize your own work as soon as possible.

SIX CRITICAL QUESTIONS

Discussions about a story or novel tend to cover six general areas. If you are working on your own, these are the critical questions which you should ask yourself as you begin to plan your revisions.

I list them here in the order in which they frequently are raised. There is a tendency, for example, to discuss characters and scene construction before the theme because they are in some respects more visible, more immediately available. Setting and tone, on the other hand, are often brought up toward the end of a discussion since they depend on what the thematic concerns are.

But it would be a great mistake to insist on any particular order. A good discussion is in a sense an organic development: It should move in whatever direction appears productive. The point of this list is not to restrict or direct discussion but to encourage as broad a range of analysis as possible.

First, *are the primary characters vivid or convincing?* I use the word *or* here because in the case of satire a character may stand out sharply the way a cartoon figure does without being *convincing* the way a fully-drawn character should be. In either case, successful characters can be described as *vivid*. (It is important to recall here the warning against the word *realistic* as a sloppy synonym for *vivid*.)

Secondary characters, of course, don't have to meet the same standards. We don't insist on getting to know Jesse Pruit in "The Windmill Man" or the host at the speak-easy in "Sausage and Beer." But even in these cases, these characters must be presented in such a way as to appear a natural part of the story. If the reader feels that a character has been added needlessly or blatantly for a specific purpose, then the story is in need of revision.

In analyzing characters, don't rely entirely on general impressions. Look closely at the narrative modes which have been used. Is the dialogue convincing? Do we enter the inner world of thoughts? Do we see the character *doing* enough? And most important of all, has exposition been used too heavily to develop character? Are there ways some of those aspects can be shown through another mode like action or dialogue?

If you are looking over your own story without benefit of an objective reader, you will have to ask the same questions. It helps if you can set the story aside for a few days between finishing the first draft and planning your second.

Second, *is the story constructed successfully?* It is often helpful to analyze just how many scenes there are before beginning to evaluate how they are handled. Once this is done, it is natural enough to discuss which scenes seem to be the most successful ones. Some may be too brief to provide the reader with a sense of being present; others may seem to drag. Frequently, a scattering of scenes may be combined to give the story a more solid base.

After discussing the scenes individually, it is important to examine the order: Is this the most effective sequence? If the opening is slow, for example, it might be worth starting with a livelier scene and returning to the original situation at a later point in the story. If the order is complicated with a storyteller or with numerous flash-backs, consider whether the advantage of such a sequence is worth the risk of confusion and distraction. Keep in mind that while there is no "right" way for any one story, every approach has both advantages and disadvantages—and in different proportions. The critic's job is not to make pronouncements like, "You can't write a story that way," but, rather, to describe what seems to be successful from the reader's point of view and what is confusing or dull. Frequently, such reactions stem from the handling of the plot.

Third, *does the story contain the type of tensions which keeps fiction alive and interesting?* It is, of course, easy to say that a story is "flat" or that "It's just plain dull." But a critic who is helpful moves directly to the problem of determining what kinds of tensions might be established. In some cases this may be a matter of creating a conflict between the protagonist and another character or some other force. This could mean basic revisions in plot. In other cases it might be solved by adding some kind of dramatic question to arouse the curiosity of the reader.

Fourth, *what is the theme, and is it sophisticated enough to be fresh and evocative?* You may have started with a clear idea of what your central concern was, but it is wise to look at the finished story objectively to see if your aim has shifted. If your work is being discussed by a group, let them talk about what they see as the theme before you say anything. Ask them to be specific.

When dealing with theme, make sure that every scene and most of the small details contribute in some way to that central concern. Sometimes elements in a story remain merely because they were a part of the original experience or an earlier draft of the story. In those cases, careful cutting is needed.

Fifth, *is the setting vivid, and does it contribute to the theme?* This is not to suggest that the setting is always a major factor in fiction, but look closely at what you have and see if it does all you want it to. Could the same plot be moved to a place which would make more of an impression on the reader? Don't reach for the exotic, however, since that makes the setting an end in itself. Your goal is to place the story in an environment which contributes to the theme.

Remember, too, that in longer stories you can contrast settings such as the asylum and the speak-easy in "Sausage and Beer" and the farmhouse set against Joanna's comfortable and affluent home in "The Nightingales Sing."

Finally, *is the tone of the story effective?* If your story is unrelentingly dark and brooding, could it use an occasional light or at least neutral element? If the plot is strong and the action dramatic as in "The Windmill Man," would it be wise to add a descriptive or reflective passage to keep the story from becoming a simple thriller?

The two greatest dangers in the area of tone are sentimentality and melodrama. In the first, the story appears to make an unjustified appeal to emotions such as pity or love. In the second, drama is pushed too far and becomes blatant and unconvincing. Group response is very helpful in determining whether you have moved in either of these directions. But if you have no critics available, you will have to read your own work with a cool, objective approach.

LEARNING FROM PUBLISHED FICTION

Writing courses are valuable because they encourage you to produce a great deal in a short period of time and because they offer you a lot of feedback on your work. Also an occasional writers' conference (all listed in *Literary Market Place* (*LMP*), available at most libraries) may be useful because it will introduce you to many other writers at least some of whom are serious about their craft. But in the long run your best teachers will be authors speaking to you through their fiction.

The word *reading* can refer to two quite different activities. The first is a form of entertainment. If there were not a great pool of individuals who find reading a pleasure in itself, writers would have no function. But for the writers themselves, *reading* is also a professional act. Some, for example, cannot read without a pencil in their hand; others keep notes on stories and novels they have found effective. Unlike casual readers, they are often willing to study work they don't really enjoy if a technique is being used which seems interesting or valuable. This does not mean that there is no pleasure in reading; it means only that the pleasure stems from personal growth rather than the immediate experience.

At first, writers of fiction, like poets, have a problem knowing what to read. Anthologies provide a good, initial step. They will introduce you to the best of the past thirty or so years. It will help if you keep a literary journal and record at least briefly your impressions (and a bit of the plot) of stories you found effective. Be sure to include where the stories were published so that you can refer to them later.

More recent short stories can be found in two annual collections, the *O. Henry Prize Stories* and *The Best American Short Stories*. These can be found in almost every library and can be ordered through your bookstore. In addition, the University of Illinois Press has been publishing four volumes of paperback collections (one author to each collection) since 1975. A list of these can be obtained by writing to the publisher, and individual volumes can be ordered directly or through your bookstore.

As for magazines, there are the major sources of fiction like *The New Yorker* (two stories a week, 52 weeks a year) and *The Atlantic*. Then there are about one hundred little magazines of which some, like the *North American Review* and *Antaeus,* publish three or more stories in most issues. Start by reading the fiction in whatever magazines are available in your library. Then subscribe. When you have your own copy of the magazine you will be sure to read it, will be free to mark it up, and will have it for reference.

Writers of fiction are even more isolated than poets. They do not have regular access to anything like poetry readings, and they are less likely to find individuals who are willing to read and criticize their work. But they are in touch through their published work.

If you decide to invest your time and energy in writing fiction, make sure you invest at least as much time in reading what others have written. If you value fiction, the cost of books and subscriptions is far from excessive. Your development as a writer will depend in large measure on how active and perceptive you are as a reader.

Part 3
The Writing of Drama

Chapter 25

Theater: A Live Performance

Drama as a "live" performance; the special attributes of drama: its dramatic impact, visual quality, its appeal to the ear, the fact that it is physically produced and is a continuous art performed for spectators; getting started with a concept, primary characters, and an outline of plot.

The transition from writing fiction to writing plays is not as great as one might think. Both depend heavily on plot. Both reveal character through action and dialogue. Both are presented with a distinctive tone and are unified with some kind of central concern or theme.

The primary difference, however, is that a play is a "live" performance. It is produced physically in front of an audience and is performed by actors. This is theater's greatest asset and explains why it is flourishing today in spite of competition with film and television.

Ever since the first "talking movie," critics have predicted the end of legitimate theater. But not even the competition of television has slowed the constant growth of new theaters. Many middle-sized cities have resident companies which have been formed within the past ten years, and this activity has been augmented with university theater programs of high quality. It is clear from this growing activity that there is a genuine need for performances given by actors on a stage.

Every genre has its special attributes—qualities which distinguish it fundamentally from other forms of writing. It is a mistake to think of a play as fiction acted out on the stage or as a poem performed or as a low-budget version of film. It is none of these things. Before you begin writing your first play script, consider carefully what the special characteristics of the genre are.

THE SPECIAL ATTRIBUTES OF DRAMA

The unique qualities of drama stem from the fact that the genre is intended to be a live performance. You will be able to find plays which do not contain one or two of the following characteristics just as some poems can be found which make little use of rhythm and some stories are written without dialogue. Clearly these are not rules; they are merely recurring characteristics. Most playwrights consider them the assets of the genre.

First, drama is by definition a *dramatic art*. That is, it generally has an emotional impact or force. In the case of comedy, we call it vitality. This is not just a tradition; it is a natural aspect of an art form which requires an audience to give its undivided attention for two-and-a-half to three hours.

This impact is often established early in a play with a *dramatic question* which seizes the attention of the audience long before the theme becomes evident. Dramatic questions are usually blunt and simple: Is this stranger a threat? Whom are they waiting for? Why do these characters hate each other? In most cases, these initial questions develop into specific conflicts. Although the need for tension like this is not as strong in very short plays and in comedies, it is usually greater in drama than in either fiction or poetry.

As in fiction, irony and satire often add to the dramatic aspect of a play. And still another device is the use of shock. Unusual or violent situations can explode where the audience least expects them.

Dramatic impact is hard to sustain, however. For this reason, most plays work up to a series of peaks, allowing the emotions of the audience to rest in between. This system of rising and falling action does not follow any prescribed pattern and is often intuitive on the part of the playwright—just as it is in the writing of short stories. But the need for such structure tends to make drama more sharply divided into scenes and acts, divisions which help to control the dramatic impact.

Second, drama is a *visual art*. Action on the stage is usually a significant and an organic part of the whole production. It is not enough in the twentieth century to have characters simply walk back and forth reciting poetry as they did in the highly stylized tradition of Greek theater. In most cases, the movement of characters on the stage is as important as the lines themselves.

And the visual concern extends beyond the characters. The set itself is often another important part of the production. Sophisticated lighting boards can convert the set from a static backdrop to a dynamic factor in developing the moods of each scene. The addition of projected images and even movie sequences—experiments in mixed media—offers one more appeal to the visual aspect of theater.

Third, drama is an *auditory art*. It appeals to the ear. Except for stage directions, every word is dialogue and intended to be spoken out loud. The sound of those lines becomes very important. In some respects, this brings playwrights closer to poets than to writers of fiction. Playwrights often read their lines out loud or have others read them, listening to the composition rather than studying it on the page.

This special attention to the sound of language applies as much to plays which are in the tradition of realism as to those which create the dreamlike distortions of expressionism. Not only are the sounds important, but the space between the lines can be utilized. In Harold Pinter's work, for example, the pauses are occasionally as important as the lines themselves.

Fourth, drama is a *physically produced art*. At first, this may seem like a limitation—sets have to be constructed with wood and nails, and there is not the freedom to shift from scene to scene as quickly or as frequently as there is in fiction and film. But there are compensating assets in the impact of live performers. Regardless of whether a play is realistic or expressionistic, it has a kind of intense credibility. And it offers a variety of techniques which bring actors into the audience and blur the distinction between performers and spectators, approaches which are simply not possible in any other genre, including cinema.

Fifth, drama is a *continuous art*. Members of the audience, unlike readers of fiction or poetry, must receive the play at whatever pace the playwright sets. They cannot linger on a sage observation or a moving episode. They cannot turn back a page or review an earlier scene.

Again, this characteristic does not make the genre "better" or "worse" than others. But as you get into playwriting you will find that this is an aspect which you can utilize. There is a certain momentum in a play and you can make use of this, knowing that your work will be taken in at a single sitting and at exactly the pace you determine. With practice, you can make one portion of a scene move rapidly and another move slowly.

This means, of course, that you have to be far more conscious of pace than you were when writing fiction. A slow scene which is extended just a bit too long can do real damage.

Finally, and closely connected, is the fact that drama is a *spectator art*. Even more than with spectator sports, audience reaction is important. Poets are relatively far removed from such concerns. It is rare indeed for poets to change lines of their verse because of critical reviews or poor public response. Novelists are slightly more susceptible to "audience" reaction. Their circle of readers is potentially larger than a poet's and authors tend to be aware of this. Many novelists will make fairly extensive revisions on the basis of their editors' suggestions. Usually, however, the publication of the work marks the end of the revisions process.

Not so with plays. Playwrights often revise when their work is in rehearsal and after the opening-night reviews and even later if changes seem necessary. They frequently base their revisions on audience reaction—those awful moments when it laughs at the wrong moment or collectively squirms with boredom.

This does not mean that dramatists are slaves to the reactions of audiences and critics. In most cases playwrights have a basic conception of the work which remains unalterable. But there is a direct and dynamic relationship between playwrights and their audiences. For many, this is one of the real pleasures in writing for the legitimate stage.

GETTING STARTED

Poems frequently begin with an image and stories with a character in a situation. Plays more often begin with what is called *a concept.*

A dramatic concept includes a basic situation, some type of conflict or struggle, and an outcome all in capsule form. You can, of course, start a play as tentatively as you might begin a story, hoping to shape and develop the plot as you work through the first draft. But such an approach is generally not as successful in playwriting because so much depends on the whole dramatic structure.

Plays, like stories, often evolve from personal experience, but the need to create a dramatic situation involving conflict or struggle between two or more people often requires metamorphosing of the original episode from the start. Although this is a risky generalization, it is probably fair to say that plays tend to be less closely tied to direct personal experience than stories. In any case, you should feel free to explore newspaper stories and accounts told to you about individuals you have not met, as long as the situation is familiar enough for you to make it appear authentic.

If you keep a literary journal, it helps to jot down a number of possible concepts. And if one seems to take shape in your mind, add the name and a brief description of one or two characters. Actually giving these characters names at the outset will help stimulate your imagination.

Next, try some sample dialogue. It helps if you can begin to hear two characters interact. See if you can create a little scene which at least roughly contributes to the concept you have in mind. Read the lines out loud. Imagine actors (male or female) saying those lines. Close your eyes and visualize the scene.

If you have done all this and you still feel that the concept has potential, begin to block out the action. This is quite different from the approach you may have used in fiction. Needless to say, there is no one approach and whatever works is fine; but the reason many playwrights block out the action at this point has a good deal to do with the nature of the genre.

Even if you are writing a one-act play with a single set—which is a good pattern to start with—you will want to think in terms of "scenes." I will have more to say about this in the chapter on plot (Chapter 27), but essentially a dramatic scene is a unit of action and dialogue which begins and ends with a character coming on stage or leaving. Some short plays have been written without these subtle but important divisions, but they are rare. *Hello Out There,* which is presented as the next chapter, is an excellent example. When you read it, mark these divisions and see how they provide structure for the play.

As for the form of the script, follow the pattern used by the two plays included in this volume. It may seem monotonous to you at first repeating the name of each speaker, but it is the customary practice and one which actors depend on in rehearsal. Stage directions are written in italics (underlined when you are typing). Place them in parentheses when they are short. It is helpful to include the names of characters after the title, listing them in order of appearance.

There are two plays included in this section. The first is serious and realistic while the second is fanciful, frequently comic, with elements of expressionism. These sharply contrasting plays should assure you that you have enormous latitude when it comes to tone.

Getting started, then, involves finding a good concept, creating vivid characters, fleshing them out with some samples of dialogue, and then blocking out the action by outlining a plot in the form of scenes. Keep in mind, however, that what you are writing down is not primarily a work to be read on the page. You are creating a live performance for a live audience. Make their experience a memorable one.

Chapter 26

A Play by William Saroyan

Hello Out There

For George Bernard Shaw

Characters:

A YOUNG MAN
A GIRL
A MAN
TWO OTHER MEN
A WOMAN

Scene: There is a fellow in a small-town prison cell, tapping slowly on the floor with a spoon. After tapping half a minute, as if he were trying to telegraph words, he gets up and begins walking around the cell. At last he stops, stands at the center of the cell, and doesn't move for a long time. He feels his head, as if it were wounded. Then he looks around. Then he calls out dramatically, kidding the world.

YOUNG MAN: Hello—out there! (*Pause.*) Hello—out there! Hello—out there! (*Long pause.*) Nobody out there. (*Still more dramatically, but more comically, too.*) Hello—out there! Hello—out there!

A GIRL'S VOICE is heard, very sweet and soft.

THE VOICE: Hello.
YOUNG MAN: Hello—out there.
THE VOICE: Hello.
YOUNG MAN: Is that you, Katey?
THE VOICE: No—this here is Emily.
YOUNG MAN: Who? (*Swiftly.*) Hello out there.
THE VOICE: Emily.
YOUNG MAN: Emily who? I don't know anybody named Emily. Are you that
                girl I met at Sam's in Salinas about three years ago?
THE VOICE: No—I'm the girl who cooks here. I'm the cook. I've never been
                in Salinas. I don't even know where it is.
YOUNG MAN: Hello out there. You say you cook here?
THE VOICE: Yes.
YOUNG MAN: Well, why don't you study up and learn to cook? How come I
                don't get no jello or anything good?
THE VOICE: I just cook what they tell me to. (*Pause.*) You lonesome?
YOUNG MAN: Lonesome as a coyote. Hear me hollering? Hello out there!
THE VOICE: Who you hollering to?
YOUNG MAN: Well—nobody, I guess. I been trying to think of somebody to
                write a letter to, but I can't think of anybody.
THE VOICE: What about Katey?
YOUNG MAN: I don't know anybody named Katey.
THE VOICE: Then why did you say, Is that you, Katey?
YOUNG MAN: Katey's a good name. I always did like a name like Katey. I
                never *knew* anybody named Katey, though.
THE VOICE: *I* did.
YOUNG MAN: Yeah? What was she like? Tall girl, or little one?
THE VOICE: Kind of medium.
YOUNG MAN: Hello out there. What sort of a looking girl are *you?*
THE VOICE: Oh, I don't know.
YOUNG MAN: Didn't anybody ever tell you? Didn't anybody ever talk to you
                that way?
THE VOICE: What way?
YOUNG MAN: You know. Didn't they?
THE VOICE: No, they didn't.
YOUNG MAN: Ah, the fools—they should have. I can tell from your voice
                you're O.K.
THE VOICE: Maybe I am and maybe I ain't.
YOUNG MAN: I never missed yet.
THE VOICE: Yeah, I know. That's why you're in jail.
YOUNG MAN: The whole thing was a mistake.
THE VOICE: They claim it was rape.
YOUNG MAN: No—it wasn't.
THE VOICE: That's what they claim it was.
YOUNG MAN: They're a lot of fools.
THE VOICE: Well, you sure are in trouble. Are you scared?
YOUNG MAN: Scared to death. (*Suddenly.*) Hello out there!
THE VOICE: What do you keep saying that for all the time?

YOUNG MAN: I'm lonesome. I'm as lonesome as a coyote. (*A long one.*) Hello—out there!

THE GIRL *appears, over to one side. She is a plain girl in plain clothes.*

THE GIRL: I'm kind of lonesome, too.
YOUNG MAN   (*turning and looking at her*): Hey—No fooling? Are you?
THE GIRL: Yeah—I'm almost as lonesome as a coyote myself.
YOUNG MAN: Who *you* lonesome for?
THE GIRL: I don't know.
YOUNG MAN: It's the same with me. The minute they put you in a place like this you remember all the girls you ever knew, and all the girls you didn't get to know, and it sure gets lonesome.
THE GIRL: I bet it does.
YOUNG MAN: Ah, it's awful. (*Pause.*) You're a pretty kid, you know that?
THE GIRL: You're just talking.
YOUNG MAN: No, I'm not just talking—you *are* pretty. Any fool could see that. You're just about the prettiest kid in the whole world.
THE GIRL: I'm not—and you know it.
YOUNG MAN: No—you are. I never saw anyone prettier in all my born days, in all my travels. I knew Texas would bring me luck.
THE GIRL: Luck? You're in jail, aren't you? You've got a whole gang of people all worked up, haven't you?
YOUNG MAN: Ah, that's nothing. I'll get out of this.
THE GIRL: Maybe.
YOUNG MAN: No, I'll be all right—*now*.
THE GIRL: What do you mean—now?
YOUNG MAN: I mean after seeing you. I got something now. You know for a while there I didn't care one way or another. Tired. (*Pause.*) Tired of trying for the best all the time and never getting it. (*Suddenly.*) Hello out there!
THE GIRL: Who you calling now?
YOUNG MAN: You.
THE GIRL: Why, I'm right here.
YOUNG MAN: I know. (*Calling.*) Hello out there!
THE GIRL: Hello.
YOUNG MAN: Ah, you're sweet. (*Pause.*) I'm going to marry *you*. I'm going away with *you*. I'm going to take you to San Francisco or some place like that. I *am*, now. I'm going to win myself some real money, too. I'm going to study 'em real careful and pick myself some winners, and we're going to have a lot of money.
THE GIRL: Yeah?
YOUNG MAN: Yeah. Tell me your name and all that stuff.
THE GIRL: Emily.
YOUNG MAN: I know that. What's the rest of it? Where were you born? Come on, tell me the whole thing.
THE GIRL: Emily Smith.

YOUNG MAN:	Honest to God?
THE GIRL:	Honest, That's my name—Emily Smith.
YOUNG MAN:	Ah, you're the sweetest girl in the whole world.
THE GIRL:	Why?
YOUNG MAN:	I don't know why, but you are, that's all. Where were you born?
THE GIRL:	Matador, Texas.
YOUNG MAN:	Where's that?
THE GIRL:	Right here.
YOUNG MAN:	Is this Matador, Texas?
THE GIRL:	Yeah, it's Matador. They brought you here from Wheeling.
YOUNG MAN:	Is that where I was—Wheeling?
THE GIRL:	Didn't you even know what town you were in?
YOUNG MAN:	All towns are alike. You don't go up and ask somebody what town you're in. It doesn't make any difference. How far away is Wheeling?
THE GIRL:	Sixteen or seventeen miles. Didn't you know they moved you?
YOUNG MAN:	How could I know, when I was out—cold? Somebody hit me over the head with a lead pipe or something. What'd they hit me for?
THE GIRL:	Rape—that's what they *said*.
YOUNG MAN:	Ah, that's a lie. (*Amazed, almost to himself.*) She wanted me to give her money.
THE GIRL:	Money?
YOUNG MAN:	Yeah, if I'd have known she was a woman like that—well, by God, I'd have gone on down the street and stretched out in a park somewhere and gone to sleep.
THE GIRL:	Is that what she wanted—money?
YOUNG MAN:	Yeah. A fellow like me hopping freights all over the country, trying to break his bad luck, going from one poor little town to another, trying to get in on something good somewhere, and she asks for money. I thought she was lonesome. She *said* she was.
THE GIRL:	Maybe she was.
YOUNG MAN:	She was *something*.
THE GIRL:	I guess I'd never see you, if it didn't happen, though.
YOUNG MAN:	Oh, I don't know—maybe I'd just mosey along this way and see you in this town somewhere. I'd recognize you, too.
THE GIRL:	Recognize me?
YOUNG MAN:	Sure, I'd recognize you the minute I laid eyes on you.
THE GIRL:	Well, who would I be?
YOUNG MAN:	Mine, that's who.
THE GIRL:	Honest?
YOUNG MAN:	Honest to God.
THE GIRL:	You just say that because you're in jail.
YOUNG MAN:	No, I mean it. You just pack up and wait for me. We'll highroll the hell out of here to Frisco.
THE GIRL:	You're just lonesome.

YOUNG MAN: I been lonesome all my life—there's no cure for that—but you and me—we can have a lot of fun hanging around together. You'll bring me luck. I know it.

THE GIRL: What are you looking for luck for all the time?

YOUNG MAN: I'm a gambler. I don't work. I've *got* to have luck, or I'm a bum. I haven't had any decent luck in years. Two whole years now—one place to another. Bad luck all the time. That's why I got in trouble back there in Wheeling, too. That was no accident. That was my bad luck following me around. So here I am, with my head half busted. I guess it was her old man that did it.

THE GIRL: You mean her father?

YOUNG MAN: No, her husband. If I had an old lady like that, I'd throw her out.

THE GIRL: Do you think you'll have better luck, if I go with you?

YOUNG MAN: It's a cinch. I'm a good handicapper. All I need is somebody good like you with me. It's no good always walking around in the streets for anything that might be there at the time. You got to have somebody staying with you all the time—through winters when its cold, and springtime when it's pretty, and summertime when it's nice and hot and you can go swimming—through *all* the times—rain and snow and all the different kinds of weather a man's got to go through before he dies. You got to have somebody who's right. Somebody who knows you, from away back. You got to have somebody who even knows you're wrong but likes you just the same. I know I'm wrong, but I just don't want anything the hard way, working like a dog, or the *easy* way, working like a dog—working's the hard way and the easy way both. All I got to do is beat the price, always—and then I don't feel lousy and don't hate anybody. If you go along with me, I'll be the finest guy anybody ever saw. I won't be wrong any more. You know when you get enough of that money, you *can't* be wrong any more—you're right because the money says so. I'll have a lot of money and you'll be just about the prettiest, most wonderful kid in the whole world. I'll be proud walking around Frisco with you on my arm and people turning around to look at us.

THE GIRL: Do you think they will?

YOUNG MAN: Sure they will. When I get back in some decent clothes, and you're on my arm—well, Katey, they'll turn around and look, and they'll see something, too.

THE GIRL: Katey?

YOUNG MAN: Yeah—that's your name from now on. You're the first girl I ever called Katey. I've been saving it for you. O.K.?

THE GIRL: O.K.

YOUNG MAN: How long have I been here?

THE GIRL: Since last night. You didn't wake up until late this morning, though.

YOUNG MAN: What time is it now? About nine?

THE GIRL: About ten.

YOUNG MAN: Have you got the key to this lousy cell?

THE GIRL: No. They don't let me fool with any keys.

YOUNG MAN: Well, can you get it?

THE GIRL: No.

YOUNG MAN: Can you *try*?

THE GIRL: They wouldn't let me get near any keys. I cook for this jail, when they've got somebody in it. I clean up and things like that.

YOUNG MAN: Well, I want to get out of here. Don't you know the guy that runs this joint?

THE GIRL: I know him, but he wouldn't let you out. They were talking of taking you to another jail in another town.

YOUNG MAN: Yeah? Why?

THE GIRL: Because they're afraid.

YOUNG MAN: What are they afraid of?

THE GIRL: They're afraid these people from Wheeling will come over in the middle of the night and break in.

YOUNG MAN: Yeah? What do they want to do that for?

THE GIRL: Don't *you* know what they want to do it for?

YOUNG MAN: Yeah, I know all right.

THE GIRL: Are you scared?

YOUNG MAN: Sure I'm scared. Nothing scares a man more than ignorance. You can argue with people who ain't fools, but you can't argue with fools—they just go to work and do what they're set on doing. Get me out of here.

THE GIRL: How?

YOUNG MAN: Well, go get the guy with the key, and let me talk to him.

THE GIRL: He's gone home. Everybody's gone home.

YOUNG MAN: You mean I'm in this little jail all alone?

THE GIRL: Well—yeah—except me.

YOUNG MAN: Well, what's the big idea—doesn't anybody stay here all the time?

THE GIRL: No, they go home every night. I clean up and then I go, too. I hung around tonight.

YOUNG MAN: What made you do that?

THE GIRL: I wanted to talk to you.

YOUNG MAN: Honest? What did you want to talk about?

THE GIRL: Oh, I don't know. I took care of you last night. You were talking in your sleep. You liked me, too. I didn't think you'd like me when you woke up, though.

YOUNG MAN: Yeah? Why not?

THE GIRL: I don't know.

YOUNG MAN: Yeah? Well, you're wonderful, see?

THE GIRL: Nobody ever talked to me that way. All the fellows in town—(*Pause.*)

YOUNG MAN: What about 'em? (*Pause.*) Well, what about 'em? Come on—tell me.

THE GIRL: They laugh at me.

YOUNG MAN: Laugh at *you?* They're fools. What do they know about any-
                thing? You go get your things and come back here. I'll take
                you with me to Frisco. How old are you?
THE GIRL: Oh, I'm of age.
YOUNG MAN: How old are you—Don't lie to me! Sixteen?
THE GIRL: I'm seventeen.
YOUNG MAN: Well, bring your father and mother. We'll get married before
                we go.
THE GIRL: They wouldn't let me go.
YOUNG MAN: Why not?
THE GIRL: I don't know, but they wouldn't. I know they wouldn't.
YOUNG MAN: You go tell your father not to be a fool, see? What is he, a
                farmer?
THE GIRL: No—nothing. He gets a little relief from the government be-
                cause he's supposed to be hurt or something—his side hurts,
                he says. I don't know what it is.
YOUNG MAN: Ah, he's a liar. Well, I'm taking you with me, see?
THE GIRL: He takes the money I earn, too.
YOUNG MAN: He's got no right to do that.
THE GIRL: I know it, but he does it.
YOUNG MAN   (*almost to himself*): This world stinks. You shouldn't have been
                born in this town, anyway, and you shouldn't have had a man
                like that for a father, either.
THE GIRL: Sometimes I feel sorry for him.
YOUNG MAN: Never mind feeling sorry for him. (*Pointing a finger.*) I'm going
                to talk to your father some day. I've got a few things to tell that
                guy.
THE GIRL: I know you have.
YOUNG MAN   (*suddenly*): Hello—out there! See if you can get that fellow
                with the keys to come down and let me out.
THE GIRL: Oh, I couldn't.
YOUNG MAN: Why not?
THE GIRL: I'm nobody here—they give me fifty cents every day I work.
YOUNG MAN: How much?
THE GIRL: Fifty cents.
YOUNG MAN   (*to the world*): You see? They ought to pay money to *look* at you.
                To breathe the *air* you breathe. I don't know. Sometimes I fig-
                ure it never is going to make sense. Hello—out there! I'm
                scared. You try to get me out of here. I'm scared them fools
                are going to come here from Wheeling and go crazy, thinking
                they're heroes. Get me out of here, Katey.
THE GIRL: I don't know what to do. Maybe I could break the door down.
YOUNG MAN: No, you couldn't do that. Is there a hammer out there or any-
                thing?
THE GIRL: Only a broom. Maybe they've locked the broom up, too.
YOUNG MAN: Go see if you can find anything.
THE GIRL: All right. (*She goes.*)
YOUNG MAN: Hello—out there! Hello—out there! (*Pause.*) Hello—out
                there! Hello-out there! (Pause.) Putting me in jail. (*With con-*

tempt.) Rape! Rape? *They* rape everything good that was ever born. His side hurts. They laugh at her. Fifty cents a day. Little punk people. Hurting the only good thing that ever came their way. (*Suddenly.*) Hello—out there!

THE GIRL (*returning*): There isn't a thing out there. They've locked everything up for the night.

YOUNG MAN: Any cigarettes?

THE GIRL: Everything's locked up—all the drawers of the desk, all the closet doors—everything.

YOUNG MAN: I ought to have a cigarette.

THE GIRL: I could get you a package maybe, somewhere. I guess the drug store's open. It's about a mile.

YOUNG MAN: A mile? I don't want to be alone that long.

THE GIRL: I could run all the way, and all the way back.

YOUNG MAN: You're the sweetest girl that ever lived.

THE GIRL: What kind do you want?

YOUNG MAN: Oh, any kind—Chesterfields or Camels or Lucky Strikes—any kind at all.

THE GIRL: I'll go get a package. (*She turns to go.*)

YOUNG MAN: What about the money?

THE GIRL: I've got some money. I've got a quarter I been saving. I'll run all the way. (*She is about to go.*)

YOUNG MAN: Come here.

THE GIRL (*going to him*): What?

YOUNG MAN: Give me your hand. (*He takes her hand and looks at it, smiling. He lifts it and kisses it.*) I'm scared to death.

THE GIRL: I am, too.

YOUNG MAN: I'm not lying—I don't care what happens to me, but I'm scared nobody will ever come out here to this Godforsaken broken-down town and find you. I'm scared you'll get used to it and not mind. I'm scared you'll never get to Frisco and have 'em all turning around to look at you. Listen—go get me a gun, because if they come, I'll kill 'em! They don't understand. Get me a gun!

THE GIRL: I could get my father's gun. I know where he hides it.

YOUNG MAN: Go get it. Never mind the cigarettes. Run all the way. (*Pause, smiling but seriously.*) Hello, Katey.

THE GIRL: Hello. What's *your* name?

YOUNG MAN: Photo-Finish is what they *call* me. My races are always photo-finish races. You don't know what that means, but it means they're very close. So close the only way they can tell which horse wins is to look at a photograph after the race is over. Well, every race I bet turns out to be a photo-finish race, and my horse never wins. It's my bad luck, all the time. That's why they call me Photo-Finish. Say it before you go.

THE GIRL: Photo-Finish.

YOUNG MAN: Come here. (THE GIRL *moves close and he kisses her.*) Now, hurry. Run all the way.

THE GIRL: I'll run. (THE GIRL *turns and runs. The YOUNG MAN stands*

	at the center of the cell a long time. THE GIRL *comes running back in. Almost crying.*) I'm afraid. I'm afraid I won't see you again. If I come back and you're not here, I—
YOUNG MAN:	Hello—out there!
THE GIRL:	It's so lonely in this town. Nothing here but the lonesome wind all the time, lifting the dirt and blowing out to the prairie. I'll stay *here.* I won't *let* them take you away.
YOUNG MAN:	Listen, Katey. Do what I tell you. Go get that gun and come back. Maybe they won't come tonight. Maybe they won't come at all. I'll hide the gun and when they let me out you can take it back and put it where you found it. And then we'll go away. But if they come, I'll kill 'em! Now, hurry—
THE GIRL:	All right. (*Pause.*) I want to tell you something.
YOUNG MAN:	O.K.
THE GIRL	(*very softly*): If you're not here when I come back, well, I'll have the gun and I'll know what to do with it.
YOUNG MAN:	You know how to handle a gun?
THE GIRL:	I know how.
YOUNG MAN:	Don't be a fool. (*Takes off his shoe, brings out some currency.*) Don't be a fool, see? Here's some money. Eighty dollars. Take it and go to Frisco. Look around and find somebody. Find somebody alive and halfway human, see? Promise me—if I'm not here when you come back, just throw the gun away and get the hell to Frisco. Look around and find somebody.
THE GIRL:	I don't *want* to find anybody.
YOUNG MAN	(*swiftly, desperately*): Listen, if I'm not here when you come back, how do you know I haven't gotten away? Now, do what I tell you. I'll meet you in Frisco. I've got a couple of dollars in my other shoe. I'll see you in San Francisco.
THE GIRL	(*with wonder*): San Francisco?
YOUNG MAN:	That's right—San Francisco. That's where you and me belong.
THE GIRL:	I've always wanted to go to *some* place like San Francisco—but how could I go alone?
YOUNG MAN:	Well, you're not alone any more, see?
THE GIRL:	Tell me a little what it's like.
YOUNG MAN	(*very swiftly, almost impatiently at first, but gradually slower and with remembrance, smiling, and* THE GIRL *moving closer to him as he speaks*): Well, it's on the Pacific to begin with—ocean water all around. Cool fog and seagulls. Ships from all over the world. It's got seven hills. The little streets go up and down, around and all over. Every night the fog-horns bawl. But they won't be bawling for you and me.
THE GIRL:	What else?
YOUNG MAN:	That's about all, I guess.
THE GIRL:	Are people different in San Francisco?
YOUNG MAN:	People are the same everywhere. They're different only when they love somebody. That's the only thing that makes 'em different. More people in Frisco love somebody, that's all.
THE GIRL:	Nobody anywhere loves anybody as much as I love you.

YOUNG MAN   (*shouting, as if to the world*): You see? Hearing you say that, a man could die and still be ahead of the game. Now, hurry. And don't forget, if I'm not here when you come back, get the hell to San Francisco where you'll have a chance. Do you hear me?

THE GIRL *stands a moment looking at him, then backs away, turns and runs.* The YOUNG MAN *stares after her, troubled and smiling. Then he turns away from the image of her and walks about like a lion in a cage. After a while he sits down suddenly and buries his head in his hands. From a distance the sound of several automobiles approaching is heard. He listens a moment, then ignores the implications of the sound, whatever they may be. Several automobile doors are slammed. He ignores this also. A wooden door is opened with a key and closed, and footsteps are heard in a hall. Walking easily, almost casually and yet arrogantly, a MAN comes in.*

YOUNG MAN   (*jumps up suddenly and shouts at* THE MAN, *almost scaring him*): What the hell kind of a jailkeeper are you, anyway? Why don't you attend to your business? You get paid for it, don't you? Now, get me out of here.

THE MAN: But I'm not the jailkeeper.

YOUNG MAN: Yeah? Well, who are you, then?

THE MAN: I'm the husband.

YOUNG MAN: What husband you talking about?

THE MAN: You know what husband.

YOUNG MAN: Hey! (*Pause, looking at* THE MAN.) Are you the guy that hit me over the head last night?

THE MAN: I am.

YOUNG MAN   (*with righteous indignation*): What do you mean going around hitting people over the head?

THE MAN: Oh, I don't know. What do *you mean* going around—the way you do?

YOUNG MAN   (*rubbing his head*): You hurt my head. You got no right to hit anybody over the head.

THE MAN   (*suddenly angry, shouting*): Answer my question! What do you mean?

YOUNG MAN: Listen, you—don't be hollering at me just because I'm locked up.

THE MAN   (*with contempt, slowly*): You're a dog!

YOUNG MAN: Yeah, well, let me tell you something. You *think* you're the husband. You're the husband of nothing. (*Slowly.*) What's more, your wife—if you want to call her that—is a tramp. Why don't you throw her out in the street where she belongs?

THE MAN   (*draws a pistol*): Shut up!

YOUNG MAN: Yeah? Go head, shoot—(*Softly.*) and spoil the fun. What'll your pals think? They'll be disappointed, won't they. What's the fun hanging a man who's already dead? (THE MAN *puts the gun away.*) That's right, because now you can have some fun yourself, telling me what you're going to do. That's what you came here for, isn't it? Well, you don't need to tell me. I *know* what you're going to do. I've read the papers and I know. They have fun. A mob of 'em fall on one man and beat him, don't they? They tear off his clothes and kick him, don't they? And women and little children stand around watching, don't they? Well, before you go on *this* picnic, I'm going to tell you a few things. Not that that's going to send you home with your pals—the other heroes. No. You've been outraged. A stranger has come to town and violated your women. Your pure, innocent, virtuous women. You fellows have got to set this thing right. You're men, not mice. You're home-makers, and you beat your children. *(suddenly)* Listen, you—I didn't know she was your wife. I didn't know she was anybody's wife.

THE MAN: You're a liar!

YOUNG MAN: Sometimes—when it'll do somebody some good—but not this time. Do you want to hear about it? (THE MAN *doesn't answer.*) All right, I'll tell you. I met her at a lunch counter. She came in and sat next to me. There was plenty of room, but she sat next to me. Somebody had put a nickel in the phonograph and a fellow was singing *New San Antonio Rose*. Well, she got to talking about the song. I thought she was talking to the waiter, but *he* didn't answer her, so after a while *I* answered her. That's how I met her. I didn't think anything of it. We left the place together and started walking. The first thing I knew she said, This is where I live.

THE MAN: You're a dirty liar!

YOUNG MAN: Do you want to hear it? Or not? (THE MAN *does not answer.*) O.K. She asked me to come in. Maybe she had something in mind, maybe she didn't. Didn't make any difference to me, one way or the other. If she was lonely, all right. If not, all right.

THE MAN: You're telling a lot of dirty lies!

YOUNG MAN: I'm telling the truth. Maybe your wife's out there with your pals. Well, call her in. I got nothing against her, or you—or any of you. Call her in, and ask her a few qestions. Are you in love with her? (THE MAN *doesn't answer.*) Well, that's too bad.

THE MAN: What do you mean, too bad?

YOUNG MAN: I mean this may not be the first time something like this has happened.

THE MAN *(swiftly)*: Shut up!

YOUNG MAN: Oh, you know it. You've always known it. You're afraid of your pals, that's all. She asked me for money. That's all she wanted. I wouldn't be here now if I had given her the money.

THE MAN (slowly): How much did she ask for?

YOUNG MAN: I didn't ask her how much. I told her I'd made a mistake. She said she would make trouble if I didn't give her money. Well, I don't like bargaining, and I don't like being threatened, either.

I told her to get the hell away from me. The next thing I knew she'd run out of the house and was hollering. (*Pause.*) Now, why don't you go out there and tell 'em they took me to another jail—go home and pack up and leave her. You're a pretty good guy, you're just afraid of your pals.

THE MAN *draws his gun again. He is very frightened. He moves a step toward the* YOUNG MAN, *then fires three times. The* YOUNG MAN *falls to his knees.* THE MAN *turns and runs, horrified.*

YOUNG MAN: Hello—out there! (*He is bent forward.*)

THE GIRL *comes running in, and halts suddenly, looking at him.*

THE GIRL: There were some people in the street, men and women and kids—so I came in through the back, through a window. I couldn't find the gun. I looked all over but I couldn't find it. What's the matter?

YOUNG MAN: Nothing—nothing. Everything's all right. Listen. Listen, kid. Get the hell out of here. Go out the same way you came in and run—run like hell—run all night. Get to another town and get on a train. Do you hear me?

THE GIRL: What's happened?

YOUNG MAN: Get away—just get away from here. Take any train that's going—you can get to Frisco later.

THE GIRL (*almost sobbing*): I don't want to go any place without you.

YOUNG MAN: I can't go. Something's happened. (*He looks at her.*) But I'll be with you always—God damn it. Always!

He falls forward. THE GIRL *stands near him, then begins to sob softly, walking away. She stands over to one side, stops sobbing, and stares out. The excitement of the mob outside increases.* THE MAN, *with two of his pals, comes running in.* THE GIRL *watches, unseen.*

THE MAN: Here's the son of a bitch!

ANOTHER MAN: O.K. Open the cell, Harry.

The THIRD MAN *goes to the cell door, unlocks it, and swings it open. A* WOMAN *comes running in.*

THE WOMAN: Where is he? I want to see him. Is he dead? (*Looking down at him, as the* MEN *pick him up.*) There he is. (*Pause.*) Yeah, that's him.

Her husband looks at her with contempt, then at the dead man.

THE MAN (*trying to laugh*): All right—let's get it over with.

THIRD MAN: Right you are, George. Give me a hand, Harry.

They lift the body.

THE GIRL (*suddenly, fiercely*): Put him down!
THE MAN: What's this?
SECOND MAN: What are you doing here? Why aren't you out in the street?
THE GIRL: Put him down and go away.

She runs toward the MEN.

THE WOMAN *grabs her.*

THE WOMAN: Here—where do you think *you're* going?
THE GIRL: Let me go. You've no right to take him away.
THE WOMAN: Well, listen to her, will you? (*She slaps* THE GIRL *and pushes her to the floor.*) Listen to the little slut, will you?

They all go, carrying the YOUNG MAN'S *body.* THE GIRL *gets up slowly, no longer sobbing. She looks around at everything, then looks straight out, and whispers.*

THE GIRL: Hello—out—there! Hello—out there!

CURTAIN

Chapter 27

The Dramatic Plot

Choosing a concept; planning scene construction; creating dramatic impact through the use of conflict, dramatic questions, and occasionally shock; varieties of comedy including humor, wit, satire; the use of comic relief.

A good dramatic plot starts with a good concept. As I explained in Chapter 25, a concept includes a basic situation, some type of conflict or struggle, and an outcome. It is far more fruitful to think in terms of a situation involving specific characters than it is abstract ideas because drama, even more than fiction, depends on events.

We can be fairly certain, for example, that in *Hello Out There,* William Saroyan did not start out with a determination to reveal aspects of hypocrisy in society and the fundamental need for individuals to make contact with one another.

The basic concept of *Hello Out There* might be described more like this: "A drifter is held in a small-town jail on a false rape charge. He almost manages to escape with the help of a young woman who is as lonely as he, but a mob, filled with a hypocritical sense of justice, reaches him first and kills him."

Turning from concept to the characters, brief descriptions might read like this: "Young man is a drifter and is genuinely lonely. Has always taken chances (named Photo-Finish). Appears to take advantage of girl to get out of jail, but is sincerely concerned about the plight of her life as well. Does his best to get her to leave town before he is killed."

At this point, you are ready to start outlining the plot.

SCENE CONSTRUCTION

The word *scene* is generally used to describe those divisions which are actually written into many scripts. Frequently they are subdivisions of *acts*.

For the dramatist (and the actor), however, the word *scene* also refers to each unit of action which begins with an entrance or an exit and ends with the next shift of characters on the stage. Those whose introduction to drama has been wholly literary are apt to miss the significance of these *secondary scenes*. But anyone who has had any experience in the production of a play knows how important they are both to the actor and to the playwright.

Occasionally, a secondary scene may have a strong dramatic unity. That is, it may build to a climax which is dramatically punctuated by the departure of one or more characters. Often, the unity is more subtle. It establishes the almost unnoticed rise and fall of action which distinguishes the play which is "interesting" from the play which appears to be "flat" or "dull."

Hello Out There is an excellent example. It is a one-act play presented in one primary scene. There is one stage set and one apparently uninterrupted flow of action. But from a playwright's point of view, the work is divided into eight secondary scenes. Each of these is marked by an exit or entrance and each has an influence on the rise and fall of dramatic impact.

The play opens with a long sequence of dialogue between the man and the girl. But notice how Saroyan maintains interest by keeping the girl off stage for a while. Her arrival marks the beginning of the second secondary scene. The impact of this may be somewhat muted for the reader, but for the audience it is visually a new situation. And Saroyan highlights this in the dialogue itself: "You're a pretty kid, you know that?" and so forth.

The third scene is a very brief one. She goes out to look for tools, and he is left on the stage alone. But it is important because it allows him to lash out vehemently against what he sees as injustice. The fact that he is alone on the stage indicates to the audience that he is speaking his inner conviction. Were it not for this little scene, we might feel that he was cynically lying to the girl simply to save himself.

The fourth scene is one in which Emily and Photo-Finish make the pact to meet in San Francisco. Notice that their relationship has grown with surprising speed. In a story, one might be tempted to spread the action out over the course of a day or so; but Saroyan's dramatic sense leads him to keep the action continuous.

The girl leaves, ending the fourth scene, and there is only a moment of sound effects before a new character suddenly appears on stage. The tension mounts as we learn that this is the angered husband.

The scene builds to new levels when the husband draws his gun, and the scene culminates with three shots. This is the natural termination of the scene, and it is highlighted by the return of the girl.

In the sixth scene, the hero and heroine are alone on the stage. If this were opera, it would be the point where the final duet is sung. As realistic drama, it is a brief, terse, yet at the same time tender moment.

But a problem arises here. How is the playwright going to maintain dramatic interest in that brief yet important section which follows the death of the protagonist? Once again, a new secondary scene is prepared for—the seventh. First the audience hears activity building off stage. Saroyan is careful to include this in his stage directions: "The excitement of the mob outside increases." And then the husband, the wife, and another man all burst in on stage, running. Visually, this is explosive enough to cap even the shooting scene. And it is here that Emily demands that they put the body down—what we can assume is the first dramatically assertive act of her life. And she is slapped to the floor.

The last of these secondary scenes is so brief that it consists of only one line. But to understand just how powerful the device is, imagine the girl delivering that last line with the other characters still on stage, struggling to drag the body off. Emily would be literally upstaged. In addition, her line would be a mere continuation of the preceding dialogue. Having her alone on the stage, probably with a single beam of light on her, isolates the final words. Her plight—now matching that of Photo-Finish at the very beginning of the play—becomes the focal point of the play.

When one first reads a play like this, it is easy to assume that it is one continual flow of action from beginning to end. Such an approach would, of course, be possible. But it would be far more difficult to hold the audience's emotional involvement for that length of time. Exits and entrances in this play provide the basic organizational structure with which the dramatic impact is heightened and lowered and then heightened again in regular succession, holding the audience from beginning to end.

Don't confuse what I am referring to here as secondary scenes with those primary scenes which are designated in the script and which often involve a change in time or locale. Movies, of course, make many rapid shifts like this; but drama on the stage tends to be less fragmentary. This is partly due to the physical difficulty of changing sets. But more than this, there is significant loss of impact every time the continuity is broken. A play cannot flick instantly to a new setting. Even if there is no curtain to drop, there must be a lowering of lights and a pause in the action. The members of the audience shift in their seats and make comments to their friends. Attention has been broken.

To avoid disruptive breaks in the flow of action, many full-length dramas and most short plays maintain a single set and an apparently unbroken flow of action. Exits and entrances provide structure without breaking the attention of the audience.

CREATING DRAMATIC IMPACT

What is going to hold the members of your audience in their seats? When you write fiction you can allow yourself periods of reflection in which the plot moves more slowly. But a play asks an audience to experience the entire performance in one sitting—often in uncomfortable seats. Productions which succeed usually provide some kind of conflict, one or more dramatic questions, and occasionally some form of shock.

Conflict can take many forms just as it does in fiction. Almost always, though, it is presented in terms of individuals pitted against each other rather than a struggle within a single character. Remember that as a dramatist you have very limited access into a character's mind. Monologues can be used sparingly, but they tend to slow the action. The genre thrives on scenes in which two or more individuals are involved in some type of struggle.

This does not necessarily require antagonism. In *Hello Out There* there is an initial struggle between the young man and the girl as he tries to persuade her to find a way of releasing him. There is no hostility involved, but his efforts hold the attention of the audience.

Later, of course, the conflict in that play shifts to the more traditional type—a person pitted against a group. This is augmented by Emily's own struggle to free him and free herself from this town.

When creating conflict, be careful not to indulge in hackneyed situations or allow your characters to turn into clichés. Saroyan skirts on the very edge of some well-used conventions, but notice that he has been careful not to make his hero perfect. Photo-Finish has been an almost-loser for some time and at the beginning of the play there is some question of whether he is trying to use the girl for his own selfish interests. Only the few lines which he speaks when she is off stage assure us that he really does feel compassion for the girl.

As for Emily, she is not the bright and beautiful woman she might have become if the script had been written for a budget film. She is simple, naive, and specifically described as "plain."

Notice too that the man who kills Photo-Finish is far from coldblooded. He seems to be aware of the fact that his wife is a tramp, and just before he shoots he is described as "very frightened."

After you have determined the major pattern of conflict or some type of struggle with which to dramatize your work, consider the value of *dramatic questions*. Most plays—including comedies—provide some type of dramatic question to hold the attention of the audience even before the primary conflict is revealed. As in fiction, the dramatic question arouses curiosity; but in drama the fact that you are dealing with a live audience makes the device even more important.

The opening dramatic question, also known as the *hook,* is important; but most plays move from one question to the next so that the audience is kept wondering about immediate outcomes as well as what the ultimate resolution will be. *Hello Out There* is a good example of how one can create a new question just as an old one has been resolved.

The play begins with a man in jail, and the audience immediately wonders why he is there. What did he do? Should we sympathize with him? Through the girl we begin to get answers to these questions, but at the same time a new cluster of dramatic questions is forming: Will she help him? And if she does, will they succeed? Toward the end of the play, we have a sense of foreboding: It is not likely that the ending will turn out to be happy. But as in all tragedies, we still concern ourselves with the survival of the protagonist. There is for most members of the audience a lingering hope that he will live up to his nickname and win by a photo-finish.

These questions, of course, are not the theme. Saroyan's thematic concern is with the loneliness of individuals; he is comparing life in a small and hostile town with being in jail. Even the wife whose unjust accusation begins the tragedy is described as probably being lonely. I will return to these more subtle aspects of character and theme in later chapters. My concern here is for dramatic questions which tend to be fairly blunt. They are theatrical devices which are important if a play is to hold the attention of the audience.

Looking at the full range of drama from Sophocles to our own decade, there are certain dramatic questions which recur frequently. This does not make the plays redundant; one hardly notices the similarity. But their widespread use does suggest just how important the dramatic question is.

1. *Will he come?* Shakespeare charged the first act of *Hamlet* with this question, applying it to the ghost. More recently, it has been broadened to cover the full length of plays. Clifford Odets' *Waiting for Lefty*, written in the 30s, Samuel Beckett's *Waiting for Godot*, and Harold Pinter's *The Dumb Waiter* all rely heavily on anticipation of a character who never appears. And to some degree, the question is a factor in *Hello Out There* as soon as the threat of a lynching is raised.

2. *Who did it?* This is, of course, the literary version of "Who-dunit?" We find it running the full length of drama from *Oedipus Rex* to Tennessee Williams' *Suddenly Last Summer*. The trial scenes in *The Caine Mutiny Trial* and, in a loose sense, *Tea and Sympathy* and *The Crucible* are simply variations of this. In many cases, of course, the audience knows who is guilty; the dramatic question arises out of the attempt on the part of the *characters* to determine guilt. It is a highly variable device, though the trial scene, when portrayed literally, has become overused.

3. *Will he or she succeed?* This is by far the most used of all dramatic questions. It has been applied both to noble and evil characters alike.

4. *Will he or she discover what we know?* The classic example is *Oedipus Rex* in which the audience is held by the drama of a character gradually discovering terrible truths about himself. It is also a factor in *Othello*. And it has more recently been adapted in plays of psychological self-discovery such as Arthur Miller's *Death of a Salesman*.

5. *Will a compromise be found?* This question has held audiences in such varied plays as *Antigone,* John Galsworthy's *Strife,* and more subtly in Tennessee Williams' *Streetcar Named Desire.* In all three of these examples, by the way, the dramatic question is merged with the theme itself—a connection which none of the other questions have.

6. *Will this episode end in violence?* This is frequently used in contemporary drama. In fact, it is one of the final questions in *Hello Out There.* Even though almost every indication points to a tragic ending, we are still deeply concerned. The plot which hints at a dire result without predicting it is also used in fiction—as we saw in "The Windmill Man."

7. *What's happening?* This is the question most frequently asked of plays in the absurdist tradition. Like dream fiction, these works plunge the audience into a confusing, often inexplicable environment. Playwrights like Pinter, Beckett, Ionesco, and occasionally Albee utilize ambiguity as a dramatic question.

    This is, however, a risky device for the novice. Like free verse, it seems easy at first but often slides into meaninglessness. Frequently it requires wit or ingenuity of thematic suggestion to keep the play alive. In short, a dull play is not improved by making it an obscurely dull play.

Dramatic questions sustain the reader's interest by arousing curiosity. Another and more violent method of creating dramatic impact is *shock.*

There has been a long tradition of violence on the stage. The Greeks kept their death scenes off stage, but they made use of self-mutilation as in *Oedipus Rex.* The Romans pushed violence of all sorts to an extreme—some plays reaching the level of our own horror films. Elizabethan drama often borrowed some of this taste for death and mutilation from Roman drama.

Contemporary drama seems to be testing the limits once again. If you look at the use of shock in its historical context, however, you will see that it has never taken over drama at any period. Most playwrights are aware that it has its own limits.

Used as the natural development of a dramatic plot, shock can be an effective device. In *Hello Out There,* the death occurs on stage and is in the tradition of Elizabethan tragedies. Notice, however, that it has been prepared for. It comes as a natural and almost inevitable climax to the play as a whole.

Before considering the use of shock in your own work, remember that there is a point at which physical violence no longer provides impact. Audiences have a "turn-off point," and once that is passed, what was intended as shock will result in laughter. It is not just the degree of violence or the frequency, it is also the kind of preparation which is provided. Violence which appears to be used for its own sake or to revive an otherwise banal play tends to reduce the work to the simplest level. The same applies to the excessive use of profanity, obscenity, and nudity. The fact that one *can* exercise these freedoms is important to any dramatist; whether one wants to and, if so, in what manner, is a more subtle matter and rests with the maturity of the writer.

There are, then, a number of ways of creating dramatic impact. They are important if the play is to have energy and vitality. But they are only means to an end and should never be allowed to obliterate the subtleties of theme and character.

THE PLOT IN COMEDY

Comedy also has plot. And it must also hold an audience. It helps to think of comic plots in terms of three closely related and frequently overlapping forms: *humor, wit,* and *satire.*

Humor tends to be warm and appreciative and usually focuses on character. The playwright adopts a fond tone and the audience in a sense laughs *with* the characters rather than *at* them.

Gently humorous plays are often nostalgic, presenting a slightly (and sometimes not so slightly) sentimental view of an earlier or idealized time. The protagonists of such plays are often slightly incompetent—a recent divorcé or divorcée, a kindly alcoholic, or aging spinster sisters. The plots focus on their humorous efforts to straighten out their lives. The outcome is almost always positive since our concept of comedy is one in which disorder is finally remedied and order is reestablished.

Such plays tend to be rather simple in terms of thematic suggestion and in characterization, but they are popular fare both on Broadway and in summer stock. The greatest danger of these comedies (aside from not being funny) is slipping into outright sentimentality or banality.

There is no sharp line dividing humor and wit, but the latter tends to have more bite. It is sharper and often more ingenious. Frequently it stems from the lines themselves rather than situation or character. Playwrights who employ wit are closer to "standup" comics since they depend so heavily on phrasing.

Satire is a form of wit. It involves two basic elements: exaggeration and ridicule. Drama is an excellent medium for satire since the group response of an audience is infectious.

The plot of a satiric play requires special thought. Consider first just what it is that you are satirizing. Is it a personality type or some kind of institution? Once you have defined your intent, it sometimes helps to list all the characteristics which you find objectionable. With this kind of precise information, you are ready to create both characters and plot which ridicule those elements.

Keep in mind that there is a wide range between mild satire, which tends to be subtle and often relatively kindly and, on the other hand, bitter or corrosive satire, which is frequently presented in plots which are wildly exaggerated and farcical. Your play will be more effective if the level of satire remains consistent.

Just as serious drama depends on conflict, dramatic questions, and the occasional use of shock to hold the attention of an audience, a comedy depends on the regular unfolding of a humorous situation or the higher voltage of wit and satire. You will have to keep inventing new material to sustain the comedy and gradually increase the tempo toward the end. Be careful not to peak too early. If the material midway seems more effective than your last scene, see if you can shift the stronger episode to the end so as to strengthen the climax. Pacing is just as important as in tragedy.

In addition to the varieties of comedy, consider the value of comic relief in otherwise serious plays. Light touches here and there or, in longer plays, comic characters used as contrast with the protagonist are often highly effective. Such comic elements are one of the best ways to counter the risk of melodrama in a highly dramatic plot. They also take the pressure off temporarily and keep a play from seeming to peak too early.

Although plot is important in fiction, it is crucial in drama. The importance of plot is somewhat softened in a story by the fact that you can occasionally use exposition and slip into the inner thoughts of a character. But a play is all right out there: action and dialogue is all you have to work with. A lapse in plot development will be painfully evident in production.

But don't let this deter you. On the positive side, plot gives you an opportunity to attract and hold the attention of your audience from start to finish. This direct and charged contact between artist and viewer is one of the special rewards for the playwright.

Chapter 28

A Play by George Dennison

The Service for Joseph Axminster
A Vaudeville Play

Characters:

MISTRESS OF CEREMONIES
BB
RAGE-IN-AGE
STAGEHAND
WC
LISA

The stage is bare except for some cardboard boxes stage left. A paper backdrop painted as by a child of eight depicts a couple of dead trees and some far-off pastures and cows.

    The MISTRESS OF CEREMONIES, *dressed as a hobo, enters right carrying a battered fedora in one hand and some road signs in the other. She stands upstage and holds a sign with an arrow: "Topeka."*

Two elderly tramps enter right, trudging. BB *carries a sack on a stick.* RAGE-IN-AGE *carries a shopping bag. They trudge. The* MC *holds up a sign that says "Dodge City." We hear "whoo ... whoo" and a* TRAIN *comes toward them. The* TRAIN *is a painted cardboard flat about waist high, equipped with a shoulder strap and carried by a stagehand dressed in blue jeans, who also toots a whistle that simulates the mournful whistle of a train.* BB *and* RAGE-IN-AGE *step aside and the* TRAIN *passes off. The* MC *reverses the roadsign. "Dodge City" now lies to the rear. She lowers the sign and moves a few feet away, watching.*

RAGE: (*pulls a piece of paper from his pocket, reads*) Bastinado, blow, cuff, kick, buffet, lash ... (*He is interrupted by a distant train whistle.*) ... castigation, beating, flagellation, pummel, torture, rack, pillory, hanging, electrocution, shooting, decapitation, strangling, crucifixion, impalement, hemlock, tar and feather ...

The TRAIN *crosses, whistling. They jump aside and let it pass.*

RAGE: ... keelhaul, strike, smite, bethwack, wham, thump, thrash, lace, drub, belabor, cowhide, lambaste, flog, scourge, horsewhip, pelt, stone, drown, banish, beat black and blue, sandbag, blackjack.

They trudge.

BB: Who wrote that poem?
RAGE: I did.

They trudge.

RAGE: It's not finished.

They trudge.

RAGE: Wrote it yesterday in that little library, before they kicked me out.
BB: You think if you'd have stayed longer, you might've got to the happy part?
RAGE: You should have come in with me!
BB: I took a nap in the bushes.
RAGE: Well, you should've come in and done some research on that strange disease of yours. Maybe you'd make some progress.
BB: You've got it all twisted around, lad. It's not a disease.
RAGE: Stop calling me *lad*. I'm older than you are.
BB: In the first place, I don't *really* forget. And in the second place, it's not the forgetting that's a problem, it's the remembering. Right now, for example, I can see my father's face as plain as day. And my mother's. The only thing I've forgotten is the vital statistics ... dates of birth and death.
RAGE: And their names.
BB: Yes, I've forgotten their names.
RAGE: And your own name.
BB: Yes, I've forgotten my own name. But that's not a problem. A man is not the same thing as his name. I'm in perfect possession of who I am. In fact, I think I went about it deliberately. I had a technique, I'm sure I did.

RAGE: What was it?

BB: I forget. Are we stopping here?

> RAGE *sets up two old boxes, takes plates, napkins, forks out of his shopping bag.* BB *opens his kerchief pack, revealing a pillow, which he places on one of the boxes. The* MC *puts on the old fedora, runs downstage left and sprawls on the floor.*

BB: I'd rather we found a place with some shelter. I think it might rain. Oh, look at those ugly blackbirds!

RAGE: They're only going south for the winter . . . the bastards. We'll have our lunch and then move on.

> RAGE *produces a can of sardines from his shopping bag, opens it. They begin to eat. A Sousa march blares out of an unseen loudspeaker.* RAGE *and* BB *go on eating, but the* MC *sits up, takes off the hat, and watches the entrance of* WC, *who comes on stepping vigorously to the march. He is dressed in a style of battered pomp, with a homburg or derby. He carries a suitcase and flourishes a cane. As he crosses the stage the music becomes slower and deeper, and his footsteps drag accordingly. He exits and re-enters, walking more slowly still. The music grinds to a halt before he is half-way across the stage.*

> *We hear the mournful whistle of the* TRAIN. *The* TRAIN *enters very rapidly.* WC *leaps aside.*

WC: Pass! Pass, doleful carriage! Pass and be damned! (*Aside to the audience.*) Sick and tired o' these things. About all you see on the railroad tracks. (*He sees the others.*) Great Scott! What's this? An open-air café! A bistro by the tracks! (*He sniffs.*) Sardines! (*He hurries across.*) What ho! Well met! Good day to you, sir. And you, sir. Banquetizing, I see. (*He sniffs, comes front.*) An imposing vista! Municipal garbage dump . . . (*He sniffs*) . . . state prison . . . Allow me to introduce myself.

BB: I've seen you before somewhere, haven't I? Your face is familiar.

WC: In me you behold the figure of the former mayor of the encampment outside of Wichita. Yass. Thank you. Thank you. (*The "thank you's" are gratuitous.*) Three miles outside of Wichita. Perhaps you were there during my incumbency.

BB: I believe I was. Well! Come and join us. There's enough for three.

WC: I shall be with you immediately. (*He turns toward the backdrop, but pauses and speaks an aside, savoring the word.*) . . . incumbency . . .

> *He opens his suitcase. There is nothing in it but a short line to which are pinned two pairs of socks. He attaches the line to the painted trees on the backdrop.*

RAGE: What's the man doing?

BB: He's hanging up his laundry.

WC: Laundry? Laundry? I am running up my flags . . . in case an admiral comes by. (*feels them*) They are still wet . . . and they have not been mended. (*salutes them*) By virtue of the power invested in me, I claim this land for the United States of America. (*comes forward, cane aloft*) In the name of the King, Ronny Reagan. I believe you mentioned sardines.

> *The* MC *claps on the fedora and sprawls face down.*

RAGE: You'll see a fork and a plate in that bag there.
BB: Go find yourself a box, lad, and sit here beside us.

WC locates a box in the pile of junk. He sees the MC's body.

WC: Agh! My God! Come here! Come here! Look!

They come running, napkins flapping from their collars.

RAGE: By God . . . there's a man there.
BB: I don't like the looks of that.

They draw closer.

RAGE: (*kneeling and touching the body*) He's cold.
BB: Turn him over. Aghhh! It's little Joey Axminster!
RAGE: By God, it is.
WC: Little Joe.
BB: There's his pack over there. And look—a tin cup. (*He steps over the body and picks up the cup.*) There's a bit of coffee in it. He keeled over right in the middle of breakfast . . . or lunch . . .
WC: . . . or supper.
BB: Ahhhh . . . what a sad thing.

They gaze at the body for a while in silence.

BB: How the man aged.
RAGE: (*softly*) The man is dead and you say he's aged.
BB: (*softly*) Well, he has aged. Look at the lines on his face.
RAGE: (*softly*) You say he's aged. What will you say when he's buried?
BB: I'll say he's dead.
WC: Little Joe. The last time I saw him was five years ago . . . in Wichita.
BB: I saw him more recently than that. Three years. He was in much better health.

RAGE looks at him sharply.

BB: I mean he looks like he might have been sick! He was always thin . . . but he's wasted away.
WC: (*gravely*) He had a bad diet, that's what the trouble was. Not enough vegetables. Too much candy.
RAGE: Died of candy, is that it? I would say old age myself.
BB: (*reflectively, to* WC) Yes, that peppermint candy. He always had a sack of it. (*imitating a New England accent*) "Would ye like a peppermint? An after-dinner mint?" Wasn't that the way he sounded? Can't you hear him?
RAGE: (*sadly*) They think if they avoid candy they'll live forever.
WC: To tell the truth, I never much liked him. Yet I always looked him up when I was in Wichita, I don't know why.
BB: How sad for a man to die on the road like this . . . so far from . . . from . . .
RAGE: California.
BB: Yes, He was on his way to California, I'll bet . . . to take advantage of the sunshine. There's nothing else out there to take advantage of.

WC: How predictable . . . yet how surprising when it happens . . .

RAGE: Lend me a hand. There's a box over here in this pile of junk. Well, under the circumstances we're his next of kin! The least we can do is dig him in.

They fetch a cardboard box shaped like a coffin and place it center. The MC stands up and stretches, steps into the coffin and sits. WC hands her Little Joe's pack and coffee pot. She places them beside her in the coffin. BB hands her his own pillow and she makes a show of getting comfortable. She lies down out of sight. WC is holding Little Joe's tin cup. He places it in the coffin, beside the body. All three stand silently a moment.

BB: You're supposed to cross his hands on his chest.

WC does so. They regard the effect.

WC: It would be more realistic if we put his hands in his pockets.

BB: It's true . . . he always stood like that, with his hands in his pockets. If you asked him which way the highway was, he'd point it out to you with his nose. We should say a few words while the coffin is open.

All three sit down, conjuring with this thought. Their wooden boxes are in a row upstage of the coffin, so that by leaning forward they can peer into it. They stand and take off their hats. There is an awkward silence.

BB: I'm not really familiar with the proper forms of these things. *(He sits.)*

RAGE: I could never stand funerals. *(He sits.)*

After a moment WC sits.

BB: Funerals, weddings, high school graduations, Armistice Day, Christmas, Fourth of July . . . I'm well acquainted with the things you can't stand.

RAGE: Don't bother me on a day like this! *(He stands.)* "Man, thou art dust." Those are the main words. We should have a book of some kind, something to read from. *(He pulls a newspaper clipping from his pocket, shoves it back in. Takes out the other piece of paper.)* "Blow, cuff, kick, rack, pillory, hanging, electrocution, shooting . . . " *(His voice trails off and he puts it away.)* What we need is a bible or prayer book. "Man, thou art dust." Oh, I hate those words! Damn those words! *(He sits.)* Man, thou art not even dust, thou art absurd! They got you comin' and goin'. Sometimes I wake up and stand at the window and look out at the world, and my God, it just sits there, you'd think it would last forever. Where is time? You can't see it anywhere. Point to it! Where is it? Time does not exist! Same thing at night. I fall asleep and hear all these voices from fifty years ago. Some little girl you never heard of, a little girl named Betty Lou Jenkins, a shameless erotic creature, age ten, says something in my dreams about six times a year, roughly every other month, and I don't even know what she says, but the fact that she says it, I know what that means, it means time is nothing, time does not exist. Except then I wake up. I'm surrounded by time. Time is everywhere. I'm drowning in time. The windows are dusty, the lamp cord is frayed, the paint is peeling, the doorknob is busted, my socks are filthy, my money's all gone. Time, time, time. Do you call this serious? Can you find some meaning in this? *(He shouts into the coffin.)* Axminster, you're lucky to be out of it!

An abashed silence.

BB: One of us . . . should say a few words about Little Joey here.

WC: (*rises*) "Man, thou art dust." (*Tips his hat to* RAGE.) No offense. (*Holds the hat at his breast.*) We are gathered together on this solemn occasion . . . (*aside*) . . . a merely solemn occasion would be a relief . . . (*continuing*) . . . we are gathered together on this catastrophic day . . . (*His eyes drop to the coffin.*) . . . Joseph Axminster. Little Joe. I'll wager there's a handful of peppermint candy in his pocket at this very moment. I asked him once why he ate so much peppermint candy. He replied to me that he ate so much peppermint candy . . . because he liked it. As a matter of fact, I am not an expert on the details of his life. (*He pauses a moment, then sits.*)

We hear the muffled whistle of a distant TRAIN.

BB: (*sitting*) He was part-time cook in the camp outside of Wichita last time I saw him. He specialized in a dish he called the One-Eyed Connelly. He'd take a piece of bread and tear a hole out of the middle. He'd put the bread in the frying pan and break an egg so it cooked in the hole, sunny-side up. That was the One-Eyed Connelly. I asked him once to put two eggs in the hole, and I mistakenly referred to it as a Two-Eyed Connelly. Little Joe corrected me. He said the name of that dish was the Double One-Eyed Connelly.

He had an amazing grasp of world history . . . up to the year 1920. That was the year, as far as I could tell, that he stopped collecting postage stamps. He came from a wealthy family, you know . . . but they threw him out, disowned him. Or maybe he disowned them, I forget which.

The TRAIN *comes by silently.*

WC: I wonder if I might . . . I wonder if while we are sitting here I might sample the sardines?

BB: Oh sure, lad, sure. (*He gives* WC *a plate and fork out of the shopping bag and serves him some sardines. All three eat silently awhile.*)

BB: We're traveling to California.

WC: California! I've been there eighteen times. It's as far west as you can go.

RAGE: Where you bound for?

WC: California. Shall we join forces? Shall we travel *en masse?*

RAGE: We set a fast pace. If you can stand the gaff, you're welcome.

WC: You shall find me willing. And for the most part able. Allow me. (*He gathers the plates, produces a pint bottle from his pocket and pours for them.*) I propose a toast. (*All rise.*) To Joseph Axminster. The truth is, he was a well-known man . . . though he had few friends. To a restless spirit . . . come to rest. (*They drink and sit down.*) Let us say nothing of the place in which he has come to rest.

RAGE: The place is all right. There's no caretaker, that's true. But if you took all the bones out of a place like this, and you took all the bones out of a fancy cemetery like Forest Lawn, and you mixed them all together . . . tell me, do you think the caretaker of Forest Lawn could sort them out? "Man, thou art dust." (*pause*) I've had a run of bad dreams lately. All in color. Last night I dreamt I was running . . . running up and down the streets. I was wearing tennis shoes. It was early summer. I'd go up one street . . . and turn the corner . . . and go down another. Not running fast, just loping. And then I came to this sycamore tree . . . and I ran underneath it . . . and I kept on going . . . down the street . . . and I turned the corner. (*pause*) It put me in a bad mood. I've been in a bad mood all day.

WC: (*uncapping the bottle*) Allow me . . . I myself no longer distinguish between my good moods and my bad moods. Style is everything. Style. (*The bottle is dry.*) Damnation! (*He starts to throw the bottle away, but BB stops him.*)

BB: Whoa! Let's put it here. Yes. Because we drank the toast out of it. I've read somewhere that that was a custom in the ancient days in Egypt. Since we're short on customs, we might as well use it. (*He puts the bottle in the coffin. He glances towards Little Joe's feet, then examines them closely.*) I thought so! He's wearing the shoes I gave him three years ago. Those old brogans that Eddie Riley gave me, that you gave him.

RAGE: (*peering at them*) They pinched me.

BB: It was during that hike to the Grand Convention. He'd worn right through his shoes. Every mile he'd sit down and say, (*imitating*) "I've got a pebble between my toes." We'd walk another mile and he'd sit down again. "I've got a pebble between my toes." I gave the shoes to him. He quizzed me that night about boyhood games. I think his upbringing was very strict. Kick-the-can, capture-the-flag, mumblety-peg . . . I played them all, but he never did. He took a keen interest in what I said.

WC: Kick-the-can . . . Kick-the-can . . . I never played that game myelf. My entire boyhood was spent at the movies . . . "transfixed before the silver screen." Actually, we never paid that much attention. The second balcony. Ah, yes. The dark places . . . the giggling . . . you see before you the living proof that popcorn and penny licorice *will* sustain human life. (*pause*) Astigmatism, constipation, and headaches. (*pause*) Happiness. Little Joe here was a despiser of films. He refused to accompany me one time to a patriotic film entitled *Sink the Bismarck!* He said . . . I remember his exact words . . . (*imitating*) "I get sleepy in the movies and there's no place to lie down."

BB: He was a strange, lonely man, now wasn't he? I don't know what he did with his time. I never saw him reading books or magazines . . . and that's odd, you know, because his background was very interesting. He was an educated man.

WC: Educated! So that was it! (*He gestures at Little Joe.*) Snob! I remember an argument I had with him. I do not remember the subject of the argument, but I remember that I won it. He was a bad loser. He called me a philistine. It is true that I have read only one book in my life. But it is also true that the name of that book is . . . *Don Quixote!* (*Stands. Brandishes cane.*) Stand, cowards! Ignoble creatures! (*He tucks the cane under his arm like a lance and shuffles forward a few steps.*) Windmill scene. I loved the speeches. He was always making speeches. The noble Don. (*cane*) Stand, cowards!(*Takes a stance.*) "I pray thee therefore get up off thy ass, good Sancho, and follow me once more; for God's providence that relieves every creature will not fail us.

Thou seest He even provides for the little flying insects in the air, the wormlings in the earth, and the spawnlings in the water; and in His infinite mercy He makes His sun shine on the righteous and on the unjust."

BB: Amen.

WC: I used to speak that speech in New York . . . when they closed the bars. In fact, I spoke that speech to Little Joey here. It was in Wichita. We heard there was a shortage of human blood at the blood bank . . . the First National Blood Bank of Wichita . . . and we walked three miles to donate—for cash—one pint apiece. They refused us. They returned us out of doors. The authority in charge of that establishment, a man who, according to the nurse who worked under him, so to speak, was divinely inspired, informed us that in the case of Little Joe . . . one pint of blood was very likely all there was. As for me, he suggested . . . he hinted . . . that my blood was tainted with gin. Tainted. I said to him, "Sir, on the open market gin will bring you three dollars a pint!" They turned us out of doors. (sits) Little Joe was glum. We had an argument on the way back and he called me a philistine. I forgive him.

The TRAIN *passes—clanging.*

RAGE: Educated. Studied One-Eyed Connellys, did he?

BB: He wasn't much for work, that's true. He figured out some timetables once for hopping the freights, switching-yard times, and when they stopped for water. He sold them and made a bit of money. They're outmoded now. They're all outmoded . . . like the free-lunch map for the city of New York . . . Ah! Somebody's coming! Somebody's coming up the tracks!

RAGE *runs to the tracks, peers down, comes back to* WC.

RAGE: Are you wanted?

WC: Alas! Hardly at all.

All three peer down the tracks.

BB: It's a woman!

WC: Indeed it is. And if it is not a woman, it is certainly a very strange man.

BB: High-heeled shoes on the railroad ties! Look at the way she wobbles.

RAGE: There's a history in that walk of hers and I can read every page of it. Women! Bah!

WC: For every ill that flesh is heir to, I can give you the name of a woman. Jealousy—Sylvia. Betrayal—Marilyn. Ruined marriages—Martha, Gloria, Jane . . .

BB: Insomnia . . .

WC: Doris!

RAGE: Migraine headaches . . .

WC: Catherine Sue!

RAGE: Women! Bah! I was cursed from the start.

BB: The very start?

The three men take their seats. The MC *gets out of the coffin and stretches.* WC *stands and comes front.*

WC: Ladies and gentlemen, you are about to witness the arrival of the fourth member of our little band, a woman of mature years, but high spirit. Her name is Lisa. Her mission, in this desolate locale, has to do with the state prison . . . to which reference has already been made. (*He indicates the prison, then looks off down the tracks again.*) She has walked the entire distance from town. During the first mile she skipped along and hummed a song from the top ten. During the second mile she rehearsed her plans, she looked for flowers by the tracks and didn't find any; occasionally she whistled. In the third mile she tired, she slowed to a slow walk, and rather quietly but with deep feeling sang the songs of her youth. Since we missed this entire performance, I shall regale you with my own favorite.

He tilts his hat to an angle, plants his cane before him, one hand on the other, and with much tremolo whistles "Moonlight Bay." When the song is ended, all three men rush back to the railroad tracks and peer down them. The MC *claps on the old fedora and lies down in the coffin.*

LISA *enters, purse dangling from one hand, whiskey bottle—unopened—from the other. Her style is feminine, seedy, baroque. She jumps when she sees the men and hurries past them.*

LISA: Out of my way! I've got enough men in my life!
(*She straightens her hat, glances off at the prison.*) I have to wait here for somebody, so don't think I'm . . . selling whiskey or something. (*An attempt at toughness.*) If you'll take my advice you'll clear out!

BB: (*to* WC) We shouldn't be staring at the lady like this.

WC: Indeed we should not. Though frankly I have seen nothing better to stare at for many years. (*He approaches* LISA.) Forgive us, my dear. I assure you we have been gazing not in rudeness but astonishment. I myself have never before seen such a lovely lady walking on the railroad tracks. As for the clearing out . . . I am afraid we cannot . . . (*He gestures to escort her toward the coffin.*) Please.

LISA *looks in the coffin, cries out, jumps back.*

RAGE: Now don't be alarmed. This man was a friend of ours. He passed away . . . right here . . . on the road.

BB: We've been holding a service—in our own way.

LISA: Well, I don't want to interfere. Live and let live. I mean . . . I'll stand over here and you go right ahead.

WC: We would feel honored if you would join us.

LISA: Join you? I can't join you. I'm busy. I mean I'm going to be busy. I mean I only have a minute. (*She glances at her watch.*)

WC: (*taking her aside*) The brevity of your presence will be matched by the eternity of his.

LISA: Oh! How lovely. And sad. I like that combination.

WC *ushers her to the wooden boxes. Each man offers his own.* RAGE *brings another. They all sit. She clutches the whiskey bottle in one hand and the purse in the other, unaware of them.*

LISA: How far did you get? (*She glances at her watch, looks off toward the prison.*)

BB: Are you familiar with the proper forms?

LISA: I remember a bit from my husband's service. He died while I was still in my twenties. If he were alive today, he'd be sixty-five. God knows how old I would be. There's a part at which the minister says, "We brought nothing into this world, and it is certain we can carry nothing out. The Lord gave, and the Lord hath taken away." Oh, that's true, isn't it! And yet we carry on as if we'd live forever. (*Looks at watch, looks toward prison.*) What was your friend's name?

BB: His name was Joseph Axminster. We called him Little Joe . . . because he was tiny . . . as you can see . . .

LISA: I'm getting so nervous. I'm afraid I'll spoil it for you.

RAGE: Why do you keep looking at the prison?

LISA: Because I hate it, that's why!

BANG BANG BANG

LISA: That's him! (*She jumps up, waves the bottle grandly.*) Clear the hell out!

The men cluster at one side. LISA *runs to the other, looking off toward the prison.*

BANG BANG BANG

LISA: He made it! He made it! Run, Louie, run!

BANG BANG BANG

LISA: Faster, Louie, faster!

BANG BANG BANG

LISA: (*turns to the men happily, speaks without exultation, only pleased indulgence*) Louie shot a cop.

BANG BANG BANG

LISA: He shot another one! *The men come closer.*

BANG BANG BANG

LISA: Two that time!

The men rush to her side.

BANG BANG BANG

ALL: Hooray!

BANG BANG BANG

They raise their hats.

ALL: Hooray!

The MC jumps out of the coffin and joins them.

BANG BANG BANG

ALL: Hooray! Hooray!

The TRAIN *comes out.*

BANG BANG BANG

ALL: (*including train whistle*) Hooray! Hooray!

BANG BANG BANG

ALL: Hooray! Hooray!
        BANG BANG BANG

Silence.

ALL: Awwwwww . . . .

Silence.

BB: They caught him.
RAGE: They're taking him back.

A pause.

WC: All that work for nothing.

TRAIN off. LISA staggers back with a cry and faints. The three men kneel beside her. The MC fans her with the old fedora, then comes front.

WC: In such moments as these the resources of the theater are powerless. We beg of you to imagine her anguish and bitter disappointment. But please bear in mind that she is a woman of spirit, and has seen many crises in her life.

LISA sits up. The MC claps on her hat and lies down in the coffin. WC ushers LISA to her seat. All sit as before. LISA is still clutching the bottle. She looks off toward the prison, sniffs, wipes away a tear with the back of her hand.

LISA: (*glancing into the coffin*) How far did you get?
BB: That's hard to say, Lisa. We've just been going along . . . talking over old times, more or less.
LISA: Well . . . tell me about your friend.
RAGE: He traveled back and forth like we do . . . staying here awhile and there awhile . . . and now here.
LISA: I don't know what I can contribute. Perhaps I could give a lecture. I used to be in the rehabilitation line. But lecturing was never my strong point. Maybe it's best if I just sit here and listen.

She notices the bottle, hands it to WC who gives her his own cup and pours for her. The others hold out their cups. He pours, is short a cup, reaches into the coffin and takes Little Joe's. They toast LISA.

BB: To your health.

They drink.

WC: We were speaking, my dear, of the accomplishments of the deceased . . . though his later years were not marked by accomplishment.

BB: I was telling of the timetables he worked out for hopping the freights. And he made a map one time, too, of all the free-lunch saloons in the city of New York. Beside each one he would mark the best time. You see, Lisa, if you came too early the lunch wasn't out yet. And it you came too late, the working men rushed in and cleaned the plates.

LISA: (*looking at Little Joe*) I wouldn't have guessed that he was a practical man. He seems . . . possibly . . . more of a dreamer.

BB: Well, he was both, he was both.

WC: The days of the free lunch! The days when, on a hot summer afternoon, the Third Avenue el cast a benign shadow over the street! (*Rises, paces about.*) New York was relatively poor then, but it was a cornucopia of the free lunch, the national capital of the free lunch, the Imperial Rome of the free lunch! The richer it got the meaner it got. There is scarcely a free lunch to be had now—nothing but plastic-coated pretzels and disgusting contorted wafers referred to humorously as potato chips. Even so, there are things I miss about it.

LISA: (*impressed*) What do you miss?

WC: The prospect of riches! . . . Ha. Yass. (*Points with cane.*) Do you know what I carry in that suitcase?

LISA: Shall I guess?

WC: No! I will tell you. Nothing. Nothing is what I carry in that suitcase. Nothing but these socks you see drying in the sun. (*He feels them.*) They are still wet, and they have not been mended. Lisa!

She jumps up.

WC: (*pointing to suitcase*) That is my estate. These are my flags. I have nothing to offer you but the fact that I am heading west. All I can guarantee is . . . that I will not walk too fast.

LISA: Offer?! Oh, my goodness . . . I hadn't thought at all of traveling . . . though I have no reason to stay . . .

WC: My dear . . . when I saw you coming down the railroad tracks . . .

RAGE: This is no time for autobiographical remarks!

WC: (*to* RAGE) I beg your pardon. (*to* LISA) Think about what I have said.

LISA: I will.

TRAIN comes by with a whistle. WC and LISA sit.

LISA: It's a pity the country here is so barren. We should have some flowers. (*She takes off her hat, removes some artificial flowers, and places them in coffin.*) They are not much. But they are something.

BB: He would appreciate the sentiment. Your mascara is smudged, Lisa. Right here. (*Indicates on himself.*)

LISA: Thank you.

BB: Lisa, imagine a man of unusual peace and serenity, a man with no more memory than a child, one to whom the past is nothing but a cluster of images . . . lovely images.

LISA: (*with interest*) Yes . . . ?

BB: Do you find him interesting?

LISA: Why yes, I believe so. Are you speaking of yourself?
BB: Yes, Lisa, I am that man.

WC *fidgets while the others talk.*

RAGE: Ha ha ha ha ha! If he and I could swap diseases, we'd both be cured! I'm plagued by the past! Plagued by memory! Plagued by dreams! What do you think of that?
LISA: Well . . . it all depends.
RAGE: Of course it depends! I *struggle* with fate. My goal is self-mastery.
LISA: (*toasting him*) Very good. You show strength of character.
RAGE: (*to BB*) You should struggle with yourself on that issue of the past.
BB: Not at all, man, not at all.
RAGE: (*to LISA*) It used to be worse. I used to daydream, too . . . but I fought with myself and I won.
BB: You fought with yourself and you lost.
RAGE: I said I won.
BB: The other guy lost.
RAGE: (*to LISA*) I can tell you the exact date of the last daydream of my life. October second, 1961. I was looking out the window of a furnished room, and I saw a cop jabbing one of the old-timers with his nightstick. I imagined it was me he was jabbing. I imagined they took me down to the station. They got me in a room and pushed me around . . . especially this one man, a man with a bull neck and a red face. I said to him, "I'll fight you fair and square if you'll take off that badge!" He was a good bit bigger than me. The other cops let up a laugh. They made him take his badge off. I was counting on speed. He threw the first punch and I ducked it. I jammed a left under his guard. He dropped his hands and I caught him with a right. He rushed me and cut my lip. I hit him with a combination. He came back and knocked me down. I got up again and jabbed with my left until my head cleared. He hit me a hard one on the shoulder, but I caught him on the chin. He backed away . . . and we circled each other . . . and I heard a voice . . . one of the onlookers, one of the cops. The voice said, "The kid's okay." The kid is okay. At that point my daydream ended. I was still sitting by the window. I got up from the chair and walked around the room . . . and every step I took I could hear that voice. "The kid's okay." I was, at that time, fifty-four years of age. I stood at the mirror and looked at myself, and I said, "Man, come to your senses." And by God I did!
LISA: Bravo! Bravo! You are a man of great warmth and determination. And I quite agree with you on the subject of daydreams. Real life does *not* have much to recommend it, *but*—don't take your eyes off it. (*She sips.*)
RAGE: Lisa . . . let me read you this . . . (*He takes out his newspaper clipping and stands in front of her.*) Dateline: Minneapolis. October eleventh, 1924. "Unvanquished North End High was handed a stunning defeat by the underdog eleven, sparked by the brilliant running . . . " (*He looks up and grunts as he catches a punt; he doubles up and turns slowly in a crouch; he straight-arms a tackler; he runs, spins, sidesteps, straight-arms again, and touches the ball in the end zone. He throws up his arms in victory, goes back to his seat, and stands there a moment staring straight ahead. Sits. He is panting.*) Listen to me. (*He coughs and wheezes.*) In those days my lungs were a furnace. And do you know

what they burned? They burned the whole bloody afternoon is what they burned! All that October air, just that amount of sun, just that amount of chill . . . and the shouts of the admiring throng . . . I breathed it in and burned it up. I'm the wreck of what I was, Lisa, and that's a fact. But there's fire in this wreck!

LISA: Indeed there is! I was spellbound by your enactment of the game. (*She throws up her hands.*) Victory! (*She claps.*) It would be a great mistake to give up memories like those. (*She takes a handkerchief from her sleeve and pats his brow. WC turns away in disgust.*) It has been many years since I have found myself in such company. (*She beams at* RAGE *and* BB, *glances quickly at* WC.)

WC looks at her intently. He takes off his hat, lays down his cane, comes front and beckons to her in a lordly fashion. She stands in front of him. He looks at her a long while, then lifts his arms and moves toward her. As they meet, we hear, at a good volume and from an unseen source, a piano rendition of "The Tennessee Waltz," player-piano style, with a great many trills. He very gallantly whirls her in the waltz. The MC sits up on the edge of the coffin and watches, her hat removed. After WC and LISA have danced awhile, the MC and RAGE form a couple and join them. BB remains seated, but swings his arms to the music. The TRAIN comes in and adds the tinkle of a triangle to the music. After a few moments the TRAIN exits in reverse. The MC sits on the edge of the coffin. RAGE sits down. WC and LISA dance on. The music is momentarily suspended. They freeze in the posture of the dance.

LISA: (*lost in a dream*) Is it true that the streets of California are paved with gold?
WC: My dear . . . nothing about California is true.
LISA: How wonderful.

The music comes back and they dance to the end of the song. He bows to her and she curtsies. He leads her back to the seats. All are sitting in a row as before. The MC is once again out of sight in the coffin. Faintly and flatly, as on a child's xylophone, the refrain of the waltz can be heard. There is an extra "plink," and WC responds as if he had felt a drop of rain. A moment later—without accompanying sound—BB feels a drop. He holds out his hand and looks up.

BB: (*standing*) It's going to rain. I felt a drop. We'd best finish our service and be moving on.
RAGE: It's only a matter of saying good-bye now. That's the heart of it. (*He leans forward, almost shouting into the coffin.*) Good-bye—but not for long . . . (*To the others, almost roughly.*) That's the heart of it. I noticed a shovel in that pile of junk. I mean the remains of one. (*He goes upstage.*)
LISA: How strange! I could never have guessed this morning that I would find myself just here. (RAGE *returns with a broken shovel. She turns her head, studying in the figure of Little Joe.*) There's an upward turn to his lips. Not like he was smiling exactly, but like he was thinking of something for the millionth time.
RAGE: He was like that. He had his thoughts and he kept them to himself. Sometimes you'd say something and he wouldn't reply . . . then he'd chuckle . . . and he'd say, "Eyeh . . . eyeh" to himself.
BB: Yes, that's the way he sounded. "Eyeh . . . eyeh."

WC: "Eyeh."

LISA: His forehead must have been all wrinkled up. I can see where the lines were. It's smoothed-out now. There's something I like about his face . . . something romantic . . . or noble . . . or distinguished.

WC: Romantic?

BB: Noble?

RAGE: Distinguished?

All three look down at him.

LISA: Well . . . I see a young man in his features somehow. A man of about twenty.

BB: He was that age when the family threw him out. I know the whole story. (*with growing agitation*) He was going to Harvard or someplace. There was some girl—I don't quite have that part of it straight. She was a waitress or some such. He was a heavy drinker, dating back to grade school. And he did something crazy in one of the Boston churches . . . something wild . . . drove in a flock of geese at High Mass. Father was always paying damages. Then there was a series of things. I can't think straight. My head's about to split. I'll be damned, I couldn't survive if I had to be normal! (*He moves away from them.*) Everything's coming back to me. Everything's coming back and I can't handle it. (*To* RAGE.) Don't talk to me about it! I know what you're going to say, so be quiet!

Silence for a moment.

BB: I'll show you a technique for blotting out the past. A way of cutting your memories down to a reasonable size. Yes. It's a way of taking all the vital statistics and detaching them from the facts. Take the case of my father. His name was Jonathan. Now that name goes with a certain face, and the face is exactly what it is—a face. It's what I call a *fact*. Now . . . I want to remember the face and *forget all the vital statistics*. Well! Jonathan was married to Claire, my mother, a woman with a lovely face. So I say to myself, "Jonathan was married to Claire and they had a son named Charles." That was my name—Charles. So I repeat it to myself, those vital statistics. "Jonathan was married to Claire and they had a son named Charles." (*He changes his tone and repeats it.*) "Jonathan was married to Claire and they had a son named Charles." It's changing. (*He folds his hands in the manner of a preacher. Still another voice.*) "Jonathan was married to Claire and they had a son named Charles." (*Now in his usual voice.*) The vital statistics are changing slowly into a legend. (*He sits again on his box by the coffin and speaks to them storyteller-fashion.*) Once upon a time a man named . . . (*a gesture of "shall we say?"*) Jonathan . . . was married to a woman called . . . Claire . . . who gave birth to an infant. Now what else could she have given birth to? She gave birth to an infant and they named him—(*He goes blank.*)

RAGE: Charles.

BB: Charles is a good name. (*He gets up and looks into the coffin, as if he has forgotten who is there. Sits again.*) There's a type of Irish face that I really admire. They call them the Black Irish . . . swarthy, with shining eyes and broad cheekbones . . . a great shock of hair . . . a black mustache.

A train whistle is repeated several times, muffled, as in the distance.

LISA: So that's your name? Charles?
BB: Charles?
RAGE: Your name.
BB: I forgot what my name is.
LISA: You were telling us a story about Jonathan, Claire, and Charles.
BB: Yes, I was. And there's a great deal more to it. I'll tell you sometime. We've been neglecting our duty. There's a piece of prayer has come back to me. It's for the side of the grave. The very last moment. (*They all stand at the coffin.*) "Man, that is born of a woman, hath but a short time to live . . . He cometh up and is cut down like a flower . . . We commend the soul of our brother . . . and we commit his body to the ground."
ALL: Amen.
RAGE: (*picking up the shovel*) We'll round it off with hard labor.

A loud peal of thunder is heard and the light flickers and dims, as in a sudden downpour. They begin hopping about, cringing in the rain. They speak in singsong shouts.

RAGE: Owww! It's raining cats and dogs!

The TRAIN comes by, going fast, with a repeated clanging.

RAGE: (*shaking his fist at the sky*) Can't you see we have no shelter?! (*to the others*) It's going down my neck like a river! (*He picks up one of the tin plates and holds it over his head.*) It's like standing in a doorway that's got no building attached! Ha ha ha! I'm drenched!

BB also holds a plate over his head, jiggling back and forth. WC lifts up his suitcase to shield LISA and himself.

RAGE: (*to BB*) If that plate was made of gold, you'd be wearing a halo! You'd swap if for an umbrella, wouldn't you?! There's an inch of mud inside my shoes!

WC drops the suitcase.

WC: Damnation! (*As he picks it up, it flops open.*) Damnation! (*He shows it empty and points to the ground.*) My winter clothes, my jewels, my documents . . . lying in the mud. (*He raises the suitcase over their heads again.*)
RAGE: (*pointing to the clothesline holding WC's socks, shouting across to WC*) They are still wet! And they have not been mended!
WC: Damnation!

LISA walks back to the boxes by the coffin. The others follow her. All sit as before. Lights back to normal.
WC comes front and picks up what appears to be a short stick. It has been visible all along, standing near or among the footlights. He fans it out into a huge sunflower, which he presents to LISA. As he sits beside her again, she rises and fastens the sunflower into brackets at the head of the coffin so that it stands up straight. As she takes her seat, WC comes halfway front and beckons toward the wings. The TRAIN comes out. The train-bearer hands him a towel and continues off.

WC: (*coming forward, dabbing fastidiously at his face*) Ladies and gentlemen . . . good evening. (*He bows.*)

BLACKOUT

When the actors take their curtain call, the MC *plucks the sunflower from the coffin
and carries it off.*

Chapter 29

Characterization

Characterization revealed through *action* and *dialogue;*
the importance of *first impressions;* character *develop-*
ment seen as a shift in attitude or an expansion of our
view; *comic characters* in satire, humor, or as foils.

Characterization in a play is based almost entirely on action and dialogue.
True, "action" can include such subtle devices as a gesture or a change of expression and "dialogue" can include, on occasion, a monologue which resembles thought; and costuming has its effect too. But the major impression
of a character on stage is made by what that character does and what he or
she says to others.

Compare this with the devices available in fiction. In that more flexible
genre you as author can use the character's own thoughts, the thoughts of
others, quick glimpses into the past through flashbacks, and direct exposition. Since the devices available to the dramatist are more limited, the tendency is to use them more boldly.

Audiences are used to this. Just as the makeup is heavier and the voice
louder, characterization is applied more bluntly. It seems natural to use the
word "theatrical" or "dramatic" to describe individuals whose personalities
are vivid or striking.

Although it is possible to analyze action and dialogue separately from a
critical point of view, the playwright deals with them simultaneously. For

this reason it is more useful to examine them together as you do in the writing: introducing new characters and then developing them.

FIRST IMPRESSIONS

When you meet people at a social gathering, first impressions are very important and frequently inaccurate. The first appearance of a character in a play is equally important, and if it is inaccurate in some way make sure that this is intentional and not just misjudgment in the writing.

Take a close look at the way Saroyan introduces Photo-Finish in *Hello Out There*. The character, known then only as "Young Man," is alone on the stage. In a sense, his opening lines are a monologue, though they have some suggestion of lines spoken to the audience—an impression which is repeated by the girl at the very end of the play. The tone is hesitant, appealing, and as suggested in the stage directions, slightly comic:

> YOUNG MAN: Hello—out there! (*Pause.*) Hello—out there! (*Long pause.*) Nobody out there. (*Still more dramatically, but more comically, too.*) Hello—out there! Hello—out there!

There are more stage directions here than are used elsewhere. It helps to keep them to a minimum generally, but this is the first impression the audience has of the protagonist, and the playwright is concerned about the right delivery of the lines.

For more than a page Photo-Finish is the only character visible on the stage. The spotlight is on him both literally and figuratively. We are learning a great deal about him—both why he is there and how he feels about it. But Emily, identified so far only as "The Voice," is hardly revealed at all. In fact when the young man says that she sounds "O.K.," she says "Maybe I am and maybe I ain't." The audience is kept as much in the dark about her as he is.

As soon as she appears, though, she reveals her own feelings. "I'm kind of lonesome, too," she says, and this is no casual line. Not only is it our first glimpse into her own feelings, it is the first suggestion of a link which is going to become very important later, the parallel between his being held in a jail and her being captive in a town which is not much better than a jail.

Plays often provide the audience with what is known as a *handle* for each important character—an easy way to identify her or him. This may be achieved by a character's situation as it is in the case of Photo-Finish, or it may be more a matter of attitude as it is with Emily Smith.

Providing quick visibility is also important in comedy. If anything, the "handle" is apt to be more pronounced. This is certainly the case in *The Service for Joseph Axminster*, which is described as *A Vaudeville Play*. As in old vaudeville comedy routines, the characters are almost cartoonlike with little apparent depth. But they are highly individualized right from our first impression.

The character known as Rage-In-Age begins with a "poem" which consists of all the varieties of brutal punishment which one might find in a thesaurus. Aside from serving as a satire of monotonously hostile protest poetry, it provides for him a quick identity which matches his name.

His friend, BB, on the other hand, is a gentler soul. How do we know? First, because of his charming response to the poem Rage has just recited. "You think," he asks, "if you'd stayed longer, you might've got to the happy part?" That is his opening. Then we learn that he was taking a nap in the bushes when Rage was looking up all those hostile words.

Next we learn that BB has forgotten the names of his parents and even his own name, preferring to remember faces. He says:

> Yes, I've forgotten my own name. But that's not a problem. A man is not the same thing as his name. I'm in perfect possession of who I am.

Through lines like these we quickly come to know him as one who accepts himself and others for what they are.

The opening scene of a play is demanding no matter how much writing experience you have had. Much of your attention necessarily is focused on starting the plot quickly. Be careful, however, not to become so involved in establishing the situation that you forget about characterization. Try to give your characters lines which—in addition to starting the play—provide us with an immediate impression of what they are like.

CHARACTER DEVELOPMENT

What we see at first is seldom the whole story. This is true when we meet people in life; it is usually true with characters in a play.

Development of this sort is sometimes called "character change," but that term implies a fundamental transformation in personality, a phenomenon rarely seen in drama and almost never in short plays. Generally, characters simply shift their attitude or, as in many short stories, our understanding of them is widened so that we see aspects we hadn't suspected at first.

Hello Out There provides two good examples. Most viewers (and readers) are uncertain as to whether to trust the motives of the protagonist in that opening scene. He is obviously in trouble and has had a good deal of experience in getting out of trouble. It seems likely that he is lying to this rather trusting girl with the hope of getting out of jail.

But the playwright provides two different speeches in which Photo-Finish speaks to himself—the first with Emily present and the second when he is alone on the stage. We acquire a different view of him when he says almost to himself:

> This world stinks. You shouldn't have been born in this town anyway, and you shouldn't have had a man like that for a father either.

And later after she leaves to see if she can find something with which to break the door down:

> Rape! Rape? *They* rape everything good that was ever born. . . .They laugh at her. Fifty cents a day. Little punk people. Hurting the only good thing that ever came their way.

These do not represent any kind of personality change. They do, however, broaden and clarify our perception of a character who while very much a drifter and a loser, is in addition someone who has genuine and warm feelings.

These glimpses into his finer side are also necessary if the audience is to accept his actions at the very end. After he has been shot he urges her to "run—run like hell—run all night," and he seems genuinely concerned for her future. If he had been portrayed as a selfish and scheming man throughout the play and revealed such warm feelings at the very end, we might very well feel that such a change was too great and too rapid.

Our perception of Emily also undergoes an expansion, though the development is not as great. She is pictured at first as a passive young woman who merely does what she is told. She cooks what they tell her to cook and works for a pittance. She shows some strength when she makes an effort to help Photo-Finish. But her greatest moment is when she tells the group to put down the body and to go away. She is slapped down, but the moment of courage has shown her in a different light.

In the end, of course, she has returned to the same position that Photo-Finish was in at the beginning of the play. But she is hardly the passive innocent she appeared to be at first.

Character revelation and development are extraordinarily rapid in this play. When you study the script on the page as you would a story, it seems almost unconvincingly compressed. The couple meet as strangers and are in love within minutes. In less than an hour of playing time he has been killed and her perception of the world has changed. Yet in production, these events are convincing. This is often true of drama. The fact that it is a performance creates a pace which is greater than what we expect in fiction.

Character development is usually less pronounced or even nonexistent in comedy. The more farcical the play, the less important characterization usually is. Cleverness of lines and the wit of satiric ridicule take over.

But *Joseph Axminster* provides an interesting exception. The play is presented as a kind of vaudeville farce with cartoon-like characters; yet

Rage-In-Age is given a moment of depth which is the sort one might expect in a serious drama. Our first view of him, you remember, is as he recites that absurd "poem" which is a list of hostile words. But like the fool in *King Lear*, he keeps saying things which have a significance below the comic surface. When they first look at the body of Joe Axminster and BB utters the commonplace statement, "How the man aged," Rage asks, "What will you say when he's buried?" And later when he tries to create some type of funeral service he recalls the phrase, "Man, thou art dust," and this causes him to make a speech which reveals the central concern of this essentially comic play:

> "Man, thou art dust." Oh, I hate those words! Damn those words!. . . .Man, thou art not even dust, thou art absurd.

His speech, which is far from comic, ends with the cry, "Do you call this serious? Can you find some meaning in this?"

The character of Rage has clearly developed far beyond the level of the clown we first met. And the play has developed from the merely comic level of vaudeville. I will have more to say about the theme of this play in Chapter 31, but my concern here is for character. It is often true in drama that the range of suggestion in the theme is directly dependent upon the degree to which the characters—comic or serious—have been developed.

COMIC CHARACTERS

If there is anything more difficult than creating a comic character, it is trying to explain to a playwright why a certain character isn't funny. It seems as if the ability to write good comedy is intuitive, but actually it may depend more on how much comedy you have read.

The easiest type of comic character to create is the satiric lampoon of a particular type. Satire of a rather blunt sort is familiar to almost all students through *Mad* and *National Lampoon* magazines. Television has also produced a long series of satiric skits over the years.

The satiric character is an exaggeration both in lines of dialogue and in action. The more specific characteristics you can find and develop, the better the satire will be. Notice, by the way, that it is difficult to satirize a comic type of person, just as it is next to impossible to satirize a funny magazine or story, without simply imitating the object of your ridicule. The most likely sources for satiric attack are individuals who take themselves very seriously.

Satire, however, has its limitations. What George Dennison has done in *Joseph Axminster* is to combine satiric elements with what is essentially a warm and wry comedy. The character called Rage is on the simplest level a caricature of a type we have all met—the individual who is brimming with random hostilities. Yet we soon see in him those fuller, deeper qualities of a man who is dealing with the apparent absurdity of life. The lengthy speech he delivers primarily for Lisa is an example. He explains in great detail how he fought a policeman face to face and with great difficulty finally did well enough so that one of the onlookers said "The kid's okay." What a victory! But then Rage admits that it was all a daydream of a man in his fifties.

That scene is a comic deception, but the satire is kindly, even compassionate. We have all had dreams in which someone assured us with the phrase "The kid's okay." Our smile is not as much *at* him as in the case of blunt satire but *with* him, sharing a familiar dream.

In longer plays, you may want to create a comic character as a *foil*—a character who sets off the protagonist by contrast. The efficient businesswoman, for example, living with a younger and totally irresponsible brother; the politician with a charming but alcoholic uncle. Such characters may help you avoid the heaviness which eventually can turn a drama into melodrama. And a wry, irreverent comic character is a good antidote to sentimentality.

There are plays in which characters are not developed: farce, for example, melodrama, and highly propagandistic or didactic dramas. But if you are working toward a play which has a range of suggestion and resonance, a play which will remain with the audience as vividly as a personal experience, you will need at least one and preferably two characters who are complex and who develop in the course of a play. Sophisticated drama is, among other things, the experience of meeting new and interesting people.

Chapter 30

Realistic and Nonrealistic Approaches

Realistic and *nonrealistic* drama defined; the *conventions of realism;* nonrealistic approaches; methods of combining realistic and nonrealistic elements; selecting your own approach; illustrations of realism and nonrealism used in a single set design.

Realistic drama creates the illusion of the world about us. Costume, set, and plot appear to be borrowed from what we see or might expect to see in life. Nonrealistic drama, on the other hand, creates its own world in somewhat the same manner as a dream does. Costumes may be symbolic, the set fanciful or bare, and the plot is not bound by the patterns of our waking life.

Realistic and *nonrealistic drama* are descriptive terms. They don't imply that one form of drama is better than the other. While it is true that we sometimes say that a play or movie was "so realistic" when we mean "convincing," the fact is that highly fanciful, dreamlike productions can appear equally convincing.

These are also nonhistorical terms. In previous editions, the term *expressionism* was used to describe nonrealistic approaches. But because *expressionism* also refers to a specific historical movement in drama, it is less confusing to adopt the more neutral term of *nonrealistic drama.*

As we shall see, realistic and nonrealistic approaches are not entirely exclusive. They are often used in combination. But because they describe two significantly different types of dramatic imagination, each deserves a close look.

THE CONVENTIONS OF
REALISM

The conventions of realism are seen in the set, the costumes, the dialogue, and most of all in the action. Since the set is what strikes the audience first, it is often a signal as to whether the play as a whole will be realistic or nonrealistic. As soon as you see an interior with, say, tables and chairs and bookcases with what appear to be real books, you tend to make an assumption that the characters and the events which will unfold will have an outward similarity to waking life.

Remember, though, that the set, like all the elements of a realistic play, is only an illusion. The audience accepts the fact that the living room has only three walls and that the performers speak most of their lines facing this missing wall. And in arena-style productions we even accept the notion of "realistic" interiors with no walls whatever. The point to remember, however, is that the *imagination* of the viewer is picturing an "as-if-real" scene because of the way the playwright has employed certain conventions.

In plays which are highly realistic, costume is an important element as well. Period costumes give the illusion of accuracy even if they are not; contemporary costumes provide those subtle cues with which we make judgments (often inaccurate) about people we meet. A rumpled suit has one set of connotations, while a dirty T-shirt and tattered sneakers have another.

At the heart of realism, however, is dialogue and action. The audience has the same expectations of realistic drama as it does when reading realistic fiction. Motivation has to be convincing. If a character says or does something which seems "out of character," some explanation has to be provided later—perhaps the character turns out to be a liar or kinder than expected or stronger or more cowardly.

As for action, it should seem to flow naturally from character and not violate the patterns of chance we are used to in our own lives. The term *deus ex machina*, literally a god lowered by a stage machine, refers to any extraordinary and unconvincing way of manipulating the plot. It is a violation of expectations in a realistic play and so breaks the illusion, but in nonrealistic plays such twists can be made effective.

Hello Out There is a good example of a play which is in some respects highly stylized and yet remains essentially realistic. The set, of course, will vary with different productions, but the playwright's description in the script calls for "a small-town prison cell" and this is specific. Both characters are dressed as we might expect individuals in that situation to be, and the di-

alogue is natural, containing the interrupted sentences and occasional colloquial expressions which seem appropriate.

The outcome is "theatrical" in that it is highly dramatic and almost
choreographed in a way that will be described shortly. Nevertheless the ending is plausible and does not violate what we might conceivably read in a
newspaper account. Therefore it is realistic.

NONREALISTIC APPROACHES

There are a great variety of nonrealistic approaches, and examples can be
found in every historical period. Greek drama used gods, mythical creatures, and supernatural occurrences; Elizabethans enjoyed ghosts, witches,
and magic. In our own century, these dreamlike effects are best seen in the
works of Eugene O'Neill (*The Emperor Jones* and *The Hairy Ape*), Elmer Rice
(*The Adding Machine*), and others who focused on the psychological suggestion in drama as opposed to the outer reality. Their work during the 1920s
and '30s is referred to as *expressionism*, although the term is also used to suggest nonrealistic plays in general.

Varied as these plays were, they all used highly symbolic details literally. In *The Adding Machine,* for example, the protagonist, a cipher in a
highly mechanical society, is named Mr. Zero, and he lives in a room surrounded by numbers. His associates have higher numbers than he does.
Costume, set, action, and dialogue are all distorted as they are in a dream;
but as in a dream there is also an internal consistency which allows us to
"make sense" of it all. We know what it is, after all, to be in some way a cog in
a machine.

In the 1950s and '60s a new interest in nonrealistic drama emerged
and was called *theater of the absurd.* It was best represented in the works of
Eugene Ionesco, Samuel Beckett, Harold Pinter, and occasionally Edward
Albee.

These playwrights were influenced by the existential notion that life is
absurd in the sense of being without ultimate purpose or meaning. Their
plays offer no hope of solution, though the pessimistic outlook is often
countered with wit. In Ionesco's *The Chairs,* for example, a couple live in a
castle in the middle of the ocean and hope that an orator will eventually tell
the world about the fundamental purpose of their lives. After a lengthy
buildup, the orator turns out to be an idiot who can utter only unintelligible
syllables. The play would be difficult to endure if it were not for a great variety of satiric scenes.

Theater of the absurd seems to have run its course, but nonrealistic
drama continues in various forms. In *Joseph Axminster,* for example, George
Dennison makes use of fanciful details which intentionally keep the audience from seeing the action as a realistic portrayal of the life of bums on the

road. Yet unlike plays in the tradition of theater of the absurd, he has a compassion for his characters and a qualified optimism about our ability to make some sense of our lives.

The nonrealistic elements are unmistakable even before a single line is spoken. The backdrop is described as having been painted "by a child of eight" and the Mistress of Ceremonies, dressed as a hobo, holds a sign reading "Topeka." And if that does not set the tone, the cardboard "train" which is carried by a stagehand certainly does.

Notice too that the body of Joseph Axminster is played by the MC who, much later in the play, sits up and is clearly the MC. This is not to suggest that their friend Joseph Axminster does not exist; it only breaks the illusion momentarily and keeps our attention focused more on the ideas than on the emotional content.

This is one of the side effects which frequently (though not necessarily) is associated with nonrealistic treatment. The more the play departs from realism, the less it generates emotions of concern for its characters or their situation. Instead, such plays rely increasingly on wit, humor, and philosophical suggestion. It is as if the playwright knowingly creates a distance between the play and the audience, stressing the intellectual aspects over direct feeling.

There are two potential dangers in the writing of nonrealistic drama which you should keep in mind before you try writing one. The first is that total fragmentation is boring. If you write a play which you feel is *absurdist*—in the tradition of theater of the absurd—and your audience can't see any coherent pattern, they will simply walk out. A poorly written realistic play sometimes holds interest because of characterization or the familiarity of the situation; nonrealistic plays do not have these elements.

Second, nonrealistic plays which are humorless open with two strikes against them from the start. Even the most pessimistic playwrights in the absurdist school are able to keep their works afloat with wit, humor, and satire. Remember that as you reduce the pulling power of a dramatic plot and a realistic situation, you must provide some other attraction for the audience. Shock is one alternative, but it is very difficult to sustain. Wit is a natural energizer and unifier for nonrealistic drama.

COMBINING REALISTIC AND NONREALISTIC ELEMENTS

Until now I have been describing these two approaches as if they were mutually exclusive. This is handy for analysis, but in practice these approaches are used together, and there is no sharp division.

One can see this best by looking at different stage sets. A conventional interior on a picture-frame stage is realistic; but as we have seen, it has one highly unrealistic detail which we choose to ignore. An arena stage with no backdrop pushes our imaginations further, but still we will see it as realistic if the details indicate that we should. The next step is to split the stage so that we see two or more rooms or a portion of the street as well as an interior. At the end of this chapter there are illustrations of the set designed by William Ritman for Harold Pinter's *The Collection*. Although the stage was small, three different playing areas were included, representing two different apartments and a telephone booth. The attention of the audience was directed by raising and lowering the lights. The play is highly realistic, but the set has used an essentially nonrealistic technique.

Much depends on our perception of the playwright's intent. In Pinter's play, the intention was to create an "as-if-real" situation on stage and even though the set is in many respects unrealistic, the audience accepts the illusion as an imitation of life. In *Joseph Axminster*, on the other hand, George Dennison calls for a far simpler set, but it is clear that his intention is to create a fanciful situation. When you turn to your own play, consider the possibility of signaling to the audience what kind of imagination you are using through their first view of your set.

The techniques of realistic and nonrealistic drama are also mixed in terms of action and dialogue. *Hello Out There* is in most respects realistic; but as I have pointed out before, the action is compressed in a way which is nonrealistic. And there is an element of choreography in the way the opening scene, which features the Young Man alone in the jail, matches the final scene in which The Girl takes that same position and speaks the same lines. This is as stylized and "unrealistic" as the symmetry one might expect in a ballet. Yet we still see the play as essentially realistic.

The bare stage is yet another way to blend the techniques of both approaches. Shakespeare used minimal staging, suggesting a set with the dialogue. Contemporary dramatists have used the bare stage to present both fairly realistic plays like Thornton Wilder's *Our Town* as well as highly nonrealistic ones such as Samuel Beckett's *Waiting for Godot*. The bare stage is neutral in that it does not indicate what kind of imagination will be used. Through the lines, however, the audience quickly places the type of play. *Our Town* takes place in Grover's Corners, New Hampshire, and even the lack of a set and the presence of a stage manager who acts like a Greek chorus do not keep the audience from imagining themselves in a typical New England town. *Waiting for Godot* is also presented without visual cues, but it is clear from the first three minutes of dialogue that we are in a dream world created by the playwright.

Although the action and dialogue in *Joseph Axminster* are unmistakably nonrealistic, there is one moment in the play in which Rage is presented as a convincing and realistically developed character. It is the scene in which he describe to Lisa what we almost assume is an actual experience fighting a policeman. When he finally confesses it was only a fantasy, we see him as a perceptive man. But when that scene is over, the playwright has the cardboard train pass through and the slapstick mood of the vaudeville play is reestablished.

SELECTING YOUR OWN APPROACH

The decision of how realistic and how nonrealistic to make a play is never simple. It depends on three factors: your own preferences, what kind of plays you have read, and the needs of the particular dramatic concept you have in mind.

The first two of these factors are a part of the same process. You cannot really have preferences until you have read or, better yet, have seen a large number of plays. The analysis in this text and the two sample plays are intended only to give a notion of what to look for in future reading and viewing. How many plays should you read and see? Four is better than two, and forty is better than four. To be reasonable, though, if you are starting out and are taking a course, you will only be able to read a few additional short plays. But if you are at the point of writing drama with more than an exploratory concern, it is essential that you read and see as many plays as time and funds will permit.

You will come to know not only what kind of plays you prefer but how enormous the range of possibilities is. It is important to discover how many major playwrights have written plays which are at almost opposite ends of the spectrum. Arthur Miller, for example, does not use a single nonrealistic device in his play *The Price*, yet in *After the Fall* he places his protagonist in a dreamlike environment in which characters from his past come forward to confront him. Edward Albee is perhaps best known for his realistic drama, *Who's Afraid of Virginia Woolf?* Yet he is also known for his highly nonrealistic plays, of which the very short *The Sandbox* is an excellent example. Those four plays would serve as a fine introduction to the spectrum of possibilities.

The approach you adopt will be determined not only by your own preferences, but by the material you have in mind. Some concepts lend themselves to realistic treatment, and you shouldn't feel that this approach is in some way not "modern." Whatever survey you wish to make—Broadway, off-Broadway, repertory companies, or universities—you will find that realistic drama is as well represented as the varieties of nonrealistic.

Some drama ideas, on the other hand, will come to you in highly symbolic or dreamlike form. When that happens, see if there are ways to organize and shape the material so that the audience will see it as an artistic whole.

There are liabilities and assets to each approach. Try to weigh these in terms of a specific drama idea and see which is appropriate .

The greatest danger when working with realistic drama is making use of stock characters, hackneyed dialogue, and conventional situations. Many of the clichés I warned against in the section on fiction appear in drama as well. Be consciously aware of all those worn-out television plots which may be floating around in the back of your mind.

The great advantage of realistic drama, on the other hand, is that it is rooted in character. The audience comes to believe in a carefully developed character more fully than is possible in nonrealistic plays. And the plot—whether serious or gently humorous—can seize hold of the audience as deeply as an important episode in life itself. This emotive potential is extraordinary.

The liability in nonrealistic drama is different. Although one also has to be careful to avoid hackneyed characters and situations, the most common problem is inaccessibility. The humorless and obscure dream-plot is cruel punishment for any audience. It seems at first to be an approach which allows the spontaneity that every artist wants. But it also eliminates the kind of structure that every artist needs. Aimlessness and lack of cohesion often lead to inaccessibility. Martin Esslin puts it this way in *The Theatre of the Absurd:*

> Mere combinations of incongruities produce mere banality. Anyone attempting to work in this medium simply by writing down what comes into his mind will find that the supposed flights of spontaneous invention have never left the ground, that they consist of incoherent fragments of reality that have not been transposed into a valid imaginative whole.

The assets of nonrealistic drama are, in a broad sense, intellectual rather than emotional. Ideas presented with wit and flashes of satire flourish with such an approach. The tone need not be cold, however. George Dennison, for example, draws his plot together through his characters' need to create a burial service for a dead friend, and their efforts, no matter how blundering and comic, are an affirmation of the human spirit. As with free verse, nonrealistic drama offers freedoms and also the obligation to find new and effective structures.

Your reading and your experiences as a theatergoer will influence your feelings about realistic and nonrealistic approaches. But let the needs of your projected play have a voice too. And don't forget your audience. No matter whether your approach is realistic or not, the world you create on the stage is one you will want to share with them.

The Collection, showing emphasis on the modern apartment, with the other areas dark.

The Collection, showing emphasis on the telephone booth, which is, in the play, some distance from either home.

The Collection, showing emphasis on the ornate apartment, with the other areas dark.

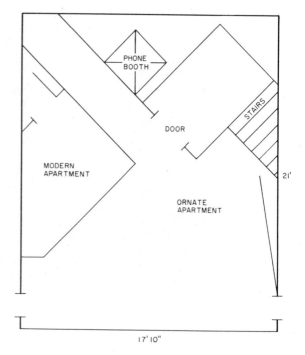

The Collection: a diagram of the stage, showing the technique of representing three entirely different scenes simply by shifts in lighting. Note how the unusual angles add both variety and depth even on a small stage.

Chapter 31

Suggestion and Statement

Theme distinguished from *thesis;* themes in *Hello Out There* and in *Joseph Axminster,* techniques of *highlighting* thematic concerns; themes of *black identity;* finding your *own themes.*

Most plays make suggestions, not pronouncements. That is, they imply more than they state directly. It is true, of course, that the genre is influenced by the fact that it is given in performance and must therefore be bold and vivid. But the thematic suggestions in a sophisticated play rarely give precise answers to the questions being raised, and frequently a number of peripheral concerns are also explored. *Hamlet,* after all, doesn't tell you any more about how to deal with stepfathers than *Hello Out There* does about how to avoid mob action.

There is, on the other hand, a significant minority of plays which do make unequivocal statements. These plays are built around a *thesis* or argument as opposed to a theme or central concern. They often present the views of a minority such as blacks or an under-represented group such as women.

Both the plays included in this text deal with a cluster of themes. As a theatergoer you might have the impression that the theme of each can be summed up rather easily in a single sentence, but as a playwright you will want to study them in greater detail.

THEMATIC SUGGESTION IN
HELLO OUT THERE

This play is remembered for its dramatic impact. If it had nothing more to offer than that, it would be a melodrama. The terror of an individual facing a lynch mob has been repeated frequently in film and television dramas. The elevation of the play above the level of a simple thriller is partly achieved through characterization; but the real complexity lies in its thematic suggestion.

Even a rapid reading of the play suggests that the theme deals with the loneliness of individuals and the need to reach out in friendship or love. The protagonist is held in jail and the girl is trapped in a small town which seems to be no better than a jail. It appears that they might escape together; but in the end his luck runs out and so, apparently, has hers.

Perhaps that is all the casual reader will ever know about the play. But a writer has to examine the technique more closely. Saroyan has used three devices in this play which dramatize his thematic concerns to the point where they are unmistakable: repetition of certain key words throughout the length of the play like refrains, reiteration of the same words in "runs" or clusters, and the use of symbolic names.

The most pronounced use of the refrain is "hello out there." No one could miss the fact that this key phrase is used in the title, at the opening, and again at the closing of the play. More significant, however, is the fact that it is repeated a total of twenty-five times!

This is no accident. If you check the first twelve uses (all of which occur before the girl appears on stage), you will see how Saroyan has established the refrain early with a "run" or cluster of three and then spaced them increasingly farther apart. After the girl appears, they occur only occasionally. The next "run" occurs when the man is left alone in the cell again. He repeats it five times in the course of one short monologue. Once again the phrase is used sparingly until the very end when the girl, trapped and alone, repeats it twice as the curtain descends.

A second series is made up of the two words "scared" and "afraid." They are used interchangeably. They are repeated sixteen times and are used to apply not only to the young couple but to the men in the town and to the husband who eventually kills Photo-Finish. Notice the redundancy in the following "run":

THE GIRL: . . . They were talking of taking you to another jail in another town.
YOUNG MAN: Yeah? Why?
THE GIRL: Because they're afraid.
YOUNG MAN: What are they afraid of?
THE GIRL: They're afraid these people from Wheeling will come over in the middle of the night and break in.

YOUNG MAN: Yeah? What do they want to do that for?

THE GIRL: Don't *you* know what they want to do it for?

YOUNG MAN: Yeah, I know all right.

THE GIRL: Are you scared?

YOUNG MAN: Sure I'm scared. Nothing scares a man more than ignorance.

First he uses "afraid" in a string of three successive lines, and then he uses "scared" three times in an almost poetic sequence.

There are two other refrains in this play which, though they are not as pronounced, still serve to dramatize the thematic concerns. One is "lonesome." It is used a total of twelve times, six of which occur in a "run" just before and just after the girl appears for the first time. Finally, there is "luck" which turns up ten times, six of which are in a cluster in about as many consecutive lines.

These, then, are five phrases or words which are repeated throughout the play and also bunched in clusters: "hello out there," "scared/afraid," "lonesome," and "luck." They also lie at the heart of what the playwright is working with: the loneliness and fear that we all experience, the reaching out, and the element of luck with which we must always deal.

How does Saroyan get away with so much redundancy? He has, after all, violated a basic "rule" which is still generally honored in the writing of exposition and most fiction. This shows how far the technique of playwriting is from other types of prose.

Saroyan's approach here is actually closer to that of free verse. The use of repeated words and phrases either scattered or in clusters is, as I pointed out in Chapter 7, one of the characteristics found in the Bible, in the works of Walt Whitman and more recently in the poetry of Allen Ginsberg, Lucille Clifton and others.

A second device found in *Hello Out There* is the rather direct use of symbolic names. The town where the protagonist is about to meet his death is called "Matador." And the town from which the freewheeling, irresponsible men come is "Wheeling." Saroyan makes sure that the audience does not miss these names by repeating each one twice—a recognition of the fact that drama is a "continuous art form" which does not permit any hesitation.

He puts the same care into the young man's nickname, "Photo-Finish." Through the character's own dialogue we learn exactly what it means and how it is linked with the central theme of luck.

More subtle than the name is the symbolic action. The play begins with an isolated, frightened individual crying out for contact with someone—anyone. It turns out that this same longing for companionship was what got him into this spot in the first place. Ironically, it is fear rather than rage which leads the husband to commit murder. And in the end, the girl has taken the role of the isolated, frightened individual crying out for contact with someone—anyone.

When one looks closely at these devices of repetition and symbolic details, they appear extraordinarily blatant. This is often true of drama. Remember that what one is analyzing here line by line is the written version of a performance which will slide through the consciousness of an audience in about twenty-eight uninterrupted minutes. For this reason, playwrights often repeat key phrases; and when they develop a symbol, they return to it at least once and often frequently. Drama, more than any other genre, thrives on reiteration.

THEMATIC SUGGESTION IN
JOSEPH AXMINSTER

In a nonrealistic comedy the themes are apt to be less visible than in a tragedy. And the playwright's subtitle, *A Vaudeville Play*, seems to suggest that the work will be a simple and themeless series of skits.

Actually it is held together by both a sustained plot and a cluster of rather important concerns. It may help to separate the two. The *plot* revolves about a burial. The characters find the body of a friend and they decide that some kind of burial service is necessary. There is a minor complication in the fact that none of them can remember the traditional words to be said, but they improvise. That done, they move on. Simple enough, but worth noting since it provides the necessary structure with which to work through various themes.

The first of several related *themes* concerns the futility of life. Rage attempts to say something appropriate over the coffin and what comes to mind is "Man, thou art dust." He adds that "Those are the main words." They are central for this play as well.

A central theme in a play this diffuse has to be repeated several times. And this one is. Shortly after Rage introduces that phrase from the Bible, he returns to it and adds his own interpretation:

> "Man, thou art dust." Oh, I hate those words! Damn those words! . . .Man, thou art not even dust, thou art absurd!

The third repetition of this same phrase is given by WC:

> Man, thou art dust. . . . We are gathered together on this solemn occasion . . . (*Aside*) . . . a merely solemn occasion would be a relief . . . (*Continuing*) . . . we are gathered together on this catastrophic day . . .

The fourth repetition comes when Rage is comparing the simple burial spot where they must inter Joseph Axminster with the famous cemetery, Forest Lawn. He suggests that the bones would all look alike and then repeats, "Man, thou art dust."

Although Lisa's contribution to the burial service does not contain exactly the same phrase, it echoes and amplifies it:

> We brought nothing into the world, and it is certain that we can carry nothing out. The Lord gave, and the lord hath taken away." Oh, that's true, isn't it!

This, then, becomes a repeated motif somewhat like the refrain in *Hello Out There*. And it appears visually in Rage's dream of endless, pointless running as well as, on a broader level, the wandering in which all the characters are engaged.

This reiteration of the apparent absurdity and meaninglessness of life is an echo of the thematic pessimism associated with plays of the theater of the absurd. But Dennison counters this theme with one which is more positive: If we recall individuals as they really were and honor their passing, we establish meaning.

The first hint of this comes when Rage states that he hates funerals and BB associates them with a whole array of ceremonies:

> Funerals, weddings, high school graduations, Armistice Day, Christmas, Fourth of July . . . I'm well acquainted with the things you can't stand.

Odd associations for funerals! But if you look at the list carefully you will see that each is an attempt to honor individuals and their achievements. These are rituals in which we give meaning to the past and, in a broader sense, to life.

These hobos are not very adept at ceremony, of course. They can't remember the right words, and they continually interrupt their efforts with other concerns. As BB says, "We're short on customs." We smile at their efforts, but how adept are we as a society at giving true meaning to such ceremonies as Armistice Day and Christmas?

"Saying good-bye. That's the heart of it," Rage says toward the end of the play. And that says a good deal about the more positive side of the play's theme. If we say good-bye with feeling and not just with pomp or empty ritual, we provide what meaning there is to a life completed.

How do we manage that? For one thing, we should recall the person and not all the statistics and facts which are usually listed in obituaries. That's what BB is implying when, early in the play, he says that he can recall his parents' faces but not their "vital statistics . . . dates of birth and death."

Another way we give meaning to individuals and their achievements is through the sincerity of our ceremonies. In *Joseph Axminster*, the funeral service is ridiculous of course, but it is also genuine. This is indicated not by the characters telling each other and the audience how deeply they feel the loss of their friend but through a simple use of flowers. Lisa says:

It's a pity the country here is so barren. We should have some flowers.

She removes some artificial flowers from her hat and places them on the coffin. "They are not much," she admits, "but they are something."

This detail would be lost if it were not repeated; so it is in a most noticeable way at the end of the play. BB recalls another part of the burial service which includes the words "Man, that is born of a woman, hath but a short time to live. . . . He cometh up and is cut down like a flower."

In the final scene, a stick which has been lying nearby is picked up by WC and fans out into "a huge sunflower." This flower, which has miraculously grown, is placed at the head of the coffin.

At the very end—even after the actors take their curtain call, the MC "plucks the sunflower from the coffin and carries it off." The MC, remember, has played the part of Joseph Axminster. It is fitting that the spirit of the dead man carry the flower which has sprung like a miraculous event from the concern of these simple friends.

HIGHLIGHTING THEMATIC CONCERNS

Because drama is continuous, flowing by the audience without pause, themes have to be stressed. *Joseph Axminster* and *Hello Out There* are strikingly different in most respects, but they use surprisingly similar methods of highlighting their themes. Key lines, for example, are repeated like the recurring refrain in free verse. The device appears obvious on the page, but it blends with the fabric of the whole work when the plays are seen.

Second, both plays use symbolic detail not only in names but in the situation of each play. A jail traps a man, just as a town traps a young woman, just as both are trapped by society; a man dreams of running, just as the characters all are wandering, just as, by implication, all of us wander until our time is up.

Incidentally, even the tone becomes a part of the thematic suggestion in *Joseph Axminster*. The childish backdrop, that ridiculous train, a dead man obviously played by a mistress of ceremonies—all these establish the absurd tone of a comic vaudeville skit. Yet ultimately we take these characters seriously because of the way they act and the feelings they express and especially from the simple concern they have for a departed friend. When we in the audience take them seriously and see them as individuals, we have created a sense of worth as if from nothing. The audience too has performed a minor miracle.

Finally, both plays avoid the temptation of having a character explain the playwright's intent in the final scene. Instead, they use symbolic action and an absolute minimum of dialogue. The jail in one case and the flower in the other are physical properties which are not explained. They come from the play itself and are meaningful only in the context of everything which has gone on.

As you read other plays, look for the ways in which the dramatist has repeated key lines or significant action and make a list of them. Trace symbolic patterns and identify them in the margin. Study endings and see how it is possible to show in dramatic terms what you might have been tempted to explain through dialogue.

THEMES OF BLACK IDENTITY

Drama is a natural medium for expressing the history, frustrations, and aspirations of any group. The Irish have had a major impact in this area of the theater, and women are beginning to contribute to the stage as they have in film. In addition, black theater has already come of age and is here to stay as a continuing influence.

The development of black theater is surprisingly recent. With a few rare exceptions, theater was a white art form until well into the 1960s. Black playwrights like Langston Hughes, Ossie Davis, and Lorraine Hansberry are known to most for one successful play each, but few white theatergoers can name the others they wrote. Langston Hughes alone turned out more than twenty plays. As a result, black playwrights, as well as black directors and actors, have been deprived of audiences and of the training which comes from regular production. This backlog of artistic frustration amplifies a deep sense of social injustice, to produce themes of bitter denunciation.

The harshest of these are written consciously and directly to a white audience. Plays like *The Toilet* by Amiri Baraka (LeRoi Jones) are intentionally designed to shock white, middle-class theatergoers. Rather than themes, these plays present theses—strong statements which often recommend specific social action.

Paul Carter Harrison's *Tabernacle* is another fine example. The play, described in his subtitle as *A Black Experience in Total Theater*, is a conglomerate of, in his words, "role playing, dance movement, choral chants, animism of masks, pregnancy of light and silence—integrated in such a manner as to create concrete images of a unique quality of Black expression."

The plot is based on a trial which took place after the Harlem riots of 1964. For all the varied techniques used in this play, it too is aimed primarily at a white audience. This is clear from the start when a preacher addresses the audience directly telling them that they are about to "witness all the infernal ashes of Cain poured down on our souls." And at the end of this extraordinarily powerful and biting play this same preacher lambastes the audience for sitting in stunned silence. By convention, theatergoers withhold their applause until after the action of the play is over; Harrison has utilized this convention as what he describes as a "pregnant silence," turning it into a metaphor for the political inaction on the part of whites and many middle-class blacks. Like Baraka, Harrison deals with strong arguments, and he thrusts them directly at a particular audience.

Conscious appeal to a white audience is also found in plays which are thematic and less accusatory. In Charles Gordone's *No Place to Be Somebody*, for example, the plot of the play is stopped twice for lengthy monologues which are delivered like prose poems from the center of the stage. One of these is formally titled "There's More to Being Black than Meets the Eye." The other is a verse narrative of what it is like for a black to try living like white suburbanites, suffering the scorn of both urban blacks and white neighbors.

Other plays address themselves more specifically to black audiences. The seven plays selected originally by the Free Southern Theater group for their pilot program are good examples: *Purlie Victorious* by Ossie Davis, *Do You Want to Be Free?* by Langston Hughes, *Lower Than the Angels* by John O. Killens, *Day of Absence* and *Happy Ending* by Douglas Turner, *Great Gettin' Up Morning* by Ann Flagg, and a modern adaptation of *Antigone*. To this list should be added Martin Duberman's *In White America*, which was actually this group's first production.

Only a few plays in the black theater movement are unmistakably written for white audiences. A larger proportion are concerned with black awareness and black identity. But perhaps a majority of plays deal with themes which are significant to all audiences. They tend to be thematic rather than thetic.

Goin' a Buffalo by Ed Bullins and *Ceremonies in Dark Old Men* by Lonne Elder III, are two excellent examples. Both involve the problems of black identity, economic survival, and moral corruption in urban life. Both are unmistakably about aspects of the black experience. But neither proposes solutions. They do not present theses; instead, they develop a tragic view of men and women caught in a highly destructive society.

FINDING YOUR OWN THEMES

If the thematic core of your play does not genuinely reflect your convictions, the play will probably not ring true. Further, you may find that this occasionally unconscious insincerity will result in characters which are stereotypes and situations which are hackneyed.

On the other hand, don't feel that if you do not have a social cause to defend that you should turn to another genre. What you need is a situation which is potentially dramatic and which involves characters whose lives are somewhat like the lives of people you know.

In some respects, your search will be similar to finding material for fiction. But the themes tend to be broader. It may strike you that Thornton Wilder's *Our Town* is a very mild piece of drama. The lives of reasonable and kindly people are depicted in episodic fashion. But there is drama in the way the tragedy of death in childbirth is finally resolved as a part of a universal harmony. Domestic situations make good plays if you can find a way of drawing a larger truth from them in a fresh and convincing way.

Don't forget your own roots. If you have a distinctive racial or national background, there will be tensions and perhaps successes and defeats associated with it. If your own life has been secure, what of your parents'?

Your life style is also a source. Whether you live in a city apartment or on a farm your experiences are in some ways unique. Do they have dramatic potential? Even if you see your environment as a "typical American surburban home," look again. When it comes to specific families (or individuals), there is no such thing as "typical." Each is individual.

Finally, draw on drama itself. What you read and what you see in production will suggest themes. And the play does not have to be contemporary. *Oedipus Rex* is about sons and parents in any age; *Antigone* is about the conflict between a woman's personal values and the laws of the society; *Othello* raises questions of trust and honesty in those who mean the most to us; *Hamlet* explores, among other things, the uneasy relationship between young men and their stepfathers.

Costumes change. Language changes. Theatrical conventions change. But themes remain so constant that we still feel emotionally involved with works written more than two thousand years ago. Whenever you feel this emotional pull, stop and ask what that play has revealed about your own situation, your own life, and your own society. You won't be borrowing a theme; you will be allowing another work of art to stimulate your own artistic imagination.

Chapter 32

Writing for Film

The *transition* from playwriting to script writing; a new approach to *scene formation;* patterns in *dramatic structure; adaptations* vs. *original scripts;* the *mechanics* of the script itself.

Shifting from playwriting to script writing for television or motion pictures is in some ways like shifting from one musical instrument to another. Much of the basic approach is similar, but there are specific differences which are more significant than you might expect.

Starting with the similarities, everything you have learned about creating dramatic impact applies to script writing. In some respects, dramatic impact becomes more important since your audience is more easily distracted. It is far easier to turn a dial than to leave a theater! So there is an even greater need for an initial hook to capture interest and a series of dramatic questions to hold it through to the end. If you have had practice writing drama for stage, all this will be familiar to you when you turn to script writing.

If you choose to write comedy, the approaches to creating a humorous situation or employing the sharper impact of wit and satire are essentially the same. And comic relief in more serious scripts is just as important as it is on the stage.

Characterization is also the same. Whatever skills you have developed in that area will serve you well as a scriptwriter. You still must depend on action and dialogue. Individuality is just as important, and you will have to maintain enough consistency to make your characters credible. As with a play script, your central characters will be filled in (*round*), and your minor characters or those providing comic relief will be presented in less detail (*flat*).

At first it may seem that the script itself will be the major hurdle. It *is* different. But getting used to the new format is surprisingly easy. The sample script which appears in the next chapter will help you to make that transition without trauma.

This script format, incidentally, is a fairly standard style. Since most dramatic television projects are shot on film, the script is essentially the same as a motion picture screenplay. What I have to say about writing for film will in almost every case apply to both media. Mastering the form is not a major problem.

There are, however, fundamental differences which distinguish film writing of either sort from playwriting. They will have to be understood in principle and then mastered with practice. The film script has a different concept of *scene* which will affect the way you think of your material and how you compose. This, in turn, will alter your pacing and your use of setting.

THE "SCENE" IN A FILM SCRIPT

A film scene is a unit of action (with or without dialogue) which occurs in a single place and time. As soon as the camera shifts to a different location, the scene changes.

Since you are not limited to a stage set, you now have enormous liberty. You will find yourself much more visually oriented when writing for film. Each unit of dialogue will be associated with a particular visual impression.

This is more than simply a different approach to setting. Your sense of pacing will be different. You are now thinking of your material in much shorter units.

These scenes may be extended to several minutes during, for example, a lengthy speech. But often they may be as short as a three-second shot of a character's face or a close-up shot of an object. Most scriptwriters avoid long scenes, especially in the 30-minute shows. The passive viewer of a television program may have the impression of long, unbroken sequences of action, but the script was probably made up of surprisingly short units.

Although you should keep your stage directions to a minimum, it is important for you to visualize each separate scene as you write your dialogue. Once you are used to the script format, you will find that your writing will move from scene to scene as if you were visualizing a series of still shots. You can train yourself by watching television dramas in the same way, scene by scene, rather than viewing the action as an apparently uninterrupted flow.

Although most scenes contain dialogue, remember the value of the visual impression with no spoken words: the close-up of a character's face, a visual impression of a house or neighborhood, a minute detail like a character's hands as he or she lights a cigarette, or a leaf falling.

DRAMATIC STRUCTURE

When writing for the stage, we think of a full-length production as being between two and three hours and a "one act" as anywhere from ten minutes to an hour. Total length is highly flexible, and the division of acts and scenes is determined mainly by the material itself. With television writing, on the other hand, there are more conventional lengths which are designed to fit the half-hour modules of the medium. These have resulted in a more regular pattern of rising action and periodic climaxes.

If you are planning a standard 30-minute show, think of it as a two-act production. Each act will come to about thirteen or fourteen typewritten pages, though of course you should calculate the playing time by giving the script a dramatic reading. Be sure to allow for action which has no accompanying dialogue.

The first act frequently ends with some kind of dramatic event or statement. Although this initial climax shouldn't overshadow the conclusion of the drama, it may provide a fresh insight or create an unexpected twist in the plot which will serve as a hook to bring your audience back after the break.

In comedy it is important to end the first act with a good line or unit of action. Be careful not to muffle it by a closing line like "See you tomorrow" or "Drive carefully." Let your comic line be the very last one for best impact.

This two-act form is less rigid in public television, which is not punctuated by commercials, but it provides a structure which many scriptwriters find valuable.

A 60-minute show is divided into four acts. They are about the same length and frequently have the same type of climax or peak of interest. And with the 90-minute show you increase the number of acts to six.

If you are just starting out, the 30-minute format is a good one to work with. You can train yourself to think in the short units of the filmed scene and still keep in mind the longer cycle of rising action which gives dramatic structure to each act.

ADAPTATIONS VS. ORIGINAL
SCRIPTS

Consider carefully whether you wish to start off with an adaptation of a story or an original screenplay. The advantage of an adaptation is that you can concentrate on the script and the individual scenes. It is best to select a fairly short work and one in which there is visual potential. You will want to outline your approach since significant changes may have to be made. But you can begin the actual writing sooner than if you are developing your own plot and characters. You can use any published work as long as you do not reproduce it or submit it for production. If you do plan to enter it in a contest or send it to a producer, be sure to secure permission in writing from the author first. Many authors will grant you permission to develop an adaptation in return for an agreed-upon payment to be made if and when the script is accepted for production.

The next chapter consists of a sample script based on the first third of the short story, "Sausage and Beer." It has been designed to illustrate the mechanics of a script, but it is only an opening fragment. You may find it helpful to complete that script, drawing on the story itself, which appears as Chapter 14 of this text. If you are able to do this in a group or in a writing class, you can learn a good deal by comparing various approaches to the same fictional scenes.

If you prefer to create an original script, begin with an outline which includes the characters and the basic plot. Keep in mind all the special needs of a theatrical performance and add to that the mobility and the pacing of film. Remember that while you were doing your best to make imaginative use of a single set for the stage, you are now working with a medium which lends itself to a constantly shifting environment. Don't trap your characters in a single room or a car. Take advantage of your freedom.

THE MECHANICS OF A FILM
SCRIPT

You may wish to read a page or two of the sample script in the next chapter before you study the following details. The actual layout of the script is relatively simple.

The title page is a separate sheet with the title of your project typed in capital letters and underlined. Below that, describe the project briefly—"A 30-minute Television Drama," "A 60-minute Situation Comedy," or the like. Your name goes below that. On the lower half of the page you may write "First Draft" or "Final Draft" on the left, and it is essential that you place your *contact address* (your home, agent, or office) on the right.

The first page of your script begins with your title again—in capital letters and underlined. The first words are "<u>FADE IN:</u>" typed at the left margin. The script will end with "<u>FADE OUT</u>" typed on the right after the last line. The sample script does not have this since it is only a portion of a full script.

Assuming that you are using pica type (preferred for play scripts and fiction as well), set your left margin at 20 spaces (2 inches) for stage directions. Dialogue begins at 30 spaces, and the name above each unit of dialogue begins 40 spaces in. If you set these tabs on your typewriter, this is a convenient arrangement.

Each new scene begins with "EXT." if it is an exterior shot or "INT." if it is an interior. It should also be identified the first time as "DAY" or "NIGHT." This information with a very brief phrase or word of identification is called a *slug line*. It will look like this:

INT. KITCHEN--DAY

or

EXT. WOODS--NIGHT

Once you have identified the action as interior or exterior and as day or night, you don't have to repeat this information until there is a complete shift to a new location.

If you shift from, say, the interior of a car to an exterior view and then return to the same interior, you can indicate this as "BACK TO SHOT."

After your slug line, double space and describe the setting and characters in single space, using the 20-space margin. (See p. 289) Keep this material fairly brief and be careful not to over-direct. If your work goes into production, a *shooting script* will be developed with much more technical advice. That is when the scenes will be numbered and certain revisions may be made by the director. He or she is the camera expert; your job is to provide an effective, playable script.

The name of each new speaker is placed in capital letters which start 40 spaces in. This is much easier than trying to center each name. Brief directions regarding tone or gesture can be placed below the name, but usually this will be unnecessary. As with a play script, most lines can and will be interpreted by both the director and actors.

If a speaker is *off screen* but physically nearby, put "(O.S.)" after the name. If the speaker's voice is a memory of someone else's voice, commentary (as in introductions), or thoughts, use "(V. O.)" for *voice over*.

Here are a few more abbreviations which you may find helpful. All are used in the sample script which follows.

BEAT   a pause in dialogue
cont.   continued; place at top of each page after the first

CU	close-up shot
MED SHOT	medium shot (use camera instructions sparingly)
P.O.V.	a scene shot from a character's point of view; that is, what he or she sees
f.g.	foreground
b.g.	background

Try not to let the terminology and the somewhat different format distract you from the essential fact that you are writing a dramatic script. If you study the sample in the next chapter and continue it for practice, following the story line printed in the fiction section, you will find that the mechanics will soon become almost automatic. When this occurs, you are ready to strike out on your own with a fresh adaptation or an original script.

Chapter 33

A Film Script

ASYLUM

(A partial adaptation of "Sausage and Beer" by Stephen Minot as a
30-minute television drama)

by
Stephen Minot

FIRST DRAFT

c/o Prentice-Hall
Englewood Cliffs, NJ 07632

<u>ASYLUM</u>

<u>FADE IN</u>:

INT. CAR--DAY

Profile of a boy, 12, in the passenger seat of a 1929 car. b.g.
through window of the moving car shows New England winter farm
land with patchy snow, a bleak scene. Boy watches farm land roll by, absolutely expressionless. Occasionally he rubs his hands or tries to
warm them under his armpits.

NEW ANGLE

Profile of father, driving. He is lean, gray, and also expressionless.

BACK TO SHOT

Boy takes a furtive look at his father, then back to the scene ahead.

> BOY
>
> Is it very far?

> FATHER (O.S.)
>
> We're about halfway now.

Long silence again. Boy takes furtive look at his father just like the
first one, then turns to the view out front and speaks without looking
at his father.

> BOY
>
> I didn't know I had an Uncle
> Theodore.

> FATHER (O.S.)
> (voice flat)
>
> He's my brother.

EXT. BOY'S P.O.V. DOWN THE ROAD

cont.

>   BOY (O.S.)
>   (musing silently to self)
>   How can anybody have a
>   brother and not talk about him?
>   Maybe he's a hermit.

                                        CUT TO

EXT. SHACK IN FOREST--DAY

Fantasy: Imaginary uncle played by father steps out of shack and
smiles warmly, waving a greeting to unseen visitors.

BACK TO SHOT

>   BOY (O.S.)
>   (still as if thinking)
>   No. They wouldn't keep that a
>   secret. This Theodore's done
>   something terrible.

                                        CUT TO

INT. CELL BLOCK IN PRISON--DAY

Fantasy: Imaginary uncle played by father again is in prison uniform
but smoking a cigar. He waves a "tough-guy" greeting to unseen
visitors.

                                        CUT TO

INT. CAR--CU BOY

>   BOY (V.O.)
>   (thinking)
>   A real gangster! That's it-- "my
>   Uncle Ted, you know, the cop
>   killer."

Just the hint of a smile crosses his face.

cont.

EXT. HIGH ANGLE

From an AERIAL SHOT, we see the car make its way along a deserted road. Patchy snow of fields and scrub land give a look of isolation and desolation.

INT. IN CAR

f.g. father and son as seen from back seat. b.g. view of long, bleak institutional buildings. Old man in a gray, nondescript uniform seen pushing a two-wheeled cart. Car moves slowly by several such buildings.

> BOY
> (awed)
> Where are all the guards?

> FATHER
> They don't have guards in a hos-
> pital.

> BOY
> Hospital?

> FATHER
> A kind of hospital.

CUT TO

EXT. FRONT STEPS

CU large, somewhat unshaven face of ATTENDANT who looks threatening at first.

MED SHOT shows ATTENDANT in doorway looking less threatening.

> ATTENDANT
> Well now, Mr. Bates, you
> brought the boy I see.

CU--FATHER who looks gray against the gray background of snow and puddles in road.

cont.

                    FATHER
            I brought the boy.

MED SHOT--FATHER AND ATTENDANT

                    FATHER
            How's Ted?

                  ATTENDANT
            Same as when you called. A lit-
            tle gloomy, maybe, but calm.
            Those boils have just about
            gone.

                    FATHER
            Good.

                  ATTENDANT
            Funny about those boils. I don't
            remember a year but what he's
            had trouble. Funny.

                    FATHER
            Funny.

INT. HALLWAY AND WAITING ROOM

LONG SHOT shows ATTENDANT, FATHER, and BOY pass through
dark hall and into waiting room in silence. Benches around four
walls. Long table in middle. Old men shuffling about; younger men
wheeling cars of linen. Everyone moving slowly. Dreamlike effect.

MED SHOT: Father and son sit on bench. Father looks straight ahead.
Boy keeps his head motionless but moves his eyes in quiet
astonishment.

                    BOY
            (Softly to his father)
            Smells like where we bring old
            clothes and things before
            Christmas.

cont.

>   FATHER
>   (A touch of a smile)
>   The Refuge? Yes, it does smell
>   like the Refuge. Sort of.

BOY'S P.O.V.--WAITING ROOM

He sees an old man stretched out on the bench beside him, one hand
over his eyes, the other resting on his crotch. He is snoring.

BACK TO SHOT

Boy inches his way further from the sleeping man. Then looks
sideways at father, hoping his attempts weren't seen. Father stares
straight ahead.

BOY'S P.O.V.

He sees another patient scratching his back on the dark-varnished
door frame.

BACK TO SHOT

Boy scratches his shoulder blade. Father looks up abruptly and the
son, seeing this, looks, too. Then he opens his eyes wide.

LONG SHOT--WAITING ROOM

Black attendant is leading a man in who must be Uncle THEODORE.
THEODORE is a heavy, sagging man with rounded shoulders. He has
a clean white shirt, no tie, and pants hung up on suspenders patched
with twine. He shuffles toward the others. The attendant points out
the visitors and leaves. THEODORE shuffles to within inches of his
visitors who stand.

>   FATHER
>   Hello there, Ted, how have you
>   been?

>   THEODORE
>   (blank-faced)
>   Been?

A BEAT. No one knows what to say.

cont.

                    FATHER
          I brought the boy

                    THEODORE
          The boy?

                    FATHER
          My boy. Young Will.

The boy attempts to hold out his hand but Theodore makes no move
to shake it.

                    THEODORE
                 (to his brother)
          But you're Will.

                    FATHER
          Right, but we've named our boy
          William, too.

CU THEODORE

His face lights up in a broad and genuine smile which radiates charm
and dispels all uneasiness about the situation.

                    THEODORE
                 (chuckling)
          Well now, there's one on me.
          You know, I'd forgotten I even
          had a boy.

Chapter 34

Developing
as a Playwright

Evaluating your own work through a silent reading, a spoken delivery, and a group reading; *five core questions*
concerning the dramatic impact, plot, characterization,
themes, and degree of originality; the importance of
embracing the medium.

The preceding chapters on drama and script writing are designed to increase your awareness of what the genre requires and what it offers. But the
actual growth process will depend, as it did with poetry and fiction, on how
well you learn to evaluate and revise your own work and, on a broader level,
how successfully you can learn from studying professional work.

EVALUATING YOUR OWN WORK

In evaluating your dramatic scripts, the opinion of friends may be
helpful—more so, in fact, than with poetry because the work is probably intended for a broader audience. And the advice of teachers and the profes-
sionals you may meet at conferences will be invaluable. But ultimately *you*
are the one who has to decide what revisions to make.

Begin with a silent reading. You have been doing that in the process of
writing, of course; but this reading is different. Give the script your undivided attention and don't stop even to make corrections or notes.

As you read, picture all the action. Visualize each scene. And try to hear the lines as they would be spoken by actors and actresses. Don't analyze. Just experience. Then, when you are through, imagine yourself the director at the end of the first dress rehearsal and write an objective critique.

That's the first step. The second is reading the script out loud. One mechanical purpose is timing. The total playing time can be estimated fairly accurately if you allow for action which occurs without lines. If it is a play which is divided into acts and scenes, it will be important to know how long they are. Use this information when deciding where to cut and expand. If it is a television script, see if you are fairly close to the structural pattern of acts outlined in Chapter 32. In either case, you will want to know the total playing time.

In addition to these mechanical concerns, the spoken reading is an effective way for you to judge the quality of your dialogue before anyone else hears it. Lines which looked satisfactory on the page may sound awkward or out of character. Long speeches which you may have read silently just a bit fast will, when you read out loud, reveal themselves to be ponderous or heavy with thematic pronouncements.

After making corrections and revisions, you are ready for the third step, an informal group reading. Your readers should be familiar with the script, but there is no need for them to memorize the lines. If possible, the reading should be taped for further study. Naturally, some of the parts will appear better or worse depending on the skills of your readers, but no matter how informal the performance may be, it will give you your first real notion of what the play might be like in full production.

It is helpful to have a small audience of friends in addition to your readers, but it is not at all essential. The real value comes from translating the written script into something close to what it is intended to become: a dramatic and convincing performance for stage or film.

If possible, allow time after the reading for a discussion of the play's dramatic impact, its theme, or any of the five critical questions suggested below. Those who have taken part in the reading are apt to have insights into the work which you may not have considered.

One note of caution: Be careful not to let such sessions deteriorate into general conversations about the issues suggested by the play. Remind your critics that the subject is the play or script itself. You may wish to reproduce the following five questions (giving credit, of course) so that they may serve as guidelines for the discussion.

FIVE CORE QUESTIONS

These five questions are central to the analysis of a dramatic script. And they will help to keep the discussion from digressing. They should also serve as a way of looking at your own work in early-draft stages.

First, *does the play have dramatic impact?* Specifically, does it present some type of hook at the outset? And is this followed by dramatic questions strong enough to hold the interest of the audience? If shock is used, does it make the scene or the play melodramatic? Or is it an effective method of elevating the dramatic punch? And if wit and satire provide dramatic energy, do they work? Is the play really funny? Or, more helpful, which characters and which specific scenes were successfully comic as compared with which less successful ones? Precise comparisons are usually more useful than general pronouncements.

Second, *is the structure of the plot effective?* Even if your critics are not sure what improvements to suggest, you will learn a good deal if you ask them where the high points were. If they are unable to describe the work in terms of rising action and periodic climaxes, you should take a second look at the structure of your plot.

Third, *were the characters convincing and interesting?* Since characterization depends on dialogue and action, this question will necessarily include the effectiveness of the lines and the appropriateness of what each character does. As playwright you may have to discourage such subjective comments as "I really didn't like that character." What you have to find out is whether it was the *characterization* that failed in some way.

The group should understand that we don't make the same demands about secondary characters and those presented for comic relief or as satiric sketches. These may not be "convincing" as fully developed characters are, but they still must serve some function and in most cases provide interest.

Fourth, *what themes are being explored and how are they developed?* It is important to find out just which themes reached your audience. Sometimes their views will differ from what you thought was clearly suggested. In such cases, don't be too quick to explain what your intent was. Encourage your critics to explain the play as they understood it. This will help you to see it objectively.

If your themes were too subtle, the play is not going to be improved by convincing your critics that they should have seen what you had in mind. See if you can work out actual approaches to revision which would highlight the ideas that didn't come through before. If, on the other hand, the group feels that the themes were too obvious, find out if the main ideas appeared to them hackneyed or preachy or just commonplace. Again, the most profitable approach you can take is not one of defense but exploration.

The fifth and final question is linked to the previous two: *Does the play or script show originality?* There is nothing wrong in having your piece reflect the work of some playwright you admire. But your treatment should be fresh. Much will depend on characterization and how you shape your thematic concerns; yet originality goes beyond that. What you hope to hear is the feeling that this is a memorable script, one which was new and convincing. But if you don't get quite that sort of support, try to find out which elements of the play were too familiar to hold full interest and which were like a new experience for your audience.

EMBRACING THE MEDIUM

Writing a play or film script can be valuable even if you never do it again. You will learn a good deal about the medium and your capacity to enjoy performances will be far greater. But if you want to go on from there and develop as a playwright or scriptwriter, you will have to immerse yourself in the medium.

In playwriting, this will involve a lot of reading. While the finished production is the best teacher, your ability to see plays may be limited by what is being presented in your area and how much money you can spend. Your library, on the other hand, will have more plays than you can read in a year.

The collections of so-called best plays may not always strike you as the best, but you can learn from any script. And don't feel that you should limit yourself to recent works. The ingenuity with which Shakespeare presents a dramatic question early in his tragedies is a skill well worth studying; the cleverness with which Shaw masks highly didactic themes with wit and satire is a technique which can be used in any period.

As for seeing plays in production, do so as much as you can. Often students are given special rates just before opening night. If you are in college, it would be well worth volunteering your time to act or to serve on a stage crew. The mechanics of producing a play should be a part of any playwright's education.

If television or motion-picture writing is what interests you, it is important to study the best productions carefully. It may also be necessary to go where the action is. Unlike the poet, you cannot develop your talents in isolation. A good school will provide contacts, and even a non-writing job in a studio or production agency will help. You will probably discover that less of your time will be spent in actual script writing than in the intricate process of marketing. This you will have to learn directly from the men and women who have made a success of it.

Developing as a playwright or scriptwriter has one aspect in common with the process of developing as a poet or writer of fiction: Your greatest resource is the published work in your field. Remember that there are tens of thousands of individuals who have published in the very genre you hope to master. They have faced just about every technical problem you will consider in a lifetime; they have shared many of your feelings. You bring a unique set of experiences and sensitivities to the field, but you won't know what approaches you can take unless you become familiar with what has been done by others. Your finest teachers are the works themselves. Listen to them.

Part 4

Appendices

Appendix A

Submission of Material for Publication

Unfounded *myths* about publishing; the *tests* of whether one is ready to submit material; *mechanical considerations* of the manuscript itself; *what to submit; where to* submit; the *vanity presses;* the use of *personal contacts;* the dangers of *double submissions;* the value of *agents; placing a play;* and the reasonable approach to publication.

The number of novice writers who submit material long before there is any chance of publication is matched by the number of those who are reluctant to submit even when they should enter the public market. This is due to the fact that there are so many writers who have only a hazy notion about the whole area of marketing.

First, let's clear away a number of unfounded myths about publishing. One hears, for example, that nothing is published without "pull," that neither fiction nor drama can succeed without sex, that poetry must be unintelligible, that agents are generally dishonest, and that Madison Avenue has a death grip on every phase of publication. Equally fanciful is the claim that if a piece of writing is "good" it will eventually be published without the slightest effort on the part of the writer.

In addition, there are a number of personal delusions which occur so frequently that they are almost archetypal. This country is full of individuals who have lost a trunk, suitcase, or even a crate of manuscripts which, if it were found, would astound the literary world. Meanwhile, they populate writers' conferences. And then there are those who have written a brilliant work which was "stolen" and published under another title with "only minor revisions."

There are two essential facts to remember: First, publication is no more fair than life itself; there will always be good works which are not accepted as well as thoroughly rotten material which is. Second, if talent, practice, and a practical system of submission are combined, one can alter the odds in one's favor.

The test of whether you are ready to submit material is twofold. First, you should have written in that particular genre for some time. So-called "first novels" usually have been preceded by considerable practice in short stories and quite frequently by two or three unpublished novels.

During this difficult period of apprenticeship you should also be reading a good deal and familiarizing yourself with the publications which might be interested in your work. I have repeatedly stressed the need to read carefully and regularly in the genre of your choice. Writers who do not do this are at such a great disadvantage that they eventually quit. Those who study their genre actively become perpetual students. They not only develop writing ability, they become increasingly familiar with the publications which may help them later.

If you have been writing for some time and have been an active, conscientious reader, you may be ready for the long and sometimes frustrating program of submitting material.

MECHANICAL CONSIDERATIONS

The manuscript must be typed with a dark ribbon on a good grade of standard typewriter paper (16- or 20-lb. weight with at least 25% rag content). The type should be pica (not elite or the new varieties). The margins at left and at the top should be 1½ inches, the bottom one inch, and the right roughly one inch without excessive hyphenation. All material except name and address should be double spaced.

Place your name and address on the left about two inches down from the top and "Fiction" or "A Poem" on the right. Some authors add the approximate length there, but this is done less now, and publishers do not require it.

The title is normally placed in capital letters (not underlined or placed in quotation marks) about a third of the way down the page in this fashion:

Harley Q. Author
205 Main St.   Fiction
Middletown, IL 62666

LOOKING FORWARD

The story begins two double spaces below this. Title pages on a separate sheet are used only for novels, plays, and film scripts.

The pages (after the first) should be numbered in Arabic numerals along with your last name in the *upper right* corner: Author 2, Author 3, and so on.

Do not place the manuscript in a folder or binder, and do not staple it. A simple paper clip will do. Novels should be sent loose in a box. Covering letters are not at all necessary, but if you do include one, make it brief and factual. Never defend your own work.

If all this seems rather restrictive, remember that originality belongs in the art form itself, not in the manuscript.

For mailing, the envelope should be large enough so that the manuscript need not be folded. This applies to single poems as well. If one buys 9½″ × 12½″ envelopes for sending, one can include a self-addressed, stamped 9″ × 12″ envelope for its return. If this is too complicated, merely fold the second 9½″ × 12½″ envelope so that it can be placed inside the first with the manuscript. In either case, be sure that your address and proper postage is on it. Failure to do this not only infuriates the editor but increases your chances of never seeing it again.

Poems are usually sent first class. Heavier manuscripts should be labeled "SPECIAL FOURTH CLASS—MANUSCRIPT" so that they will be sent at the more economical book rate. United Parcel rates vary by zone but are often almost as inexpensive as the Postal Service book rate.

Allow about four weeks for poetry and short stories and an agonizing three months for novels. Resist that temptation to enquire about work sent until at least twice the expected time has passed.

If you know no one on the staff, merely send the manuscript to the fiction or poetry editor at the address given in the magazine. But if you have met or have corresponded with an editor or even a junior reader, send it to him or her.

Keeping records is extremely important. It is impossible to remember what went out when and to which magazine. In addition, it is invaluable to have a record not only of which editors had a kind word or two but of which magazines sent specifically worded rejection slips. The lowest level of rejection slip is merely a printed statement saying that they appreciated receiving your work and were unable to use it. In addition, most magazines have one or two special slips with wording like "this was of particular interest to us" or "we hope to see more of your work." Take these seriously. Next on the scale is the penned comment on the bottom of the slip like "good dialogue" or "try us again." These are infuriatingly brief, but they are worth recording. Be careful, however, not to inundate a magazine with weekly submissions. An editor who has commented on one poem is not going to be impressed with a flood of inferior work. Treat such individuals as potential allies who deserve only your best efforts.

The highest point on this scale is the *letter* of rejection. Even if brief, this is close to acceptance. If they suggest specific revisions which seem wise, revise and resubmit. If not, send your next really good piece. These are two situations in which you should definitely include a short covering letter.

WHAT TO SUBMIT

This decision must rest ultimately with you. Although the advice of other serious writers can be helpful, don't be swayed by friends who do not know what you are doing. Classmates or neighbors who never read poetry are not going to be very helpful as critics.

This does not hold for drama or television scripts, however. Since such work is designed to reach a larger audience, the advice of non-writers may be of real value.

Poets should select a group of three or four poems. Writers of fiction should limit each submission to one story. Once the choice is made, keep sending the work out repeatedly. A single editorial rejection means absolutely nothing. A manuscript is not "dead" until it has been turned down by at least ten magazines. The best approach is to send the work out on the very day it is returned—otherwise you are apt to lose courage. As a practical matter, just as many manuscripts are accepted after six or eight rejections as after only one. This is largely due to the fact that so many nonliterary factors go into selecting a work for publication, such as the number and kind of manuscripts on hand, the balance of a particular issue, and the personal preferences of the first reader.

There is no easy rule concerning what should be sent out; but once the decision is made, stand by it until you have cumulative proof that the work is unpublishable.

WHERE TO SUBMIT

As I have suggested in earlier chapters, the place to start studying publications is your library. Read the little magazines and quarterlies and find out which ones are printing your kind of work. Keep a file on each publication with a brief description of the works which you found successful so that you will remember them and can look them up later.

You can find additional titles listed in *Literary Market Place* (*LMP*) and *Writer's Market*. But never submit material to a magazine on the basis of these listings alone. Always review at least one issue of the magazine and make sure that they would be interested in your kind of work. "Blind submissions"—those made without being familiar with the publication—not only waste your time and money, they are a terrible burden for the editors who frequently work for little or no salary.

Novels and book-length collections of poems or stories should be handled the same way. Make sure that the publishing house you select has taken work similar to yours. Once you make up a list (again from *LMP*, the most complete resource book available), keep submitting until you have sent to thirteen or fourteen major publishers. This will take you about three years—time enough to complete the next novel or collection.

Circulating novels and book-length collections of short works raises four questions which are asked at every writer's conference. First, what about vanity presses?

A vanity press is one which charges the author a large fee for publication costs and sometimes for revisions. Many such organizations are perfectly honest, but it is rare indeed that a vanity press with its minimal system of distribution can do much with a novel which has been rejected by major publishers.

Don't confuse these commercially oriented vanity houses with small presses which are often run by individuals who love books and are willing to live a marginal economic life to work with them. Private presses still can't do much with a novel, but they are an increasing outlet for collections of poems and stories. The author still has to pay, but the venture is a cooperative one.

Another question raised by those submitting book-length manuscripts is whether it is appropriate to make use of a personal contact at a publishing house. Yes, it most certainly is. Even if your acquaintance is not in the editorial department, submit through him or her. Using such a connection will not, generally, get a bad manuscript published, but it may bypass that first reader who has a great many manuscripts to review. In the case of rejections, the writer is apt to receive a lengthier comment if the reader has some personal interests. I can testify to the fact that such personal contact is not a prerequisite for having stories or novels accepted; but it is neither unethical nor a waste of time to make use of any interested reader or publisher.

Third, should you submit copies of the same work to different publishers at the same time? No, you should not. This applies to individual stories and poems as well. Such double submissions are acceptable only from novelists who have repeatedly been on the best-seller list and who have a high-powered agent who can referee what may resemble a kind of manuscript auction. For the rest of us, it's one at a time.

Publishers assume that if they accept a novel, they are investing in an author. Standard contracts usually insist on a first refusal on whatever book-length manuscript you may submit next. This does not apply to individual stories or poems you may be circulating at the same time, but it does mean that you should not have two copies of a book-length manuscript or even two different novels circulating at the same time.

This is frustrating and, to my mind, unfair to writers who have two novels which they would like to keep in circulation. As for taking a chance, remember that the publishing world is small and closely connected. It is not worth trying to violate what editors call "publishers' ethics."

Finally, what about agents? Reputable agents charge a flat 10 percent of all material sold through them and make no other charges whatever, regardless of how much postage or time they may spend. In return they expect to see *all* your fiction. With rare exceptions, agents do not handle poetry. If you are unpublished, it is sometimes difficult to find an agent who is willing to handle your work. But it is not impossible. Write letters of inquiry to agents you have heard about through friends or have located through *LMP*. Be sure to ask them to recommend an agent if they cannot take on your work themselves. Often they will know of younger agents who are looking for new clients. Once an agent has decided to handle your work, she or he may be willing to represent you through a decade of absolutely profitless submissions.

Certain agents charge for reading manuscripts of unpublished writers. Some of them may be of help to those in specialized fields like juveniles or mysteries, but any writer whose interest is at least partially literary will have little to learn from them. More serious, some of these agents have a way of flattering incompetent writers into paying one fee after another for such services as "editorial analysis" and "professional revision" which end up finally with an expensive offer from a vanity press. The only way you can be sure that you are dealing with a reputable agent is to have an agreement in writing which makes no financial demands except the flat 10 percent for work sold.

There is not much point in seeking an agent if you plan to submit primarily to little magazines. Placing material in such publications is an honor well worth struggling for, but they pay relatively little and 10 percent of that hardly covers postage. Agents cannot afford to work for love alone.

You may be able to interest an agent if you have a group of five or six potentially publishable stories which might be considered by quality magazines (*Atlantic, The New Yorker*), the women's magazines (*McCalls, The Ladies' Home Journal*) or what are now being called the flesh magazines (*Playboy, Penthouse*). Manuscripts submitted to such magazines through agencies usually receive more careful scrutiny by readers with more editorial authority.

Most agents, however, are reluctant to take on new clients unless they have a novel manuscript ready for submission. Agents perform a real service in this area, handling not only the tedious (and emotionally draining) ritual of submissions but also negotiating a contract. Although magazines do not offer contracts (you merely accept the rate offered), publishers do. And they are negotiable—especially after the first. If you do not have an agent and have reached this fortunate stage, be sure to secure a sample contract from the Authors Guild (234 West 44th St., New York, NY 10036).

All this should not deter you if you are unable to find an agent. You are your own best agent when it comes to submitting to little magazines. And many first novels and stories have been accepted directly from authors.

All this has only partial relevance to the problem of marketing a play. There are several directions the playwright can take—none of them as neat and simple as the methods of submitting fiction and poetry.

First, the playwright can try working through an agent. Most large agencies have drama departments, and some small agencies specialize in this field. Second, try every drama contest in the country—and there are many. Announcements of contests are usually found on bulletin boards in colleges and universities. Third, those who are fortunate enough to be on campuses with a good stage and active drama group can try to have their work produced locally. This may not be Broadway, but the satisfaction is deep and lasting. It is also professionally valuable. Fourth, submit to those publishers who specialize in plays; though here is it much more important to know exactly what their editorial policy is than it is in the case of novels. Most of these concerns have a particular type of play which they consider acceptable for publication. Fifth, one-act plays can sometimes be placed in magazines. It is well worth writing a letter of inquiry first. Finally, one can try to find a producer directly. There is probably no other branch of the arts which is more committed to personal contact than drama. To put it more brutally, "pull" is extraordinarily valuable. If you know a producer, director, actor, or even a stagehand, write him or her. This situation is not merely a matter of commercial corruption. The fact is that although book publishers come to know potential writers through little magazines (which they read with professional care), producers have little contact with the young playwright whose work has not yet appeared on the stage. This situation will continue until there are more little magazines willing to specialize in original plays and more low-budget stage companies in the smaller cities. Meanwhile, playwrights must struggle with the particularly difficult task of presenting their material.

Marketing television and motion picture scripts is a world unto itself. There is no art form which plunges the writer so deeply into the marketplace. There are three areas to consider, each with its own approaches: commercial television, public television, and motion-picture studios. For a clear introduction to the television world, I recommend *Television Writing* by Richard A. Blum (Communication Arts Books, Hastings House,

Publishers, NY). For news of recent events in television, theater, and film, consider a newsletter called *ScriptWriter News* which is published twice monthly (250 West 57th St., Suite 224, New York, NY 10019). Write them or check *LMP* for current subscription rates.

If you are serious about your art, you must be realistic when considering publication. It is naive to assume that marketing your work is crass and demeaning. Publishers have no way of discovering you if you make no effort to circulate your work. Yet on the other hand, a mania to publish at all costs can be damaging to the creative process. It often leads to imitative and conventional work and to feelings of hostility toward editors and publishers.

To avoid these most unrewarding extremes, begin with an honest evaluation of your own work. Then follow through with a planned, long-range program of submissions. There are, of course, writers who achieve wide recognition very suddenly; but this is rare and not always a blessing. Ideally, creative work is a way of life, and the effort to publish is an important but not a central portion of that life.

Appendix B

Resources for Writers

GENERAL REFERENCE BOOKS

The following three reference books are published annually and can be found in almost every library.

- *Literary Market Place,* R.R. Bowker Co.
  LMP contains the most complete listings of magazines (though scant on poetry journals), book publishers, literary agents, contests, writers' conferences, television and motion picture addresses. It is entirely factual and does not have articles on how to write or market your material.
- *The Writer's Handbook,* The Writer, Inc.
  The listing of magazines and book publishers is adequate, but more than half of this volume is devoted to a large number of short, practical articles on the writing of fiction, nonfiction, verse (mostly popular), plays, TV scripts, juveniles, and the like.
- *Writer's Market,* Writer's Digest Books
  This volume strikes a balance between listings of magazines and informative articles on writing and marketing. The section on poetry journals is more comprehensive than those in the two books described above.

INFORMATIVE MAGAZINES

These magazines provide information and advice for writers, poets, and to a lesser degree, dramatists. They do not generally publish fiction or poetry. Consult library copies for current subscription rates.

- *Coda: Poets and Writers Newsletter,* 201 W. 54th St., New York, NY 10019
  This nonprofit publication is a must for anyone who writes poetry, fiction, or dramatic scripts. It is published five times a year. Its articles deal with problems faced by all literary writers: how to find time to write when teaching, how to arrange readings, how to find out about writers' conferences and colonies, publishing translations, and negotiating book contracts. It is also the best source of contest and grant application deadlines, dates of conferences and readings, winners of awards.
- *The Writer,* 8 Arlington St., Boston, MA 02116
  Both this magazine and *Writer's Digest* (see below) focus more on writing for mass markets than does *Coda.* Articles give advice on writing and marketing a great variety of material from gothic novels to "confessionals" and from poetry to greeting card verse.
- *Writer's Digest,* 9933 Alliance Rd., Cincinnati, OH 45242
  A highly popular magazine for those who wish practical, "how-to" advice from successful writers of fiction, drama, and popular verse.
- *Publishers Weekly,* 1180 Avenue of the Americas, New York, NY 10036
  Of particular interest to those in the business end of publishing, this magazine covers what books are about to be released, who is doing what in the field, author profiles, and future trends.

POETRY JOURNALS

Although almost all literary quarterlies ("little magazines") contain some poetry, the following publications are of special interest to poets. They represent only a small sampling of the many fine poetry journals publishing today. Be sure to buy and read carefully at least one copy before submitting. If you write poetry, you will want to subscribe to at least one journal.

- *The American Poetry Review,* 1616 Walnut St., Rm. 405, Philadelphia, PA 19103
  Printed bimonthly in tabloid form, *APR* is a relatively large-circulation (26,000) publication which contains not only new poetry but news and opinion about and by poets.
- *Beloit Poetry Journal,* Box 2, Beloit, WI 53511
  Published quarterly, the issues average about 40 pages, all poetry.
- *Paris Review,* 45-39 171 Place, Flushing, NY 11358
  Published four times a year, *Paris Review* contains fiction, interviews with writers and poets, as well as many poems. The magazine, once published in Paris, enjoys a circulation of 10,000.

- *Poetry,* 601 S. Morgan St., P.O. Box 4348, Chicago, IL 60680
  Known as "Poetry Chicago," this distinguished monthly was established in 1912 and has a circulation of about 8,000.
- *Poetry Northwest,* 4045 Brooklyn Ave., NE, University of Washington, Seattle, WA 98105
  This excellent quarterly has been edited by David Wagoner for a number of years.
- *Sewanee Review,* University of the South, Sewanee, TN 37375
  Most issues contain one story and several articles on literature and the arts, but the poetry section is a regular and important feature.

POETRY ANTHOLOGIES AND COLLECTIONS

The following anthologies are just a few of many which focus on modern work. Most are available in paperback.

- *A Geography of Poets,* Edward Field, ed., Bantam Books
  Arranged by geographic area, Field's anthology avoids most literary biases and presents a balanced view of what is being published by poets today. Women poets are well represented.
- *The Modern Poets,* J.M. Brinnin and B. Read, ed., McGraw-Hill
  A broad, inclusive anthology.
- *The New Naked Poetry: Recent American Poetry in Open Forms,* S. Berg and R. Mezey, ed., The Bobbs-Merrill Co.
  The subtitle is more accurate than the title. Don't expect to find metered verse here.
- *No More Masks! An Anthology of Poems by Women,* F. Howe and E. Bass, ed., Anchor/Doubleday
  From Amy Lowell to Nikki Giovanni—a full spectrum of women poets in this century.

Magazines and anthologies are both excellent ways of discovering poets whose work you enjoy and can learn from. Collections (as opposed to anthologies) have the advantage of giving you a far greater appreciation of the work of a single poet.

Many such volumes can be found in any good library. But consider buying your own copies when you can. Since many bookstores do not stock more than a few titles, the best approach is to list the poets whose work you admire and check the "Authors" section of *Books in Print* in any library or bookstore to see which poets have published collections. Then order them through your bookstore or directly from the publisher (addresses in *LMP*). The cost of each volume will be less than a single meal at a restaurant, and the rewards will be long-lasting.

LISTENING TO POETRY

There are two ways of hearing poets read their own work. First, attend poetry readings. Almost every college and university offers a series of poetry readings which are open to the public. Often colleges will place you on a mailing list if you are not a student. In addition, larger libraries and organizations like the Y.M.C.A., Y.W.C.A., and Y.M.H.A. invite poets to read their works. Attending writers' conferences in the summer (listings in *LMP*) is also a good way to hear poets read their own work.

The second approach is through recordings. Many libraries have good record collections. Records and tapes may also be ordered through any music store.

MAGAZINES WHICH PUBLISH FICTION

Anyone who writes fiction should make a habit of reading the stories which appear in the four big-circulation magazines:

- *Atlantic Monthly* (one or two stories each issue)
- *Esquire* (usually one story; published fortnightly)
- *The New Yorker* (normally one light and one serious story each week)
- *Harper's* (usually one story; monthly).

In addition, here are five important journals which place a special emphasis on short stories. If fiction is important to you, subscribe to at least one and make sure your library takes the other four.

- *Antaeus,* 1 W. 30th St., New York, NY 10001
  This quarterly occasionally has special issues devoted to poetry or criticism, but most issues are balanced, with a good representation of short stories.
- *Fiction International,* St. Lawrence University, Canton, NY 13617
  They are presently publishing one large issue each fall plus a collection by a single author. Their publishing policy is subject to change, but their standards remain high.
- *Mississippi Review,* University of Southern Mississippi, Southern Station, Box 5144, Hattiesburg, MS 39401
  Edited by Frederick Barthelme, *MR* publishes a wide range of fiction from traditional to innovative. It is published three times a year.
- *The North American Review,* University of Northern Iowa, Cedar Falls, IA 50614
  The oldest quarterly in the United States, *NAR* maintains a strong commitment to new fiction. In 1981 it received the National Magazine Award for Fiction (with *The New Yorker* and *Esquire* as runners-up!)

- *Ploughshares,* Box 529, Cambridge, MA 02139
  Relatively new, this quarterly rotates its editorship for variety. Special issues are occasionally devoted to poetry, but most contain several stories. Their all-fiction issues are excellent and, when available, serve well as an inexpensive anthology for writing classes.

FICTION ANTHOLOGIES AND COLLECTIONS

There are two widely read annual publications made up of short stories published in magazines during the previous year. While no two editors will agree on the "best" stories published in any year, these volumes provide a fine overview of good, contemporary fiction.

- *The Best American Short Stories,* Houghton Mifflin Co.
  This volume has been published annually since 1915. Edited for 36 years by Martha Foley, the collection is still referred to informally as "the Foley collection." The editorship is now changed each year.
- *Prize Stories, The O. Henry Awards,* William Abrahams, ed., Doubleday and Co.
  Better known as "the O. Henry collection," this is another view of the best fiction published during the previous year. It serves as an excellent companion work to *The Best American Short Stories.*

In addition to these two annuals, there are many short-story anthologies designed mainly for college use. They offer an opportunity to discover authors you may not have read. Here are four as an introduction.

- *Modern Short Stories,* A. Mizener, ed., W. W. Norton and Co.
  A good, comprehensive collection.
- *Short Stories From the Literary Magazines,* J.A. Thurston and C. Johnson, ed., Scott, Foresman and Co.
  As the title indicates, this volume is limited to stories published fairly recently in literary magazines. Your favorite authors may not be represented, but a valuable sampling of fairly recent fiction is provided.
- *Short Story Masterpieces,* R.P. Warren and A. Erskine, Dell Publishing Co.
  This inexpensive paperback has been used for years in college courses. It has excellent stories by such favorites as Faulkner, Fitzgerald, Hemingway, and Salinger.
- *The Story, A Critical Anthology,* M. Schorer, Prentice-Hall Inc.
  In addition to a solid list of stories, this anthology includes valuable commentary by Mark Schorer, biographer and short-story writer.

As with poetry anthologies, these volumes will introduce you to a variety of work. But when you find an author you admire, see if he or she has published a collection of stories. In many cases you can find such volumes in your local library. But if you wish to order your own copy, turn to the "Author" section of *Books in Print* in your library or bookstore.

A number of university presses have begun to publish collections of short stories by a single author in paperback. Among the first to do this was the University of Illinois Press (Urbana, IL 61801). They have been publishing four paperback collections a year since 1975. This admirable policy has been adopted in modified form by The Johns Hopkins University Press (Baltimore, MD 21218), the University of Pittsburgh Press (Pittsburgh, PA 15260), and a few others. Write these publishers if you wish a list of their short story collections and prices.

MAGAZINES FOR PLAYWRIGHTS AND SCRIPTWRITERS

- *Coda: Poets and Writers Newsletter*, 201 W. 54th St., New York, NY 10019
  Although *Coda* was listed earlier for poets and writers of fiction, it is also valuable for dramatists. It lists deadlines for drama contests and occasionally gives advice on marketing scripts. A special issue was devoted to "Writing for Television."
- *Drama Review*, 51 West 4th St., Rm. 300, New York, NY 10012
  This quarterly focuses on contemporary, avant-garde drama. Articles are often in depth and cover a wide range of generally innovative drama: women's theater, European trends, mixed-media productions, and so on.
- *ScriptWriter News*, Writer's Publishing Co., 250 West 57th St., Suite 224, New York, NY 10019
  Published twice monthly, this tightly-packed newsletter reports on events and trends in television writing with some attention paid to legitimate theater. A good source for learning who needs what kind of scripts and, on the personal level, "who's hot" in video, theater, and film.

BOOKS FOR PLAYWRIGHTS AND SCRIPTWRITERS

- *Best Short Plays*, Chilton Book Co.
  This annual has been published for decades. Back issues can be found in many libraries.
- *Best Short Plays of the World Theatre*, Crown Publishers, Inc.
  Published irregularly, these volumes are similar to *Best Short Plays* but with most of the work coming from abroad.
- *Television Writing*, Richard A. Blum, Communication Arts Books, Hastings House, Publishers, Inc.
  A brief, practical introduction to writing television scripts and marketing them.

PUBLISHERS OF PLAY SCRIPTS

These publishers buy, print, and sell play scripts—both one-act and full length. Since they deal largely with schools and regional companies, their selections tend to be conservative and easily playable. Each publisher puts out a catalogue describing its plays briefly.

- *Baker's Plays,* 100 Chauncy St., Boston, MA 02111
  In business since 1845, Baker's Plays offers not only a great many rather light comedies and mysteries, but also a number of serious dramas which have had Broadway success. Their scripts are relatively inexpensive and offer a good way to study plays which are not found in drama anthologies.
- *The Dramatic Publishing Co.,* 4150 N. Milwaukee Ave., Chicago, IL 60641
  Established in 1885, this company prints from 40 to 60 titles a year.
- *Samuel French, Inc.,* 25 W. 45th St., New York, NY 10036
  The oldest (1830) of these three venerable publishing houses, Samuel French, Inc. has branches in England and Canada and publishes about 50 titles a year.

In addition to these publishers specializing in drama, many other houses print paperback editions of plays. They may be difficult to find, however, because few bookstores stock more than a sampling. The best solution is the same as it is for poetry and fiction: Start with the card file in your library. If you want to order a copy, turn to the "Authors" section of *Books in Print* and order through your bookstore or directly from the publisher (address in *LMP*).

Remember, finally, that whether your interest is in theater, television drama, or film, it is essential that you see as many productions as you can. Whenever possible, combine your study of the script with the experience of seeing the work performed. Each approach will provide insights the other cannot.

Appendix C

Glossary-Index

This appendix may be used both for quick review of literary terms and as an index. The explanations are limited to the way terms are used in this text. Numbers refer to pages; those in italics indicate lengthier treatment. Italicized expressions indicate cross-references either in the same or a closely related form, e.g., *metered* may be found under **meter,** *rhyming* under **rhyme,** etc.

Absurdist, 266. See *theater of the absurd.*

Alliteration, 10, *39.* See *sound devices.*

Ambiguity, 72. That which suggests two or more different meanings. Ambiguity in theme which is not resolved frequently leads to obscurity. But ambiguities can be effective when the two alternative meanings join to make a broader, more profound suggestion.

Ambivalence, *70,* 175. Conflicting or contrasting emotions which are held at the same time. Lack of ambivalence sometimes results in *simple writing.*

Anapestic foot, 50. See *meter.*

Archaic diction, 26. Words which are primarily associated with an earlier period and are no longer in general use.

Arena stage, 265. See *stage designs.*

Assonance, 10, *39.* See *sound devices.*

Automatic writing, 115. See *stream of consciousness.*

Ballad, 82. A *narrative poem* often written in quatrains (see *stanza*) of alternating iambic tetrameter and trimeter *rhyming abcb.* "Folk ballads" are often intended to be sung and are relatively *simple.* "Literary ballads" are a *sophisticated* use of the old form.

Beat, 286. A pause in a line of dialogue in a television or film script.

Black humor, 202. Macabre, grim, or tragic events treated in a comic fashion so that the reader (or audience) is caught between laughter and *shock*. The technique is seen in the works of James Purdy, Joseph Heller, Bruce Jay Friedman, and Roald Dahl. It is sometimes referred to as "dark humor" to distinguish it from works written by black authors.

Black theater, *279ff.* Plays written by black Americans. Although playwrights like Langston Hughes and Ossie Davis wrote hundreds of works in the 1930s and 40s, the term is most frequently used to refer to those who have come into prominence since the 1960s such as Amiri Baraka (LeRoi Jones), Paul Carter Harrison, Lonne Elder III, and Adrienne Kennedy.

Black verse, 13, 67. *Verse* written by black Americans like Lucy Smith, David Henderson, Conrad Kent Rivers (p.98), Lucille Clifton (p.99), Maya Angelou (p. 92), and Gwendolyn Brooks (p. 92).

Blank verse, 50. Unrhyming iambic pentameter (see *verse* and *meter*).

Breath units, 62. See *rhythm*.

Caesura, 48. A pause or complete break in the *rhythm* of a line of *verse* frequently occurring in the middle. It is particularly noticeable in Old English alliterative verse such as *Beowulf*. It is also found in *metered verse*.

Canto, 81. A relatively lengthy unit, often numbered, found in both *metered* and *free verse*. It may consist of several *stanzas*.

Central concern, *199ff.* See *theme*.

Characterization, *168ff, 258ff.* The illusion in *fiction* or *drama* of having met someone. The illusion depends on consistency of details, complexity of insight, and on individuality. *Simple* characterization stresses consistency at the expense of complexity and often results in a *stock character*, a form of *simple writing*.

Cinquain, 43. See *stanza*.

Cliché, 15, *23ff.* A *metaphor* or simile which has become so familiar from overuse that the vehicle (see *metaphor*) no longer contributes any meaning whatever to the tenor. It provides neither the vividness of a good metaphor nor the strength of a single, unmodified word. "Good as gold" and "crystal clear" are clichés in this specific sense. The word is also used to describe overused but nonmetaphorical expressions such as "tried and true" and "each and every."

Comedy, *239 ff., 262 ff.* Drama which is light in *tone* and ends happily. Such plays are usually characterized by humor, wit, and *satire*.

Commercial writing, 109. *Prose*—both *fiction* and nonfiction—which is *simple* and conforms to certain rigid *conventions* of *plot* and *character* usually for the sake of publication and profit. Fictional forms include the "pulps" (confessionals such as *True Romance*) and the "slicks" (*McCalls, Redbook,* and the like). The so–called slick magazines, however, have also published a great deal of *sophisticated fiction*.

Concrete poetry, 58. *Verse* in which *typography* is employed in an extreme fashion to make the words and word fragments suggest a shape or picture which becomes of greater importance than rhythm or sound. Also called "shaped poetry."

Conflict, *181ff.,* 236. See *tension*.

Connotation, 19, *65.* The unstated suggestion implied by a word, phrase, passage, or any other unit in a *literary* work. This term includes everything from the emotional overtones or associations of a word or phrase to the symbolic significance of a character, setting, or sequence of actions.

Consonance, 39. See *sound devices*.

Convention, *11, 111*. Any pattern or device in literature which is repeated in a number of different works by a number of different writers. It is a broad term which includes basic devices like *plot, dialogue, meter,* the division of a play into acts and *scenes,* and the division of a *sonnet* into *octave* and *sestet*. It also refers to recurring patterns in subject matter such as men pitted against nature in fiction, women compared with a summer's day in verse, and the recognition scene in drama. Conventions can be subtle or hackneyed. The term includes everything which is not unique in a work of literature.

Cosmic irony, 71, 185. See *irony*.

Couplet, 42, 80. See *stanza*.

Creative writing, 4, 119. Any form of *sophisticated literary writing*. This term is generally used to describe college courses in the writing of fiction, poetry, and drama, or any combination of these. It excludes courses in expository writing, assertive writing, and (usually) *commercial writing*. Although all forms of writing require creativity in the broad sense, *creative writing* normally applies to *literary* as opposed to *descriptive* writing.

Dactylic foot, 50. See *meter*.

Descriptive writing, 4, *104ff*. Any verbal system in which meaning is ultimately linked with the real world and so can be judged as generally valid or invalid. This is in contrast with *literary writing* which contains its own system of *internal logic* and cannot be judged as valid or invalid. *Descriptive writing* is synonymous with "assertive writing" and includes such forms as the essay, thesis, editorial, article, text, and the varieties of journalism.

Deus ex machina, 265. Literally, "god from a machine," formerly used to describe stage machinery which was designed to save a character at the last moment. It now refers to any artificial or improbable event or device used in a play to turn the plot in the desired direction. It is often used in *simple fiction* or *drama*. It lacks *internal logic*.

Dialogue, 108, *174ff.*, 217. Any word, phrase, or passage which quotes a character's speech directly. It normally appears in quotation marks to distinguish it from thoughts. "Monologue" is reserved for relatively lengthy and uninterrupted speeches. "Soliloquy" refers to monologues spoken in plays. "Indirect dialogue" (p.176) is the same as "indirect discourse"; it echoes the phrasing of dialogue without actually quoting. Dialogue and thoughts constitute two of the five *narrative modes*.

Diction, *21ff.*, 204. The choice of words in any piece of writing. Diction is a major factor in determining *style*. "Poetic diction" is a special term used by those who argue that certain words are appropriate for poetry and others are not.

Dimeter, 51. See *line*.

Distance, 201 ff. That aspect of *tone* which describes how closely identified an author (or narrator) appears to be to his or her fictional character. Highly autobiographical and subjective works tend to have very little distance. *Metamorphosing* the *protagonist* or adding an *ironic* or humorous *tone* increases the *distance*.

Double rhyme, 42. See *rhyme*.

Drama, *216ff*. That form of *literary writing* intended primarily for presentation by performers speaking and acting on a stage. Drama is characterized, generally speaking, by the following: it is a "dramatic art" in the sense that it has an emotional impact or force; it is a visual art; it is an auditory art; it is physically produced on a stage; it moves continuously; and it is intended for spectators.

Dramatic conflict, *181ff.*, 236ff. See *tension*.

Dramatic irony, 71, 185. See *irony*.

Dramatic question, 184, 216, *236ff.* The emotional element in a play which holds the attention of an audience before the *theme* or thesis becomes clear. The dramatic question (or series of questions) is usually a *simple,* emotional appeal based either on *curiosity* or *suspense.* When the dramatic question is stressed at the expense of *theme,* the result is usually *melodrama.*

End-stopped line, 52. See *run-on line.*

Epiphany, 134 ff. The moment of awakening or discovery on the part of a fictional character, the reader, or both. This use of the term was suggested by James Joyce. It is generally limited to *fiction.*

Expressionism, 264, *266.* See *realistic drama.*

Eye rhyme, 42. See *rhyme.*

Falling meter, 51. See *meter.*

Feet, *49ff.* See *meter.*

Feminine rhyme, 41, 80. See *rhyme.*

Fiction, *103ff.* That form of *literary writing* which tells an untrue story in *prose.* It may be very *simple* like most *commercial writing* or it may be *sophisticated.* In either case, it establishes its own special world which is guided primarily by *internal logic.* Fiction is also classified by length and breadth: The short story is usually less than forty manuscript pages and explores the lives of only one or two characters; the novel is usually over two hundred manuscript pages long, frequently develops more than two characters, and explores a wider variety of themes. The novella is an ill-defined term designating works of fiction which fall between the story and the novel.

Figure of speech, *30ff.* See *image.*

First person narration, *148ff.* See *person.*

Flashback, *131ff.* See *plot.*

Focus, *152 ff.* The character or characters who are the primary concern of a story. When it is a single individual, he or she is also referred to as the *protagonist.* If the protagonist has an opponent (especially in drama), this character may be referred to as the *antagonist.*

Foil, 263. A secondary character in *fiction* or *drama* who sets off a primary character by contrast in attitude, appearance, or in other ways.

Foot, *49.* See *meter.*

Formula, 113. Popular *conventions* which characterize *simple fiction* and *drama.* These conventions are usually patterns of *plot* combined with stock characters. Sample: The–sincere–brunette who competes with The–scheming–blonde for the attentions of The–rising–young–executive who at first is "blind to the truth" but who finally "sees the light."

Frame story, 132. See *plot.*

Free verse, *56ff.* Verse which is written without meter, depending instead on *rhythmical* patterns derived from *typography,* syntactical elements, the repetition of words and phrases, *syllabics,* or breath units. Free verse contains no regular *rhyme,* depending instead on *sound devices* such as assonance, consonance, and alliteration.

Genre, 5ff., 103ff., 216ff. Any of several types of *literary* writing. In common usage, genres refer to *fiction, poetry,* and *drama.* Classifications like "mysteries," "Westerns," and "science fiction" are often referred to as "sub-genres," though the word does not yet appear in most dictionaries.

Gimmick, 114. A somewhat colloquial synonym for *convention* or literary trick, usually applied to *plot.* Although this word is generally used in its pejorative sense as a too-clever or contrived twist of plot, it is occasionally used to describe any unusual element in a piece of fiction.

Hackneyed language, 24. A broad term which includes clichés as well as nonmetaphorical phrases and words which have been weakened by overuse. Such language is closely associated with *sentimentality* and with *stock characters*.

Haiku, *36ff.*, 61, 82. Originally a Japanese verse form. In English it is usually written as a three-line poem containing five syllables in the first line, seven in the second, and five in the third.

Heptameter, 51. See *line*.

Hexameter, 51. See *line*.

Hyperbole, 32. A figure of speech (see *image*) employing extreme exaggeration usually in the form of a simile or *metaphor*.

Iambic foot, 49ff. See *meter*.

Image, 16, *28ff.* Any significant piece of sense data in a poem. It may be used in a literal statement, as a symbol, or in a figure of speech. A figure of speech (also called figurative language) uses an image in a stated or implied comparison. *Metaphors* are the most common figures of speech. When several contain images which are closely related, the result is an "image cluster" (p.33). Other figures of speech include similes, *puns,* and *hyperbole*.

Indirect dialogue, 176. See *dialogue*.

Internal logic, 4, 105. A system of consistencies within a literary narrative which determines what is possible, impossible, likely or unlikely for that particular piece. In this way, each piece of literature "creates its own world." This is an inductive system which makes use of every detail in a work—action, *dialogue*, descriptive material, *style*, and the like. It is a writer's primary method of establishing credibility.

Irony, 71ff., 185ff. A reversal in which the literal statement or actual event is contrasted with the intended meaning or expected outcome. Irony can take three forms. The first is "verbal irony," in which a statement by the author or a character is knowingly the opposite of the actual meaning (like saying, "Great day for a sail" during a hurricane). The second is "dramatic irony," in which events, not words, are reversed (like the messenger in *Oedipus Rex* who says "Good news" when unknowingly he brings disastrous information). The third is "cosmic irony," which is usually thought of as a reversal on the part of fate or chance (like the fire fighter who dies from smoking in bed).

Journalistic writing, 104. See *descriptive writing*.

Legitimate theater, 215. Plays performed by actors on a stage as contrasted with television drama, cinema, and the like.

Line, 5ff., *50ff.* A unit of *verse* which when printed normally appears without being broken, the length of which is determined by the poet alone. The inclusion of the line as a part of the art form rather than merely a printer's concern is one of the fundamental distinctions between *verse* and *prose*. In *metered verse*, lines usually contain the same number of feet (see *meter*); in *sprung rhythm* and *alliterative verse*, lines are linked by having the same number of stressed syllables; and in *free verse*, the length of lines is more of a visual concern (see *typography*). The following represent eight types of lines used in metered verse: (1) monometer (one foot), (2) dimeter (two feet), (3) trimeter (three feet), (4) tetrameter (four feet), (5) pentameter (five feet), (6) hexameter (six feet), (7) heptameter (seven feet), (8) octometer (eight feet).

Literary writing, 4, *105.* Any verbal system in which meaning is ultimately self-contained because it has created its own system of logic (see *internal logic*) which may or may not resemble that with which we interpret aspects of the real world. In essence, literary writing creates its own universe, as opposed to *descriptive writing* which is designed to explain or comment on some aspect of the real world. Literary writing, a synonym for *literature*, is a nonevaluative term and includes both *simple* and *sophisticated* samples of *fiction, poetry,* and *drama.*

Lyric, 47. Originally a Greek term referring to verse to be accompanied by a lyre. Today, it generally refers to a short poem which presents a single speaker who is concerned with a strongly felt emotion. Thus, poems of love, observation, and contemplation are "lyrics" in contrast with *ballads* and other types of *narrative poetry.* "Lyrical" is often used loosely to describe poetry which sounds musical because of its *sound devices* and *rhythm.*

Means of perception, *145ff.* The agent through whose eyes a piece of fiction appears to be presented. This character is also the one whose thoughts are revealed directly. The term is synonymous with "point of view" and "viewpoint." It is generally limited to a single character in short fiction.

Melodrama, 114ff., 211. *Simple writing* (usually drama or fiction) which is dominated by *suspense* and exaggerated forms of dramatic *tension. Sophisticated literature* also uses conflict, but melodrama does it blatantly and at the expense of other literary concerns. It usually makes use of *stock characters* as well.

Metamorphosis, *117ff.* Radical transformations of an experience or of an existing draft of a story or play in order to create fresh literary work. This process can be either conscious or unconscious. It is usually employed either to clarify existing patterns or to break up patterns which appear to be too neat or contrived. It may also help a writer to regain control over an experience which in its original form is still too personal to develop in literary form.

Metaphor and **simile,** *30ff.* A simile is a figure of speech (see *image*) in which one item is compared with another which is different in all but a few significant respects. Thus, "She fought like a lion" suggests courage but not the use of claws and teeth. The item being described is called the tenor (the true subject) and the one utilized is the vehicle. (Terms originally suggested by I. A. Richards.) A metaphor implies rather than states this same sort of comparison and so becomes a statement which is literally untrue, but when successful, figuratively stronger than a simile. "She was a lion when fighting for civil rights" is not taken literally because the reader recognizes it as a literary *convention.* In both cases, the base or starting point is the tenor. The reverse of this—using the vehicle as base and merely implying the tenor—is a *symbol* ("It was the lion, not the lamb that ruled England in those years").

Meter, 49ff. A system of *stressed* and unstressed syllables which creates *rhythm* in certain types of verse. The *conventionalized* units of stressed and unstressed syllables are known as *feet.* Metered verse normally contains the same number of feet in each *line* and the same type of foot throughout the poem. The effect, however, is usually muted by substituting other types of feet occasionally. The following six feet are in common use, but the iamb is the most popular form in English. Those which end on a stressed syllable are called "rising meter"; those which end on an unstressed syllable are called "falling meter."

iamb	(iambic)	ĕxcépt
trochee	(trochaic)	Mídăs
anapest	(anapestic)	dĭsăppoínt
dactyl	(dactylic)	háppĭlў
spondee	(spondaic)	héartbréak
pyrrhic	(pyrrhic)	ĭn thĕ

Modes, 108, *206ff.* See *narrative modes.*

Monologue, 280. See *dialogue.*

Monometer, 51. See *line.*

Mood and **tone,** *65ff.,* 87, *201ff.,* 210. See *tone.*

Narrative modes, 108, *206ff.* The five methods by which *fiction* can be presented: *dialogue,* thoughts, action, description, and exposition. Most writers use all five in varying proportions.

Narrative poetry, 79. Verse which tells a story. This may take the form of the *ballad,* the epic, or a tale in verse such as Hecht's "Lizards and Snakes" (p. 90).

Octave, 43, 70, 80. An eight-lined *stanza* in *metered verse.* Also the first eight lines of a *sonnet.*

Octometer, 51. See *line.*

Off rhyme, 40, 44. See *rhyme.*

Omniscient point of view, 147. The *means of perception* in which the author enters the mind of all major characters. "Limited omniscience" restricts the means of perception to certain characters. Most short fiction and a majority of novels limit the means of perception to a single character.

Onomatopoeia, 40. See *sound devices.*

Orientation, *188ff.* The sense in *fiction, drama,* or *narrative poetry* of being somewhere specific. This includes awareness of geography, historical period, season, and time.

Overtone and **connotation,** 9, 19. See *connotation.*

Pace, *133ff.,* 207. The reader's sense that a story or play "moves rapidly" or "drags." This is determined by the *rate of revelation* and by the *style.*

Paradox, 72. A statement which on one level is logically absurd yet on another level implies a reasonable assertion. Example from Heller's *Catch-22:* "The Texan turned out to be good-natured, generous, and likable. In three days no one could stand him."

Pentameter, 50ff. See *line.*

Person, *148ff.* Any of several methods of presentation by which fiction is given the illusion of being told by a character, about a character, about the reader and the like. The third person ("he") is the most common; the first person ("I") can be written either in a neutral *style* or "as-if told" style. The second person singular ("you") and the third person plural ("they") are seldom used. *Person* is how a story is presented; the *means of perception* is who appears to present it.

Persona, 69. Broadly, a character in a poem, story, or play. The term is more frequently used to identify a fictitious narrator (implied or identified) in poetry.

Plot, *129ff., 233ff.* The sequence of events, often divided into *scenes,* in fiction, drama, or narrative poetry. This may be chronological, or it may be nonchronological in any of three ways: by flashback (inserting an earlier scene), or by multiple flashbacks (as in Vonnegut's *Slaughterhouse-Five* and Conrad's *Lord Jim*), or by using a frame (beginning and ending with the same scene).

Poetic, 5ff. In addition to being an adjective for "poetry" (*see verse*), this term is used to describe fiction or drama which makes special use of *rhythm, sound devices, figurative language, symbol,* and compression of meaning and implication.

Poetic diction, *21ff.* See *diction.*

Poetry, *5ff.* See *verse.*

Point of view, *145ff.* See *means of perception.*

P.O.V., 287. An abbreviation used in television scripts to indicate a scene shot from a character's point of view—that is, what the character sees.

Prose, 5. Those forms of writing in which the lines are continuous and have nothing to do with the statement or the form. This is in contrast with *verse.*

Prose rhythm, 6,59. See *rhythm.*

Protagonist, 148ff. The main character in a piece of *fiction,* play, or *narrative poem.* This character is often opposed by an antagonist. The term is broader than "hero" which suggests greatness. Protagonists who are perpetual victims are sometimes referred to as "anti-heroes."

Pun, 33,73. A figure of speech (see *image*) in which two different but significantly related meanings are attached to a single word. Most *sophisticated* uses of the pun are a form of *metaphor* with the tenor and the vehicle combined in a single word as in the case of Dylan Thomas's "some grave truth."

Pyrrhic foot, 50. See *meter.*

Quatrain, 43, 80. See *stanza.*

Quintet, 43, 80. See *stanza.*

Rate of revelation, 133. The rate at which new information or insights are given to the reader regarding character, theme, or plot. It is one of the primary factors which determine *pace.*

Realistic drama, *264ff.* Drama which creates the illusion of the world about us. Costume, set, and *plot* appear to be borrowed from what we see or might expect to see in life. This is opposed to nonrealistic drama which creates its own world in somewhat the same manner as a dream. "Expressionism" is sometimes used as a synonym for nonrealistic drama, but more strictly it refers to a dramatic school culminating in the 1920s and 30s with the works of O'Neill, Rice, and others.

Refrain, *82,* 274. A phrase, line, or stanza which is repeated periodically in a poem.

Reportorial style, 104, *152.* The style of writing used in newspaper articles (see *descriptive writing*) and in fiction which echoes this style.

Resonance, 203. That aspect of *tone* in *sophisticated writing* which is created by the use of *symbolic* and suggestive details. It is a layering of meaning and implication not found in *simple writing.*

Rhyme, *40ff.* A device found exclusively in *verse* and consisting of two or more words linked by an identity in sound which begins with an accented vowel and continues to the end of each word. The sounds preceding the accented vowel in each word must be unlike. This is "true rhyme." "Slant rhyme" and "off rhyme" use similar rather than identical vowel sounds. "Double rhyme," also called "feminine rhyme," is a two-syllable rhyme as in "running" and "sunning." In an "eye rhyme," the words look alike but sound different. "Rhyme scheme" is a pattern of rhymed endings which is repeated regularly in each *stanza* of *metered verse.*

Rhyme royal, 43. A stanza form of metered verse in which each septet is rhymed *ababbcc.*

Rhythm, 8, *47ff.* A systematic variation in the flow of sound. In *metered* verse this is achieved through a repeated pattern of stressed and unstressed syllables. In "alliterative verse" and "sprung rhythm" the pattern is determined by the number of stresses in each line without regard for the unstressed syllables. In "syllabic verse," the number of syllables in any one line matches the number in the corresponding line of the other *stanzas.* In "free verse," rhythms are achieved by *typography,* repeated syntactical patterns, and breath units. Rhythms in prose are achieved by repeating key words, phrases, and syntactical patterns.

Rising meter, 51. See *meter.*

Run-on line, 52. *Lines* in *verse* in which either the grammatical construction or the meaning or both are continued from the end of one line to the next. One function of this technique is to mute the rhythmical effect of *meter*. It is contrasted with "end–stopped lines," which are usually terminated with a period or a semicolon.

Satire, *73ff.,* 186, 239. A form of wit in which a distorted view of characters, places, or institutions is used for the purpose of criticism or ridicule. At least some measure of exaggeration (if only through a biased selection of details) is necessary for satire to be effective.

Scanning, 50. The analysis of *meter* in a sample of verse, identifying the various feet (see *meter*) and the type of *line* used.

Scansion, 50. The noun which refers to *scanning*.

Scene, *129ff., 234ff.,* 283. In *drama*, a formal subdivision of an act marked in the script and shown to the audience by lowering of the curtain or dimming of the lights; or a more subtle subdivision of the plot marked only by the exit or the entrance of a character. The former are here called "primary scenes" and the latter "secondary scenes." In *fiction*, the scene is a unit of action marked either by a shift in the number of characters or, more often, a shift in time or place. In television and film scripts a scene is a unit of action (with or without dialogue) which occurs in a single place and time. As soon as the camera shifts to a different location, the scene changes. Also called a "take."

Sentimentality, 113, 211. A form of *simple writing* which is dominated by a blunt appeal to the emotions of pity and love. It does so at the expense of subtlety and literary *sophistication*. Popular subjects are puppies, grandparents, and young lovers.

Septet, 43, 80. See *stanza*.

Sestet, sextet, 43, 70, 80. A six-lined *stanza* in *metered* verse. Also the last six lines of the *sonnet*.

Set, 217, 265, 271. See *setting*.

Setting, *188ff.,* 265. Strictly, the geographic area in which a *plot* takes place; but more generally, the time of day, the season, and the social environment as well. In *drama* the setting is usually specified at the beginning of the script. What the audience sees on the stage (excluding the actors) is the "set." Set design of *The Collection* appears on pp. 271–272.

Shock, *184,* 238. A method of creating dramatic impact through violence or morbid surprise. When it follows naturally from *plot* and *character*, it can be effective, as in the death which occurs in "Hello Out There." But when used for its own sake or without preparation, it results in *melodrama*.

Short story, *103ff.* See *fiction*.

Simile, 30ff. See *metaphor*.

Simple writing, *7ff., 105ff.* Writing in which the intent is made blatant, the *style* is limited to a single effect, or the *tone* is limited to a single emotion. It includes the adventure and horror story (*melodrama*), many love stories, most greeting-card verse (*sentimentality*), most patriotic *verse* and politically partisan *fiction* and *drama* (propaganda), and that which is single-mindedly sexual or sadistic (pornography). It also includes work which is so personal or so obscure that its intent fails to reach even a conscientious reader. The antonym for *simple* is *sophisticated*.

Slant rhyme, 40, 44. See *rhyme*.

Slug line, 286. The brief identification of a *scene* in a television script. If a new scene, it begins with "EXT." (exterior) or "INT." (interior), then has a word or phrase of description, and "DAY" or "NIGHT." Example: INT. KITCHEN—DAY.

Sonnet, 70, *83.* A metered poem of fourteen lines usually in iambic pentameter. The first eight lines are known as the "octave" and the last six as the "sestet." The Italian or Petrarchan sonnet is often rhymed *abba, abba; cde, cde.* The Elizabethan sonnet is often thought of as three quatrains and a final rhyming couplet: *abab, cdcd, efef, gg.*

Sophisticated writing, *7ff, 105ff.* Writing in which the intent is complex, having implications and ramification, the *style* makes rich use of the techniques available, and the *tone* has a range of suggestion. It is normally unified with a system of *internal logic.* It is the opposite of *simple writing.* Not to be confused with the popular use of "sophisticated."

Sound devices, 5, *38ff.* The technique of linking two or more words by alliteration (similar initial sounds), assonance (similar vowel sounds), consonance (similar consonantal sounds), onomatopoeia (similarity between the sound of the word and the object or action it describes), or *rhyme* (40ff.). In addition, "sound clusters" link groups of words with related vowel sounds which are too disparate to be called true samples of assonance.

Spondaic foot, 50. See *meter.*

Sprung rhythm, 49. A technique of *rhythm* in *verse* which is based on the number of *stressed* syllables in each *line,* disregarding those which are unstressed. It is primarily associated with the work of Gerard Manley Hopkins (see "Pied Beauty," p. 97).

Stage designs, 217, 265, 271. The "conventional stage" has a raised playing area which is set behind a "proscenium arch" from which a curtain is lowered between acts and *scenes.* The effect is like seeing a performance in an elaborate picture frame. "Theater in the round," "theater in the square," and "arena theater" place the action in a central arena with the audience seated on all sides. Compromise designs include a variety of apron stages with the audience on three sides.

Stanza, 42ff., *80ff.* Normally, a regularly recurring group of lines in a poem which are separated by spaces and frequently (though not necessarily) unified by a metrical system and by rhyme. Common forms include the couplet (two lines); tercet or triplet (three lines); quatrain (four lines); quintet or cinquain (five lines); sestet or sextet (six lines); septet (seven lines); octave (eight lines). The term is occasionally applied to irregular divisions in free verse which are used more like paragraphs in prose.

Stock character, *111ff.* Characters in *fiction* or *drama* which are *simple* and which also conform to one of a number of types which have appeared over such a long period and in so many different works that they are familiar to readers and audiences. Their dialogue is often *hackneyed* and their presence can reduce a work to the level of *simple fiction* or *drama.*

Stream of consciousness, 115, *151ff.* Fiction in the form of a character's thoughts directly quoted without exposition. Although wandering and disjointed, it is designed to reveal character. This is in sharp contrast with "automatic writing" in which the writer's goal is not *characterization* (or even *fiction*), but self-exploration.

Stress, *48ff.* In metered verse, the relative force or emphasis placed on a particular syllable. In "awake," the second syllable is stressed. See *meter.*

Style, *204ff.* The manner in which a work is written. It is determined by the author's decision, both conscious and unconscious, regarding diction (the type of words used), syntax (the type of sentences), *narrative mode* (relative importance of dialogue, thoughts, action, description, and exposition), and *pace* (the reader's sense of progress). It is closely connected with *tone.*

Substitution, 53. The technique in *metered verse* of occasionally replacing a foot (see *meter*) which has become the standard in a particular poem with some other type of foot. A common form of substitution is the use of a trochee for emphasis in a poem which is generally iambic.